Practical Statecharts in C/C++

Quantum Programmming for Embedded Systems

Miro Samek, Ph.D.

CMP**Books**

San Franciso, CA

Published by CMP Books
an imprint of CMP Media LLC
Main office: 600 Harrison Street, San Francisco, CA 94107 USA
Tel: 415-947-6615; fax: 415-947-6015
www.cmpbooks.com
email: books@cmp.com

Acquisitions editor:	Robert Ward
Technical editor:	Jeff Claar
Editors:	Catherine Janzen, Julie McNamee, and Rita Sooby
Layout design & production:	Justin Fulmer
Managing editor:	Michelle O'Neal
Cover art design:	Rupert Adley and Damien Castaneda

Distributed to the book trade in the U.S. by:
Publishers Group West
1700 Fourth Street
Berkeley, CA 94710
1-800-788-3123

Distributed in Canada by:
Jaguar Book Group
100 Armstrong Avenue
Georgetown, Ontario M6K 3E7 Canada
905-877-4483

For individual orders and for information on special discounts for quantity orders, please contact:
CMP Books Distribution Center, 6600 Silacci Way, Gilroy, CA 95020
Tel: 1-800-500-6875 or 408-848-3854; fax: 408-848-5784
email: cmp@rushorder.com; Web: www.cmpbooks.com

Printed in the United States of America

04 05 06   5 4

ISBN: 1-57820-110-1

CMP*Books*

Table of Contents

Preface

What we do not understand we do not possess.
— Goethe

Almost two decades ago, David Harel invented statecharts as a powerful way to describe complex reactive (event-driven) systems [Harel 87]. Subsequently, statecharts have gained almost universal acceptance as a superior formalism and have been adopted as components of many software methodologies, most notably as part of the Unified Modeling Language (UML). Nevertheless, the use of statecharts in everyday programming has grown slowly. Among the many reasons, the most important is that statecharts have always been taught as the use of a particular tool, rather than the way of design.

This heavy reliance on tools has affected the software community in three ways. First, the aggressive marketing rhetoric of tool vendors has set unrealistically high expectations for purely visual programming and fully automatic code generation. Second, the rhetoric of the argument for automatic code synthesis depreciated the role of manual coding. Finally, the accidental association between statecharts and CASE (computer-aided software engineering) tools gave rise to a misconception that the more advanced UML concepts, such as statecharts, are only viable in conjunction with sophisticated code-synthesizing tools.

The reality is that CASE tools haven't made manual coding go away. Even the best-in-class code-synthesizing tools can generate only a fraction of the software (the so-called housekeeping code [Douglass 99]). The difficult, application-specific code still must be written explicitly (although it is typically entered through the dialog boxes of a tool rather than typed into a programming editor). This also means that the models are not purely visual, but a mixture of diagrams and textual information (mostly snippets of code in a concrete programming language).

Moreover, for many projects, a design automation tool is not the best solution. The fundamental problem, as always, is the cost versus the return. Even if you ignore the dollar cost of the tool, you must ask whether the benefits outweigh the compounded complexity of the problem *and* the tool. The complete cost function must also include training and adaptation of the existing infrastructure to the tool (e.g., the compiler/linker/debugger tool chain, the host and target operating systems, the directory structure and file names, version control, and the software build process). After weighing all the pros and cons and struggling with a tool for a while, many teams notice that they spend more time fighting the tool than solving problems. For many developers, the tool simply can't pull its own weight and ends up as shelfware or a not-so-simple drawing tool.

Mission

My primary mission in this book is to offer a simple, lightweight alternative to a design automation tool by providing concrete, efficient, and proven implementations of statecharts that every practitioner reasonably proficient in C or C++ can start using within days.

To achieve these goals, I describe the major components of every typical code-synthesizing tool.

- The techniques needed to implement and use UML statecharts — the main *constructive* element in the UML specification (presented in Part I).

- A real-time application framework — a complete software infrastructure for executing statecharts, tailored to embedded real-time systems and based on active objects and asynchronous event passing (presented in Part II).

At first glance, the approach can be classified as a set of common elaborative techniques for implementing UML models. Even as such, it spares many practitioners from reinventing the wheel. In this book, I present ready-to-use, generic, and efficient elements that you can use to implement and execute hierarchical state machines; generate, queue, and dispatch events; integrate state machines with real-time operating systems (RTOSs); and much more. These software elements vary little from system to system but are hard to find in the literature. It's even harder to make them work well together. The value of this book is similar to that of a multivitamin pill: in one fell swoop (or a few chapters in this case), you get all the necessary ingredients, well balanced and complementing each other. If you use this book only in this manner, my most important goal is already accomplished.

Why Quantum Programming?

By providing concrete implementations of such fundamental concepts as statecharts and statechart-based computing models, the book lays the groundwork for a new programming paradigm, which I propose to call Quantum Programming (QP). I chose this name to emphasize the striking and fundamental analogy between reactive software systems and microscopic objects. As the laws of quantum mechanics describe, at the fundamental level, most microscopic objects (such as elementary particles, nuclei, atoms, and molecules) exhibit state behavior. Quantum objects are, in fact, little state machines, which spend their lives in strictly defined, discrete quantum states and can change state only in certain ways via uninterruptible transitions known as quantum leaps. Correspondingly, QP models state transitions with run-to-completion (RTC) steps. The only way quantum systems interact with one another is through an exchange of field quanta (intermediate vector bosons), which are mediators of fundamental forces.[1] Similarly, QP requires reactive systems to interact only by exchanging event instances. I explain more about this quantum analogy in Chapters 1, 2, and 7.

As a programming paradigm, QP has much more to offer than merely the snippets of code published in this book. I see and use QP as a set of techniques that increases the level of abstraction of a conventional programming language (such C or C++). The additional abstractions in QP allow me to efficiently model reactive systems directly in C++ or C. The role of QP can be compared to that of an object-oriented (OO) programming language. Just as Smalltalk, C++, or Java enable object-oriented programming (OOP) through direct support for the three fundamental OO design meta-patterns — abstraction, inheritance, and polymorphism — QP enables statechart modeling directly in C or C++ through another fundamental meta-pattern: the hierarchical state machine (HSM). Currently, the fundamental HSM pattern is an external add-on to C++ or C, but there is no reason it couldn't be natively supported by a quantum programming language in the same way that abstraction, inheritance, and polymorphism are natively supported by OO programming languages. (Indeed, in Appendix A, you see that OOP can be supported as an "add–on" in procedural languages such as C by explicitly applying the three fundamental OO patterns. I subsequently use this augmented C, which I call "C+", to develop the C implementation of the HSM pattern.)

The relationship between QP and OOP is interesting. On one hand, the most important aspects of QP, such as the HSM design pattern and the asynchronous communication paradigm, are orthogonal to OOP, which is an indication that these aspects of QP might be fundamental. On the other hand, however, these concepts work best when applied with OOP. In fact, a deep analogy exists between OOP and

---

1. For example, photons mediate the electromagnetic force, gluons the strong force, and bosons $W^{\pm}$ and Z^{o} the weak interactions.

QP, which I discuss in Chapter 1. In this sense, QP builds on top of OOP, complements it, and extends it into the domain of reactive systems.

Most of the concepts that form QP are not new, but, rather, draw on a broad range of long-known techniques and methodologies from programming and other disciplines such as quantum field theory. Most inspiring to me was the real-time object-oriented modeling (ROOM) method described by Bran Selic and colleagues [Selic+ 94]. Specifically, the real-time framework, or Quantum Framework, first began as a radically simplified ROOM virtual machine. Other influences were the classical Gang of Four design patterns [Gamma+ 95], the UML specification [OMG 01] (especially the state machine package), the original works of Harel [Harel 87, Harel+ 98], and books by Bruce Douglass [Douglas 99, Douglas 99a]. The Douglass writings in many ways are on the opposite end of the spectrum from QP, because QP offers mostly alternative views and complementary techniques to those he describes. For example, the state patterns he pioneered rely heavily on orthogonal regions, whereas QP shows how to implement some of these more elegantly using state hierarchy (Chapter 5).

For over four years, I have been using and refining QP in real-life projects — for example, in hard real-time implementations of GPS receivers. I am excited and thrilled by the potential of this approach to the point that I wrote this book so I could share QP with the largest audience I can reach. However, I am realistic — I do not see QP as a silver bullet. QP does not promise you the royal road, as do some design automation tools; however, it offers arguably the fastest road to better designed, safer, and more efficient event-driven software, because nothing stands between you and the solution. When you start using QP, you'll find, as I did, that your problems change. You no longer wrestle with convoluted `if` or `switch` statements; rather, you spend more time thinking about how to apply state patterns and how to partition your problem into active objects. Nonetheless, even with QP (or any CASE tool, for that matter), programming reactive systems remains difficult because it is by nature difficult. As Frederick Brooks [Brooks 87] notes in his classic essay "No Silver Bullet," you can only attack the accidental difficulties and can't do much about the essential ones, at least not in software alone. In this context, QP exactly follows Brooks' advice — to attack and remove the accidental difficulties associated with developing event-driven software.

QP versus XP and Other Agile Methodologies

QP is not a programming methodology; it is a set of concrete techniques for modeling and implementing reactive systems. Nevertheless, the QP approach is an expression of a basic programming philosophy, which is closely aligned with the recent trends in software development known collectively as *light* or *agile* methodologies. Some of these technologies include eXtreme Programming (XP), Crystal methodologies, SCRUM, Adaptive Software Development, Feature-Driven Development, and

Agile Modeling. The basic philosophy behind the new approaches is best summarized in the "Agile Manifesto" [Fowler 01], in which the "seventeen anarchists" agree to value (1) individuals and interactions over processes and tools and (2) working software over comprehensive documentation.

In the context of QP, valuing individuals and interactions over processes and tools means putting emphasis on understanding the underlying implementations and mechanisms rather than on hiding the complexity behind a tool (the practice that Anders Hejlsberg [Hejlsberg 01] denounced as *simplexity–complexity wrapped in something simple*). Real-life experience has shown repeatedly that if an individual understands the underlying implementation model, then he or she can code more efficiently and work with greater confidence. For example, determining which actions fire in which sequence in a nontrivial state transition is not something you should guess at or discover by running a tool-supported animation of your statechart. The answer should come from your understanding of the underlying implementation (discussed in Chapters 3 and 4). Even if you decide to use a design automation tool and even if your particular tool uses slightly different statechart implementation techniques than those I discuss in this book, you will still be a better, more productive, and confident user of the tool because of your understanding of the fundamental mechanisms.

In addition to putting value on individuals and interactions by explaining low-level fundamental software patterns, QP also offers powerful high-level metaphors, such as the quantum-mechanical and object-oriented analogies. A metaphor is valuable because it promotes the conceptual integrity of a software product and provides a common vocabulary, which dramatically improves communication among all of the stakeholders. Agile methodologies recognize the importance of such metaphors (e.g., XP proposes the development of a metaphor as a key practice).

As an elaborative approach, QP values working software over comprehensive documentation. In fact, QP offers nothing but the working code. I have made every attempt to provide only executable code, so that you can try out virtually every listing and code snippet you find in this book, as well as the code available only on the accompanying CD-ROM. Because only executable code is testable, this aspect of QP goes hand-in-hand with the requirement for continuous testing, which is inherent to all agile methodologies.

In addition to offering techniques for creating executable code, QP also offers highly readable, self-documenting code. For example in Chapter 4, I give directions on how to make the structure of a statechart clearly apparent from the code and almost equivalent to a UML state diagram. This is not to say that QP abandons UML diagrams or makes them obsolete. To the contrary, in this book, you will see quite a few diagrams that follow UML notation strictly (although because I used a simple drawing tool, they cannot be called UML-compliant). When it comes to diagrams and other visual models, QP shares the commonsense view of Agile Modeling [Ambler 01]. The most important role of visual models is to help you think through the designs and communicate them to programmers, customers, or management. For that purpose, simple tools like paper and pencil, whiteboard, or sticky notes are usually sufficient. It is also OK to discard the visual models after they have fulfilled their purpose. The specific value of visual modeling lies in tapping the potential of high bandwidth spatial intelligence, as opposed to lexical intelligence used with textual information.

Incomplete, disposable visual models, however, can't be used for code synthesis. In this respect, the agile approach fails to take advantage of the constructive aspect of some visual representations, such as UML statecharts. QP complements agile methodologies by enabling high-level modeling directly at the code level. With the concrete, ready-to-use building blocks provided by QP, you can construct, compile, and execute concurrent state models rapidly, even if they are nothing more than vastly incomplete skeletons. As you will see in Chapter 4, you can change the state machine topology (e.g., add, remove, or rearrange states and transitions) at any stage, even late in the process, by changing a few lines of code and recompiling. Then you can test your executable model on the host or target environments. Plenty of such executable models are included throughout this book. In that way, you can quickly try out many alternatives before committing to any one of them. This process is rightly called modeling, rather than coding, because your goal isn't the generation of a final product or even a prototype, but rather the fast exploration of your design space.

Admittedly with such lightweight modeling, you lose the benefits of spatial intelligence. As mentioned earlier, modeling at the code level does not preclude using UML diagrams or low-fidelity sticky notes as models of user interfaces. Indeed, spatial intelligence is best at grasping high-level structures and patterns when the models are relatively high level and uncluttered. As the models become more detailed, lexical intelligence usually takes over anyway because, in the end, *programming is all about text* [Hejlsberg 01].

Audience

This book is intended for the following computer professionals interested in reactive, or event-driven, systems.

- Embedded programmers and consultants will find practical advice, explanations, and plenty of code that they can use as is or modify to build event-driven software.

- Real-time systems designers will find a lightweight alternative to heavyweight CASE tools for modeling real-time systems. The Quantum Framework, combined with a preemptive RTOS, can provide deterministic behavior and can be embedded in commercial products.

- Users of design automation tools will better understand the inner workings of their tools, helping them to use the tools more efficiently and confidently.
- GUI developers, interactive Web page designers, and computer game programmers using C or C++ will find nontrivial, working examples of how to code and integrate UML statecharts with GUI environments such as the Microsoft Windows API.
- Hardware designers exploring the extension of C or C++ with class libraries to model SoC (System on Chip) designs will find one of the most succinct and efficient implementations of hierarchical state machines.
- Graduate-level students of Computer Science or Electrical Engineering will learn many design patterns that are backed up by numerous examples and exercises.

This book is about extending object-oriented techniques to programming reactive systems in C++ and C. I assume that you are familiar with fundamental object-oriented concepts and are reasonably proficient in one of these two languages. To benefit from Part II of the book, you should be familiar with fundamental real-time concepts. I am not assuming that you have prior knowledge of the UML specification in general or statecharts in particular, and I introduce these concepts in a crash course in Chapter 2.

Guide to Readers

This book has two main parts. In Part I (Chapters 1–6), I describe state machines — what they are, how to implement them, and the standard ways or patterns of using them. This part is generally applicable to any event-driven system, such as user interfaces (graphical and otherwise), real-time systems (e.g., computer games), or embedded systems. In Part II (Chapters 7–11), I describe the Quantum Framework, which is a software architecture designed specifically for embedded real-time systems.

Surveys of programmers[2] consistently indicate that C and C++ clearly dominate embedded systems programming. The vast majority (some 80 percent) of embedded systems developers use C; about 40 percent occasionally use C++. Consequently, every practical book genuinely intended to help embedded systems programmers should focus on C and C++. For that reason, I consistently present two complete sets of code: C++ and C. The C++ implementations are typically more succinct and natural because the underlying designs are fundamentally object oriented. In Appendix A,

---

2. For example, the Embedded Systems Programming survey (published annually by *ESP* magazine) or the Annual Salary Survey (published by *SD* magazine).

I present a description of "C+" – a set of three design patterns (abstraction, inheritance, and polymorphism), which I've used to code object-oriented designs in portable ANSI C. The "C+" patterns appear in many nontrivial examples throughout the book contrasted side-by-side with C++ implementations of the same designs. If you are interested only in C++, you can skip the C implementations on the first reading. However, I found that understanding the underlying mechanisms of implementing object orientation vastly improved my OO designs and allowed me to code them with greater confidence. For that reason, you might want to study the C code, concentrating primarily on the "C+" specifics. Conversely, if you are interested only in C, you should still read the explanations pertaining to C++ code. Often, I don't repeat clarifications for design decisions because they are the same for C++ and C. As a C programmer, you should have no problems understanding my C++ implementations because I use only very straightforward inheritance and hardly any polymorphism (except in Chapter 6).

My goal is not only to give you fish (i.e., the source code) but to teach you how to fish (i.e., to model reactive systems). Unfortunately, if you want to learn to fish, you should be ready to sweat a little. I try to provide you with executable implementations whenever possible. I believe that nothing builds more confidence in a new technique than actually executing a piece of example code. Sometimes, I ask you to step through a few instructions with a debugger; other times, I suggest that you make alterations to the code and rerun it. In the end, however, it is up to you to actually do it.

Most of the chapters in this book contain exercises. The exercises are intermixed with the text, rather than grouped at the end of a chapter, to put them closer to the relevant text. Most of the time, the exercises are not intended to test your comprehension of the chapter, but rather to suggest an alternative solution or to introduce a new concept. I provide a complete set of answers in order to pass on as much information as possible. If you usually skip over exercises, at least consider looking at the answers provided on the CD-ROM so that you don't miss the guidelines or techniques I introduce there.

I describe the CD-ROM that accompanies this book in more detail in Appendix C and the HTML browser included on the disc. Here, I want to mention that the examples (although written in portable C++ or C) are designed to run under Microsoft Visual C++ v6.0 on a 32-bit Windows machine (9x/NT/2000). If you don't have Visual C++, I recommend you get a copy so that you will be able to run the examples without redoing the makefiles, libraries, and so on. It is also important to have a good, easy-to-use debugger.

The source code for this book is available on the CD-ROM and can be freely distributed to students by accredited colleges and universities without a license. You can use the code as is or modify it to embed in your products, but you must obtain a

Source Code Distribution License to distribute QP source code. I may choose to assess a license fee for such situations, and you need to contact me for pricing (see below).

I intend to continue advancing QP and am interested in any constructive feedback you may have. I have opened a Web site devoted to promotion of this book and QP at the URL http://www.quantum-leaps.com. I plan for this site to contain application notes, ports of QP to different platforms, state patterns, useful links, bug fixes, frequently asked questions and much more. Please feel free to contact me via e-mail at miro@quantum-leaps.com.

Acknowledgments

I would like to thank Robert Ward, my acquisitions editor at CMP Books, in whom I found excellent editor, extremely knowledgeable software professional, and a resonating mind. I feel very lucky that Robert accepted my book for publication and offered his guidance throughout this book's lengthy birthing. I couldn't have dreamed of a better editor for this book.

The team of CMP Books has been wonderful. It was a great pleasure to have Michelle O'Neal as the managing editor. I'd like to thank Julie McNamee, Catherine Janzen, and Rita Sooby, for putting up with my writing. I'm amazed how many times they managed to turn my convoluted technical jargon into something actually readable. Reviewing their corrections was for me the best possible lesson in lucid writing. I also thank Justin Fulmer, for polishing my drawings and integrating them into the final version of the book.

I am indebted to Jeff Claar, for the technical review of the manuscript and for scrutinizing the accompanying code. Jeff's contributions include the complete C++ state machine implementation compliant with multiple inheritance, which is available on the companion CD-ROM.

I'd like to thank Michael Barr, for letting me publish my earlier article on the subject in the Embedded Systems Programming magazine, and for reviewing an early copy of this book.

This book has had a long gestation, of which the actual writing was merely the final step. I owe a lot to my former colleagues at GE Medical Systems, specifically to John Zhang, for infecting me with his enthusiasm for design patterns and state machines. In addition, I'd like to acknowledge my current team at IntegriNautics Corporation—one of the highest concentrations of Ph.D.s per square foot in Silicon Valley. I am particularly grateful to Paul Montgomery, for brainstorming many of the ideas, unforgettable pair-programming sessions, and for patiently enduring all my early iterations of the Quantum Framework.

I wholeheartedly thank my parents, who from over 7,000 miles away were still able to provide plenty of support and encouragement. The perseverance they instilled in me was critical for completion of this project. Quite specially, I thank my sister Barbara, for her faith in me and for always taking care of her "little brother".

Most of all, however, I would like to thank my wife Kinga and our lovely daughter Marie for tolerating far too many nights and weekends, which I spent in front of a computer rather than with them. Without their love, help, and continuous encouragement this book could never be finished. I love you so much!

Miro Samek
Palo Alto, California
April 2002

STATECHARTS

State machines are a superb formalism for specifying and implementing event-driven systems that must react to incoming events in a timely fashion. The UML statecharts represent the current state of the art in state machine theory and notation.

Part I of this book introduces the concept of statecharts, describes concrete techniques of coding statecharts directly in C and C++, and presents a small catalogue of basic statechart-based design patterns. You will learn that statecharts are a powerful way of design that you can use even without the assistance of sophisticated code-synthesizing tools.

Chapter 1

Whirlwind Tour of Quantum Programming

I have found out there ain't no surer way to find out whether you like people or hate them than to travel with them.
— *Tom Sawyer Abroad* [Mark Twain]

The triumph of the graphical user interface has been one of the most impressive developments in software during the past three decades.[1] Today the concept is so familiar as to need no description. Although from the beginning, windows, icons, menus, and pointing have been intuitive and easy to grasp for users, they remain a challenge for programmers. The internal GUI architecture baffles many newcomers, who often find it strange, backwards, mind-boggling, or weird. GUI programming is different because unlike traditional data processing, it is entirely *event-driven*. Events

---

1. The concept of the windows, icons, menus, and pointing (WIMP) interface was first publicly displayed by Doug Englebart and his team from the Stanford Research Institute at the Western Joint Computer Conference in 1968 [Englebart+ 68].

can occur at any time in any order. The application always must be prepared to handle them. GUI is an example of a complex *reactive system*.

You don't need to look far to find other examples of reactive systems. In fact, CPUs of all PCs, Macs, and other general-purpose computers consume only about 1 percent of the worldwide microprocessor production. The other 99 percent of microprocessor chips sold every year end up in various embedded systems, which are predominantly reactive in nature. Yet, in spite of this ubiquity, the code found in most of these systems is notoriously difficult to understand, fix, and maintain. Theoretical foundations on how to construct such software have been around for more than a decade; however, these ideas somehow could not make it into the mainstream. *Quantum Programming* (QP) is an attempt to make the modern methods more approachable for programmers. QP is a set of straightforward design patterns, idioms, concrete implementations, and commonsense techniques that you can start using immediately without investing in sophisticated tools.

1.1   The Ultimate Hook — Anatomy of a GUI Application

The early GUI designers faced a formidable task. On the one hand, a GUI application must be virtually infinitely customizable to allow anything from nonrectangular windows to splash screens and dazzling screen savers. On the other hand, the system ought to impose a consistent look and feel, and applications content with this standard behavior should be simple. How would you reconcile such conflicting requirements?

Today the problem seems easy — the trick is to use the "Ultimate Hook" [Petzold 96]. The idea is brilliantly simple. The GUI system (e.g., Windows) dispatches all events first to the application (Windows calls a specific function inside the application). If not handled by the application, the events flow back to the system. This establishes a hierarchical order of event processing. The application, which is conceptually at a lower level of hierarchy, has a chance to react to every event; thus, the application can customize every aspect of its behavior. At the same time, all unhandled events flow back to the higher level (i.e., to the system), where they are processed according to the standard look and feel. This is an example of *programming-by-difference* because the application programmer has to code only the differences from standard system behavior.

Independently, David Harel applied the same idea to the finite state machine formalism [Harel 87]. Around 1983 he invented statecharts as a powerful way of specifying complex reactive systems. The main innovation of statecharts over classical finite state machines was the introduction of *hierarchical states*. To understand what it means, consider the relation between the nested state (substate) and the surrounding state (superstate) depicted in Figure 1.1a. This statechart attempts to process any

Figure 1.1   **(a) Statechart notation for nesting states**
(b) Statechart representing Ultimate Hook design pattern

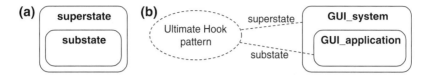

event, first, in the context of the substate. If the substate cannot handle it, the state-chart *automatically* passes the event to the next higher level (i.e., to the superstate). Of course, states can nest deeper than one level. The simple rule of processing events applies then recursively to an arbitrary level of nesting.

Harel's semantics of state hierarchy is at the heart of the Ultimate Hook design underlying GUI systems; in other words, the statechart supports the Ultimate Hook pattern *directly*. This becomes obvious when renaming the superstate to GUI_system and the substate to GUI_application, as shown in Figure 1.1b. Now this is an interesting result: The fundamental Ultimate Hook design pattern turns out to be a very simple statechart! This powerful statechart is unusually simple because, at this level of abstraction, it does not contain any state transitions.

Traditionally, the hierarchy of states introduced in statecharts has been justified as follows.

> *As it turns out, highly complex behavior cannot be easily described by simple, "flat" state-transition diagrams. The reason is rooted in the unmanageable multitude of states, which may result in an unstructured and chaotic state-transition diagram —* [Harel+ 98].

Certainly, hierarchical diagrams are often simpler and better structured than traditional flat diagrams. However, this is not the fundamental reason for the significance of state hierarchy, merely one of the side effects. State hierarchy is fundamentally important even without the multitude of states and transitions, as demonstrated clearly by the GUI example. The powerful statechart shown in Figure 1.1b contains only two states and not a single state transition; yet, it is powerful. The only essential feature is state hierarchy, in its pure form.

Figure 1.1b is so unusually simple because it shows only the highest level of abstraction. All nontrivial GUI applications have many modes of operation (states) with typically complex rules of switching between these modes (state transitions), regardless of whether you use a statechart, a classical flat state transition diagram, brute force, or any other method. However, designs based on the statechart formalism seem to be the most succinct, robust, and elegant, if for no other reason than their direct support for programming-by-difference (Ultimate Hook pattern).

Although statecharts in some form or another have gained almost universal acceptance as a superior formalism for specifying complex reactive systems, their actual adoption into mainstream programming has been slow. In particular, GUI designs traditionally have not used statecharts. You will not find them in standard GUI architectures such as Microsoft Foundation Classes (MFC), Borland's Object Windows Library (OWL), or the more recent Java Abstract Window Toolkit (AWT). You also will not find support for statecharts in rapid application development (RAD) tools such as Microsoft Visual Basic or Borland Delphi. Among the many reasons, the most important is that statecharts have been taught as a high-level, visual language, mandating the use of sophisticated computer-aided software engineering (CASE) tools, rather than as a type of design. This has created many misconceptions in the industry and has resulted in a lack of practical advice on how to code statecharts in mainstream programming languages such as C or C++.

1.2   A Better Way of Programming — A Calculator That Works

Coding a statechart directly in C or C++ is not that hard. This section shows you how. I decided to include this example early in the text so you could start experimenting with it as soon as possible. The example comes from the book *Constructing the User Interface with Statecharts* by Ian Horrocks [Horrocks 99]. The author presents a desktop calculator application distributed with Microsoft Visual Basic. He first identifies a number of problems with the original implementation and then proposes an alternative statechart design. Here, I will pick up where he left off by actually implementing his statechart[2] in C++ and integrating it with the Windows GUI (Figure 1.2). Although this section concentrates on a C++ implementation, the accompanying CD-ROM also contains the equivalent version in C.

1.2.1   Shortcomings of the Traditional Event–Action Paradigm

Before getting into the implementation; however, I'll examine some problems that Ian Horrocks found in the Visual Basic Calculator because they turn out to be emblematic of inconsistencies in handling modal behavior. Most of the time, the

---

2.   Actually, the statechart is modified slightly compared to the original Horrocks design.

calculator correctly adds, subtracts, multiplies, and divides. However, in certain cases, the application provides misleading results, freezes, or crashes altogether.

Exercise 1.1   After familiarizing yourself with the contents of the accompanying CD-ROM (see Appendix C and the HTML browser on the disc) find the Visual Basic Calculator example and launch it. Try the following sequence of operations and watch the application crash: 1, /, –, =, 2, =. Try the sequence 2, ×, CE, 2, =, and observe that Cancel Entry had no effect, even though it appeared to cancel the '2' entry from the display. Try different ways of breaking the calculator or of producing misleading results.

The Visual Basic Calculator often has problems dealing with negative numbers. This is because the same button (–) is used to negate a number and to enter the subtraction operator. The correct interpretation of the '–' event, therefore, depends on the context, or mode, in which it occurs. Likewise, Cancel Entry (CE button) occasionally works erroneously. Again, Cancel Entry makes sense only in a particular context, namely, just after the user has entered a number or operator. As it turns out, the calculator tries to handle it in other contexts as well. At this point, you probably have noticed an emerging pattern. Just look for events that require different handling depending on the context, and you can break the calculator in many more ways.

The faults just outlined are rooted in the standard bottom-up implementation of this application. The context (state) of the computation is represented ambiguously as a group of flags and variables, so it is difficult to tell precisely in which mode the application is at any given time. There is no notion of any single mode of operation, but rather tightly coupled and overlapping conditions of operation. For example, the calculator uses `DecimalFlag` to indicate that a decimal point has been entered,

Figure 1.2   **(a) Visual Basic Calculator GUI and (b) Quantum Calculator GUI**

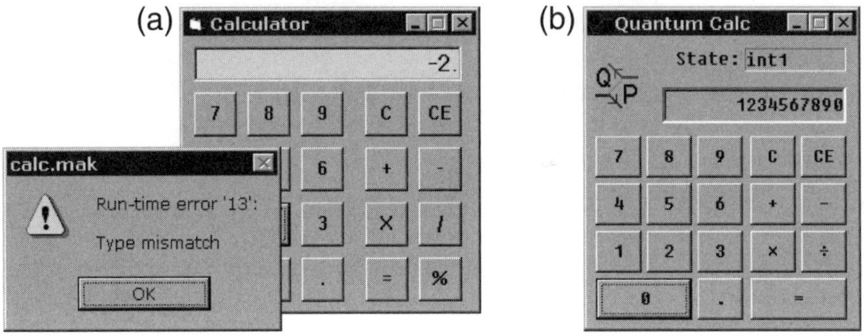

OpFlag to represent a pending operation, LastInput to indicate the type of the last key press event, NumOps to denote the number of operands, and several more state variables. With this representation, determining whether the '−' key should be treated as negation or subtraction requires the following conditional logic (in Visual Basic).[3]

```
Select Case NumOps
    Case 0
    If Operator(Index).Caption = "-" And LastInput <> "NEG" Then
        ReadOut = "-" & ReadOut
        LastInput = "NEG"
    End If
    Case 1
    Op1 = ReadOut
    If Operator(Index).Caption = "-" And LastInput <> "NUMS" And
                                  OpFlag <> "=" Then
        ReadOut = "-"
        LastInput = "NEG"
    End If
. . .
```

Such an approach is fertile ground for bugs for at least two reasons: examining the current mode requires evaluating a complex expression, and switching between different modes requires modifying many variables, which can easily lead to inconsistencies. Expressions like these, scattered throughout the code, are not only unnecessarily complex but expensive to evaluate at run time. They are also notoriously difficult to get right, even by experienced programmers, as the bugs still lurking in the Visual Basic Calculator attest.

1.2.2 Calculator Statechart

The good news is that there is a better way of approaching reactive systems. Statecharts, like the one depicted in Figure 1.3, eliminate the aforementioned problems by design. Arriving at this statechart was definitely *not* trivial, and you shouldn't worry if you don't fully understand it at the first reading (I wouldn't either). At this point, my goal is just to introduce you to the statechart approach and convince you that it isn't particularly hard to code in C or C++.[4] I want to walk you quickly through the main points without slowing you down with full-blown detail. I promise to return to

---

3. The complete Visual Basic source code for the calculator application is available on the accompanying CD-ROM.
4. Here, I discuss a C++ implementation. However, the implementation in plain C is available on the accompanying CD-ROM.

Figure 1.3 **Calculator statechart; the standard `IDC_` Windows event prefixes are omitted for clarity**

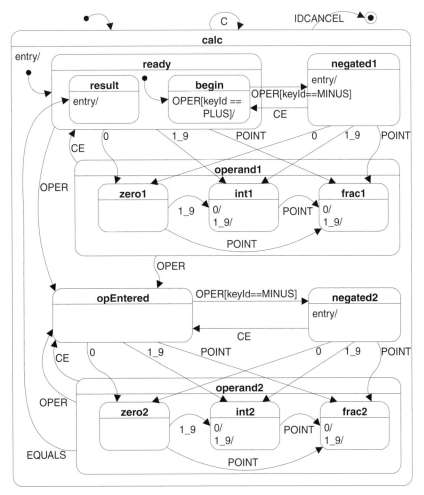

this statechart on more than one occasion in the following chapters, for a closer study of statechart design, and to discuss concrete implementation techniques later.

The calculator statechart from Figure 1.3 contains 15 states[5] (the topmost Windows system state is not included) and handles 11 distinct events: IDC_0, IDC_1_9,

---

5.   At first, you might be disappointed that the statechart for such a simple calculator is so complicated. After analyzing the problem, I feel that the diagram in Figure 1.3 represents the complexity of the problem just about right. Section 2.3.1 in Chapter 2 explains in more detail the reasons for complexity in this case.

IDC_POINT, IDC_C, IDC_CE, IDC_PLUS, IDC_MINUS, IDC_MULT, IDC_DIVIDE, IDC_EQUALS, and IDCANCEL.

Exercise 1.2   Find and launch the Quantum Calculator application (try both the C++ and C implementations). Try to understand the behavior of the application by comparing it with the statechart from Figure 1.3 (you might find the current state display handy). Try to break it or produce misleading results. Test the Quantum Calculator to see how it handles the '–' and '+' unary operators.

   This state machine takes advantage of hierarchy in several places. For example, Cancel (the 'C' button) is handled explicitly only in the highest level state, calc (look for the arrow labeled "C" at the top of Figure 1.3). This event triggers a self-transition in the calc state. You can understand how the statechart handles the Cancel event based solely on the Ultimate Hook semantics of state nesting introduced earlier. Assume, for example, that when the user clicks the 'C' button, the active state is opEntered. This state doesn't "know" how to handle the Cancel event, so it automatically passes this event for processing to the next higher level state, that is, to calc. The calc state knows how to handle the Cancel event by executing the aforementioned self-transition. This causes exit from calc followed by entry, first to calc, then ready, and finally begin, by the recursive execution of initial transitions. At this point, the calculator ends processing of the Cancel event and waits for the next event.

   To restate: The statechart started in opEntered and ended in begin. Actually, the statechart could have been in any of the other 11 substates of calc (refer to Exercise 1.3) and would still end up in begin. The classical flat state machine would require specifying each of the 11 transitions explicitly. The statechart allows reusing one transition 11 times. The gain is not only the drastic reduction in the sheer number of transitions but also a more accurate representation of the problem at hand. There is only one Cancel transition in the calculator problem. A natural language specification might read as follows: Whatever state the calculator is in at the time the user clicks the 'C' button, the calculator should clear its display and other internal registers and become ready for another computation. The statechart represents this specification faithfully, whereas the classical flat state machine would add repetitions and artificial complexity.

Exercise 1.3   Not all 15 substates of calc can be active. For example states ready, operand1, and operand2 can never become active. Explain why.

The following implementation of the calculator statechart is straightforward because all the state machine functionality is inherited from the QHsm (quantum hierarchical state machine) class. Listing 1.1 shows the C++ declaration of the calculator statechart.

Listing 1.1   Declaration of the calculator statechart; the unusual indentation of state handler methods (lines 14–29) indicates state nesting

```
1 #include <windows.h>
2 #include "qf_win32.h"                      // include the Quantum Framework (QF)
3
4 struct CalcEvt : public QEvent {
5    int keyId;                              // ID of the key depressed
6 };
7
8 class Calc : public QHsm {         // calculator Hierarchical State Machine
9 public:
10    Calc() : QHsm((QPseudoState)initial) {}
11    static Calc *instance();                 // Singleton accessor method
12 private:
13    void initial(QEvent const *e);          // initial pseudostate-handler
14    QSTATE calc(QEvent const *e);                      // state-handler
15      QSTATE ready(QEvent const *e);                   // state-handler
16        QSTATE result(QEvent const *e);                // state-handler
17        QSTATE begin(QEvent const *e);                 // state-handler
18      QSTATE negated1(QEvent const *e);                // state-handler
19      QSTATE operand1(QEvent const *e);                // state-handler
20        QSTATE zero1(QEvent const *e);                 // state-handler
21        QSTATE int1(QEvent const *e);                  // state-handler
22        QSTATE frac1(QEvent const *e);                 // state-handler
23      QSTATE opEntered(QEvent const *e);               // state-handler
24      QSTATE negated2(QEvent const *e);                // state-handler
25      QSTATE operand2(QEvent const *e);                // state-handler
26        QSTATE zero2(QEvent const *e);                 // state-handler
27        QSTATE int2(QEvent const *e);                  // state-handler
28        QSTATE frac2(QEvent const *e);                 // state-handler
29    QSTATE final(QEvent const *e);                     // state-handler
30 private:                                        // action methods...
31    void clear();
32    void insert(int keyId);
33    void negate();
34    void eval();
35    void dispState(char const *s);
36 private:                                            // data attributes
37    HWND myHwnd;
38    char myDisplay[40];
```

```
39    char *myIns;
40    double myOperand1;
41    double myOperand2;
42    int myOperator;
43    BOOL isHandled;
44    friend BOOL CALLBACK calcDlg(HWND hwnd, UINT iEvt,
45                                 WPARAM wParam, LPARAM lParam);
46 };
```

Events dispatched to the calculator are represented as instances of the `CalcEvt` class (Listing 1.1, lines 4–6). This class derives from `QEvent` and adds the `keyId` event parameter, which represents the ID of the key entered. As mentioned before, the calculator hierarchical state machine `Calc` declared in lines 8 through 46 derives from `QHsm`. The `Calc` class contains several attributes that keep track of the computation (the attributes constitute the memory of the state machine). Please note, however, that the attributes are not used to determine the state of the application. Rather, the `QHsm` superclass keeps track of the active state, which is crisply defined at all times. In fact, the calculator GUI displays it for you, so that you can easily correlate calculator behavior with the underlying statechart from Figure 1.3. You also can recognize all states declared as state handler methods in lines 14 through 29. The unusual use of indentation indicates state nesting.

1.2.3   Integration with Windows

For simplicity, this example uses the raw Win32 API rather than a higher level wrapper like MFC. The calculator GUI is a dialog box, so it declares friendship with the corresponding Windows dialog procedure (Listing 1.1, lines 44–45). Because Windows is an event-driven (reactive) system, it already provides a complete environment within which a state machine can execute and needs only minor customizations for this particular application. The main Windows procedure, `WinMain()`, performs only basic initializations and then invokes the dialog procedure.

```
int WINAPI WinMain(HINSTANCE hInst, HINSTANCE hPrevInst,
                   PSTR cmdLine, int iCmdShow)
{
    InitCommonControls();                       // load common controls library
    locHinst = hInst;                           // store instance handle
    DialogBox(hInst, MAKEINTRESOURCE(IDD_DIALOG), NULL, calcDlg);
    return 0;                        // exit application when the dialog returns
}
```

The dialog procedure (Listing 1.2) starts the state machine (by invoking the `init()` method in response to the `WM_INIT_DIALOG` Windows message), translates the Windows events to calculator events, and dispatches the events for processing (by invoking the `dispatch()` method) in response to the `WM_COMMAND` Windows message.

Listing 1.2   Initializing and dispatching events to the Quantum Calculator statechart from a dialog procedure

```
static HINSTANCE locHinst;                                    // this instance
static HWND locHwnd;                                          // window handle

BOOL CALLBACK calcDlg(HWND hwnd, UINT iMsg,
                      WPARAM wParam, LPARAM lParam)
{
    CalcEvt e;
    switch (iMsg) {
    case WM_INITDIALOG:
        Calc::instance()->myHwnd = locHwnd = hwnd;
        SendMessage(hwnd, WM_SETICON, (WPARAM)TRUE,
                    (LPARAM)LoadIcon(locHinst, MAKEINTRESOURCE(IDI_QP)));
        Calc::instance()->init();                   // take the initial transition
        return TRUE;
    case WM_COMMAND:
        switch (e.keyId = LOWORD(wParam)) {
        case IDCANCEL:
            e.sig = TERMINATE;
            break;
        case IDC_1:
        case IDC_2:
        case IDC_3:
        case IDC_4:
        case IDC_5:
        case IDC_6:
        case IDC_7:
        case IDC_8:
        case IDC_9:
            e.sig = IDC_1_9;
            break;
        case IDC_PLUS:
        case IDC_MINUS:
        case IDC_MULT:
        case IDC_DIVIDE:
            e.sig = IDC_OPER;
            break;
        default:
            e.sig = e.keyId;
            break;
        }
        Calc::instance()->isHandled = TRUE;
        Calc::instance()->dispatch(&e);                      // take one RTC step
        return Calc::instance()->isHandled;
    }
    return FALSE;
}
```

1.2.4   State Handler Methods

State handler methods perform the actual work of the application. As members of the Calc class, state handlers have direct access to all the attributes. A state handler takes a pointer to an immutable event instance (QEvent const *) and returns either 0, if it handled the event, or the superstate (more precisely, the pointer to the superstate handler method), if not.

Listing 1.3 contains handlers for states calc, ready, and begin (you can refer to the accompanying CD-ROM [Appendix C] for the code of the other state handlers). The structure of all state handlers is similar: They all start with an identical switch statement (with an event signal e->sig used as the discriminator) and all end in the same way by returning the superstate (i.e., a pointer to superstate handler method). For example, state begin returns ready, ready returns calc, and calc returns top (the ultimate superstate that contains the entire state machine). The body of the switch statement contains all signals that the corresponding state handles, coded as separate case statements. For example, the begin state handles signals Q_ENTRY_SIG and IDC_OPER (Listing 1.3 lines 41–50). Most case statements end with return 0 to indicate that the state handler processed this event. State transitions are coded using the Q_TRAN() (quantum transition) macro. For example, event IDC_OPER in state ready triggers a transition to state opEntered, so you code it as (line 33) Q_TRAN(&Calc::opEntered).

Listing 1.3   **State handlers for** calc, ready, **and** begin **states. Boldface indicates housekeeping code (see the last paragraph of this section)**

```
1 QSTATE Calc::calc(QEvent const *e) {
2     switch (e->sig) {
3     case Q_ENTRY_SIG: dispState("calc");               return 0;
4     case Q_INIT_SIG: clear(); Q_INIT(&Calc::ready);  return 0;
5     case IDC_C:        clear(); Q_TRAN(&Calc::calc);   return 0;
6     case TERMINATE:    Q_TRAN(&Calc::final);           return 0;
7     }
8     if (e->sig >= Q_USER_SIG) {
9         isHandled = FALSE;
10    }
11    return (QSTATE)&Calc::top;
12 }
13
14 QSTATE Calc::ready(QEvent const *e) {
15    switch (e->sig) {
16    case Q_ENTRY_SIG:    dispState("ready");     return 0;
17    case Q_INIT_SIG:     Q_INIT(&Calc::begin);   return 0;
18    case IDC_0: clear(); Q_TRAN(&Calc::zero1);   return 0;
19    case IDC_1_9:
20        clear();
```

```
21          insert(((CalcEvt *)e)->keyId);
22          Q_TRAN(&Calc::int1);
23          return 0;
24      case IDC_POINT:
25          clear();
26          insert(IDC_0);
27          insert(((CalcEvt *)e)->keyId);
28          Q_TRAN(&Calc::frac1);
29          return 0;
30      case IDC_OPER:
31          sscanf(myDisplay, "%lf", &myOperand1);
32          myOperator = ((CalcEvt *)e)->keyId;
33          Q_TRAN(&Calc::opEntered);
34          return 0;
35      }
36      return (QSTATE)&Calc::calc;
37  }
38
39  QSTATE Calc::begin(QEvent const *e) {
40      switch (e->sig) {
41      case Q_ENTRY_SIG:    dispState("begin");    return 0;
42      case IDC_OPER:
43          if (((CalcEvt *)e)->keyId == IDC_MINUS) {
44              Q_TRAN(&Calc::negated1);
45              return 0;                           // event handled
46          }
47          else if (((CalcEvt *)e)->keyId == IDC_PLUS) {    // unary "+"
48              return 0;                           // event handled
49          }
50          break;                                  // event unhandled!
51      }
52      return (QSTATE) &Calc::ready;
53  }
```

As you can see, the housekeeping code[6] (i.e., state machine declaration and state handler skeletons, indicated in boldface in Listing 1.3) you need to write to translate a statechart to C++ is almost trivial. In fact, it is not more complicated than the code you need to write to translate a Unified Modeling Language (UML) class diagram to C++ (i.e., class declaration and method skeletons). You probably don't even think that you translate a class diagram to C++; you simply code an object-oriented system directly in C++. This is so because C++ provides the right (object-oriented) level of abstraction. The practical techniques for implementing statecharts raise the level of

---

6. Douglass [Douglass 99] uses the term "housekeeping code" to denote sections of code that are used repetitively to represent common constructs such as states, transitions, events, and so on. Some CASE tools can automatically generate such *representational invariants* from statechart diagrams.

abstraction further (to the "quantum" level) and, in the same sense, enable direct modeling of reactive systems in C++.

1.3 Object-Oriented Analogy

I hope you experienced déjà vu when you read about programming-by-difference and *reuse of behavior* in the context of statecharts. Haven't you encountered similar concepts before? Doesn't a state hierarchy resemble an object-oriented taxonomy of classes? As this section explains, hierarchical states don't simply resemble classes of objects in object-oriented programming (OOP); the analogy is deep and fundamental. Such a close analogy has many practical implications.

1.3.1 State Hierarchy and Class Taxonomy

One of the cornerstones of OOP is the concept of class inheritance, which allows you to define new classes of objects in terms of existing classes, and consequently enables you to construct hierarchically layered taxonomies of classes. A hierarchy of states introduces another type of inheritance, which is equally fundamental. I will call it *behavioral inheritance* [Samek+ 00].

To understand how state hierarchy leads to inheritance and how it works, consider again the statechart depicted in Figure 1.1a. This time, however, suppose that the substate is completely empty, with no internal structure (no transitions and no reactions). If such a state becomes active, it will automatically forward all events to the superstate. Therefore, the behavior of such a substate will be externally indistinguishable from the superstate — the empty substate *inherits* the exact behavior from its superstate. This is analogous to an empty subclass, which does not declare any methods or attributes. An instance of such a subclass is, in every respect, equivalent to an instance of its superclass. The child class is indistinguishable from the parent class because everything is inherited exactly.

Although checking the corner case of exact inheritance is instructive, inspecting ways in which nested states can differ from their ancestors is more interesting. As class inheritance allows subclasses to "adapt" to new environments, behavioral inheritance allows substates to "mutate" by adding new behavior or by overriding existing behavior. Nested states can add new behavior by adding new state transitions or reactions for events that are not recognized by surrounding states. This corresponds to adding new methods to a subclass. Alternatively, a substate may also process the same events as the surrounding states but will do it in a different way. Thus, the substate can override the inherited behavior, which corresponds to a subclass overriding a method defined by its parents, which leads to polymorphism.

In a typical class taxonomy, classes lower in the hierarchy are more specialized than their ancestors; conversely, classes higher in the hierarchy are generalizations of their descendants. The same holds true in state hierarchies. For example, consider a hypothetical "failed" state that turns on an alarm bell upon entry (as part of its entry action) and turns it off upon exit (as part of its exit action). If this state has a substate, say "unsafe," and this substate becomes active, the alarm bell will ring because being in the unsafe state also means being in the failed state. If the system is in the unsafe state, it also is in the failed state and, recursively, is in every ancestor state of failed. The *is in* (is-in-a-state) generalization of states corresponds to the *is a* (is-a-kind-of) generalization of classes.

1.3.2 Entering/Exiting States and Instantiating/Finalizing Classes

In the previous example, the entry action executed automatically upon entry to a state (turning on the alarm bell), and the exit action (turning off the alarm bell) executed automatically upon exit from the state. These actions are analogous to class constructors and destructors. Instantiation of a class is very much like entering a state. Conversely, class finalization is like exiting a state. In both cases, special actions are invoked in a predetermined order: Constructors are invoked starting from the most remote ancestor class (destructors are invoked in reverse order). Entry actions are invoked starting from the topmost superstate (exit actions are invoked in reverse order).

1.3.3 Programming-by-Difference

Class inheritance is commonly used for programming-by-difference. This programming style is the essence of reuse: A subclass needs to define only the differences from its superclass and otherwise can *reuse* (share) implementation defined in the superclass.

Behavioral inheritance is identical in this respect. A substate needs to define only the differences from its superstate and can otherwise reuse the behavior defined in the superstate. In other words, supporting programming-by-difference behavioral inheritance enables reuse of behavior.

1.3.4 Behavioral Inheritance as a Fundamental Meta-Pattern

OOP can be viewed as a consistent use of three fundamental concepts — abstraction, inheritance, and polymorphism — that are actually *meta*-patterns because they provide the underpinnings for all other object-oriented (OO) design patterns [Gamma+ 95]. QP introduces and implements another, equally fundamental, meta-pattern: behavioral inheritance. The meta-pattern is truly enabling because it raises the level of abstraction to allow direct modeling of complex state behavior in C or C++ in the same way that fundamental OO meta-patterns (natively supported in OO languages) enable direct OO modeling in C++, Smalltalk, or Java.

As you will see in Chapter 4, the implementation of the behavioral inheritance meta-pattern often uses the object analogy and borrows many solutions from the C++ object model implementation. Again, this is a direct application of the OO analogy.

1.3.5   State Patterns

As Gamma and colleagues [Gamma+ 95] write: "*One thing expert designers know not to do is solve every problem from the first principles.*" The maturity of object technology shows through the emergence of OO design patterns that capture, name, and catalog proven OO designs. In analogy, *state patterns*, which are concerned with useful ways of structuring states rather than objects, have begun to appear [Douglass 99], reflecting the increasing maturity of statechart technology.

By providing a concrete implementation for the behavioral inheritance meta-pattern, QP enables a much more precise description of state patterns than the traditional graphical statechart notation alone, in the form of concrete, executable code. In this respect, QP acts much like an OO programming language, which also captures OO patterns in the form of concrete executable code. In both cases, bubbles and arrows of graphical representation, although very helpful, are not sufficient to capture all the details necessary to understand and successfully apply a pattern. Bertrand Meyer summarized elloquently the shortcomings of graphical-only descriptions when he said [Meyer 97a]:

> the good thing about bubbles and arrows, as opposed to programs, is that they never crash.

State patterns in QP revolve predominantly around the central concept of behavioral inheritance, rather than the orthogonal component. Therefore, they represent alternatives to the solutions presented elsewhere (e.g., Douglass [Douglass 99]). Chapter 5 presents a minicatalog of quantum state patterns.

1.3.6   Refactoring State Models

Another aspect in which state models and OO models are similar is their evolution during the software life cycle. Both state hierarchies and class hierarchies undergo similar development phases, and both, at some point of their life cycle, need restructuring to continue to evolve.

The main objective of software restructuring, or *refactoring* (see e.g., [Opdyke 92], [Fowler+ 99]), is not to change how the software behaves — indeed, the changes should be transparent to black-box testing. The goal of refactoring is rather to actively counteract the natural increase in the degree of chaos (architectural decay) that gradually renders any software system prohibitively expensive to maintain and modify.

Because of the similarities between behavioral inheritance and class inheritance, the same general refactorings are applicable both to OO systems and to statecharts.

- *Refactoring to generalize* — creating a common superclass–creating a common superstate
- *Refactoring to specialize* — deriving subclasses from a common base–nesting substates in a common superstate

In addition, like OO design patterns, state patterns capture many structures that result from refactoring state models. Using these patterns early in the life of a statechart design can prevent later refactorings. Alternatively, when restructuring becomes inevitable, state patterns can provide convenient *targets* for your refactorings.

1.3.7 Beyond Object-Oriented Programming

Recent years have seen several attempts to extend and augment traditional OOP. Trends that have gained particular attention are components, patterns, and frameworks. Software components are capable of encapsulating complete business functions and therefore are usually at a higher level of granularity than objects. OO design patterns try to capture and reuse proven patterns of collaboration among whole groups of objects. At a higher level still are frameworks, which are entire, albeit incomplete, applications. The common themes of all these developments are ways of combining many fine-granularity objects into systems. All these trends are examples of programming-in-the-large.

QP, based on behavioral inheritance, takes the opposite route. The traditional OO method stops short at the boundary of a class, leaving the *internal* implementation of individual class methods to mostly procedural techniques. Behavioral inheritance and the OO analogy allow many OO methods to be extended and applied *inside* classes.

1.4 Quantum Analogy

To help you understand how Quantum Programming fits with other trends, it is helpful to compare software developments to modern physics. Traditionally, OOP would correspond to classical mechanics: beautifully able to describe everyday experience but unable to accurately describe either very large or very small scale phenomena. Components, patterns, and frameworks try to expand the macroscale frontier. You could compare them to thermodynamics or general relativity pertinent to large-scale, complex objects like galaxies or black holes. In this picture, QP would correspond to *quantum mechanics*, because it expands the microscale frontier.

As described by the laws of quantum theory, microscopic objects have the following two most characteristic properties.

- Quantum objects spend their lives in strictly defined quantum states and can change their state only by means of uninterruptible transitions known as quantum leaps. Because of various symmetries, the quantum states are naturally hierarchical (degenerate in quantum terminology).

- Quantum systems cannot interact with one another directly; rather, every interaction proceeds via an intermediate artifact (intermediate boson). The various intermediate bosons are mediators of fundamental forces (e.g., photons mediate the electromagnetic force, gluons the strong force, and bosons $W^{\pm}$ and Z^{o} the weak forces).

QP follows the quantum model quite faithfully. Part I of this book corresponds to the first characteristics of quantum systems — their discrete, statelike behavior. Part II, on the other hand, covers the second aspect of the quantum analogy — the interactions. The fundamental units of decomposition in QP are concurrently active hierarchical state machines (active objects). These software machines can interact with one another only by asynchronous exchange of various event instances.

1.5   Summary

This chapter provided a quick tour of Quantum Programming. QP is concerned with reactive systems, which are systems that continuously interact with their environment by means of exchanging *events*. Over the years, several techniques have evolved that can be used to design and implement such systems. One of the most powerful ideas has proved to be the concept of hierarchical event processing, which GUI programmers know as the Ultimate Hook pattern. Almost two decades ago, David Harel generalized this concept and combined it with finite state machines to create the formalism known as statecharts. Although statecharts have gained almost universal acceptance in software methodologies and modeling languages, like UML, their adoption into everyday programming has been slow. The main reason is the widespread misunderstanding that statecharts are only usable when supported by sophisticated CASE tools. The result is a lack of practical advice on how to efficiently hand-code statecharts in mainstream programming languages such as C or C++. However, as you saw in the Quantum Calculator example, you can easily implement the fundamental concepts of statecharts directly in C++ by applying the behavioral inheritance meta-pattern. This pattern is central to QP, just as abstraction, inheritance, and polymorphism are patterns central to OOP.

The analogy between QP and OOP goes deeper. They are both unified around the concept of inheritance. Just as class inheritance is a cornerstone of OOP, behavioral inheritance is a cornerstone of QP. This analogy allows almost direct application of many OO techniques to state models, such as programming-by-difference, the construction of proper state taxonomies, the application of similar refactorings, or the use of exit and entry actions. In addition, the implementation of the behavioral inheritance meta-pattern shares many commonalities with the internal implementation of the C++ object model, which you can view as a native realization of the three fundamental OO design patterns: abstraction, inheritance, and polymorphism.

QP, like OOP, introduces its own (quantum) state patterns. These patterns are concerned with useful ways of structuring statecharts to solve recurring problems. QP, like an OO programming language, allows more precise descriptions of the patterns than can be achieved with graphical-only representation.

QP goes beyond traditional OOP by modeling the internal structure of reactive classes. The governing laws in this microcosm turn out to be similar to those of quantum physics, where objects spend their lives in discrete states, make uninterruptible state transitions (quantum leaps), and interact only by exchanging event instances (intermediate virtual bosons).

Chapter 2

A Crash Course in Statecharts

Nothing is particularly hard if you divide it into small jobs.
— Henry Ford

If you look through enough real-life code in use across the industry, you probably agree that the code pertaining to the reactive parts of various systems is riddled with a disproportionate number of convoluted conditional execution branches (deeply nested if–else or switch–case statements in C/C++). This highly conditional code (recall the Visual Basic Calculator from Chapter 1) is a testament to the basic characteristics of reactive systems, which respond to an input based on not only the nature of the input but the history of the system (i.e., on past inputs in which the system was involved).

If you could eliminate even a fraction of these conditional branches, the code would be much easier to understand and test, and the sheer number of convoluted execution paths through the code would drop radically, perhaps by orders of magnitude. Techniques based on state machines are capable of achieving exactly this — a dramatic reduction of the different paths through the code and simplification of the conditions tested at each branching point.

The state machines described in the UML specification represent the current state of the art in the long evolution of these techniques. UML state machines, known also as *UML statecharts* [OMG 01], are object-based variants of Harel statecharts [Harel 87] and incorporate several concepts defined in ROOMcharts, a variant of the statechart defined in the real-time object-oriented modeling (ROOM) language [Selic+ 94].

This chapter briefly introduces UML statecharts with a fresh, unorthodox perspective on the role of state machines and state modeling. My intention is not to give a complete discussion of UML statecharts, which the official OMG specification [OMG 01][1] covers formally and comprehensively. Rather, my goal in this chapter is to lay a foundation quickly by establishing basic terminology, introducing basic notation,[2] and clarifying semantics. This chapter is restricted to only a subset of those statechart features that are arguably most fundamental. The emphasis is on essence rather than formality.

2.1 The Essence of Finite State Machines

A system exhibits *state behavior* when it operates differently during different periods and when its behavior can be partitioned into finite, nonoverlapping chunks called *states*.

Not all systems or their components reveal state behavior; certain system components exhibit only simple behavior. For example, basic mathematical functions, such as $\sin(x)$, return the same result for a given input x regardless of the history of previous inputs $\{x_i\}$. Conversely, a continuous behavior depends on the history of inputs but cannot reasonably be divided into a finite number of states. System components in this category include, for example, digital filters [Douglass 99].

A common, straightforward way of modeling state behavior is through a *finite state machine* (FSM). FSMs are an efficient way to specify *constraints* of the overall behavior of a system. Being in a state means that the system responds only to a subset of all allowed inputs, produces only a subset of possible responses, and changes state directly to only a subset of all possible states.

2.1.1 States

A state is a situation or condition in the life of a system during which some (usually implicit) invariant holds, the system performs some activity, or the system waits for some external event [OMG 01].

A state captures the relevant aspects of the system's history very efficiently. For example, when you strike a key on a keyboard, the character code generated will be either an uppercase or a lowercase character, depending on whether the Caps Lock is

---

1.   The official UML specification [OMG 01] is included in PDF on the accompanying CD-ROM.
2.   Appendix B contains a comprehensive summary of the notation.

active. Therefore, the keyboard *is in* the capsLocked state, or the default state (most keyboards have an LED that indicates when the keyboard is in the capsLocked state). The behavior of a keyboard depends only on certain aspects of its history, namely whether Caps Lock has been activated, but not, for example, on how many and which specific characters have been typed previously. A state can abstract away all possible (but irrelevant) event sequences and capture only the relevant ones.

2.1.2   Extended States

One possible interpretation of state for software systems is that each state represents one distinct set of valid values of the whole program memory. Even for simple programs with only a few elementary variables, this interpretation leads to an astronomical number of states. For example, a single 32-bit integer could contribute to 2^{32} (4,294,967,296) different states. Clearly, this interpretation is not practical, so program variables are commonly dissociated from states. Rather, the complete condition of the system (called the *extended state*) is the combination of a qualitative aspect — the state — and the quantitative aspects — the *extended state variables*. In this interpretation, a change of variable does not always imply a change of the qualitative aspects of the system behavior and therefore does not lead to a change of state [Selic+ 94].

State machines supplemented with memory are called *extended state machines*. Extended state machines can apply the underlying formalism to much more complex problems than is practical with the basic (memoryless) state machines. For instance, suppose the behavior of the keyboard depends on the number of characters typed on it so far and that after, say, 100,000 keystrokes, the keyboard breaks down and enters a broken state. To model this behavior in a state machine without memory, you would need to introduce 100,000 states (e.g., pressing a key in state stroke54312 would lead to state stroke54313, and so on), which is clearly an impractical proposition. Alternatively, you could construct an extended state machine with a 32-bit counter. The counter would be incremented by every keystroke without changing state. When the counter reached the critical value of 100,000 keystrokes, the state machine would enter the broken state.

This wider range of applicability of extended state machines comes with a price, however, because of the blurry distinction between the qualitative aspects (state) and the quantitative aspects (extended state variables). For example, if the keyboard was to enter the broken state after just three keystrokes (rather poor mileage), then adding three states (e.g., stroke1, stroke2, and stroke3) might be more advantageous than introducing a keystroke counter, which has to be properly initialized and then incremented and checked by every keystroke event. What is the "right" way to model this particular behavior: the basic state machine with the three states or the extended state machine with the keystroke counter? The answer to this question is not always straightforward and presents a difficult design decision that will have profound effects on software performance and complexity.

2.1.3 Guards

Extended state machines often react to stimuli based not only on the qualitative state but also on the value of the extended state variables associated with that state. For instance in the keyboard example, when the keystroke counter exceeds a certain value, the state machine alters its behavior by changing state. In fact, the logical condition (comparing the counter with the threshold) is tested by every keystroke, but the change of state occurs *only* when the condition evaluates to TRUE.

This example illustrates the general mechanism by which extended state variables influence behavior. Boolean expressions, called *guard conditions* (or simply *guards*), are evaluated dynamically based on the value of extended state variables.[3] Guard conditions affect the behavior of a state machine by enabling or disabling certain operations (e.g., change of state).

The need for guards is the immediate consequence of adding memory (extended state variables) to the state machine formalism. Used sparingly, guards and extended state variables form an incredibly powerful mechanism that can immensely simplify designs. Used too liberally, however, guards can easily defeat the purpose of using state machines in the first place.

If you recall from the first paragraph of this chapter, the primary reason to use state machines is to reduce the number of conditional branches in the code and to reduce the complexity of the tests performed at each branch. The use of guards goes exactly against these goals by reintroducing testing of (extended state) variables and branching based on these tests. In the extreme case, guards effectively take over handling of all the relevant conditions in the system, which puts you back to square one. Indeed, abuse of guards is *the* primary mechanism of architectural decay in designs based on state machines.

2.1.4 Events

In the most general terms, an event is an occurrence in time and space that has significance to the system. Strictly speaking, in the UML specification, the term "event" refers to the *type* of occurrence rather than to any concrete instance of that occurrence [OMG 01]. For example, Keystroke is an event for the keyboard, but each press of a key is not an event but a concrete *instance* of the Keystroke event. Another event of interest for the keyboard might be Power-on, but turning the power on tomorrow at 10:05:36 will be just an instance of the Power-on event.

---

3. Guard conditions also can contain event parameters (see the discussion of events and event parameters in the next section).

Usually, in the day-to-day battle, it seems very tempting (especially to programmers new to state machine formalism) to add yet another extended state variable and yet another test (guard) rather than to factor out the related behavior into a new qualitative aspect of the system — the state. Therefore, perhaps the most important requirement for a *practical* state machine implementation is the ease of adding (or removing) states. The likelihood of architectural decay is directly proportional to the overhead (actual or perceived) involved in adding or removing states.

An event can have associated parameters, allowing the event instance to convey not only the occurrence of some interesting incident but also quantitative information regarding that occurrence. For example, the Keystroke event generated by pressing a key on a computer keyboard has associated parameters that convey the character scan code, as well as the status of the Shift, Ctrl, and Alt keys.

An event instance outlives the instantaneous occurrence that generated it and might convey this occurrence to one or more state machines. Once generated, the event instance goes through a processing life cycle that can consist of up to three stages. First, the event instance is *received* when it is accepted and awaiting processing (e.g., it is placed on the event queue). Later, the event instance is *dispatched* to the state machine, at which point it becomes the *current event*. Finally, it is *consumed* when the state machine finishes processing the event instance. A consumed event instance is no longer available for processing.

2.1.5   Actions and Transitions

When an event instance is dispatched, the state machine responds by performing *actions*, such as changing a variable, performing I/O, invoking a function, generating another event instance, or changing to another state. Any parameter values associated with the current event are available to all actions directly caused by that event.

Switching from one state to another is called *state transition*, and the event that causes it is called the *triggering event*, or simply *trigger*. In the keyboard example, if the keyboard is in the `default` state when the Caps Lock key is pressed, the keyboard will enter the `capsLocked` state. However, if the keyboard is already in the `capsLocked` state, pressing Caps Lock will cause a different transition — from the `capsLocked` to the `default` state. In both cases, pressing Caps Lock is the triggering event.

In extended state machines, a transition can have a guard, which means that the transition can "fire" only if the guard evaluates to TRUE. A state can have many transitions in response to the same trigger, as long as they have nonoverlapping guards; however, this situation could create problems in the sequence of evaluation of the guards when the common trigger occurs. The UML specification intentionally does not stipulate any particular order; rather, it puts the burden on the designer to devise guards in such a way that the order of their evaluation does not matter. Practically, this means that guard expressions should have *no side effects*, at least none that would influence evaluation of other guards having the same trigger.

2.1.6 Mealy and Moore Automata

Classical FSMs have two interpretations: Mealy and Moore automata. The *Mealy automaton* associates actions with state transitions. Because actions necessarily take a finite amount of time, a Mealy automaton causes conceptual difficulty, because while a system is executing actions, it is not in any state (it is between two states). In other words, the state of a Mealy automaton is not well defined at all times.[4] This problem is avoided in the alternative *Moore automaton* interpretation of FSM, which associates actions with states rather than transitions. The state of a system is always well defined in a Moore automaton because actionless transitions can be considered instantaneous (actions still take time but are executed in a well-defined state context). More formally, the output of a Moore automaton depends only on the current state, whereas the output of a Mealy automaton depends on both the current state and the current input.

Mealy and Moore automata are mathematically equivalent (i.e., one always can be transformed into the other). In general, however, a Moore automaton requires more states to model the same system because a Mealy automaton can use different transitions (transitions with different triggers) to the same state and can execute different actions. A Moore automaton must use different states to represent conditions in which different actions are performed.

2.1.7 Execution Model — Run-to-Completion Step

In practice, executing actions always takes some time to complete. The state machine therefore alternates between two modes: idle — listening for the arrival of the next event, and busy — responding to an event.

What happens in this model when a high-priority event occurs while the system is still busy handling the previous (lower priority) event? There are actually only two possibilities: the preemptive and nonpreemptive handling of events. In the preemptive model, the system can immediately suspend processing of the lower priority event and commence with the new event. In the nonpreemptive model, before the system handles a new event. it can store it until the previous event has completed processing. This model is called *run to completion*, or RTC.

---

4.   Mealy automata dismiss this problem by simply assuming that actions take no time to execute (the so-called zero time assumption).

The problem with the preemptive model is that it introduces internal concurrency within the scope of a single state machine. If preemption is allowed, handling the high-priority event might modify some internal variables that were in the process of being modified by the interrupted (low-priority) processing. After resuming, the low-priority processing might find some of these variables unexpectedly modified, which could cause errors. This creates a standard concurrency problem that requires some form of mutual exclusion. However, proper handling of this situation leads to immense complexity in the general case, rendering the preemptive model impractical.

In the RTC model, the system processes events in discrete, indivisible RTC steps. Higher priority events cannot interrupt the handling of other events, thereby completely avoiding the internal concurrency issue. This model also gets around the problem of the ill-defined state in the Mealy automaton. During event processing, the system is unresponsive (unobservable), so the ill-defined state during that time has no practical significance. The RTC model is analogous to the quantum mechanical interpretation of a quantum leap, where a transition between different quantum states (the quantum leap) is fundamentally indivisible (uninterruptible). Because a quantum system has to finish one interaction before engaging in another, it always appears to be in a well-defined quantum state. Such systems are fundamentally unobservable in the midst of a transition.

RTC does not mean that a state machine has to monopolize the processor until the RTC step is complete. The preemption restriction only applies to the task context of the state machine that is already busy processing events. In a multitasking environment, other tasks (not related to the task context of the busy state machine) can be running, possibly preempting the currently executing state machine. As long as other state machines do not share variables with each other, there are no concurrency hazards.

State machine formalisms, including UML statecharts, universally assume RTC execution semantics. The key advantage of RTC processing is *simplicity*. Its biggest disadvantage is that, within the scope of a single state machine, event handling cannot take too long to ensure a timely response to higher priority events. In order to achieve high responsiveness, timely low-latency and high-priority processing cannot be mixed in the same state machine with high-latency, low-priority processing.[5] This requirement can sometimes significantly complicate implementation.

---

5. A state machine can improve responsiveness by breaking up the CPU-intensive processing into sufficiently short RTC steps.

2.1.8   State Transition Diagrams

FSMs have an expressive graphical representation in the form of *state transition diagrams*. These diagrams are directed graphs in which nodes denote states and connectors denote transitions.[6]

For example, Figure 2.1 shows a state transition diagram corresponding to the computer keyboard model. States are represented as rounded rectangles labeled with state names. The transitions, represented as arrows, are labeled with the triggering events followed optionally by the list of triggered actions. The *initial transition* originates from the solid circle and specifies the starting state when the system first begins. Every state diagram should have such a transition, which should not be labeled, since it is not triggered by an event. However, the initial transition can have associated actions, such as setting up the extended state variables or initializing the hardware. Optionally a state transition diagram can also have a *final state*, indicating the end-of-life of the system (typically destruction of the object). The final state is represented as an empty circle with a black dot (a bull's-eye).

Figure 2.1   State transition diagram representing the computer keyboard FSM

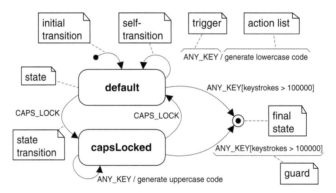

2.2   The Essence of UML Statecharts

UML statecharts are extended state machines with characteristics of both Mealy and Moore automata. In statecharts, actions generally depend on both the state of the system and the triggering event, as in a Mealy automaton. Additionally, statecharts provide optional entry and exit actions, which are associated with states rather than transitions, as in a Moore automaton.

---

6.   Appendix B contains a succinct summary of the graphical notations used throughout the book, including state transition diagrams.

2.2.1 Hierarchical States

The most important innovation of statecharts over classical state machines is the introduction of *hierarchically nested states*, which is why statecharts are also called *hierarchical state machines* (HSMs). The semantics associated with state nesting (shown in Figure 2.2a)[7] are as follows. If a system *is in* the nested state s11 (called *substate*), it also (implicitly) *is in* the surrounding state s1 (the *superstate*). This state machine will attempt to handle any event in the context of state s11 (which is in the lower level of the hierarchy). However, if state s11 does not prescribe how to handle the event, the event is not quietly discarded (as in a classical state machine); rather, it is *automatically* handled in the higher level context of state s1. This is what is meant by the system being in state s1 as well as s11. Of course, state nesting is not limited to one level only, and the simple rule of event processing applies recursively to any level of nesting.

States that contain other states are called composite states; conversely, states without internal structure are called simple states. A nested state is called a direct substate when it is not contained by any other state; otherwise, it is referred to as a transitively nested substate.

Because the internal structure of a composite state can be arbitrarily complex, any hierarchical state machine can be viewed as an internal structure of some (higher level) composite state. It is conceptually convenient to define one composite state as the ultimate root of state machine hierarchy. In the UML specification, every state machine has a *top state* (the abstract root of every state machine hierarchy), which contains all the other elements of the entire state machine. The graphical rendering of this all-enclosing top state is optional [OMG 01].

As you can see, the semantics of hierarchical state decomposition are designed to allow *sharing* of behavior. The substates (nested states) need only define the *differences* from the superstates (surrounding states). A substate can easily reuse the common behavior from its superstate(s) by simply ignoring commonly handled events, which are then automatically handled by higher level states. In this manner, the substates can share all aspects of behavior with their superstates. For example, in a state model of a simple toaster oven (Figure 2.2b), states toasting and baking share a common transition to state doorOpen, defined in their common superstate heating.

The aspect of state hierarchy emphasized most often is *abstraction* — an old and powerful technique for coping with complexity. Instead of facing all aspects of a complex system at the same time, it is often possible to ignore (abstract away) some parts of the system. Hierarchical states are an ideal mechanism for hiding internal details because the designer can easily zoom out or zoom in to hide or show nested states. Although abstraction by itself does not reduce overall system complexity, it is

---

7. The graphical notation of a statechart is a straightforward extension of the state transition diagrams.

Figure 2.2 **(a) Simple statechart with state `s11` nested inside state `s1`; (b) state model of a simple toaster oven, in which states `toasting` and `baking` share the common transition from state `heating` to `doorOpen`**

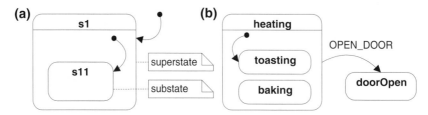

valuable because it reduces the amount of detail you need to deal with at one time. As Grady Booch [Booch 94] notes:

> *... we are still constrained by the number of things that we can comprehend at one time, but through abstraction, we use chunks of information with increasingly greater semantic content.*

However valuable abstraction might be, you cannot cheat your way out of complexity simply by hiding it inside composite states. However, the composite states can not only hide but also reduce complexity through the *reuse of behavior*. Without such reuse, even a moderate increase in system complexity often leads to an explosive increase in the number of states and transitions. Classical nonhierarchical FSMs can easily become unmanageable, even for moderately involved systems. This is because traditional state machine formalism *inflicts repetitions*. For example, if you transform the statechart from Figure 2.2b to a classical flat state transition diagram,[8] you must *repeat* one transition (from `heating` to `doorOpen`) in *two* places — as a transition from `toasting` to `doorOpen` and from `baking` to `doorOpen`. Avoiding repetitions allows HSMs to grow proportionally to system complexity. As the modeled system grows, the opportunity for reuse also increases and thus counteracts the explosive increase in states and transitions typical for traditional FSMs. As will become clear by the end of this chapter, hierarchical states enable capturing *symmetries* of the system.

2.2.2 Behavioral Inheritance

Hierarchical states are more than merely the "*grouping of [nested] state machines together without additional semantics*" [Mellor 00]. In fact, hierarchical states have simple but profound semantics. Nested states are also more than just "*great diagrammatic simplification when a set of events applies to several substates*" [Douglass 99]. The savings in the number of states and transitions are real and go far beyond

---

8.   Such a transformation is always possible because HSMs are mathematically equivalent to classical FSMs.

less cluttered diagrams. In other words, simpler diagrams are just a side effect of behavioral reuse enabled by state nesting.

The fundamental character of state nesting comes from the combination of abstraction and hierarchy, which is a traditional approach to reducing complexity and is otherwise known in software as inheritance. In OOP, the concept of class inheritance describes relations between classes of objects. Class inheritance describes the *is a* relationship among classes. For example, class `Bird` might derive from class `Animal`. If an object *is a* bird (instance of the `Bird` class), it automatically *is an* animal, because all operations that apply to animals (e.g., eating, eliminating, reproduction) also apply to birds. But birds are more specialized, since they have operations that are not applicable to animals in general. For example, flying applies to birds but not to fish.[9]

The benefits of class inheritance are concisely summarized by Gamma and colleagues [Gamma+ 95].

> *Inheritance lets you define a new kind of class rapidly in terms of an old one, by reusing functionality from parent classes. It allows new classes to be specified by difference rather than created from scratch each time. It lets you get new implementations almost for free, inheriting most of what is common from the ancestor classes.*

As you saw in the previous section, all these basic characteristics of inheritance apply equally well to nested states (just replace the word "class" with "state"), which is not surprising because state nesting is based on the same fundamental *is a* classification as object-oriented class inheritance. For example, in a state model of a toaster oven, state `toasting` nests inside state `heating`. If the toaster *is in* the `toasting` state, it automatically *is in* the `heating` state, because all behavior pertaining to heating applies also to toasting (e.g., the heater must be turned on). But toasting is more specialized because it has behaviors not applicable to heating in general. For example, setting toast color (light or dark) applies to toasting but not to `baking`.

In the case of nested states, the *is a* (is-a-kind-of) relationship merely needs to be replaced by the *is in* (is-in-a-state) relationship; otherwise, it is the same fundamental classification. State nesting allows a substate to inherit state behavior from its ancestors (superstates); therefore, it's called behavioral inheritance. Note that behavioral inheritance is an original term characteristic of QP and does not come from the UML specification. Please also note that behavioral inheritance describes the relationship between substates and superstates, and you should not confuse it with traditional (class) inheritance applied to entire state machines.

---

9. Except, of course, the flying fish.

Identifying the relationship among substates and superstates in inheritance has many practical implications. Perhaps the most important is the *Liskov Substitution Principle* (LSP) applied to state hierarchy. In its traditional formulation for classes, LSP requires that a subclass can be freely substituted for its superclass. This means that every instance of the subclass should be compatible with the instance of the superclass and that any code designed to work with the instance of the superclass should continue to work correctly if an instance of the subclass is used instead.

Because behavioral inheritance is just a specific kind of inheritance, LSP can be applied to nested states as well as classes. LSP generalized for states means that the behavior of a substate should be consistent with the superstate. For example, all states nested inside the heating state of the toaster oven, (e.g., toasting or baking) should share the same basic characteristics of the heating state. In particular, if being in the heating state means that the heater is turned on, then none of the substates should turn the heater off (without transitioning out of the heating state). Turning the heater off and staying in the toasting or baking states would be inconsistent with being in the heating state and would indicate poor design (violation of the LSP).

Compliance with the LSP allows you to build better (more correct) state hierarchies and make efficient use of abstraction. For example, in an LSP-compliant state hierarchy, you can safely zoom out and work at the higher level of the heating state (thus abstracting away the specifics of toasting and baking). As long as all the substates are consistent with their superstate, such abstraction is meaningful. On the other hand, if the substates violate basic assumptions of being in the superstate, zooming out and ignoring specifics of the substates will be incorrect.

The concept of inheritance is fundamental in software construction. Class inheritance is essential for better software organization and for code reuse, which makes it a cornerstone of OOP. In the same way, behavioral inheritance is essential for efficient use of HSMs and for behavior reuse, which makes it a cornerstone of QP. In Chapter 5, a minicatalog of state patterns shows ways to structure HSMs to solve recurring problems. Not surprisingly, behavioral inheritance plays the central role in all these patterns.

2.2.3   Orthogonal Regions

Hierarchical state decomposition can be viewed as the classical exclusive-or applied to states. For example, if a system is in state heating (Figure 2.2b), it means that it's either in state toasting or baking. That is why state hierarchy is alternatively called *or-decomposition* and the nested states are called *or-states*. UML statecharts also introduce the complementary *and-decomposition*. Such decomposition means that a composite state can contain two or more *orthogonal regions* (orthogonal means independent in this context) and that being in such a composite state entails being in all of its orthogonal regions simultaneously [Harel+ 98].

Orthogonal regions address the frequent problem of a combinatorial increase in the number of states when the behavior of a system is fragmented into independent, concurrently active parts. For example, apart from the main keypad, a computer keyboard has an independent numeric keypad. From the previous discussion, recall the two states of the main keypad already identified: default and capsLocked (Figure 2.1). The numeric keypad also can be in two states — numbers and arrows — depending on whether Num Lock is active. The complete state space of the keyboard in the standard decomposition is the cross product of the two components (main keypad and numeric keypad) and consists of four states: default–numbers, default–arrows, capsLocked–numbers, and capsLocked–arrows. However, this is unnatural because the behavior of the numeric keypad does not depend on the state of the main keypad and vice versa. Orthogonal regions allow you to avoid mixing the independent behaviors as a cross product and, instead, to keep them separate, as shown in Figure 2.3.

Note that if the orthogonal regions are fully independent of each other, their combined complexity is simply additive, which means that the number of independent states needed to model the system is simply the sum $k + l + m + ...$, where $k, l, m, ...$ denote numbers of or-states in each orthogonal region. The general case of mutual dependency, on the other hand, results in multiplicative complexity, so in general, the number of states needed is the product $k \times l \times m \times ....$

Figure 2.3   Two orthogonal regions (main keypad and numeric keypad) of a computer keyboard

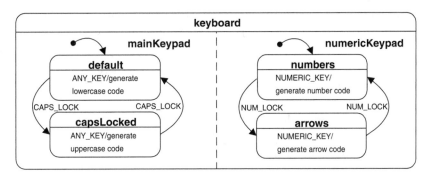

In most real-life situations, however, orthogonal regions are only approximately orthogonal (i.e., they are not quite independent). Therefore, UML statecharts provide a number of ways for orthogonal regions to communicate and synchronize their behaviors. From this rich set of (sometimes complex) mechanisms, perhaps the most important is that orthogonal regions can coordinate their behaviors by sending event instances to each other.

Even though orthogonal regions imply independence of execution (i.e., some kind of concurrency), the UML specification does not require that a separate thread of execution be assigned to each orthogonal region (although it can be implemented that way). In fact most commonly, orthogonal regions execute within the same thread. The UML specification only requires that the designer not rely on any particular order in which an event instance will be dispatched to the involved orthogonal regions.

2.2.4   Entry and Exit Actions

Every state in a UML statechart can have optional *entry actions*, which are executed upon entry to a state, as well as optional *exit actions*, which are executed upon exit from a state. Entry and exit actions are associated with states, not transitions. Regardless of how a state is entered or exited, all of its entry and exit actions will be executed. Because of this characteristic, statecharts behave like Moore automata.

The value of entry and exit actions is that they provide means for guaranteed initialization and cleanup, very much like class constructors and destructors in OOP. For example, consider the doorOpen state from Figure 2.2b, which corresponds to the toaster oven behavior while the door is open. This state has a very important safety-critical requirement: Always disable the heater when the door is open.[10] Additionally, while the door is open, the internal lamp illuminating the oven should light up.

Of course, you could model such behavior by adding appropriate actions (disabling the heater and turning on the light) to every transition path leading to the doorOpen state (the user may open the door at any time during baking or toasting or when the oven is not used at all). You also should not forget to extinguish the internal lamp with every transition leaving the doorOpen state. However, such a solution would cause the repetition of actions in many transitions. More importantly, such an approach is error-prone in view of changes to the state machine (e.g., a programmer working on a new feature, such as top-browning, might simply forget to disable the heater on transition to doorOpen).

Entry and exit actions allow you to implement the desired behavior in a much safer, simpler, and more intuitive way. You could specify that the exit action from heating (see Figure 2.2b) disables the heater, the entry action to doorOpen lights up the oven lamp, and the exit action from doorOpen extinguishes the lamp. This solution is superior because it avoids repetitions of those actions on transitions and eliminates the basic safety hazard of leaving the heater on while the door is open. The semantics of exit actions guarantees that, regardless of the transition path, the heater will be disabled when the toaster is not in the heating state.

---

10. Commonly such a safety-critical function is (and should be) realized by mechanical interlocks, but for the sake of this discussion, suppose you need to implement it in software.

Because entry actions are executed automatically whenever an associated state is entered, they often determine the conditions of operation or the *identity* of the state, very much as a class constructor determines the identity of the object being constructed. For example, the identity of the heating state is determined by the fact that the heater is turned on. This condition must be established *before* entering any substate of heating because entry actions to a substate of heating, like toasting, rely on proper initialization of the heating superstate and perform only the *differences* from this initialization. Consequently, the order of execution of entry actions must always proceed from the outermost state to the innermost state.

Not surprisingly, this order is analogous to the order in which class constructors are invoked. Construction of a class always starts at the very root of the class hierarchy and follows through all inheritance levels down to the class being instantiated. The execution of exit actions, which corresponds to destructor invocation, proceeds in the exact reverse order, starting from the innermost state (corresponding to the most derived class).

Please note, however, that although entry and exit actions are closely related to class constructors and destructors, they are also significantly different. The main difference comes about because changing the identity of a class instance (object) involves complete destruction followed by complete reconstruction, even if the initial and final objects are closely related (have common ancestors). For example, if you need to exchange an instance of a Bird class with an instance of a Fish class (e.g., in a database application), then you must completely destroy the bird object and create a fish object from scratch, even though they both descend from the common ancestor class Animal (Figure 2.4a). In a statechart, such a change of identity corresponds to a state transition; however, in contrast to objects, the change does not require complete destruction and recreation. For example, a state transition from toasting to baking (both nested inside the heating state) involves only the execution of the toasting exit actions followed by the baking entry actions but does not involve executing the heating exit or entry actions, simply because this transition never leaves the heating state (Figure 2.4b).

2.2.5 Transition Execution Sequence

State nesting combined with entry and exit actions significantly complicates the state transition semantics in statecharts compared to simple FSMs. When dealing with composite states and orthogonal regions, the simple term "current state" can be quite confusing. In an HSM, more than one state can be active at once. If the state machine is in a simple state that is contained in a composite state (which is possibly contained in a higher level composite state, and so on), all the composite states that either directly or transitively contain the simple state are also active. Furthermore, because some of the composite states in this hierarchy

Figure 2.4 **(a) Changing the identity of object :Bird into :Fish requires complete destruction and recreation of the entire object, including the part inherited from the common Animal superclass; (b) state transition from toasting to baking does not require exit and reentry into the common heating superstat**

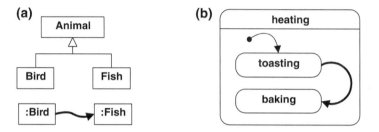

might have orthogonal regions, the current active state is actually represented by a tree of states starting with the single top state at the root down to individual simple states at the leaves. The UML specification refers to such a state tree as *state configuration* [OMG 01].

Every state transition, except for internal transitions (see the next section), causes the statechart to exit a *source* state configuration and enter a *target* state configuration. The UML specification prescribes that taking a state transition involves executing the following actions in the following sequence [OMG 01]:

- exit actions of the source state configuration,
- actions associated with the transition, and
- entry actions of the target state configuration.

This three-step transition rule is easy to interpret when the source and target state are both simple and nest at same level, as in the transition between states default and capsLocked in Figure 2.3. However in statecharts, state transition can connect any two states directly, including composite states at different levels of nesting. The problem is to discover which states need to be exited in step one. The UML specification prescribes that the first step involves exiting all nested states from the current active state (which might be a direct or transitive substate of the source state) up to, but not including, the *least common ancestor* (LCA) state of the source and target states. As the name indicates, the LCA is the lowest composite state that is simultaneously a superstate (ancestor) of both the source and the target states. As described before, the order of execution of exit actions is always from the most deeply nested state (the current active state) up the hierarchy to the LCA (but without exiting the LCA). In the last step (after executing actions associated with the transition), the target state needs to be entered. Executing entry actions commences from the level where the exit actions left off (i.e., from inside the LCA), down the state hierarchy to the target state. If the target state is composite, then its submachine is recursively entered via the default transition or the history mechanism (see the description of history pseudostates coming up in Section 2.2.7).

2.2.6 Internal Transitions

Very commonly, an event causes only some internal actions to execute but does not lead to a change of state (state transition). In this case, all actions executed comprise the *internal transition*. For example, when you type on your keyboard, it responds by generating different character codes. However, unless you hit the Caps Lock key, the state of the keyboard does not change (no state transition occurs). In UML, this situation should be modeled with internal transitions, as shown in Figure 2.3. The UML notation for internal transitions follows the general syntax used for exit (or entry) actions, except instead of the word "entry" (or "exit") the internal transition is labeled with the triggering event (e.g., see the internal transition triggered by the ANY_KEY event in Figure 2.3).

In the absence of entry and exit actions, internal transitions would be identical to *self-transitions* (transitions in which the target state is the same as the source state). In fact, in a classical Mealy automaton, actions are associated exclusively with state transitions, so the only way to execute actions without changing state is through a self-transition (depicted as a directed loop in Figure 2.1). However, in the presence of entry and exit actions, as in UML statecharts, a self-transition involves (1) the execution of exit actions followed by (2) the execution of actions associated with the transition, and finally (3) the execution of entry actions. Because a self-transition involves the execution of exit and entry actions in statecharts, it is distinctively different from an internal transition.

In contrast to a self-transition, no entry or exit actions are ever executed as a result of an internal transition, even if the internal transition is executed at a higher level of the hierarchy than the currently active state. Internal transitions are inherited by the substates (as any other behavior) and act as if they were defined directly at all the lower levels of hierarchy (unless they were not overridden explicitly).

2.2.7 Pseudostates

Because statecharts started as a visual formalism [Harel 87], some nodes in the diagrams other than the regular states turned out to be useful for implementing various features (or simply as a shorthand notation). The various "plumbing gear" nodes are collectively called *pseudostates*. More formally, a pseudostate is an abstraction that encompasses different types of transient vertices (nodes) in the state machine graph.

The UML specification [OMG 01] defines the following kinds of pseudostates.

- The initial pseudostate (shown as a black dot) represents a source for default transition. There can be, at most, one initial pseudostate in a composite state.

- The shallow-history pseudostate (shown as a circled letter "H") is a shorthand notation that represents the most recent active direct substate of its containing state. A transition coming into the shallow-history vertex (called a *transition to history*) is equivalent to a transition coming into the most recent active substate of a state. A transition can originate from the history connector to designate a state to be entered in case a composite state has no history yet (has never been active before).

- The deep-history pseudostate (shown as a circled "H*") is similar to shallow-history, except it represents the whole, most recent state configuration of the composite state that directly contains the pseudostate.

- The join pseudostate (shown as a vertical bar) serves to merge several transitions emanating from source vertices in different orthogonal regions.

- The fork pseudostate (represented identically as a join) serves to split an incoming transition into two or more transitions terminating in different orthogonal regions.

- The junction pseudostate (shown as a black dot) is a semantics-free vertex that chains together multiple transitions. A junction is like a Swiss Army knife: it performs various functions. Junctions can be used both to merge multiple incoming transitions (from the same concurrent region) and to split an incoming transition into multiple outgoing transition segments with different guards. The latter case realizes a static conditional branch because the use of a junction imposes static evaluation of all guards before the transition is taken.

- The choice pseudostate (shown as an empty circle or a diamond) is used for dynamic conditional branches. It allows the splitting of transitions into multiple outgoing paths, so the decision on which path to take could depend on the results of prior actions performed in the same RTC step.

2.2.8 Refined Event Handling

The UML specification defines four kinds of events, each one distinguished by a specific notation.

- SignalEvent represents the reception of a particular (asynchronous) signal. Its format is *signal-name* '(' *comma-separated-parameter-list* ')'.

- TimeEvent models the expiration of a specific deadline. It is denoted with the keyword `after`, followed by an expression specifying the amount of time.

- CallEvent represents the request to synchronously invoke a specific operation. Its format is *operation-name* '(' *comma-separated-parameter-list* ')'.

- ChangeEvent models an event that occurs when an explicit Boolean expression becomes true. It is denoted with the keyword when, followed by a Boolean expression.

A SignalEvent is by far the most common event (and the only one used in classical FSMs). Even here, however, the UML specification extends traditional FSM semantics by allowing the specified signal to be a subclass of another signal, resulting in *polymorphic event triggering*. Any transition triggered by a given signal event is also triggered by any subevent derived directly or indirectly from the original event.

Additionally, the UML specification provides syntax for *deferring* events. A state can specify a list of deferred events. If a received event matches one of the types in the deferred list of that state, it is not dispatched but remains in the event queue until a state is reached where the event is not deferred.

2.2.9 Semantics versus Notation

Statecharts have been invented as "a visual formalism for complex systems" [Harel 87], so from their inception, they have been inseparably associated with graphical representation in the form of statechart diagrams. However, it is important to understand that the *concept* of HSMs transcends any particular notation, graphical or textual. The UML specification [OMG 01] makes this distinction apparent by clearly separating state machine semantics from the notation.

Nevertheless, many elements of statecharts and much of the semantics are heavily biased toward graphical notation. For example, state diagrams poorly represent the sequence of processing, be it order of evaluation of guards or order of dispatching events to orthogonal regions. The UML specification sidesteps these problems by putting the burden on the designer not to rely on any particular sequencing. However, as you will see in the following chapters, when you implement statecharts (e.g., in C or C++), you will have full control over the order of execution, so the restrictions imposed by statecharts will be unwarranted. Similarly, statechart diagrams require a lot of plumbing gear (a.k.a. pseudostates, like joins, forks, junctions, choicepoints, etc.) to represent the flow of control graphically. These elements are nothing but the old flowchart in disguise, which structured programming techniques rendered obsolete[11] a long time ago.

However, the notation of UML statecharts is not purely visual, since it requires a large amount of textual information (e.g., the specification of actions and guards). The exact syntax of action and guard expressions isn't defined in the UML specifica-

---

11. You can find a critique of flowcharts in Brooks [Brooks 95].

tion, so many people use either structured English or, more formally, expressions in an implementation language such as C, C++, or Java [Douglass 99b]. Practically, this means that UML statechart notation depends heavily on the specific programming language.

This is not to criticize the graphical notation of statecharts. In fact, it is remarkably expressive and can scarcely be improved. Rather, the aforementioned difficulties stem from the inherent difficulty in visualizing the software concepts themselves. As Brooks [Brooks 95] writes:

> *More fundamentally, ... software is difficult to visualize. Whether we diagram control flow, variable scope nesting, variable cross-references, data flow, hierarchical data structures, or whatever, we feel only one dimension of the intricately interlocked software elephant.*

Later in the text, he responds to Harel:

> *... software structure is not embedded in three-space, so there is no natural mapping from a conceptual design to a diagram, whether in two dimensions or more ... one needs multiple diagrams [multiple views], each conveying some distinct aspect, and some aspects don't diagram well at all.*

2.2.10 Statecharts versus Flowcharts

It is important to distinguish statecharts from flowcharts. The UML specification adds to the confusion in this respect by including *activity graphs* in the state machine package [OMG 01]. Activity graphs are essentially elaborate flowcharts.

Figure 2.5 **Comparison of (a) Mealy state machine, (b) Moore state machine, and (c) activity graph (flowchart)**

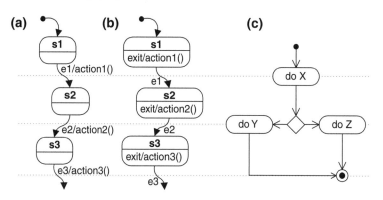

Figure 2.5 shows a comparison of Mealy and Moore state machines with a flowchart. State machines (a and b) perform actions in response to explicit triggers. In contrast, the flowchart (c) does not need explicit triggers; rather, it transitions from node to node in its graph *automatically* upon completion of an activity.

Compared to the statechart, a flowchart reverses the sense of vertices and arcs [Simons 00]. In a statechart, the processing is associated with the arcs, whereas in a flowchart, it is associated with the vertices (Figure 2.5 attempts to show that reversal of roles by aligning the arcs of the statecharts with the processing stages of the flowchart).

You can compare a flowchart to an assembly line in manufacturing because the flowchart describes the *progression* of some task from beginning to end. A statechart generally has no notion of such a progression. A computer keyboard (Figure 2.1), for example, is not in a more advanced stage when it is in the capsLocked state, compared to being in the default state. A *state* in a state machine is an efficient way of specifying *constraints* of the overall behavior of a system, rather than a stage of processing.

2.2.11 Statecharts and Automatic Code Synthesis

Statecharts provide sufficiently well-defined semantics for building *executable* state models. Indeed, several CASE tools on the market support various versions of statecharts (see the sidebar "CASE Tools Supporting Statecharts" on page 44). The commercially available design automation tools typically not only automatically generate code from statecharts but also enable debugging and testing of the state models at the graphical level [Douglass 99].

But what does automatic code generation really mean? And, more importantly, what kind of code is actually generated by such statechart-based tools?

Many people understand automatic code synthesis as the generation of a program to solve a problem from a statement of the problem specification. Statechart-based tools cannot provide this because a statechart is just a higher level (mostly visual) *solution* rather than the statement of the problem.

As far as the automatically generated code is concerned, the statechart-based tools can autonomously generate only so-called housekeeping code [Douglass 99]. The modeler explicitly must provide all the application-specific code, such as action and guard expressions, to the tool. The role of housekeeping code is to "glue" the various action and guard expressions together to ensure proper state machine execution in accordance with the statechart semantics. For example, synthesized code typically handles event queuing, event dispatching, guard evaluation, or transition chain execution (including exit and entry of appropriate states). Almost universally, the tools also encompass some kind of a real-time framework (see Part II of this book) that integrates tightly with the underlying operating system.

2.3   Examples of State Models

This section presents a short case study of two state models: the Quantum Calculator introduced in Chapter 1 and a hydrogen atom. The purpose of the first example is a step-by-step guide to developing a nontrivial statechart. The second example illuminates the deep analogy between HSMs and quantum systems and shines new light on the true role of state nesting and behavioral inheritance.

CASE Tools Supporting Statecharts

Some of the CASE tools with support for statecharts currently available on the market.

* Statemate and Rhapsody (I-Logix, www.ilogix.com)
* Rational Suite Development Studio Real-Time (Rational Software Corp., www.rational.com)
* BetterState (WindRiver Systems, www.wrs.com)
* Stateflow (MathWorks, www.mathworks.com)
* VisualState (IAR, www.iar.com)
* ObjectGeode (Telelogic, www.telelogic.com)

2.3.1   Quantum Calculator

In Chapter 1, I promised I'd come back to the Quantum Calculator statechart and explain it in more detail. Now, after introducing the most important elements of statecharts, is the right time to do so.

First, I want to comment on the high complexity of the calculator statechart from Figure 1.3 in Chapter 1. The calculator operates broadly as follows: a user enters an operand, then an operator, then another operand, and finally clicks the Equals button to get a result. From the programming perspective, this means that the calculator needs to parse[12] numerical expressions, which in itself is not trivial. For example, the following grammar formally defines such expressions.

---

12.   Parsing and state machines are related. In fact, most parsers operate as finite state machines.

Listing 2.1   Grammar of numerical expressions parsed by the calculator

```
1 expression ::= operand1 operator operand2 '='
2 operand1   ::= expression | ['+' | '-'] number
3 operand2   ::= ['+' | '-'] number
4 number     ::= {'0' | '1' | ... '9'}* ['.' {'0' | '1' | ... '9'}*]
5 operator   ::= '+' | '-' | '*' | '/'
```

The problem is not only to correctly parse numerical expressions but to do it *interactively* (on the fly). The user can provide any symbol at any time, not necessarily only the symbols allowed by the grammar in the current context. It is up to the application to ignore[13] such symbols. In addition, the application must handle inputs not related to parsing expressions, for example Cancel (C), or Cancel Entry (CE). These complications add up to a nontrivial problem, and it is not surprising that the bottom-up approach of the Visual Basic Calculator is inadequate in this case.

Figure 2.6   The first two steps in elaborating the Quantum Calculator statechart

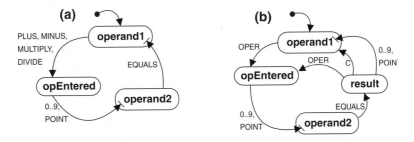

Figure 2.6 shows the first steps in elaborating the Quantum Calculator statechart.[14] In the first step (a) the state machine attempts to realize the *primary* function of the system (the primary use case), which is to compute the expression operand1 operator operand2 equals .... The state machine starts in the operand1 state, whose function is to ensure that the user can only enter a valid operand. This state obviously needs an internal submachine to accomplish this goal, but ignore that for now. The criterion for transitioning out of operand1 is entering an operator (+, -, *, or /). The statechart then enters the opEntered state, in which the calculator waits for the second operand. When the user clicks a digit (0 ... 9) or a decimal point, the state machine transitions to the operand2 state, which is similar to operand1. Finally, the

---

13. This particular application ignores invalid inputs. Often, a better approach is to actively prevent generation of the invalid inputs in the first place (e.g., by disabling invalid options).
14. Designing a statechart is not a strict science. You can arrive at a correct design in many different ways. This is just one of them.

user clicks '=', at which point the calculator computes and displays the result. It then transitions back to the operand1 state to get ready for another computation.

The simple state model from Figure 2.6a has a major problem, however. When the user clicks '=' in the last step, the state machine cannot transition directly to operand1, because this would erase the result from the display. You need another state, result, in which the calculator pauses to display the result (Figure 2.6b). Three things can happen in the result state: (1) the user clicks an operator button to use the result as the first operand of a new computation,[15] (2) the user clicks Cancel (C) to start a completely new computation, or (3) the user enters a number or a decimal point to start entering the first operand.

Figure 2.6b illustrates a trick worth remembering — the consolidation of signals PLUS, MINUS, MULTIPLY, and DIVIDE into a higher level signal OPER (operand). This transformation avoids repetition of the same group of triggers on two transitions (from operand1 to opEntered and from result to opEntered). Although most events are generated externally to the statechart, in many situations it is still possible to perform simple transformations *before* dispatching them (e.g., see Listing 1.2 in Chapter 1). Such transformations often simplify designs more than the slickest state and transition topologies.

Figure 2.7   **Applying state nesting to factor out the common Cancel (C) transition**

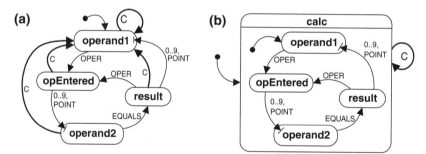

The state machine from Figure 2.6b accepts the Cancel command only in the result state. However, the user expects to be able to cancel and start over at any time. The statechart in Figure 2.7a adds this feature in a naïve way. A better solution is to factor out the common transition into a higher level state calc and let all substates *reuse* the Cancel transition through behavioral inheritance. Figure 2.7b shows this solution, except that it implements Cancel as an empty self-transition[16] rather than as a transition from the calc to operand1 substate. This solution enables even more reuse, because a self-transition triggers exit and then reentry to the state (see

---

15. See line 2 of Listing 2.1.
16. Empty self-transition is a useful idiom for resetting a composite state.

Section 2.2.6, "Internal Transitions"), thus reusing the initialization that these actions perform anyway.

The states `operand1` and `operand2` need submachines to parse floating-point numbers (Figure 2.8). These submachines consist of three substates. The `zero` substate is entered when the user clicks '0'. Its function is to ignore additional zeros that the user might try to enter (so that the calculator displays only one '0'). The function of the `int` substate is to parse the integer part of a number. This state is entered either from outside or from the `zero` peer substate (when the user clicks '1' through '9'). Finally, the substate `frac` parses the fractional part of the number. It is entered either from outside or from both of its peer substates when the user clicks the decimal point.

Figure 2.8   **Internal submachine of states `operand1` and `operand2`**

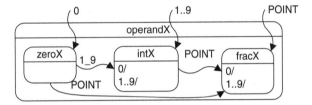

Exercise 2.1   Integrate composite states `operand1` and `operand2` into the statechart from Figure 2.7b (i.e., draw the calculator statechart with all levels of detail).

Exercise 2.2   The quantum `calc0` application on the accompanying CD-ROM implements the statechart from Figure 2.7b. Find and execute this application. Test how it performs and correlate its behavior with the underlying statechart. Examine the source code.

The last step brought the calculator statechart to the point in which it can actually compute expressions (Exercise 2.2). However, it can handle only positive numbers. In the next step, I will add handling of negative numbers, which turns out to be perhaps the toughest problem in this design because the same button (–) represents the binary operator of subtraction in some contexts and the unary operator of negation in others.

In only two possible contexts can '–' unambiguously represent negation rather than subtraction: (1) in the `opEntered` state (as in the expression 2*–2 =) and (2) at the beginning of a new computation (as in the expression –2*2 =). The solution to the first case (shown in Figure 2.9a) is simpler. You need one more state, negated2, which is entered when the operator is MINUS (note the use of the guard). Upon entry, this state sets up the display to show '–0' and subsequently does *not* clear the display when transitioning to the operand2 state. This behavior is different from opEntered because, in this state, the display must be cleared to prepare for the second operand.

Figure 2.9   Two cases of handling negative numbers

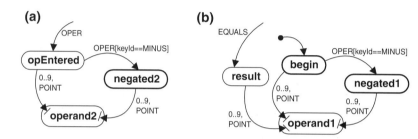

The second case in which '–' represents negation is trickier because the beginning of a new computation specification is much more subtle. Here, it indicates the situation just after launching the application or after the user clicks Cancel, but *not* when the calculator displays the result from the previous computation. Figure 2.9b shows the solution. State begin is separated from operand1 to capture the behavior specific to the beginning of a new computation (note the initial transition pointing now to begin rather than to operand1). The rest of the solution is analogous to the first case, except now state begin plays the role of opEntered.

Exercise 2.3   The state machine fragment in Figure 2.9b still offers opportunity for reuse of the identical transition from result to operand1 and from begin to operand1. Factor out this transition and place it in a common superstate, ready.

The calculator is almost ready now. The final touches (that I leave as an exercise) include adding Cancel Entry transitions in appropriate contexts and adding a transition to the final state to terminate the application.

The complete Quantum Calculator statechart is shown in Figure 1.3 in Chapter 1. Executable applications with compete source code (versions in C and C++) are available on the accompanying CD-ROM.

2.3.2 Hydrogen Atom

State behavior can be found in many systems, such as GUIs, keyboards, toaster ovens, and countless more. Indeed, state behavior is a vital aspect of virtually every computer system. However, the significance of state machines goes beyond software.

At the turn of the twentieth century, physicists realized that at the most fundamental level, all microscopic objects exhibit state behavior, rather than the continuous behavior predicted by classical mechanics. This discovery led directly to the formulation of quantum mechanics. As explained in the sidebar "Quantum States of the Hydrogen Atom" on page 51, the quantum mechanical description of a microscopic system leads naturally to *state hierarchies* that, by nature, comply with the LSP for states. Moreover, the quantum analogy clearly shows the fundamental role of behavioral inheritance, which captures *symmetries* of the system.

Because of this natural fit, virtually every quantum system provides a good case for state modeling. For instance, Figure 2.10 shows an overly simplified state model of a hydrogen atom.[17] This state diagram demonstrates many elements of the UML notation. The atom starts its life in the ground state 1S (I use traditional spectroscopic notation for naming states), as indicated by the top-level initial transition. Entry actions of the 1S state set the energy E of the system to $-13.6eV$ (a negative sign indicates binding energy), the angular momentum l to 0, and the projection of the angular momentum m to 0, which establishes the quantum mechanical identity of this state. The outgoing transitions from the ground state are triggered by photons g (signal events) of appropriate energy (indicated as a parameter associated with every "g" event). Consequently, the atom absorbs only specific (resonant) photons and "ignores" all others. The spontaneous photon emission from excited states is modeled by means of time events[18] (denoted by the keyword after followed by a time indication). Please note how state entry actions and actions associated with the transitions work together to ensure energy conservation.

The spontaneous, high-level transitions correspond to the full degeneration of hydrogen energy levels. This degeneration can be partially removed by inserting the atom into an external magnetic field (Zeeman effect) to lower the symmetry of the system. A system with lower symmetry generally requires a more complex state machine with more transitions connecting directly to more specific (more deeply nested) substates than a system with higher symmetry. Indeed, the Zee-

---

17. Theoretically, the hydrogen atom has an infinite number of states (energy levels), so strictly speaking, it cannot be modeled by a finite state machine. However, most relevant aspects of hydrogen behavior can be modeled by considering just a few of the lowest energy levels.

18. The indicated lifetimes of the corresponding decay paths are just examples and do not correspond to actual measurements.

Figure 2.10   Simplified state model of a hydrogen atom

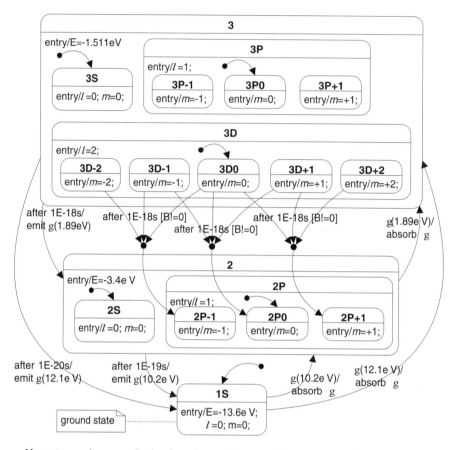

man effect introduces whole families of transitions connecting substates of different magnetic quantum number m. One example of such a family for the 3D → 2P
transitions is shown in Figure 2.10. This family of transitions is distinguished by the
guard [B != 0] on transition segments leading to a junction pseudostate. This
guard enables these specific decay channels only in the presence of an external magnetic field (otherwise the state decays via the high-level generic transitions inherited
from the superstate). Conservation of angular momentum forbids many transitions
(e.g., 3D–2 → 2P+1), because a photon can only carry one unit of angular momentum, so the magnetic quantum number can change by –1, 0, or +1 (but not by +3).
This constraint is clearly visible in that, at most, three transitions merge at any given
junction.

Although the statechart diagram from Figure 2.10 captures the basic behavior of
the hydrogen atom quite well, it also points out the main shortcomings of the graph-

ical notation. Although the diagram is by no means complete, it is already quite cluttered. Many transitions, especially those corresponding to the reduced symmetry case [B != 0], are intentionally omitted just to make this graph readable. UML notation addresses the clutter arising in virtually every nontrivial state diagram by allowing stubbed transitions and submachine states (besides, of course, using abstraction to hide the internal structure of composite states) [OMG 01]. Please note, however, that the difficulties with representation come from graphical notation rather than the fundamental inability of statecharts (as a concept) to scale up to handle the behavior of complex systems.

Quantum States of the Hydrogen Atom

In quantum mechanics, all physically observable quantities are associated with linear (Hermitean) operators, called *observables*. An outcome of a physical measurement is always an eigenvalue of such an operator, and the corresponding eigenvector is the *quantum state* of the microscopic system at the time of measurement. Typically, more than one physical quantity can be measured in a given quantum state, which means that this state is a simultaneous *eigenvector* of *many* observables (Hermitean operators). As you will see, this naturally leads to state hierarchy.

For example, in a quantum mechanical description of the hydrogen atom, the observables typically are Hamiltonian (H), orbital angular momentum (L^2), and projection of the angular momentum on the third axis (L_z). These three operators have common eigenvectors because they are commutative. This is not always the case; for example, operators of position and momentum (or energy and time) are not commutative and cannot be measured simultaneously, which is known as the Heisenberg uncertainty principle.

The simultaneous eigenvector of the three operators is denoted as |nlm> (Dirac's notation), where n is the principal quantum number, l is the orbital quantum number, and m is the magnetic quantum number. The eigenvector |nlm> fulfills the following eigenvalue equations.

$$H|nlm\rangle = \frac{-13.6\,\text{eV}}{n^2}|nlm\rangle \qquad n = 1, 2, 3, \ldots$$

$$L^2|nlm\rangle = \hbar^2 l(l+1)|nlm\rangle \qquad l = 0, 1, 2, \ldots n-1$$

$$L_z|nlm\rangle = \hbar m|nlm\rangle \qquad m = -l, -l+1, \ldots l$$

The quantum state |*nlm*> is thus hierarchical, with three levels of nesting. For every given state of energy (principal quantum number *n*), there are *n* substates of the orbital angular momentum (orbital quantum number *l*). Each substate, in turn, has $2l + 1$ different substates corresponding to different projections of the angular momentum on the third axis (magnetic quantum number *m*).

In these equations, all (direct or transitive) substates of a given energy state correspond to exactly the same energy eigenvalue ($-13.6eV/n^2$). In quantum mechanics, such a state is called degenerate. Degeneration is always an indication of some *symmetry* of the system. For example, the degeneration of the angular momentum state comes from spherical symmetry of the atom. This observation is very important: *Behavioral inheritance resulting from the nesting of states corresponds to symmetry of the system.*

A quantum mechanical state hierarchy *naturally* complies with the LSP for states. For example, if an atom *is in* a given quantum state of the projection operator L_z, it simultaneously *is in* the quantum state of angular momentum operator L^2, and simultaneously *is in* the quantum state of the Hamiltonian H. In such a hierarchy, you can efficiently use abstraction. For example, you can abstract away angular momentum and consider only energy levels of the atom (e.g., to understand its energy spectrum). This abstraction corresponds to zooming out to the highest level of nesting. On the other hand, if you destroy the spherical symmetry by subjecting the atom to an external magnetic field (e.g., to study the Zeeman effect), you might be interested in the lowest level substates of the magnetic quantum number.

Exercise 2.4 Closer inspection of hydrogen spectra reveals so-called fine structure, caused by a small magnetic moment associated with electron spin. The spin is an intrinsic angular momentum, with only two possible projections on the quantization axis ($s_z = \pm^1/_2\hbar$). How can you include electron spin in the state model of the hydrogen atom? Hint: Electron spin is mostly orthogonal to the basic electron–proton interaction.

2.4   Summary

Most reactive systems have state behavior, which means the response of a system depends not only on the nature of a stimulus but on the history of the previous stimuli. Such behavior is commonly modeled as FSMs or automata. FSMs efficiently capture overall system behavior and any applicable constraints.

States are means of partitioning behavior into nonoverlapping chunks (the divide and conquer strategy). The concept of state is a very useful abstraction of system history, capable of capturing only relevant sequences of stimuli (and ignoring all irrelevant ones). In extended state machines (state machines with "memory"), state corresponds to qualitative aspects of system behavior, whereas extended state variables (program memory) correspond to the quantitative aspects.

An event is a type of instantaneous occurrence that can cause a state machine to perform actions. Event instances are means of conveying such occurrences to state machines. Events can have parameters, which convey not only the occurrence of something interesting but the quantitative information regarding this occurrence. Upon reception of an event instance, a state machine responds by performing actions (executing code). The response might include changing state, which is called a state transition. Classical FSMs have two complementary interpretations of actions and transitions. In Mealy automata, actions are associated with transitions, whereas in Moore automata, actions are associated with states.

State machine formalisms universally assume the RTC execution model. In this model, all actions triggered by an event instance must complete before the next event instance can be dispatched to the state machine, meaning the state machine executes uninterruptible steps (RTC steps) and starts processing each event in a stable state configuration.

UML statecharts are an advanced formalism for specifying state machines. The formalism is a variant of extended state machines with characteristics of both Mealy and Moore automata. Statecharts include notations of nested hierarchical states and orthogonal regions and extend the notation of actions.

The most important innovation of statecharts over classical FSMs is the introduction of hierarchical states. The semantics of state nesting allows substates to define only differences in behavior from the superstates, thus promoting sharing and reuse of behavior. The relation between a substate and its superstate has all the characteristics of inheritance and is called behavioral inheritance in QP. Behavioral inheritance is as fundamental as class inheritance and allows the building of whole hierarchies of states, as with class taxonomies. The properly designed state hierarchies comply with the LSP, extended for states.

Statecharts introduce state entry and exit actions, which provide the means for guaranteed initialization and cleanup, very much as constructors and destructors do for classes. Entry actions are always executed starting with the outermost state, which is analogous to class constructors executed from the most general class. The exit actions, similar to destructors, are always executed in exact reverse order.

Entry and exit actions combined with state nesting complicate transition sequence. The general rule is to (1) execute exit actions from the source state, (2) execute actions associated with transitions, and (3) execute entry actions to the target. The only exceptions to this rule are internal transitions, which never cause the execution of exit or entry actions and therefore are distinctively different from self-transitions.

Statecharts were first invented as a visual formalism; therefore, they are heavily biased toward graphical representation. However, it is important to distinguish the underlying concept of the HSM from statechart notation.

The significance of HSMs goes beyond software. For example, state hierarchies arise naturally in microscopic systems governed by the laws of quantum mechanics, demonstrating the fundamental character of behavioral inheritance, which is the primary means of representing symmetries within reactive systems.

Chapter 3

Standard State Machine Implementations

*An expert is a man who has made all the mistakes which can be made,
in a narrow field.*
— Niels Bohr

Implementing state machines is not as easy as it looks. Even with classical nonhierarchical FSMs, you must make an amazing number of design decisions and trade-offs:

- How do you represent events? How about events with parameters?
- How do you represent states?
- How do you represent transitions?
- How do you dispatch events to the state machine?

When you add state hierarchy, exit/entry actions, and transitions with guards, the design becomes anything but trivial.

In this chapter, I focus on standard implementation techniques, which you can find in the literature or in the working code. They are mostly applicable to the classical flat (nonhierarchical) extended state machines because there are hardly any standard implementations of HSMs.

Typical implementations of state machines in high-level programming languages, such as C or C++, include

- the nested `switch` statement,
- the state table,
- the object-oriented State design pattern, and
- other techniques that are mostly combinations of the previous three.

3.1   State Machine Interface

The majority of published state machine code presents state machines intimately intertwined with a specific concurrency model and a particular event dispatching policy. For example, embedded systems engineers[1] often present their state machines inside polling loops or interrupt service routines (ISRs) that extract events directly from hardware or global variables. GUI programmers are typically more disciplined in this respect (although they seldom use state machines, as demonstrated in the Visual Basic Calculator example in Chapter 1), because a typical GUI environment (e.g., Microsoft Windows) handles event queuing and dispatching for the programmer. However, a typical GUI API — for instance, `WinMain()` — provides only a fixed set of event parameters and is not generally applicable outside the GUI domain (after all, the most complex external occurrence that a GUI needs to handle is a mouse click).

However, it is better to separate the state machine code from a particular concurrency model and to provide a flexible way of passing signals and event parameters. Therefore, implementations in this chapter provide a simple and generally applicable interface to a state machine. In this respect, the implementations presented are not typical because a state machine does not have a standard interface.

The interface I propose consists of just three methods: `init()`, to take a top-level initial transition; `dispatch()`, to dispatch an event to the state machine; and `tran()`, to take an arbitrary state transition. In this simple model, a state machine is externally driven by invoking `init()` once[2] and `dispatch()` repetitively. Part II of this book shows how this interface can be used in conjunction with preemptive multitasking or in a background loop.

To focus the following discussion, consider the state diagram shown in Figure 3.1. The state machine models a lexical parser that distinguishes C-style comments (/* ... */) from code and counts the number of comment characters presented to the parser. The state space of this state machine consists of four states `code`, `slash`,

---

1.   Judging by 12 years of articles (1988–2000) published on the subject in *Embedded Systems Programming* magazine.

2.   The initial transition (the `init()` method) is intentionally separated from the state machine constructor to give you better control over the initialization sequence.

comment, and star. The input alphabet of the state machine consists of signals STAR (*), SLASH (/), and CHAR (any character different from * and /).

Figure 3.1   C comment parser (CParser) state machine

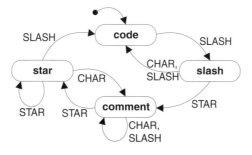

Exercise 3.1 In the spirit of eXtreme Programming (XP), first prepare a test for the C comment parser state machine. The test harness should (1) open a C source file for reading, (2) instantiate a tested state machine object, (3) take a default transition by invoking init() on this object, (4) read characters from the file (until end-of-file) and translate them into signal events (CHAR, STAR, SLASH), and (5) dispatch the event instances to the state machine by invoking dispatch() on the state machine object.

3.2   Nested switch Statement

Perhaps the most popular technique of implementing state machines is the nested switch statement, with a scalar state variable used as the discriminator in the first level of the switch and an event signal used in the second level. Listing 3.1 shows a typical implementation of the C comment parser FSM from Figure 3.1.

Listing 3.1   Comment parser state machine implemented using the nested switch statement technique

```
1 enum Signal {                          // enumeration for CParser signals
2    CHAR_SIG, STAR_SIG, SLASH_SIG
3 };
4 enum State {                           // enumeration for CParser states
5    CODE, SLASH, COMMENT, STAR
6 };
7 class CParser1 {
8 public:
9    void init() { myCommentCtr = 0; tran(CODE); }        //initial transition
10   void dispatch(unsigned const sig);
11   void tran(State target) { myState = target; }
```

```
12    long getCommentCtr() const { return myCommentCtr; }
13 private:
14    State myState;                              // the scalar state-variable
15    long myCommentCtr;                          // comment character counter
16    . . .                                       // other CParser1 attributes
17 };
18
19 void CParser1::dispatch(unsigned const sig) {
20    switch (myState) {
21    case CODE:
22       switch (sig) {
23       case SLASH_SIG:
24          tran(SLASH);                          // transition to SLASH
25          break;
26       }
27       break;
28    case SLASH:
29       switch (sig) {
30       case STAR_SIG:
31          myCommentCtr += 2;                    // SLASH-STAR count as comment
32          tran(COMMENT);                        // transition to COMMENT
33          break;
34       case CHAR_SIG:
35       case SLASH_SIG:
36          tran(CODE);                           // go back to CODE
37          break;
38       }
39       break;
40    case COMMENT:
41       switch (sig) {
42       case STAR_SIG:
43          tran(STAR);                           // transition to STAR
44          break;
45       case CHAR_SIG:
46       case SLASH_SIG:
47          ++myCommentCtr;                       // count the comment char
48          break;
49       }
50       break;
51    case STAR:
52       switch (sig) {
53       case STAR_SIG:
54          ++myCommentCtr;                       // count STAR as comment
55          break;
56       case SLASH_SIG:
57          myCommentCtr += 2;                    // count STAR-SLASH as comment
58          tran(CODE);                           // transition to CODE
59          break;
```

```
60        case CHAR_SIG:
61            myCommentCtr += 2;                    // count STAR-? as comment
62            tran(COMMENT);                        // go back to COMMENT
63            break;
64        }
65        break;
66    }
67 }
```

Signals are typically represented as an enumeration (Listing 3.1, lines 1–3), as are states (lines 4–6). The myState state variable is included in the Cparser1 class (line 14) because each instance needs to keep track of its own state. Execution of the state machine begins with the initial transition via a call to init(). The heart of the state machine is implemented in the dispatch() event handler method (lines 19–67), which the client code invokes once per RTC step. State transitions are achieved by reassigning the state variable (tran(), line 11).

Variations of this implementation include breaking up the monolithic event-handler code by moving the second level of discrimination (based on the signal) into specialized state handler functions (see Exercise 3.3). In this case, the job of the main event handler is reduced to dispatching events to appropriate state handlers. Also, the state machine is often a *Singleton* (i.e., there is only one instance of it in the system). In that case, the state machine can be coded as a module instead of a class, and the single instance of the state variable can be hard-coded in the event handler.

The nested switch statement implementation has the following consequences.

- It is simple.
- It requires enumerating states and triggers.
- It has a small memory footprint, since only one scalar state variable is necessary to represent a state machine.
- It does not promote code reuse since all elements of a state machine must be coded specifically for the problem at hand.
- Event dispatching time is not constant but depends on the performance of the two levels of switch statements, which degrade with increasing number of cases (typically as $O(\log n)$, where n is the number of cases).
- The implementation is not hierarchical, and manually coded entry/exit actions and nested initial transitions are prone to error and difficult to maintain in view of changes in the state machine topology. This is mainly because the code pertaining to one state (e.g., an entry action) becomes distributed and repeated in many places (on every transition leading to this state).
- The latter property is not a problem for code-synthesizing tools, which often use a nested switch statement type of implementation.

Exercise 3.2	Implement CParser1 in C. Hint: You can preserve the notion of the CParser1 class by following techniques described in Section A.1 of Appendix A. Please do not use the "C+" macros in this exercise.

Exercise 3.3	Implement a variation of the nested switch statement technique by breaking the monolithic Cparser1::dispatch() event handler into separate state handlers.

3.3   State Table

Another popular approach is to use state tables containing (typically sparse) arrays of transitions for each state. Table 3.1 shows the state table for the C comment parser state machine.

Table 3.1   **C comment parser state table**

Signals →

		CHAR_SIG	**STAR_SIG**	**SLASH_SIG**
States ↓	code			doNothing(), slash
	slash	doNothing(), code	a2(), comment	doNothing(), code
	comment	a1(), comment	doNothing(), star	a1(), comment
	star	a2(), comment	a1(), star	a2(), code

This table lists signals (triggers) along the top and states along the left edge. The contents of the cells are transitions represented as {action, next-state} pairs. For example, in the slash state, the STAR_SIG signal triggers a transition to the comment state, associated with the execution of the a2() action. Empty cells correspond to undefined signal–state combinations. The common policy of handling such triggers is to silently ignore them without changing the state. You can choose a different policy; for example, such events could trigger an error() action.

Listing 3.2 shows how a typical implementation using this technique might look.

Listing 3.2   State table implementation of the C comment parser FSM

```
 1 // generic "event processor" ...
 2 class StateTable {
 3 public:
 4   typedef void (StateTable::*Action)();        //pointer-to-member function
 5   struct Tran {                    // inner struct transition (aggregate)
 6     Action action;
 7     unsigned nextState;
 8   };
 9   StateTable(Tran const *table, unsigned nStates, unsigned nSignals)
10     : myTable(table), myNsignals(nSignals), myNstates(nStates) {}
11   virtual ~StateTable() {}                         // virtual xctor
12   void dispatch(unsigned const sig) {
13     register Tran const *t = myTable + myState*myNsignals + sig;
14     (this->*(t->action))();
15     myState = t->nextState;
16   }
17   void doNothing() {}                       // do-nothing default action
18 protected:
19   unsigned myState;
20 private:
21   Tran const *myTable;
22   unsigned myNsignals;
23   unsigned myNstates;
24 };
25
26 // specific Comment Parser state machine ...
27 enum Event {                             // enumeration for CParser events
28   CHAR_SIG, STAR_SIG, SLASH_SIG, MAX_SIG
29 };
30 enum State {                             // enumeration for CParser states
31   CODE, SLASH, COMMENT, STAR, MAX_STATE
32 };
33 class CParser2 : public StateTable {           // CParser2 state machine
34 public:
35   CParser2() : StateTable(&myTable[0][0], MAX_STATE, MAX_SIG) {}
36   void init() { myCommentCtr = 0; myState = CODE; }      // initial tran.
37   long getCommentCtr() const { return myCommentCtr; }
38 private:
39   void a1() { myCommentCtr += 1; }                        // action method
40   void a2() { myCommentCtr += 2; }                        // action method
41 private:
42   static StateTable::Tran const myTable[MAX_STATE][MAX_SIG];
43   long myCommentCtr;                           // comment character counter
44 };
45                        // static initialization of a (ROMable) state-table...
```

```
46 StateTable::Tran const CParser2::myTable[MAX_STATE][MAX_SIG] = {
47    {{&StateTable::doNothing, CODE },
48     {&StateTable::doNothing, CODE },
49     {&StateTable::doNothing, SLASH}},
50    {{&StateTable::doNothing, CODE },
51     {static_cast<StateTable::Action>(&CParser2::a2), COMMENT },
52     {&StateTable::doNothing, CODE }},
53    {{static_cast<StateTable::Action>(&CParser2::a1), COMMENT },
54     {&StateTable::doNothing,STAR   },
55     {static_cast<StateTable::Action>(&CParser2::a1), COMMENT }},
56    {{static_cast<StateTable::Action>(&CParser2::a2), COMMENT },
57     {static_cast<StateTable::Action>(&CParser2::a1), STAR },
58     {static_cast<StateTable::Action>(&CParser2::a2), CODE }}
59 };
```

The state table implementation can be clearly divided into a generic and reusable event processor part (class StateTable in lines 2–24) and an application-specific part (lines 27–59). As shown in Figure 3.2, class StateTable does not physically contain the array of transitions, but rather manages an array of an arbitrary number of states (myNstates) and signals (myNsignals). Allocation and initialization of this array is left to the clients. Transitions are represented as {action, next-state} pairs (Listing 3.2, lines 5–8). The generic action is represented as a pointer-to-member function of class StateTable (line 4). A pivotal aspect of this design is that the pointer-to-member function (Action) of class StateTable can also point to a member of a *subclass* of StateTable.[3]

Both events and states are represented as unsigned integers (clients typically enumerate them). The dispatch() method (Listing 3.2, lines 12–16) performs three steps: (1) it identifies the transition to take as a state table lookup (line 13), (2) it executes the action (line 14), and (3) it changes the state (line 15).

Figure 3.2   StateTable instance managing an array of transitions

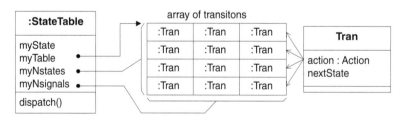

---

3.   Invoking methods of a subclass through a pointer-to-member function of the superclass can be potentially unsafe when combined with multiple inheritance — that is, if the subclass inherits from more base classes than StateTable (see the sidebar "C++ Pointer-to-Member Functions and Multiple Inheritance" on page 75).

The application-specific part requires: (1) enumerating states and signals (Listing 3.2, lines 27–32), (2) subclassing `StateTable` (line 33), (3) defining the action functions (lines 39–40), and (4) initializing the transition table (lines 46–59). Note that `CParser2` declares the table `myTable` as both `static` and `const` (line 41). The `static` specifier means that all instances of the `CParser2` class can share a single instance of the table. The `const` specifier indicates that the table is immutable and can be placed in ROM. Note the necessity of upcasting[4] pointer-to-member functions in the static initializer[5] (lines 46–59) because methods `a1()` and `a2()` are members of a subclass of `StateTable` (`CParser2`) rather than of `StateTable` directly.

There seem to be two main variations on state table implementation in C++. Concrete state machines can either *be* state tables (inheritance) or *have* a state table (aggregation). The technique presented here falls into the inheritance category. However, the aggregation approach seems to be more popular (e.g., see [Douglass 01, 99]). Aggregation introduces the indirection layer of the context class — that is, the concrete class on behalf of which the aggregated state table executes actions. Inheritance eliminates this indirection, because the `StateTable` class plays the role of the context (concrete state machine) class simultaneously. In other words, by virtue of inheritance, every concrete state machine (like `CParser2`) also *is a* `StateTable`.

The state table, like the nested `switch` statement technique, is not hierarchical. However, it is always possible to extend such nonhierarchical techniques to incorporate exit actions, entry actions, and nested initial transitions by hard-coding them into *transition action functions*, which are then placed into the state table. Figure 3.3 shows an example of such a transition action function `fromStateAAonE1()` that handles the whole hierarchical transition chain by explicitly calling the appropriate exit actions, transition actions, and entry actions [Duby 01].

The state table implementation has the following consequences.

- It maps directly to the highly regular state table representation of a state machine.

- It requires the enumeration of triggers and states.

- It provides relatively good performance for event dispatching ($O(const)$, not taking into account action execution).

- It promotes code reuse of the generic event processor, which is typically small.

- It requires a large state table, which is typically sparse and wasteful. However, because the state table is constant, it often can be stored in ROM rather than RAM.

---

4. If your C++ compiler does not support the new-style cast `static_cast<Action>(...)` (e.g., some older or EC++ compilers don't), then you should use the C-style cast `(Action)(...)`.

5. The static (compile-time) initialization requires that the inner class `StateTable::Tran` is an aggregate — that is, a class without private members or constructors [Stroustrup 91]. That's why I've declared this class as `struct` in line 6 of Listing 3.2.

Figure 3.3 **Transition chain hard-coded in a transition action function**
`fromStateAAonE1()` **[Duby 01]**

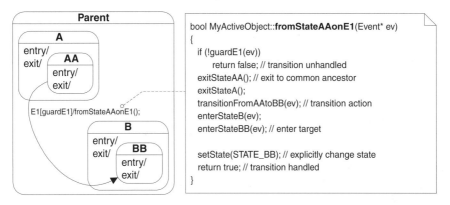

- It requires a large number of fine-granularity functions representing actions.

- It requires a complicated initialization. Manual maintenance of this initialization, in view of changes in the state machine topology, is expensive and prone to error. For instance, adding a new state requires adding and initializing a whole row in the transition array, which often discourages programmers from evolving the state machine. Instead, they tend to misuse extended state variables and guard conditions (see Section 2.1.3 in Chapter 2).

- It is not hierarchical. Although the state table can be extended to implement state nesting, entry/exit actions, and transition guards, these extensions require hard-coding whole transition chains into transition action functions, which is prone to error and inflexible.

Exercise 3.4   Implement the `CParser2` state machine in C. Hint: Sections A.1 and A.2 of Appendix A describe simple techniques for implementing classes and inheritance in C. Please use the "C+" macros `CLASS()` and `SUBCLASS()` to declare classes `StateTable` and `CParser2`, respectively.

Exercise 3.5   Implement a variation of the state table technique in which you push the responsibility of changing state into the action method (action methods must call `tran()` explicitly). This variation allows you to replace the `Transition` class with a pointer-to-member function. Note how this cuts the size of the transition array in half (storing next-states becomes unnecessary). However, you need to implement many more action methods, because now they are more specific. Modify the event processor `StateTable::dispatch()` and the transition table initialization accordingly.

3.4 State Design Pattern

The object-oriented approach to implementing state machines is known as the *State design pattern* [Gamma+ 95, Douglass 99]. An instance of this pattern applied to the C comment parser state machine is shown in Figure 3.4.

Figure 3.4 **State design pattern applied to the CParser state machine**

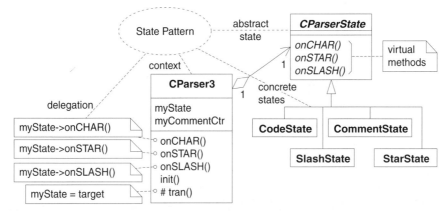

The pattern is based on delegation and polymorphism. Concrete states are represented as subclasses of an abstract state class, which defines a common interface for handling events (each event corresponds to a virtual method). A context class delegates all events for processing to the current state object (designated by the myState attribute). State transitions are explicit and are accomplished by reassigning the myState pointer. Adding new events requires adding new methods to the abstract state class, and adding new states requires subclassing this class.

Listing 3.3 shows one possible implementation of the design in Figure 3.4.

Listing 3.3 **CParser3 implemented as a State design pattern**

```
 1 class CParser3;                        // Context class, forward declaration
 2 class CParserState {                              // abstract State
 3 public:
 4      virtual void onCHAR(CParser3 *context, char ch)  {}
 5      virtual void onSTAR(CParser3 *context) {}
 6      virtual void onSLASH(CParser3 *context) {}
 7 };
 8 class CodeState : public CParserState {         // concrete State "Code"
 9 public:
10      virtual void onSLASH(CParser3 *context);
11 };
12 class SlashState : public CParserState {        // concrete State "Slash"
13 public:
```

```
14      virtual void onCHAR(CParser3 *context, char ch);
15      virtual void onSTAR(CParser3 *context);
16      virtual void onSLASH(CParser3 *context);
17 };
18 class CommentState : public CParserState {        //concrete State "Comment"
19 public:
20      virtual void onCHAR(CParser3 *context, char ch);
21      virtual void onSTAR(CParser3 *context);
22      virtual void onSLASH(CParser3 *context);
23 };
24 class StarState : public CParserState {          // concrete State "Star"
25 public:
26      virtual void onCHAR(CParser3 *context, char ch);
27      virtual void onSTAR(CParser3 *context);
28      virtual void onSLASH(CParser3 *context);
29 };
30 class CParser3 {                                      // Context class
31     friend class CodeState;
32     friend class SlashState;
33     friend class CommentState;
34     friend class StarState;
35     static CodeState     myCodeState;
36     static SlashState    mySlashState;
37     static CommentState  myCommentState;
38     static StarState     myStarState;
39     CParserState *myState;
40     long myCommentCtr;
41 public:
42     CParser3(CParserState *initial) : myState(initial) {}
43     void init() { myCommentCtr = 0; tran(&myCodeState); }
44     long getCommentCtr() const { return myCommentCtr; }
45     void onCHAR(char ch) { myState->onCHAR(this, ch); }
46     void onSTAR() { myState->onSTAR(this);  }
47     void onSLASH() { myState->onSLASH(this); }
48 protected:
49     void tran(CParserState *target) { myState = target; }
50 };
51
52 CodeState     CParser3::myCodeState;
53 SlashState    CParser3::mySlashState;
54 CommentState  CParser3::myCommentState;
55 StarState     CParser3::myStarState;
56
57 void CodeState::onSLASH(CParser3 *context) {
58     context->tran(&CParser3::mySlashState);
59 }
60 void SlashState::onCHAR(CParser3 *context, char ch) {
```

```
61     context->tran(&CParser3::myCodeState);
62 }
63 void SlashState::onSTAR(CParser3 *context) {
64     context->myCommentCtr += 2;
65     context->tran(&CParser3::myCommentState);
66 }
67 void SlashState::onSLASH(CParser3 *context) {
68     context->tran(&CParser3::myCodeState);
69 }
70 void CommentState::onCHAR(CParser3 *context, char c) {
71     context->myCommentCtr++;
72 }
73 void CommentState::onSTAR(CParser3 *context) {
74     context->tran(&CParser3::myStarState);
75 }
76 void CommentState::onSLASH(CParser3 *context) {
77     context->myCommentCtr++;
78 }
79 void StarState::onCHAR(CParser3 *context, char ch) {
80     context->myCommentCtr += 2;
81     context->tran(&CParser3::myCommentState);
82 }
83 void StarState::onSTAR(CParser3 *context) {
84     context->myCommentCtr += 2;
85     context->tran(&CParser3::myCommentState);
86 }
87 void StarState::onSLASH(CParser3 *context) {
88     context->myCommentCtr += 2;
89     context->tran(&CParser3::myCodeState);
90 }
```

The CParserState class (Listing 3.3, lines 2–7) provides the interface for handling events as well as the default (do-nothing) implementation for the actions associated with these events. The four C parser states are defined as concrete subclasses of the abstract CParserState class (lines 8–29). These subclasses override only specific event-handler methods; those corresponding to events that are handled in these states. For example, state CodeState overrides only the onSLASH() method. Class CParser3 plays the role of the context class from the pattern (lines 30–50). It grants friendship to all state classes (lines 31–34) and also declares all concrete states as static members (lines 35–38). The context class duplicates the interface of the abstract state class declaring a method for every signal event (lines 45–47). The implementation of these methods is entirely prescribed by the pattern. The context class simply delegates to the appropriate methods of the state class, which are invoked polymorphically. The specific actions are implemented inside the event handler methods of the concrete CParserState subclasses (lines 57–90).

The State design pattern has the following consequences.

• It partitions state-specific behavior and localizes it in separate classes.

• It makes state transitions efficient (reassigning one pointer).

• It provides very good performance for event dispatching through the late binding mechanism (O(const), not taking into account action execution). This performance is generally better than indexing into a state table plus invoking a method via a function pointer, as used in the state table technique. However, such performance is only possible because the selection of the appropriate event handler is not taken into account. Indeed, clients typically will use a switch statement to perform such selections.

• It allows you to customize the signature of each event handler. Event parameters can be made explicit, and the typing system of the language can be used to verify the appropriate type of a parameter at compile time (e.g., onCHAR() takes a parameter of type char).

• It is memory efficient. If the concrete state objects don't have attributes (only methods), they can be shared (as in the CParser3 example).

• It does not require enumerating states.

• It does not require enumerating events.

• It compromises the encapsulation of the context class, which typically requires granting friendship to all state classes.

• It enforces indirect access to the context's parameters from the methods of the concrete state subclasses (via the context pointer).

• Adding states requires adding concrete state subclasses.

• Handling new events requires adding event handlers to the state class interface.

• The event handlers are typically of fine granularity, as in the state table approach.

• It is not hierarchical.

Exercise 3.6   (*Advanced*)   Implement the State design pattern version of the C comment parser in C. Hint: Appendix A describes the realization of abstraction, inheritance, and polymorphism in C. Note: I consider this exercise advanced because the design makes heavy use of polymorphism, which is not necessary, even for the implementation of later hierarchical state machines.

The standard State design pattern does not use the `dispatch()` method for performing RTC steps. Instead, for every signal event, it provides a specific (type-safe) event-handler method. However, the pattern can be modified (simplified) by combining all event handlers of the state class into just one, generic state handler, `dispatch()`, as shown in Figure 3.5. The abstract state class then becomes generic, and its `dispatch()` method becomes the generic state handler. Demultiplexing events (by event type), however, must be done inside the `dispatch()` methods of the concrete state subclasses.

Figure 3.5   **Simplified State design pattern applied to C comment parser state machine**

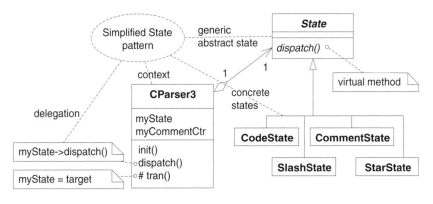

Exercise 3.7   Implement the C comment parser state machine using the Simplified State design pattern from Figure 3.5.

3.5   Optimal FSM Implementation

In previous sections, I presented the three most popular techniques for implementing FSMs. From my experience, though, none of these techniques in its pure form is truly optimal. However, one particular combination of these techniques repeatedly proved to be the most succinct and efficient implementation of the classical flat FSM. This design, which I call the Optimal FSM design pattern, is shown in Figure 3.6. Listing 3.4 shows an implementation of the C comment parser state machine.

Figure 3.6   The optimal C comment parser FSM implementation

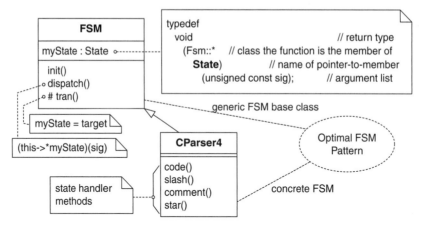

Listing 3.4   The optimal FSM pattern applied to the C comment parser

```
1 class Fsm {
2 public:
3     typedef void (Fsm::*State)(unsigned const sig);
4     Fsm(State initial) : myState(initial) {}
5     virtual ~Fsm() {}                                     // virtual xtor
6     void init() { dispatch(0); }
7     void dispatch(int sig) { (this->*myState)(sig); }
8 protected:
9     void tran(State target) { myState = target; }
10    #define TRAN(target_) tran(static_cast<State>(target_))
11    State myState;
12 };
13 enum Signal{                          // enumeration for CParser signals
14    CHAR_SIG, STAR_SIG, SLASH_SIG
15 };
16 class CParser4 : public Fsm {
17 public:
18    CParser4() : Fsm((FSM_STATE)initial) {}               // ctor
19    long getCommentCtr() const { return myCommentCtr; }
20 private:
21    void initial(int);                       // initial pseudostate
22    void code(int sig);                             // state-handler
23    void slash(int sig);                            // state-handler
24    void comment(int sig);                          // state-handler
25    void star(int sig);                             // state-handler
26 private:
27    long myCommentCtr;                   // comment character counter
28 };
```

```
29
30 void CParser4::initial(int) {
31     myCommentCtr = 0;
32     TRAN(&CParser4::code);                    // take the default transition
33 }
34 void CParser4::code(int sig) {
35     switch (sig) {
36     case SLASH_SIG:
37         TRAN(&CParser4::slash);                   // transition to "slash"
38         break;
39     }
40 }
41 void CParser4::slash(int sig) {
42     switch (sig) {
43     case STAR_SIG:
44         myCommentCtr += 2;           // SLASH-STAR characters count as comment
45         TRAN(&CParser4::comment);              // transition to "comment"
46         break;
47     case CHAR_SIG:
48     case SLASH_SIG:
49         TRAN(&CParser4::code);                     // go back to "code"
50         break;
51     }
52 }
53 void CParser4::comment(int sig) {
54     switch (sig) {
55     case STAR_SIG:
56         TRAN(&CParser4::star);                     // transition to "star"
57         break;
58     case CHAR_SIG:
59     case SLASH_SIG:
60         ++myCommentCtr;                        // count the comment character
61         break;
62     }
63 }
64 void CParser4::star(int sig) {
65     switch (sig) {
66     case SLASH_SIG:
67         myCommentCtr += 2;                    // count STAR-SLASH as comment
68         TRAN(&CParser4::code);                    // transition to "code"
69         break;
70     case CHAR_SIG:
71     case STAR_SIG:
72         myCommentCtr += 2;                       // count STAR-? as comment
73         TRAN(&CParser4::comment);                    // go back to "comment"
74         break;
75     }
76 }
```

As you can see, this implementation combines elements from the nested `switch` statement, state table, and Simplified State design pattern, but it also adds some original ideas. The design hinges on class `Fsm`. This class plays a double role as the context class from the simplified state pattern and the event processor from the state table pattern. The novelty of the optimal FSM design comes from representing states directly as state handler methods, which are members of the `Fsm` class (actually, its subclasses[6] like `CParser4`). This means that state handlers have immediate access to all attributes of the context class (via the implicit `this` pointer in C++) without breaking encapsulation. Like the context class, `Fsm` keeps track of the current state by means of the `myState` attribute of type `Fsm::State`, which is `typedef`'d as a pointer-to-member function of the `Fsm` class (Listing 3.4, line 3).

The Optimal FSM design pattern has the following consequences.

- It is simple.

- It partitions state-specific behavior and localizes it in separate state handler methods. These methods have just about the right granularity — neither too fine (as with action methods) nor monolithic (as with the consolidated event handler).

- It provides direct and efficient access to state machine attributes from state handler methods and does not require compromising the encapsulation of the context class.

- It has a small memory footprint because only one state variable (the `myState` pointer) is necessary to represent a state machine instance.

- It promotes code reuse of an extremely small (trivial) and generic event processor implemented in the `Fsm` base class.

- It makes state transitions efficient (by reassigning the `myState` pointer).

- It provides good performance for event dispatching by eliminating one level of `switch` from the nested `switch` statement technique and replacing it with the efficient function pointer dereferencing technique. In typical implementations, state handlers still need to rely on one level of a `switch` statement, with performance dependent on the number of cases (typically $O(\log n)$, where n is the number of cases). However, the `switch` can be replaced by a look-up table in selected (critical) state handlers (see Exercise 3.8)

- It is scalable and flexible. It is easy to add both states and events, as well as to change state machine topology, even late in the development cycle.

---

6.   Invoking methods of a subclass through a pointer-to-member function of the superclass can be potentially unsafe when combined with multiple inheritance — that is, if the subclass inherits from more base classes than `Fsm` (see the sidebar "C++ Pointer-to-Member Functions and Multiple Inheritance" on page 75).

- It does not require enumerating states (only events must be enumerated).
- It is not hierarchical.

Exercise 3.8 Reimplement the optimal FSM C comment parser in C. Change the implementation of one state handler — say, `CParser4comment()` — to use an internal pointer-to-function look-up table, rather than the `switch` statement, to dispatch events at a fixed time. Hint: Appendix A describes the realization of abstraction and inheritance in C. Please use the techniques directly in this exercise without the "C+" macros.

3.6 State Machines and C++ Exception Handling

Throwing and catching exceptions in C++ is fundamentally incompatible with the run-to-completion (RTC) semantics of state machines. For example, assume that the "Nested `switch` Statement" version of the C-comment parser throws an exception at line 31 of Listing 3.1. As the exception propagates up the call stack (to the caller of the `CParser1::dispatch()` method), it bypasses the state transition at line 32 and destroys the integrity of the state machine. The extended state variable (`myCommentCtr`) accounts for two new comment characters, whereas the state variable (`myState`) still corresponds to the SLASH state. The problem is fundamental and independent of the particular implementation technique. Any uncaught exceptions can play havoc with a state machine.

Therefore, you should be wary of the C++ exception handling in state machines. If you cannot avoid the mechanism altogether (e.g., you rely on a library that throws exceptions), you should be careful to catch all exceptions before returning from an action method or a state handler. This rule, of course, defeats the benefits of using exceptions in the first place.

However, state machines offer a better, language-independent way of handling exceptions. A state machine associated with a reactive system can represent all conditions of the system, including fault conditions. Instead of throwing an exception, an action should generate an exception event, which then triggers a state-based exception handling. Section 8.2.2 in Chapter 8 describes the state-based exception handling in more detail.

3.7 Role of Pointer-to-Member Functions

The efficiency of any state machine implementation technique[7] depends on how fast it can dispatch an event (`dispatch()`) and how fast it can take a state transition (`tran()`). As it turns out, the optimal FSM implementation is unbeatable[8] in both

respects. The following disassembled output shows the invocation of the in-lined
`Fsm::dispatch()` method (x86 instruction set, 32-bit protected mode, Microsoft
VC++ compiler).

```
0040118C    push    esi                          ; stack the event pointer e
0040118D    mov     ecx,407940h                  ; put 'this' pointer in ecx
00401192    call    dword ptr ds:[407944h]  ; (this->*myState)(e)
```

As you can see, the dereferencing of the pointer-to-member function and the
`(this->*myState)()` method invocation are both accomplished in just one
machine instruction (noted in bold). The two preceding instructions prepare arguments for the call (stack the e pointer and fetch the this pointer) and are needed no
matter what technique you use.

The following is the disassembled output of a state transition (the in-lined `tran()`
method).

```
0040101A    mov     dword ptr [ecx],401030h ; QFSM_TRAN(slash)
```

Again, state transition takes only one machine instruction because state transition
corresponds just to reassigning the `this->myState` pointer (the this pointer is, as
before, in the ecx register).

Exercise 3.9   In the literature, you often find implementations that apply pointers to
functions but still use a scalar state variable to resolve the state handler
through a look-up table (e.g., see [Gomez 00]). Try to implement this
technique as a variation of the optimal FSM. Look at the disassembled
output and compare it with the original implementation. What are other
disadvantages of this technique?

The point to remember from this discussion is that pointer-to-member functions
in C++ (or regular pointers to functions in C) are *the* fastest mechanism for implementing state machines in C++ (or in C). State machines are the "killer applications"
for pointers-to-functions (in C) and pointers-to-member functions (in C++).

---

7.   I am interested here only in the efficiency of the generic event processor, not the specific user actions.
8.   The C optimal FSM implementation should be truly unbeatable; however, the performance of the C++ imple-
      mentation depends on the C++ compiler.

C++ Pointer-to-Member Functions and Multiple Inheritance

In the book *Inside the C++ Object Model*, Lippman [Lippman 96, page 145] observes:

> *Use of a pointer-to-member function would be no more expensive than a non-member pointer to function if it weren't for virtual functions and multiple inheritance (including, of course, virtual base classes), which complicate both the type and invocation of a pointer-to-member. In practice, for those classes without virtual functions or virtual multiple base classes, the compiler can provide equivalent performance.*

Indeed, the high performance of C++ state machine implementations based on pointer-to-member functions can suffer slightly with virtual state handler functions, but the implementation might break altogether in the presence of multiple inheritance (MI).

The reason for the incompatibility with MI is that the C++ state machine implementations based on pointer-to-member functions (e.g., the state table or the optimal FSM) often use a pointer-to-member function of a base class (e.g., Fsm) to point to a member function of a subclass (e.g., CParser4). Such usage requires that you explicitly upcast pointer-to-member functions of a subclass to pointer-to-member functions of the superclass. However, although upcasting is legal (when implemented with static_cast<>), using the base class pointer to invoke methods declared in a derived class is not strictly correct.

For example, the optimal FSM implementation declares state handlers as methods of the CParser4 subclass (Listing 3.4), which requires assigning the state variable of the base class Fsm::myState by upcasting the pointer-to-member functions of the CParser4 subclass (see macro TRAN() in Listing 3.4, line 10). However, Fsm::dispatch() invokes the current state handler on behalf of the this pointer of the base class: (this->*myState)(sig) (Listing 3.4, line 7). Such a pointer-to-member function dereferencing (method invocation) might be a problem: MI could change the mechanism of method invocation in the subclass CParser4 from that in the base class Fsm (i.e., if CParser4 were to derive from more base classes than Fsm).

To be strictly correct and compatible with MI, you must always bind a method of class X to the object of the same class X. In other words, if a pointer-to-member function points to a method of class CParser4, you should not invoke the method through a pointer of class Fsm, even though Cparser4 descends from Fsm. Applying this rule to Fsm::dispatch() would require downcasting the this pointer to the derived class CParser4 with the following construct.

```
((static_cast<CParser4 *>(this))->*myState)(sig)
```

Such a downcast would destroy the generality of the Fsm class.

However, if MI is not important to you (which I believe is the case for the vast majority of applications), then the simple techniques presented in this chapter should be safe while offering unbeatable performance.

3.8 Implementing Guards, Junctions, and Choice Points

As described in Chapter 2, guards, junctions, and choice points are elements of flow-charts that the UML statecharts simply reuse. As such, these elements are not specific to hierarchical state machines and can be used equally well in classical flat state machines.

If you know how to code a flowchart, you already know how to implement guards, junctions, and choice points. Flowcharts map easily to plain structured code and are therefore straightforward to implement in those techniques that give you explicit choice of the target of a state transition, such as the nested switch statement, the State design pattern, and the optimal FSM pattern. Conditional execution is much harder to use in the state table technique because the rigidly structured state table implicitly selects the targets of state transitions.

A guard specified in the UML expression [*guard*]/*action* ... maps simply to the if statement: if(*guard*()) { *action*(); ...}. In the absence of orthogonal regions, a junction pseudostate can have only one incoming transition segment and many outgoing segments guarded by nonoverlapping guard expressions. This construct maps simply to chained if–else statements: if (*guard1*()) { *action1*(); } else if (*guard2*()) { *action2*(); } and so on. You can imple-ment a dynamic choice point in an identical way, except that you can precede the first if statement with an expression that dynamically affects subsequent evaluations of the guards (equivalently, your guards might have side effects).

3.9 Implementing Entry and Exit Actions

The classical nonhierarchical state machines can also reap the benefits of a guaranteed initialization of the state context through entry actions and a guaranteed cleanup in the exit actions. The lack of hierarchy vastly simplifies the problem (but at the same time, it makes the feature much less powerful). One way of implementing entry and exit actions is to dispatch reserved signals (e.g., ENTRY_SIG and EXIT_SIG) to the state machine. The tran() method could dispatch the EXIT_SIG signal to the current state (transition source) then dispatch the `ENTRY_SIG` signal to the target. For example, the implementation of `Fsm::tran()` from the optimal FSM pattern can take the following form.

```
void Fsm::tran(FsmState target) {
    (this->*myState)(EXIT_SIG);          // dispatch EXIT signal to the target
    myState = target;
    (this->*myState)(ENTRY_SIG);         //dispatch ENTRY signal to the source
}
```

Please note that the `ENTRY_SIG` and `EXIT_SIG` signals are reserved; that is, clients must not use them as their application-specific signals.

Exercise 3.10 Suppose you want the C comment parser state machine to count the number of comment blocks (/* ... */). The obvious solution is to count the number of transitions from `slash` to `comment` (Figure 3.1), but this approach is not robust against possible extensions of the state machine. A safer solution would be to use entry or exit actions. However, using the entry action to count the number of entries into state `comment` does not provide the correct number of comment blocks. Explain why. Propose a hierarchical C comment parser state machine, in which the counting of entries into the `comment` state would indeed provide the number of the complete comment blocks.

3.10 Dealing with State Hierarchy

The hierarchy of states remains difficult to address elegantly and efficiently. Some published attacks on this problem include the following.

- A ROOMchart implementation [Selic+ 94][9] attempts to generalize the state table approach by representing the state machine in a data structure, which is more efficient than an array. A generic state machine interpreter traverses (interprets) the data structure at run time when events are dispatched to the state machine. This method has essentially the same consequences as a state table but trades complexity for hierarchy and speed for memory savings.

- The UML state machine meta-model [OMG 01] is an elaborate design. The model contains such classes as `StateMachine`, `StateVertex`, `State`, `CompositeState`, `SimpleState`, `PseudoState`, `Transition`, `Action`, `Guard`, and `Event`, to name just a few. The UML statechart meta-model is similar to the ROOMchart approach, which is to realize a hierarchical state machine as a

---

9. The ROOMchart implementation published by Selic and colleagues [Selic+ 94] is different from code generated by the ObjecTime toolset.

collaboration of specialized objects. I am not familiar with any practical statechart implementation that would literally apply a UML meta-model.[10]

- Ian Horrocks [Horrocks 99] essentially applies the state table technique but
  represents hierarchy by using a separate state variable for each level of nesting. Horrocks' state-variables are much like quantum numbers used in the
  description of quantum states (see the sidebar "Quantum States of the Hydrogen
  Atom" on page 51 in Chapter 2). This approach seems simple but requires hard-
  coding the action chains for every transition; therefore, the resulting code is difficult to modify when the topology of the state machine changes. In addition, Horrocks' approach seems to neglect entry and exit actions for states.

- Carolyn Duby [Duby 01] advocates the state table technique based on
  pointer-to-member functions in C++. Her technique addresses state hierarchy
  by packaging transition chains (exit actions, transition actions, entry actions,
  and even guards) into *transition action functions* subsequently stored (as pointers to members) in a state table. This approach puts the burden on the programmer to determine the least common ancestor (LCA) state for each
  transition and to explicitly hard-code all necessary exit and entry actions. As
  in Horrocks' approach, this renders the code inflexible and, in practice,
  defeats the benefits of guaranteed initialization and cleanup through the
  entry/exit actions. Programmers can easily forget to invoke the appropriate
  entry/exit actions, or they invoke them in the wrong order. The interesting part
  of this technique is the consistent naming convention for action methods,
  which makes navigating the code significantly easier. Finally, Duby's method
  incorporates not only an event processor, but also event queueing and a sin-
  gle-task execution model for multiple state machines.

In quick review, the published approaches to manually coding HSMs seem to
fall into two broad categories: (1) heavyweight techniques that relieve the programmer from the responsibility of coding transition chains and (2) lightweight
techniques that require the programmer to explicitly hard-code transition
chains. Unfortunately, this creates the preconception that tight and efficient
manually generated HSM implementations are only possible through techniques
from the second category, which are inflexible and prone to error. In the next
chapter, I show you that it doesn't necessarily have to be that way. You can have
a lightweight HSM implementation that takes care of transition chains. In other
words, you can have your cake and eat it too!

---

10. For example, a UML-compliant design automation tool, Rhapsody, from I-Logix (www.ilogix.com) seems
    not to use the UML meta-model for code generation. Instead, the code synthesized by the tool resembles a hand-
    coded double `switch` statement technique [Douglass 99].

3.11 Summary

The standard implementation techniques and their variations discussed in this chapter can be freely mixed and matched to provide a continuum of possible trade-offs. Indeed, most of the implementations of state machines that you can find in the literature seem to be variations or combinations of the three fundamental techniques: the nested `switch` statement, the state table, and the object-oriented State design pattern. In this chapter, I provided concrete, executable code, and for each fundamental technique, I discussed the consequences of its use, as well as some of the most common variations.

One particular combination of techniques, the optimal FSM pattern, deserves special attention because it is elegant and offers an unbeatable combination of good performance and a small memory footprint. As you will see in Chapter 4, its interface can be compatible with the behavioral inheritance meta-pattern, so you could use it as a drop-in replacement for the simpler reactive classes, which don't need state hierarchy but would benefit from somewhat better performance and a smaller memory footprint.

In all techniques, state machines tend to eliminate many conditional statements from your code. By crisply defining the state of the system at any given time, state machines require that you test only one variable (the state variable) instead of many variables to determine the mode of operation (recall the Visual Basic Calculator example from Chapter 1). In all but the most basic approach of the nested `switch` statement, even this explicit test of the "state variable" disappears as a conditional statement. This coding aspect is similar to the effect of polymorphism, which eliminates many tests based on the type of the object and replaces them with more efficient (and extensible) late binding.

In the last section, I skimmed through some published attempts to implement state hierarchy. Only automatic code synthesis seems to address the problem correctly. The published manual techniques rely on explicitly hard-coding transition chains, which renders the code inflexible and practically defeats the purpose of using state hierarchy in the first place. In the next chapter, I present the QP (Quantum Programming) approach.

Chapter 4

Implementing Behavioral Inheritance

Perfection is achieved, not when there is nothing more to add
but when there is nothing left to take away.
— Antoine de Saint Exupery

In this chapter, I describe a practical realization of behavioral inheritance[1] in the form of an HSM implementation. Behavioral inheritance is one of the cornerstone concepts of QP, in the same way that abstraction, inheritance, and polymorphism are cornerstone concepts of OOP. One view of abstraction, inheritance, and polymorphism is that they are meta-patterns that provide the foundation for OOP and all other OO design patterns. In the same way, you can view behavioral inheritance as another fundamental meta-pattern, in that its various structured uses become design patterns (state patterns[2]) in their own right.

---

1. The concept of behavioral inheritance (defined in Chapter 2) is the relationship between the substate and the superstate in an HSM.
2. You can find a few such state patterns in Chapter 5.

To be practical and truly useful, the concepts of state machine and state hierarchy must map easily to mainstream programming languages like C or C++. One excellent example of how to successfully realize fundamental meta-patterns in a C-like language[3] is C++ itself (viewed as an OO extension to C). The C++ object model (e.g., see [Lippman 96]) is nothing more than a concrete implementation of the three fundamental OO meta-patterns. In view of the OO analogy between behavioral inheritance and class inheritance, a successful HSM implementation should be able to imitate the following main elements attributed to the wide-spread acceptance of the C++ object model.

1. It should be simple to use and maintain. Defining states should be as easy as defining C++ classes.

2. It should allow for easy changes in the state machine topology (state nesting and state transitions). No manual coding of transition chains should be required. The necessary modifications should be confined to one place in the code (ideally, one line), like changing superclass in C++.

3. It should provide good run-time efficiency and should have a small memory footprint. The cost of dispatching events to a state machine should be comparable to the invocation of virtual functions in C++.

4. It should follow the "zero overhead" principle of C++ (what you don't use shouldn't cost you anything). For instance, the virtual function mechanism of C++ allows you to explicitly specify class methods for which you accept the overhead of late binding (virtual functions). Other class methods (nonvirtual) will not pay the price.

Although UML statecharts support state nesting and thus enable behavioral inheritance, they also contain many more concepts of secondary importance. The full specification of the UML state machine package [OMG 01] presents a concoction of features at various levels of generality, usefulness, and implementation overhead that tends to overwhelm and obscure the really fundamental and important aspects of statecharts. More importantly, the big and heavyweight UML specification precludes a small and efficient implementation.

Therefore, in order to meet the goals enumerated earlier, the HSM implementation does not attempt to address all features specified in the UML state machine package; rather, it addresses only the following few essential elements:

- hierarchical states with full support for behavioral inheritance,
- guaranteed initialization and cleanup with state entry and exit actions, and
- support for specializing state models via class inheritance.

---

3. Some recent additions to the family of C-like languages include Java and C#.

As you can see, this minimal approach leaves out pretty much everything except support for behavioral inheritance and extensibility. In particular, the behavioral inheritance meta-pattern intentionally limits itself only to the passive event processor, which needs to be driven externally to process events. In particular, the meta-pattern does not include the standard elements traditionally associated with state machines, such as an event queue, an event dispatcher, an execution context (thread), or timing services. There are at least two reasons for this separation of concerns. First, unlike the generic event processor, the other elements necessary to execute state machines depend heavily on the concrete operating system. Second, in many cases, these elements are already available. For example, GUI systems such as Microsoft Windows offer a complete event-driven environment for executing passive state machines, so there is no need to duplicate this functionality.[4]

The goal of the behavioral inheritance meta-pattern is to provide a generic event-processor that you can use with any event queuing and dispatching mechanism.[5] The strategy is to provide just enough (but not more!) truly fundamental elements to allow for the efficient construction of all other (higher level) statechart features, including those built into the UML specification.

Note: In Chapter 5, you will see how to realize event deferral, orthogonal regions, and transitions to history as state patterns that build on top of the fundamental behavioral inheritance implementation presented here. Chapter 6 addresses the reuse of state models through the inheritance of entire state machines.

4.1   Structure

Chapter 3 detailed one particular implementation of the classical flat state machine (the Optimal FSM) that had exceptionally favorable properties. This approach can be extended to support state hierarchy without sacrificing its good characteristics.

Figure 4.1 shows the overall structure of the behavioral inheritance meta-pattern. On the left side of the diagram, the design is similar to the Optimal FSM design (compare Figure 3.6 in Chapter 3). The abstract HSM base class QHsm (quantum HSM) provides the familiar init() interface to initialize the state machine, the dispatch() method to dispatch events, and the (protected) tran() method to execute state transitions. This base class is central to the design because all concrete state machines derive from it.

---

4.   The Quantum Calculator (Chapter 1) provides an example of integrating the event processor directly with the Windows GUI.

5.   Part II of this book describes the Quantum Framework, an infrastructure for executing state machines optimized for embedded real-time systems.

As in the Optimal FSM design, the state QState (quantum state) is represented as a pointer-to-member function of the QHsm class. Class QHsm keeps track of the active state by means of the myState attribute. In addition, it uses another attribute (mySource) to keep track of the current transition source during a state transition (in HSMs, when a transition is inherited from a higher level superstate, the source of this transition is different from the active state).

On the right side of Figure 4.1, you find facilities for representing events and event parameters. The QEvent (quantum event) class represents a SignalEvent (see Section 2.2.8 in Chapter 2), which can be used as-is (for events without parameters) or can serve as a base for subclassing (for events with parameters). QEvent relates to QHsm through the signature of the state handler method (see the note attached to QState in Figure 4.1).

Figure 4.1   Structure of the behavioral inheritance meta-pattern

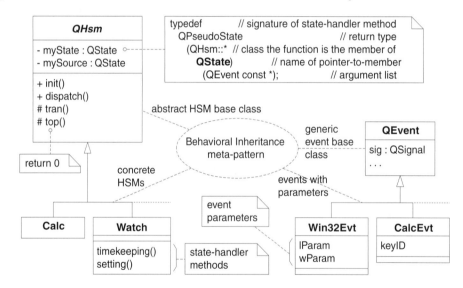

Listing 4.1 shows the complete declaration of the QHsm class, which provides the familiar public methods: init() for triggering the initial transition (line 9), and dispatch(), for dispatching events (line 10). You also can find the protected tran() method for executing transitions (line 21), but this method is not intended to be invoked directly by the clients. Instead, QHsm provides three macros to execute state transitions: Q_INIT() is exclusively for initial transitions, Q_TRAN() is for regular state transitions, and Q_TRAN_DYN() is for state transitions in which the target can change at run time. The following sections explain all these elements in detail.

As you also will see later in this chapter, an HSM implementation can do without polymorphism at the basic level. For simplicity, the QHsm class intentionally avoids virtual functions, except of the `virtual` destructor (Listing 4.1, line 8). The `virtual` destructor, however, makes the QHsm class polymorphism-ready and is important to properly synthesize pointer-to-member functions in some C++ implementations. Chapter 6 discusses these issues, as well as the legitimate use of polymorphism in conjunction with state machines. In Chapter 6, you also will see how to design extensible object models and how to reuse them through inheritance.

Listing 4.1   **QHsm class declaration**

```
 1 class QHsm {                            // Quantum Hierarchical State Machine
 2 public:
 3    typedef void (QHsm::*QPseudoState)( QEvent const *);
 4    typedef QPseudoState (QHsm::*QState)(QEvent const*);
 5    #define QSTATE QHsm::QState
 6
 7    QHsm(QPseudoState initial);                          // Ctor
 8    virtual ~QHsm();                                // virtual Xtor
 9    void init(QEvent const *e = 0);          // execute initial transition
10    void dispatch(QEvent const *e);                 // dispatch event
11    int isIn(QState state) const;               // "is-in-state" query
12    static char const *getVersion();
13
14 protected:
15    struct Tran {                           // protected inner class Tran
16       QState myChain[8];
17       unsigned short myActions;         // action mask (2-bits for action)
18    };
19    QPseudoState top(QEvent const*) { return 0; }       // the "top" state
20    QState getState() const { return myState; }
21    void tran(QState target);                    // dynamic state transition
22    void tranStat(Tran *t, QState target);       // static state transition
23    void init_(QState target) { myState = target; }
24    #define Q_INIT(target_) init_( Q_STATIC_CAST(QState, target_))
25    #define Q_TRAN(target_) if (1) { \
26       static Tran t_; \
27       tranStat(&t_, Q_STATIC_CAST(QState, target_));\
28    } else ((void)0)
29    #define Q_TRAN_DYN(target_) tran(Q_STATIC_CAST(QState, target_))
30
31 private:
32    void tranSetup(Tran *t, QState target);
33
34 private:
35    QState myState;                              // the active state
36    QState mySource;                     // source state during a transition
37 };
38 typedef QHsm::QPseudoState QSTATE;           // state-handler return type
```

If you are familiar with the standard Chain of Responsibility design pattern [Gamma+ 95], you might recognize that it addresses similar design problems to behavioral inheritance. In fact, every state hierarchy is a specific chain of responsibility, in which a request (event instance) is sent down a chain of state hierarchy in which more than one state has a chance to handle it. However, the two patterns are also significantly different. The chain of responsibility addresses the forwarding of requests among different objects, whereas behavioral inheritance addresses event handling within a single object.

4.1.1 Events

As you probably noticed from the standard state machine implementations (Chapter 3), most of the techniques (in particular, the optimal FSM approach) require a uniform representation of events, which leaves essentially only two choices for passing events to the handler methods: (1) passing the signal and generic event parameters separately or (2) combining the two into an *event object*. In Chapter 3, I demonstrated how to use the first option. Passing signals and parameters separately was fine for events with only a small and fixed set of parameters (e.g., the raw Windows API (Win32) uses the fixed-parameter technique to pass events to WinMain()), but in general, the second option offers more flexibility. Combining the signal with the parameters has an additional advantage, in that event instances (as opposed to pairs of signals and event parameters) are available in virtually every event-driven environment and can be passed around more easily and stored in event queues.

Event instances are used primarily as "bags" for packaging and passing around signals and event parameters. To generate events efficiently, it's often convenient to use statically preallocated event objects initialized with an initializer list. To allow such initialization, a class must be an aggregate; that is, it must not have private or protected members, constructors, base classes, and virtual functions [Stroustrup 91]. For that reason, the quantum event class QEvent (Listing 4.2) is declared as struct without any constructors (an obvious constructor would take one argument to initialize the sig attribute). In C++, struct is exactly equivalent to class, except in struct, the default protection level is public rather than private [Lipmann 96].

Listing 4.2   QSignal data type and QEvent class

```
typedef unsigned short QSignal;                        // Quantum Signal

struct QEvent {                                        // Quantum Event
   QSignal sig;
     . . .
};
```

New events with arbitrary parameters derive from the QEvent base class. The main responsibilities of the QEvent class are to bundle event parameters (by subclassing), to store the signal, and to provide a means of identifying the derived classes. The QEvent class combines the last two responsibilities and assigns them both to the sig attribute of scalar type QSignal.

When you derive from QEvent, obviously the subclasses are no longer aggregates. However, you should still keep your event classes simple and lightweight. Keep declaring your subclasses as structs, as a reminder that they are lightweight. In particular, you should avoid introducing constructors or virtual functions[6] in the derived event classes. As you will see in Part II, events generally do not go thorough conventional instantiation and cleanup (unless you use overloaded new and delete operators), so the constructors aren't invoked and the virtual pointers aren't set up.

Listing 4.2 declares QSignal as an unsigned short (typically a 16-bit integer). For most applications, the dynamic range of 2^{16} (65,536) should be sufficient for representing all necessary signals (even the dynamic range of a byte, 2^8 [256], typically will do). Naturally, you can redefine QSignal to use as many bits as you need.

The base class QEvent dictates that all event objects inherit the sig attribute, which provides the uniform mechanism for event processing because state handlers need to accept only the generic QEvent* pointer. On the flip side, this approach compromises type safety because a handler method doesn't know the concrete type of the event object passed as a generic pointer. All the handler knows is how to access the sig attribute to infer the concrete class of the event so that it can explicitly downcast the generic event to a concrete event. Therefore, it is crucial for the sig attribute to provide not only the signal but a unique mapping to the concrete event class. In other words, many signals can be mapped to the same QEvent (sub)class, but each QEvent subclass should have only *one* corresponding signal (otherwise, to which class would you downcast in your state handler method?).

The QEvent class contains other attributes (intentionally omitted in Listing 4.2), which I discuss in Chapter 9. I had to include them in the level of QEvent, rather than add them later via inheritance, to keep the benefits of an aggregate. For now, suffice it to say that these data members are used to automatically recycle event objects in Part II of this book (a specific garbage collection of the Quantum Framework).

Exercise 4.1   Redefine the signature of the state handler method in the optimal FSM implementation (Listing 3.4 in Chapter 3) to accept a generic immutable event pointer (QEvent const*) instead of an integer signal. Name this new class QFsm (quantum FSM). Subsequently use this quantum FSM design to implement the C comment parser from Chapter 3.

---

6.   This technique precludes using run time type identification (RTTI) for identifying event classes.

4.1.2 States

When you look at the structure of the behavioral inheritance meta-pattern shown in Figure 4.1, you might be surprised to see no State class. After all, State is the central abstraction for a state machine, and a State class falls out automatically from every OO analysis of the problem. Indeed, an earlier HSM implementation [Samek+ 00] was built around such a central State class. Using state objects seemed unavoidable because, in contrast to a basic flat state, a hierarchical state includes more than behavior. At a minimum, it must provide a data link to its superstate to represent state nesting, which is analogous to data links that chain together request-handler objects in the Chain of Responsibility design pattern. However, representing states as objects has severe drawbacks: Objects require storage and initialization, which are big inconveniences for the clients.

However, a state handler method can provide behavior and the badly needed structural link by *returning* the superstate. As simple as it seems, this was a breakthrough idea for me[7] because it allowed a straightforward extension of the optimal FSM design, preserving most of its favorable properties.

From the optimal FSM implementation in Chapter 3, you might recall that the state was represented as a pointer to the state handler method — that is, a pointer-to-member function of the QFsm class. Exercise 4.1 arrives at the following signature.

```
typedef void                                    // return type
        (QFsm::*                    // class the function is member of
            QFsmState)              // name of pointer-to-member
        (QEvent const *);                       // argument list
```

In the case of a hierarchical state, a state handler must additionally return the superstate, which leads to a recursive definition of the hierarchical state handler signature. Constructing such a signature is not possible in C++ (see [Sutter 01]), so it's approximated by the following definition of the quantum state, QState.

```
typedef void (QHsm::*QPseudoState)(QEvent const *);
typedef QPseudoState                            // return type
        (QHsm::*                    // class the function is member of
            QState)                 // name of pointer-to-member
        (QEvent const *);                       // argument list
```

The definition of the QState type nails down the signature of a hierarchical state handler. Listing 4.3 shows an example of a state handler method that handles events according to their signals (e->sig attribute) and returns the superstate if it

---

7. Perhaps the main difficulty of arriving at this obvious solution was breaking with traditional OO analysis principles, which prescribe mapping abstractions to classes.

cannot process a given event. This particular state handler method comes from the Quantum Calculator example discussed in Chapter 1.

Listing 4.3   Example of a hierarchical state handler (refer to the statechart shown in Figure 1.3 in Chapter 1)

```
 1 QSTATE Calc::operand1(QEvent const *e) {      // state-handler signature
 2   switch (e->sig) {
 3   case Q_ENTRY_SIG:
 4     dispState("operand1");
 5     return 0;                                  // event handled
 6   case IDC_CE:
 7     clear();
 8     Q_TRAN(&Calc::begin);                      // transition to "begin"
 9     return 0;                                  // event handled
10   case IDC_OPER:
11     sscanf(myDisplay, "%lf", &myOperand1);
12     myOperator = (static_cast<CalcEvt *>(e))->keyId;      // downcast
13     Q_TRAN(&Calc::opEntered);                  // transition to "opEntered"
14     return 0;                                  // event handled
15   }
16   return (QSTATE)&Calc::calc;      //event not handled, return superstate
17 }
```

The emphasized sections of Listing 4.3 demonstrate the main points. Line 1 shows the signature of the state handler method. In line 2, you see how the handler uses the sig signal attribute of the generic event pointer as the discriminator of a single-level switch statement (this is the same switch statement as in the optimal FSM implementation from Chapter 3). Line 12 demonstrates downcasting of the generic event pointer e to a derived event to get access to a specific parameter (here, CalcEvt::keyId). Finally, the handler has multiple exit points. In lines 5, 9, and 14, it returns 0, which indicates that the event has been processed. The default exit point (line 16), however, is reached only if the state handler cannot process the event, so it returns the superstate (the calc state handler in this case). Please note the casting of QState, which is necessary because the calc state (as for all other states in this state machine) is defined at the level of the Calc subclass, rather than directly in the QHsm class. This technique has the potential to be unsafe when combined with multiple inheritance (see the sidebar "C++ Pointer-to-Member Functions and Multiple Inheritance" in Chapter 3).

4.1.3   Entry/Exit Actions and Initial Transitions

In Chapter 2, you saw that UML statecharts support elements of Moore automata such as entry actions, exit actions, and initial transitions. These elements are sole characteristics of the state in which they are defined and do not depend, in particular, on the transition path through which the state has been reached. As described in Chapter 3, state handlers can (optionally) specify a state-specific behavior by responding to the following reserved signals.

```
enum {
    Q_ENTRY_SIG = 1,
    Q_EXIT_SIG,
    Q_INIT_SIG,
    Q_USER_SIG
};
```

A state handler can handle these signals by defining the appropriate cases in the usual `switch` statement. A state handler is free to execute any actions in response to those signals, but it should not take any state transitions in entry/exit actions. Conversely, it should always invoke the Q_INIT() macro to designate the initial direct substate in response to the Q_INIT_SIG signal.

Note: The UML specification allows the initial transition to target both direct and transitive substates. For simplicity and better efficiency, the HSM implementation restricts initial transitions to targeting the direct substates only.

The following code is an example of a state handler that uses these facilities.

```
QSTATE Calc::calc(QEvent const *e) {
    switch (e->sig) {
    case Q_ENTRY_SIG:
        dispState("ready");                          // entry action
        return 0;                          // entry action executed
    case Q_INIT_SIG:
        clear();
        Q_INIT(&Calc::ready);                    // initial transition
        return 0;                      // initial transition taken
    . . .
    }
    return (QSTATE)&Calc::top;        // signal unhandled, return superstate
}
```

The reserved signals take up the lowest signal IDs, which are thus not available for clients. For convenience, the public HSM interface contains the signal Q_USER_SIG, which indicates the first signal free for client use. A simple way to guarantee unique signals is to define them in a single enumeration. In this case, Q_USER_SIG can be used as follows.

```
enum MySignals {
   MY_KEYPRESS_SIG = Q_USER_SIG,
   MY_MOUSEMOVE_SIG,
   MY_MOUSECLICK_SIG,
   . . .
};
```

If you look carefully, you might notice that a reserved signal starts with a 1 rather than a 0. This is because signal 0 also is reserved but is used only in the internal implementation; therefore, it is not included in the public interface presented here. The additional reserved signal, 0 (the Empty signal Q_EMPTY_SIG), should never be handled explicitly by a state handler. Its only purpose is to force a state handler to return the superstate.

Note: The reserved signals Q_ENTRY_SIG, Q_EXIT_SIG, and Q_INIT_SIG should cause no side effects in state handler methods that do not have entry actions, exit actions, or initial transitions. The Q_EMPTY_SIG (0) signal always should cause a state handler to return the superstate without any side effects.

4.1.4   State Transitions

The example of a state handler in Listing 4.3 shows that state handler methods implement state transitions by means of the Q_TRAN() macro. More specifically, the state handler corresponding to the source of the transition invokes the macro and specifies the target as the argument.

This simple implementation cannot be compliant with the UML specification. As described in Section 2.2.5 of Chapter 2, the UML specification prescribes the following transition execution sequence: (1) exit actions from the source state configuration, (2) actions associated with the transition, and (3) entry actions to the target state configuration. Instead, the Q_TRAN() macro executes only the exit actions from the source state configuration immediately followed by the entry actions to the target state configuration. This sequence does not include actions associated with the transition, which can either precede the change of state (if you define them before Q_TRAN()) or follow the change of state (if you define them after Q_TRAN()), meaning the Q_TRAN() macro performs an *atomic* change of state, which cannot be disrupted by any other actions.

An earlier implementation of an HSM [Samek+ 00] tried to follow the UML standard strictly and ended up with a rather awkward and suboptimal design in this respect. The implementation was forced to interrupt a transition sequence after the exit from the source to give the clients a chance to squeeze in the transition-related actions before entering the target. This design not only put the burden on the clients to arrange the code appropriately, but obscured the implementation and prohibited valuable optimizations of the fragmented transition execution chain.

Yet, in my own experience with HSMs, as well as in reference statechart designs, I have never encountered a state model in which this particular alteration in the sequence of actions would really matter. If anything, then, the altered sequence implemented in the Q_TRAN() macro seems more intuitive, because even the UML specification advises: *"[You should] think of a transition as belonging to the source state"* [OMG 01, section 3.80.3]. Therefore, it seems most natural to execute the transition actions in the context of the source state (i.e., before changing the state through invocation of the Q_TRAN() macro). The notion that transition actions are executed in the source state is additionally reinforced in the QHsm implementation, because you define the transition actions in the source state handler. At the same time, the UML specification arbitrarily prescribes leaving the source state up to the LCA and then executing the transition actions. For me, choosing the context of the LCA for execution of the transition actions is not intuitive. To be more specific, I believe that the transition execution sequence specified in the UML is flawed and the proposed sequence here is correct.

More importantly, however, the altered sequence does not compromise any fundamental benefits of HSMs, like programming-by-difference or guaranteed initialization and cleanup via entry and exit actions. Please note that the altered transition sequence still preserves the essential order of exiting a nested source state (from the most deeply nested state up the hierarchy to the LCA) and entering a target state (from the LCA state down the hierarchy to the target).

4.1.5   The top State and the initial Pseudostate

Every HSM has the (typically implicit) top state, which contains all the other elements of the entire state machine (see Section 2.2.1 in Chapter 2). The QHsm class guarantees that the top state is available in every state machine by providing the protected QHsm::top() state handler inherited subsequently by all QHsm subclasses (Listing 4.1, line 19). By definition, the top state has no superstate, so the corresponding state handler always returns 0. The QHsm class implementation defines the top state entirely, and clients cannot override it (the QHsm::top() state handler is intentionally *not* virtual).

The only purpose, and legitimate use, of the top state is to provide the ultimate root of a state hierarchy, so that the highest level state handlers can return top as their superstate. In particular, you should not target the top state in a state transition (you cannot use the `top` state as a transition source either, because you cannot override the `QHsm::top()` state handler).

Figure 4.2   The top state and the initial pseudostate

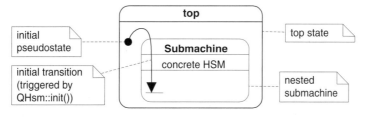

The only customizable aspect of the `top` state is the initial transition (see Figure 4.2). Clients must define the initial pseudostate handler for every state machine. The `QHsm` constructor enforces this condition by requiring a pointer to the initial pseudostate handler as an argument (Listing 4.1, line 7). The initial pseudostate handler defines only the initial transition, which must designate the default state of the state machine nested inside the `top` state (via the `Q_INIT()` macro). The initial transition can also specify arbitrary actions (typically initialization). The following code is an example of an initial pseudostate handler (from the Quantum Calculator example in Chapter 1).

```
void Calc::initial(QEvent const *) {
    clear();                              // perform initializations...
    Q_INIT(&Calc::calc);                  // designate the default state
}
```

The `QHsm` constructor intentionally does not execute the initial transition defined in the initial pseudostate because the clients don't have precise control over the timing when the C++ run time executes constructors.[8] Instead, a state machine comes out of the instantiation process in the initial pseudostate. Later, the client code must trigger the initial transition explicitly by invoking `init()` (described in the next section). This process separates instantiation of the state machine from initialization, giving the clients full control over the sequence of initializations in the system, which can be important because state machines are often Singletons[9] that are statically allocated and instantiated in an arbitrary order by the C++ run time prior to invoking `main()`. During the static instantiation, some vital objects can be missing, hardware might not be properly initialized yet, and multitasking is typically not yet enabled.

---

8. For example, state machine objects are often static, in which case the C++ run time instantiates them before invoking `main()`.

9. For example, the Quantum Calculator from Chapter 1 is a Singleton (see the Singleton design pattern in Gamma and colleagues [Gamma+ 95]).

Please note that the topmost initial transition can fire only once (actually, exactly once), because after you leave the top state, you cannot transition back. In other words, your state machine cannot reuse the initial pseudostate in its life cycle.

Exercise 4.2   Propose an alternative design for the state machine initialization that would implement an initial transition as a polymorphic initial() method (a virtual function in C++), rather than as an initial pseudostate. This method should be abstract (purely virtual) in the QHsm class so that clients would have to override it.

Exercise 4.3   Extend the previous design by adding another polymorphic method, onUnhandled(), which would be invoked from the top state handler, instead of silently discarding a user-defined signal. The default implementation should do nothing, but clients could override it to customize the treatment of such signals (e.g., treat them as errors).

4.2   An Annotated Example

Chapter 1 described one example of instantiating the behavioral inheritance metapattern. The Quantum Calculator application implemented a nontrivial statechart and integrated it with the Microsoft Windows GUI environment.

In this section, I walk you through the implementation of another nontrivial statechart, shown in Figure 4.3. This HSM contains six states — s0, s1, s11, s2, s21, and s211 — and its alphabet consists of eight signals, a through h. I have carefully designed this example to contain almost all the complex features of HSMs,[10] while still being simple enough to present the complete code.

---

10. This statechart also provides an exhaustive test case for the underlying internal implementation of the event processor described in Section 4.4.

Figure 4.3   **Statechart used in the example**

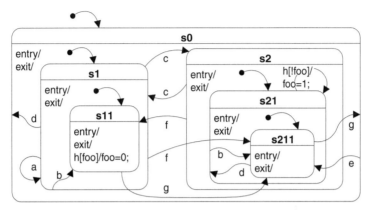

For simplicity, this statechart uses only a text-based interface. Most actions consist only of `printf()` statements that report the status of the state machine. You can regard these statements as a primitive instrumentation of the code.

In this section, I present the C++ implementation; however, I will present the C implementation of this statechart later in this chapter (Section 4.5.5). The accompanying CD-ROM contains complete code for both the C and C++ versions.

4.2.1   Enumerating Signals and Subclassing QHsm

The first step of the implementation consists of enumerating all signals (Listing 4.4, lines 3–6). Note that the user signals cannot start from zero; rather, they have to be offset by Q_USER_SIG to avoid overlapping the reserved system signals (Q_ENTRY_SIG, Q_EXIT_SIG, and Q_INIT_SIG).

Next, you derive the concrete HSM by inheriting from the QHsm class (Listing 4.4, line 8). In the derived class, you declare state handler methods with the predefined signature for all states in your statechart. The statechart from Figure 4.3 has six states, so you end up with six state handler methods (lines 13–18). Additionally, you also must declare the initial pseudostate handler (line 12) with the predefined signature. Typically, you define a default constructor (without arguments) using the initial pseudostate handler as the argument to construct the superclass QHsm (line 10). Finally, you add arbitrary data members to the state machine (line 20). State handler methods use these attributes as extended state variables.

Listing 4.4   **Enumerating signals and subclassing QHsm; the unusual indentation used to declare state handler methods indicates state nesting**

```
 1 #include "qf_win32.h"
 2
 3 enum QHsmTstSignals {
 4     A_SIG = Q_USER_SIG,          // user signals start with Q_USER_SIG
 5     B_SIG, C_SIG, D_SIG, E_SIG, F_SIG, G_SIG, H_SIG
 6 };
 7
 8 class QHsmTst : public QHsm {                    // QHsmTst derives from QHsm
 9 public:
10     QHsmTst() : QHsm((QPseudoState)initial) {}              // default Ctor
11 private:
12     void initial(QEvent const *e);                  // initial pseudostate
13     QSTATE s0(QEvent const *e);                          // state-handler
14       QSTATE s1(QEvent const *e);                         // state-handler
15         QSTATE s11(QEvent const *e);                      // state-handler
16       QSTATE s2(QEvent const *e);                         // state-handler
17         QSTATE s21(QEvent const *e);                      // state-handler
18           QSTATE s211(QEvent const *e);                   // state-handler
19 private:                                    // extended state variables...
20     int myFoo;
21 };
```

4.2.2   Defining State Handler Methods

All state handlers in this example are verbose, in that they log every signal processed (including entry and exit actions and the initial transition). Listing 4.5 shows the initial pseudostate handler as well as all six state handlers of QHsmTst class.

Listing 4.5   **Definition of the state handler methods of the QHsmTst class**

```
 1 void QHsmTst::initial(QEvent const *) {
 2     printf("top-INIT;");
 3     myFoo = 0;                          // initial extended state variable
 4     Q_INIT(&QHsmTst::s0);                         // initial transition
 5 }
 6
 7 QSTATE QHsmTst::s0(QEvent const *e) {
 8     switch (e->sig) {
 9     case Q_ENTRY_SIG: printf("s0-ENTRY;"); return 0;
10     case Q_EXIT_SIG:  printf("s0-EXIT;");  return 0;
11     case Q_INIT_SIG:  printf("s0-INIT;");  Q_INIT(&QHsmTst::s1);
           return 0;
12     case E_SIG: printf("s0-E;"); Q_TRAN(&QHsmTst::s211); return 0;
13     }
```

```
14    return (QSTATE)&QHsmTst::top;
15 }
16
17 QSTATE QHsmTst::s1(QEvent const *e) {
18    switch (e->sig) {
19    case Q_ENTRY_SIG: printf("s1-ENTRY;"); return 0;
20    case Q_EXIT_SIG:  printf("s1-EXIT;");  return 0;
21    case Q_INIT_SIG:  printf("s1-INIT;");  Q_INIT(&QHsmTst::s11);
          return 0;
22    case A_SIG: printf("s1-A;"); Q_TRAN(&QHsmTst::s1);    return 0;
23    case B_SIG: printf("s1-B;"); Q_TRAN(&QHsmTst::s11);   return 0;
24    case C_SIG: printf("s1-C;"); Q_TRAN(&QHsmTst::s2);    return 0;
25    case D_SIG: printf("s1-D;"); Q_TRAN(&QHsmTst::s0);    return 0;
26    case F_SIG: printf("s1-F;"); Q_TRAN(&QHsmTst::s211); return 0;
27    }
28    return (QSTATE)&QHsmTst::s0;
29 }
30
31 QSTATE QHsmTst::s11(QEvent const *e) {
32    switch (e->sig) {
33    case Q_ENTRY_SIG: printf("s11-ENTRY;"); return 0;
34    case Q_EXIT_SIG:  printf("s11-EXIT;");  return 0;
35    case G_SIG: printf("s11-G;"); Q_TRAN(&QHsmTst::s211); return 0;
36    case H_SIG:                              // internal transition with a guard
37       if (myFoo) {                          // test the guard condition
38          printf("s11-H;");
39          myFoo = 0;
40          return 0;
41       }
42       break;
43    }
44    return (QSTATE)&QHsmTst::s1;
45 }
46
47 QSTATE QHsmTst::s2(QEvent const *e) {
48    switch (e->sig) {
49    case Q_ENTRY_SIG: printf("s2-ENTRY;"); return 0;
50    case Q_EXIT_SIG:  printf("s2-EXIT;");  return 0;
51    case Q_INIT_SIG:  printf("s2-INIT;");  Q_INIT(&QHsmTst::s21);
          return 0;
52    case C_SIG: printf("s2-C;"); Q_TRAN(&QHsmTst::s1);  return 0;
53    case F_SIG: printf("s2-F;"); Q_TRAN(&QHsmTst::s11); return 0;
54    }
55    return (QSTATE)&QHsmTst::s0;
56 }
57
58 QSTATE QHsmTst::s21(QEvent const *e) {
```

```
59    switch (e->sig) {
60    case Q_ENTRY_SIG: printf("s21-ENTRY;"); return 0;
61    case Q_EXIT_SIG:  printf("s21-EXIT;");  return 0;
62    case Q_INIT_SIG: printf("s21-INIT;");   Q_INIT(&QHsmTst::s211);
          return 0;
63    case B_SIG:  printf("s21-C;"); Q_TRAN(&QHsmTst::s211); return 0;
64    case H_SIG:                             // self transition with a guard
65        if (!myFoo) {                       // test the guard condition
66            printf("s21-H;");
67            myFoo = 1;
68            Q_TRAN(&QHsmTst::s21);          // self transition
69            return 0;
70        }
71        break;                              // break to return the superstate
72    }
73    return (QSTATE)&QHsmTst::s2;            // return the superstate
74 }
75
76 QSTATE QHsmTst::s211(QEvent const *e) {
77    switch (e->sig) {
78    case Q_ENTRY_SIG: printf("s211-ENTRY;"); return 0;
79    case Q_EXIT_SIG:  printf("s211-EXIT;");  return 0;
80    case D_SIG: printf("s211-D;");   Q_TRAN(&QHsmTst::s21); return 0;
81    case G_SIG: printf("s211-G;");   Q_TRAN(&QHsmTst::s0);  return 0;
82    }
83    return (QSTATE)&QHsmTst::s21;           // return the superstate
84 }
```

Translating the statechart from Figure 4.3 into code is straightforward and requires adherence to just a few simple rules. Consider, for instance, the QHsmTst::s21() state handler (Listing 4.5, lines 58–74). First, look up this state in the diagram and trace around its state boundary. You need to implement all transitions originating at this boundary, as well as all internal transitions enlisted in this state. Additionally, if an initial transition is embedded directly in the state, you need to implement it as well. For state s21, the transitions that originate at the boundary are transition b and self-transition h. In addition, the state has an entry action, an exit action, and an initial transition.

Coding of entry and exit actions is the simplest. You just intercept the reserved signals Q_ENTRY_SIG or Q_EXIT_SIG, enlist actions you want to execute, and terminate the lists with return 0 (Listing 4.5, lines 60, 61).

To code the initial transition, you intercept the reserved signal Q_INIT_SIG, enlist the actions, and then designate the target substate through the Q_INIT() macro (line 62), after which you exit the state handler with return 0.

You code a regular transition in a very similar way, except that you intercept a custom-defined signal (e.g., B_SIG, line 63), and you use the Q_TRAN() macro to designate the target state. Again, you exit state handler with return 0.

Coding a transition with a guard is a little more involved. Lines 64 through 71 of Listing 4.5 show how to handle this case. As before, you intercept the custom signal (here, H_SIG), except now you test the guard condition inside an if (...) statement (line 65) first. You place the transition actions, Q_TRAN() macro, and return 0 *inside* the TRUE branch of the if statement (lines 66–69). Because the return is placed inside the if statement, the code following the if statement executes only when the guard expression evaluates to FALSE. When that happens, you break out of the switch (line 71) and return the superstate from the state handler (to indicate that the event has not been handled).

The last step of every state handler designates the superstate by returning the corresponding state handler to the caller. In the case of state s21, this is the s2() state handler (line 73). Please note the necessary type cast to QSTATE.

Listing 4.5 demonstrates many more examples of the simple rules just mentioned. Note that this implementation automatically handles the execution of transition chains — that is, the computation of the LCA state and the execution of appropriate exit actions, entry actions, and initial transitions. Consequently, no manual coding of transition chains is necessary.

4.2.3   Initialization and Dispatching Events

The test harness for this HSM (Listing 4.6) consists of a simple character interface through which you inject events to the state machine by typing the characters 'a' through 'h' on your keyboard. Typing a character outside of this range ends the test.

The interesting points in Listing 4.6 are instantiating the state machine (line 1), triggering the initial transition through QHsm::init() (line 9), and dispatching events through QHsm::dispatch() (line 17).

Listing 4.6   Test harness for QHsmTst statechart

```
 1 static QHsmTst test;              // instantiate the QHsmTst state machine
 2 static QEvent const testEvt[] = {              // static event instances
 3    {A_SIG, 0, 0}, {B_SIG, 0, 0}, {C_SIG, 0, 0}, {D_SIG, 0, 0},
 4    {E_SIG, 0, 0}, {F_SIG, 0, 0}, {G_SIG, 0, 0}, {H_SIG, 0, 0}
 5 };
 6
 7 main() {
 8    printf("QHsmTst example, v.1.00, QHsm: %s\n", QHsm::getVersion());
 9    test.init();                              // take the initial transition
10    for (;;) {                                              // for-ever
11       printf("\nSignal<-");
```

```
12      char c = getc(stdin);
13      getc(stdin);                                    // discard '\n'
14      if (c < 'a' || 'h' < c) {                       // character out of range?
15          return 0;                                   // terminate
16      }
17      test.dispatch(&testEvt[c - 'a']);               // dispatch event
18  }
19  return 0;
20 }
```

4.2.4 Test Run

As always, I strongly recommend that you run this example on your PC (Exercise 4.4) and correlate the output with the statechart shown in Figure 4.3. You can learn a lot about the mechanics of statecharts by playing with this application.

Exercise 4.4   Find the Qhsmtst.exe application on the accompanying CD-ROM and execute it. Try out all possible transitions. Compare the application output with the test log from Listing 4.7.

Listing 4.7   **QHsmTst** test session log

```
 1 QHsmTst example, version 1.00, libraries: QHsm 2.2.2
 2 top-INIT;s0-ENTRY;s0-INIT;s1-ENTRY;s1-INIT;s11-ENTRY;
 3 Signal<-a
 4 s1-A;s11-EXIT;s1-EXIT;s1-ENTRY;s1-INIT;s11-ENTRY;
 5 Signal<-e
 6 s0-E;s11-EXIT;s1-EXIT;s2-ENTRY;s21-ENTRY;s211-ENTRY;
 7 Signal<-e
 8 s0-E;s211-EXIT;s21-EXIT;s2-EXIT;s2-ENTRY;s21-ENTRY;s211-ENTRY;
 9 Signal<-a
10
11 Signal<-h
12 s21-H;s211-EXIT;s21-EXIT;s21-ENTRY;s21-INIT;s211-ENTRY;
13 Signal<-h
14
15 Signal<-x
```

Listing 4.7 shows an example of a test session log. In line 1, you see the version of the test harness, as well as the library (the QHsm implementation is linked in from a library). Line 2 shows the effect of the initial transition triggered by QHsm::init(). Injecting signals into the state machine starts from line 3. Every stimulus (odd line numbers) is followed by the response (even line numbers) in the form of the transition chain printout. From these printouts, you can always determine the sequence of actions, as well as the active state (the last state entered). For instance, in line 3, the state machine is in state s11 because it is the last state entered in the previous line. Signal a injected in this line triggers a self-transition inherited from state s1. The statechart responds in line 4 by executing the transition sequence described in Section 4.1.4.

Interestingly, in hierarchical state machines, the same transition can cause different behavior, depending on which state inherits the transition. For example, in lines 5 and 7, the injection of signal e triggers the same state transition each time (the statechart has only one transition e in state s0). However, the responses of the state model in lines 6 and 8 are different because transition e fires from different state configurations — once when s11 is active (line 6) and next when s211 is active (line 8).

Additionally, in extended state machines, the response depends not only on the stimulus and the state but on the value of the extended state variables. For example, signal h triggers a transition in line 12 but is not handled in line 14, although the state machine remains in the same state, s211. From the inspection of the statechart in Figure 4.3, you can see that transition h in state s21 has a guard, which once evaluates to TRUE and the next time to FALSE.

After experimenting for a while with the QHsmTst statechart, you might want to modify it to try out different state topologies. In fact, in this implementation of the HSM, it is easy to change any aspect of the state model, even late in the development process.[11] The following two exercises give you some ideas of how you can modify the statechart to learn even more from this example.

Exercise 4.5 Modify the state machine by moving transition e from s0 to s2 and by changing the target of transition f in state s1 from s211 to s21.

Exercise 4.6 Change the initial transition in state s2 to target the s211 state rather than s21 and observe the assertion failure on transition c. Change the target of transition g in state s211 to top (see Section 4.1.4) and observe another assertion failure. Explain the reasons for breaking the assertions.

4.3   Heuristics and Idioms

The behavioral inheritance meta-pattern presented here allows you to build executable hierarchical state models directly in C++ (and C as well; see the C implementation coming up in Section 4.5). In this section, I have collected a few coding heuristics and idioms that I found useful for constructing readable, efficient state

---

11. It is even easier to change the code than to redraw the state diagram.

machine code that is easy to maintain. Although illustrated in C++, most of the guidelines apply equally well to the C implementation.

4.3.1   Structuring State Machine Code

To code your own HSMs, you just need to subclass QHsm and implement each state in a separate state handler method. These state handlers must fulfill the simple contract of returning the superstate every time they do not handle an event or returning 0 when they do. Other than that, you can structure the state handler methods arbitrarily. However, the following suggestions should help you avoid pitfalls and make the structure of the state machine readily apparent.

You should construct *complete state handlers* — that is, state handler methods that directly include all state machine elements pertaining to a given state (such as all signals and all transitions). Consider the following code snippet.

```
QSTATE MyHsm::stateA(QEvent const *e) {
    switch (e->sig) {
    . . .
    case MYSIG1_SIG:
        onMySig1();                              // internal transition ???
        return 0;                                // event handled
    . . .
    }
    return (QSTATE)&MyHsm::top;          // event unhandled, return superstate
}

void MyHsm::onMySig1() {                 // definition of onMySig() method ...
    if (myA && !myB && myC > 0 ...) {        // conditionally transition to B
        Q_TRAN(&MyHsm::stateB);
    }
}
```

Although in principle correct, the state handler MyHsm::stateA() is incomplete, because the action MyHsm::onMySig1() hides the Q_TRAN(&MyHsm::stateB) transition. Worse, the way it is coded suggests that the MYSIG1_SIG signal triggers an internal transition, which it does not. You can easily make the handler complete again by breaking it up a little differently. Observe that the transition is conditional; that is, it has a guard condition in statechart lingo. You should code this guard explicitly, as in the following code fragment.

```
QSTATE MyHsm::stateA(QEvent const *e) {
    switch (e->sig) {
    . . .
    case MYSIG1_SIG:
        if (sig1Guard()) {                       // explicit guard condition
```

```
        Q_TRAN(&MyHsm::stateB);                     // explicit state transition
      return 0;
      }
      break;
    . . .
    }
    return (QSTATE)&MyHsm::top;
}

int MyHsm::sig1Guard() {                    // definition of sig1Guard() guard ...
    return (myA && !myB && myC > 0 ...);
}
```

Now the `MyHsm::stateA()` state handler conveys the correct information. In particular, it's clear that the transition to `stateB` has a guard.

Lucid coding requires you to include every state machine element directly and explicitly in a state handler that you would draw in a statechart diagram for this state. Instead of splitting the code ad hoc, you should partition it into elements of statecharts — that is, actions, guards, junctions, and choice points (structured if–then–else statements). This division makes the one-to-one mapping between diagrams and code obvious. In fact, complete and compact state handlers are one of the most succinct and efficient textual representations of HSMs (see Exercise 4.7).

Exercise 4.7   Most design automation tools capable of translating statechart diagrams to code internally represent statecharts in textual format. For example, the ROOM method [Selic+ 94] defines a ROOM linear form representation, which is capable of capturing HSMs among other things. Try to invent your own textual notation, succinct yet expressive, to represent statecharts. Use your notation to write down a specification for state s21 of the statechart from Figure 4.3. Compare it with the `QHsmTst::s21()` state handler code in Listing 4.5.

4.3.2   Choosing the Right Signal Granularity

Nothing affects state machine complexity and efficiency as much as the right signal granularity. The optimal granularity of signals falls somewhere between the two extremes of too fine and too coarse.

The granularity of signals is too fine if you repeatedly find the same groups of signals handled in the same way. For example, recall the Quantum Calculator example (Figure 1.3 in Chapter 1). At the statechart level, the calculator HSM handles all numerals 1 through 9 in the same way. Therefore, introducing a separate signal for each numeral would lead to a signal granularity that is too fine, which would unnecessarily bloat the state handler methods. Instead, the Quantum Calculator statechart represents the whole group of numerals 1 through 9 as one signal, `IDC_1_9`.

The granularity of signals is too coarse if you find yourself frequently using guard conditions that test event parameters. In this case, event parameters are the de facto signals. Consider the Windows message (signal) `WM_COMMAND`, frequently used in Windows GUI applications (e.g., Listing 1.2 in Chapter 1). This signal is too coarse, because clients typically must test parameters associated with the `WM_COMMAND` (most frequently `LOWORD(wParam)`) to choose the desired behavior. In other words, values of `LOWORD(wParam)` are the de facto signals. In this case, the too-coarse signal granularity results in a suboptimal (and not very elegant) additional `switch` statement.

When you encounter signals that are too coarse, the first thing you should try is to redefine or remap signals to the right level of granularity (the Quantum Calculator application exemplifies the remapping option). However, if you cannot do this, you should include all the de facto signals directly in your state handlers. All too often, the additional layer of signal dispatching is moved to separate methods, which makes state handlers incomplete (in the sense discussed in Section 4.3.1).

4.3.3   UML-Compliant HSMs

Any nontrivial language, including the graphical language of statecharts, allows making constructs that not only happen to be false but are meaningless and sometimes self-contradicting. The latter statements are said to be *malformed*. A big part of the UML specification [OMG 01] deals with specifying so-called *well-formedness rules* that allow the detection of malformed constructs. Examples of such UML rules for statecharts are: The top state cannot be a source of a transition, or: A composite state can have, at most, one initial transition. Many of these rules (e.g., the first example) are automatically enforced by the structure of the QHsm class. For instance, the `QHsm::top()` state handler cannot be overridden, so it cannot become a source of a transition. In addition, by following the basic guidelines outlined earlier, you automatically satisfy many well-formedness rules. For example, in a complete state handler, you can't define two initial transitions (the second example of well-formedness rules) because a `switch` statement with two identical cases (`Q_INIT_SIG`) will not compile.

Except for the slightly altered transition chain sequence (Section 4.4.3), the behavioral inheritance meta-pattern allows you to build UML-compliant state machines. However, it is also possible to build state machines violating the UML specification well-formedness rules. Whereas, in general, noncompliance with the UML specification can have consequences that are hard to foresee, the following extension to the UML specification is safe and often leads to simpler state models.

In the UML specification, composite states (states with substates) are significantly different from simple states (states without substates). One well-formedness rule concerning composite states is: "*If a [not concurrent] composite state is active then exactly one of its substates is active*" [OMG 01, page 2-162]. In view of the OO analogy between state hierarchies and class taxonomies, if this rule were applied to classes, it would require that every class that has subclasses must necessarily be abstract (cannot have instances). However, it often happens that an abstraction captured in a class can be used directly (instantiated) in some parts of the code. Independently, someone else might specialize this abstraction by creating subclasses, but this should not break the earlier code that instantiated the original class. You cannot foresee whether someone will subclass your class (unless it is explicitly abstract), neither can you prevent subclassing.[12]

Following the OO analogy, it is logical to relax the UML rule and allow composite states to become active without any of their substates being active. Consider, for example, the C comment parser state machine discussed in Chapter 3. Figure 4.4a shows a UML-compliant hierarchical version of the C comment parser state machine (compare it with the classical FSM shown in Figure 3.1 in Chapter 3). Unfortunately, the hierarchical version is significantly more complex than the flat FSM (it adds two more states and two more initial transitions) because the high-level code and comment states provide only groupings for their substates and add little toward semantics. The non-UML-compliant version (Figure 4.4b), on the other hand, is no more complex than the classical FSM because it has exactly the same number of states and transitions. The difference between the UML-compliant and the -noncompliant versions is that the code and comment states each has only one substate, which is not necessarily active when its superstate is active (note the lack of initial transitions in the code and comment states).

Figure 4.4   **An HSM representation of the C comment parser from Chapter 3; (a) UML-compliant, (b) not UML-compliant**

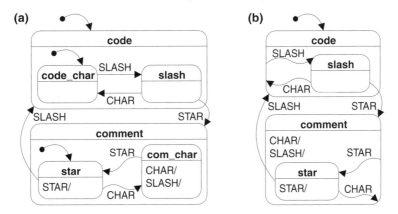

---

12. In Java, you can use the `final` keyword, but in C++, you generally cannot prevent subclassing.

The advantage of the hierarchical version over the flat state machine from Chapter 3 is that HSMs are more intuitive and extensible. For example, when the classical FSM (Figure 3.1 in Chapter 3) encounters a slash character while in the code state, it transitions to the slash state, leaving the code state. However, the slash character also can represent a division operator, so conceptually, the parser should remain in the code state until it collects enough evidence for a conclusive decision that the parser is no longer parsing code. This is the exact behavior of both hierarchical models (Figure 4.4a, b). All things being equal, however, the model in Figure 4.4b is much simpler than the model in Figure 4.4a.

Exercise 4.8   Implement the HSM from Figure 4.4b in C and in C++. Subsequently, extend the hierarchical C comment parser to count the number of comment blocks (/* ... */), as well as the number of comment characters (see Exercise 3.10 in Chapter 3). Hint: Count the number of entries into the comment state.

4.4   The Event Processor

In principle, at this point you should be able to successfully instantiate the behavioral inheritance meta-pattern in your own statechart implementations. However, you will code more efficiently and with greater confidence when you understand the internal workings of the QHsm class. In this section, I peek under the hood and examine the event processor, which performs the work of executing actions and transitions.

Design by Contract in C/C++

Design by Contract (DBC) is a method of programming based on precisely defined specifications of the various software components' mutual obligations (*contracts*). The central idea of this method is to inherently embed the contracts in the code and validate them automatically at run time.

In C/C++, you can implement the most important aspects of DBC with assertions. Throughout this book, I use customized assertion macros defined in the header file qassert.h. These macros include

- REQUIRE(), to assert a precondition,
- ENSURE(), to assert a postcondition,
- INVARIANT(), to assert an invariant, and
- ASSERT(), to assert a general contract of another type.

Each of these macros performs a function similar to that of the standard library facility `assert()`, and their different names serve only to document the purpose of the contract. Section 8.2.1 in Chapter 8 covers DBC and `qassert.h` in more detail.

4.4.1   Initializing the State Machine: The `init()` Method

As mentioned earlier, the purpose of `QHsm::init()` is to trigger the initial transition and to recursively enter the submachine of the `top` state (Figure 4.2). You must call this method only once for a given state machine *before* dispatching any events to it. `QHsm::init()` (1) triggers the initial transition defined in the `initial` pseudostate and (2) "drills" into the state hierarchy until it reaches a leaf state.

Almost all methods of `QHsm`, including `init()`, use the helper macro `TRIGGER()` internally.

```
#define TRIGGER(state_, sig_) \
   Q_STATE_CAST((this->*(state_))(&pkgStdEvt[sig_]))
```

The goal of this macro is to present one of the reserved signals (`Q_EMPTY_SIG`, `Q_ENTRY_SIG`, `Q_EXIT_SIG`, or `Q_INIT_SIG`) to a given state handler, `state_`. Please note the characteristic syntax of handler method invocation based on the pointer-to-member function (`(this->*state_)(...)`). Because `QState` is not exactly recursive (see Section 4.1.2), the value returned by the state handler from `QPseudoState` must necessarily be cast onto `QState`, which the macro `TRIGGER()` accomplishes through another macro, `Q_STATE_CAST()`. `Q_STATE_CAST()` is compiler dependent and should be defined as `reinterpret_cast<QState>(...)` for the C++ compilers that support the new type casts and as the C-style cast `(QState)(...)` for the C++ compilers that don't.[13]

Listing 4.8   Definition of the `QHsm::init()` method

```
 1 void QHsm::init(QEvent const *e) {
 2    REQUIRE(myState == top &&                         // HSM not executed yet
 3            mySource != 0);               // we are about to dereference mySource
 4    register QState s = myState;                    // save myState in a temporary
 5    (this->*(QPseudoState)mySource)(e);        // top-most initial transition
 6                                       // initial transition must go *one* level deep
 7    ASSERT(s == TRIGGER(myState, Q_EMPTY_SIG));
 8    s = myState;                                       // update the temporary
 9    TRIGGER(s, Q_ENTRY_SIG);                              // enter the state
10    while (TRIGGER(s, Q_INIT_SIG) == 0) {                  // init handled?
11                                       // initial transition must go *one* level deep
12        ASSERT(s == TRIGGER(myState, Q_EMPTY_SIG));
```

---

13. For example, embedded C++ (EC++) compilers don't support the new type casts.

```
13          s = myState;
14          TRIGGER(s, Q_ENTRY_SIG);                    // enter the substate
15      }
16 }
```

Listing 4.8 shows the definition of the init() method. The preconditions[14] in lines 2 and 3 assert that the HSM has not been executed yet (myState points to the top state) and that mySource has been initialized to the initial pseudostate handler by the QHsm constructor. The initial transition of the top submachine is triggered in line 5. According to the limitation mentioned in Section 4.1.3, the initial transition can target only a direct substate of a given state, which init() asserts in line 7. The while loop in line 10 triggers an initial transition in the current state and tests the return value to find out if the state handler has actually handled the transition. If so (the state handler returns 0), the body of the loop asserts that the target is a direct substate of the source (lines 11, 12) and then enters the target substate. The loop continues until there are no more initial transitions to take.

4.4.2   Dispatching Events: The `dispatch()` Method

The choice of the state handler signature makes the most frequently used dispatch() method almost trivial. Its only job is to scan the state hierarchy (chain of responsibility) until some state handles the event (in which case, it returns 0) or the top state is reached (in which case, it also returns 0). Listing 4.9 contains the complete code.

Listing 4.9   Definition of the `QHsm::dispatch()` method

```
1 void QHsm::dispatch(QEvent const *e) {
2     for (mySource = myState; mySource;
3         mySource = Q_STATE_CAST((this->*mySource)(e)))
4     {}
5 }
```

The dispatch() method traverses the state hierarchy starting from the currently active state myState. It advances up the state hierarchy (i.e., from substates to superstates), invoking all the state handlers in succession. At each level of state nesting, it intercepts the value returned from a state handler to obtain the superstate needed to advance to the next level.

By using the mySource attribute (instead of an automatic variable) to invoke state handlers, the current level of hierarchy (i.e., the potential source of a transition) is accessible to tran() (see the next section). Again, because QState, by definition, is

---

14. See the sidebar "Design by Contract in C/C++" on page 106.

not exactly recursive (see Section 4.1.2), the Q_STATE_CAST() type cast in line 3 of Listing 4.9 is necessary.

Exercise 4.9 The QHsm class provides the "is-in-state" query (see the declaration of isIn() in Listing 4.1, line 11). Write the body of this method. Note that in HSMs, to be in a state also means to be in all substates of that state. Hint: You can implement the is-in-state query using the same state hierarchy traversal as the dispatch() method.

4.4.3   Static and Dynamic State Transitions: Macros Q_TRAN() and Q_TRAN_DYN()

As you saw in all state handler examples presented so far, you code state transitions by invoking the macro Q_TRAN() (defined in Listing 4.1, lines 20–23). At the heart of this macro is the protected tranStat() method, which actually drives state handlers to accomplish a *static* state transition. Almost all state transitions are static, which means that both the source and the target of the transition do not change at run time. This characteristic offers an opportunity to optimize the execution of such transitions, because the expensive determination of the transition chain (finding out which exit and entry actions and initial transitions to execute) can be done only once instead of each time the transition is taken.

Nonetheless, some transitions might need to change their targets at run time (e.g., transitions to history).[15] For these rare occasions, the QHsm class offers a *dynamic* state transition that you code with the Q_TRAN_DYN() macro (defined in Listing 4.1, line 29). This macro invokes the protected method tran() rather than tranStat().

Exercise 4.10 Q_TRAN_DYN() is an optimization only with respect to Q_TRAN(), which means that you should be able to replace Q_TRAN() with Q_TRAN_DYN() (with the loss of optimization). Modify the HSM example described in Section 4.2 by replacing Q_TRAN() with Q_TRAN_DYN(). Recompile and verify that the state machine works as before.

Executing state transitions is by far the most complex part of the HSM implementation. Figure 4.5 illustrates the challenge. This diagram shows the inheritance tree of states comprising the Quantum Calculator statechart (Figure 1.3 in Chapter

---

15. Chapter 6 presents another example (related to inheritance of entire state machines) in which you need to use dynamic state transitions.

1) and two exemplary transitions. As described earlier in this chapter (Section 4.1.4), a transition execution sequence involves the exit of all states up to the LCA, then recursive entry into the target state. Exiting the current state configuration is relatively straightforward because it follows the natural direction of navigation through the state hierarchy (denoted by the behavioral inheritance arrow in Figure 4.5). However, the entry to the target requires navigating in the opposite direction (recall that state handlers return only the superstate).

Figure 4.5   **Behavioral inheritance tree of states in the Quantum Calculator statechart; the heavy-lined arrows indicate state transitions triggered by C (cancel) and OPER (operator); the natural direction of navigation through the model is from substates to superstates, as indicated by the behavioral inheritance arrow**

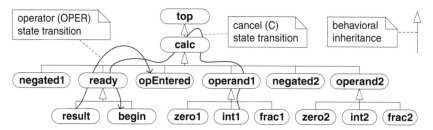

The solution to the problem of entering the target state configuration is to first record the exit path from the target to the LCA, without executing any actions. You can do this by dispatching the reserved empty signal (Section 4.1.3), which causes every state handler to return the superstate without causing any side effects.[16] After the exit path has been recorded in that way, it can easily be turned into the entry path by playing it backwards, which is the desired order.[17]

This strategy immediately suggests an optimization. Instead of rediscovering the entry path every time, one might as well store it permanently in a static object and subsequently reuse the path information for a much more efficient execution of the transition. However, this works only for static transitions (coded with Q_TRAN()), where the target never changes at run time. Dynamic transitions (coded with Q_TRAN_DYN()) cannot use this optimization and must determine the transition execution sequence every time.

---

16. It is the responsibility of the client (you) to design state handler methods in such a way that the empty signal (0) causes no side effects.
17. One of the first documented uses of this method was to get rid of the mythological Minotaur (half-man, half-bull monster on the island of Crete). The Athenian hero Theseus unraveled a ball of thread on his way to the Minotaur's labyrinth, killed the beast, and followed the thread to find his was out.

In the next section, I discuss the somewhat simpler `QHsm::tran()` dynamic transition, and in the following section, I cover the `QHsm::tranStat()` static transition as an optimization of the first technique.

4.4.4 Dynamic State Transition: The `tran()` Method

The goal of the `QHsm::tran()` method is to execute transition sequences (i.e., chains of exit and entry actions and initial transitions) by invoking the appropriate state handlers in the correct order using the appropriate standard signal for each invocation. Unlike `init()` and `dispatch()`, which are invoked directly by clients, `tran()` is protected and can be invoked only indirectly from state handlers (more precisely, from the `dispatch()` method as in Listing 4.9, line 3).

The `tran()` method consists of two major steps. In the first step, `tran()` performs a traversal of the state hierarchy similar to that of `dispatch()`, but with the objective to exit all states up to the level in which the transition is defined. This step covers the case of an *inherited* state transition — that is, the transition defined at a level higher than the currently active state. For example, Figure 4.6 shows the details of the OPER transition from Figure 4.5. This transition is defined at the level of the `ready` state, from which the `result` and `begin` states inherit. When a client calls `dispatch()` with the OPER event, `dispatch()` invokes the currently active state first, which happens to be the `result` state. This state does not "know" how to handle the OPER event, so it returns the superstate. The `dispatch()` method then loops to the `ready` state, in which OPER triggers the transition to `opEntered`. However, the correct exit of the current state configuration must include exiting `result` before exiting `ready`. Figure 4.6 shows this segment of the transition in a dashed line. The figure also shows the state of the `myState` and `mySource` pointers at the time that `dispatch()` invokes `tran()`. As you can see, `myState` still points to the previously active state (`result`), whereas `mySource` points to the state handler that invoked `tran()` (`ready`), which is the source of the transition.

Figure 4.6   Two segments of an inherited state transition

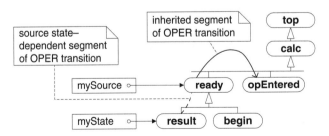

Only after exiting all states up to the source of the transition can `tran()` proceed with the second step, which is execution of the transition itself. This step tries to optimize the workload by minimizing the number of "probing" invocations of state handlers with empty signals (i.e., with the sole purpose of eliciting the superstate). The optimization relies on testing directly for all the simplest source–target state configurations, which are most likely to occur in practice. Moreover, the strategy is to order these configurations in such a way that the information about the state configuration obtained from earlier steps can be used in later steps. Figure 4.7 shows such ordering of state transition topologies, and Table 4.1 (page 115) enlists the tests required to determine a given configuration.

Figure 4.7   **Ordering of all possible source and target state configurations used in** `QHsm::tran()`

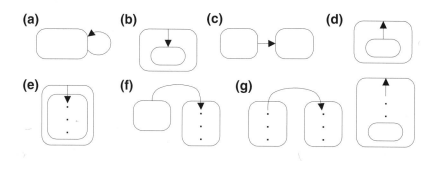

Exercise 4.11 Compare Figure 4.7 with the example statechart from Figure 4.3 on page 95. Convince yourself that transitions a through g in the example statechart correspond to the cases enumerated in Figure 4.7 (e.g., signal a triggers the state transition described in Figure 4.7a, and so on).

Listing 4.10   **Definition of the dynamic state transition** `QHsm::tran()` **method**

```
1 void QHsm::tran(QState target) {
2    REQUIRE(target != top);                      // cannot target "top" state
3    QState entry[8], p, q, s, *e, *lca;
4    for (s = myState; s != mySource; ) {
5       ASSERT(s);                                // we are about to dereference s
6       QState t = TRIGGER(s, Q_EXIT_SIG);
7       if (t) {                    // exit action unhandled, t points to superstate
8          s = t;
9       }
10      else {                          // exit action handled, elicit superstate
```

```
11          s = TRIGGER(s, Q_EMPTY_SIG);
12       }
13    }
14
15    *(e = &entry[0]) = 0;
16    *(++e) = target;                              // assume entry to target
17
18    // (a) check mySource == target (transition to self)
19    if (mySource == target) {
20       TRIGGER(mySource, Q_EXIT_SIG);             // exit source
21       goto inLCA;
22    }
23    // (b) check mySource == target->super
24    p = TRIGGER(target, Q_EMPTY_SIG);
25    if (mySource == p) {
26       goto inLCA;
27    }
28    // (c) check mySource->super == target->super (most common)
29    q = TRIGGER(mySource, Q_EMPTY_SIG);
30    if (q == p) {
31       TRIGGER(mySource, Q_EXIT_SIG);             // exit source
32       goto inLCA;
33    }
34    // (d) check mySource->super == target
35    if (q == target) {
36       TRIGGER(mySource, Q_EXIT_SIG);             // exit source
37       --e;                                       // do not enter the LCA
38       goto inLCA;
39    }
40    // (e) check rest of mySource == target->super->super... hierarchy
41    *(++e) = p;
42    for (s = TRIGGER(p, Q_EMPTY_SIG); s;
43         s = TRIGGER(s, Q_EMPTY_SIG))
44    {
45       if (mySource == s) {
46          goto inLCA;
47       }
48       *(++e) = s;
49    }
50    TRIGGER(mySource, Q_EXIT_SIG);                 // exit source
51    // (f) check rest of mySource->super == target->super->super...
52    for (lca = e; *lca; --lca) {
53       if (q == *lca) {
54          e = lca - 1;                             // do not enter the LCA
55          goto inLCA;
56       }
57    }
```

```
58      // (g) check each mySource->super->super..for each target...
59      for (s = q; s; s = TRIGGER(s, Q_EMPTY_SIG)) {
60          for (lca = e; *lca; --lca) {
61              if (s == *lca) {
62                  e = lca - 1;                        // do not enter the LCA
63                  goto inLCA;
64              }
65          }
66          TRIGGER(s, Q_EXIT_SIG);                             // exit s
67      }
68      ASSERT(0);                                      // malformed HSM
69 inLCA:                              // now we are in the LCA of mySource and target
70      ASSERT(e < &entry[DIM(entry)]);             // new entry e must fit in
71      while (s = *e--) {            // retrace the entry path in reverse order
72          TRIGGER(s, Q_ENTRY_SIG);                            // enter s
73      }
74      myState = target;                           // update current state
75      while (TRIGGER(target, Q_INIT_SIG) == 0) {
76                              // initial transition must go *one* level deep
77          ASSERT(target == TRIGGER(myState, Q_EMPTY_SIG));
78          target = myState;
79          TRIGGER(target, Q_ENTRY_SIG);               // enter target
80      }
81 }
```

Listing 4.10 shows the complete implementation of QHsm::tran(). In the first step (lines 4–13), tran() exits all states from the currently active state (myState) up to the level in which the transition is defined (mySource) to cover the case of an inherited state transition. While exiting the states, tran() must differentiate between the case in which the exit action is not handled (the state handler returns the superstate) and the case in which the exit action is executed (the state handler returns 0). In the latter case, the state handler is triggered again (lines 10–12) with the empty event just to elicit the superstate.

In the second step (Listing 4.10, lines 15–81), tran() executes all the actions associated with the change of state configuration. Although this step is rather elaborate, the most frequently used source–target configurations are handled efficiently because only a small fraction of the code is executed. As described earlier, the method uses the automatic array entry[] (Figure 4.8) to record the entry path to the target in order to execute entry actions in the correct order. Table 4.1 describes the handling of all possible source–target state configurations.

Figure 4.8   The entry path to the `target` state recorded in `entry[]`; pointer `e` points to the entry last filled; pointer `lca` points to the LCA in the steps shown in Figure 4.7f and g; `lca - 1` points to the first state that needs to be entered in the steps shown in Figure 4.7f and g (see Listing 4.10)

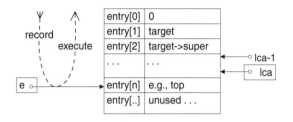

Table 4.1   Processing source–target state configurations from Figure 4.7; line numbers refer to Listing 4.10

Step	Test	Description
a	`source == target`	(Self-transition) Can be checked directly without probing any superstates. Involves exit from source and entry to target (lines 18–22).
b	`source == target->super`	Requires probing the superstate of the `target` state. Involves only entry to source but no exit from target (lines 23–27).
c	`source->super == target->super`	(Most common transition topology) Requires additional probing of the superstate of the source state. Involves exit from source and entry to target (lines 28–33).
d	`source->super == target`	Does not require additional probing. Involves only exit from source but not entry to target (lines 34–39).
e	`source == any of target->super ...`	Requires probing the superstates of the target until a match is found or until the `top` state is reached. The `target` state hierarchy is stored in the automatic array `entry[]` (Figure 4.8) and subsequently is reused to retrace the entry in the reverse order (down the state hierarchy). This transition topology is the last that does not require exiting the original source state, so if the given transition does not fall into this category, the source must be exited (lines 40–50).

f	source->super == any of target->super ...	Requires traversal of the target state hierarchy stored in the array `entry[]` to find the LCA (lines 51–57). As shown in Figure 4.8, the subsequent entry proceeds from `lca-1` (line 54).
g	any of source->super ... == any of target ...	Requires traversal of the target state hierarchy stored in the array `entry[]` for every superstate of the source. Because every scan for a given superstate of the source exhausts all possible matches for the LCA, the source's superstate can be safely exited (lines 58–67). As shown in Figure 4.8, the subsequent entry proceeds from `lca-1` (line 62).

Once `tran()` detects the state configuration and executes all necessary exit actions up to the LCA, it must enter the `target` state configuration. Thanks to the entry path saved in step e, this is straightforward (Listing 4.11, lines 71–73). The assertion in line 70 checks that the automatic array `entry[]` does not overflow, which can happen if the transition chain has more than seven[18] steps.

The target state can be composite and can have an initial transition. Therefore, in lines 74 through 80, `tran()` iterates until it detects a leaf state (the initial transition returns non-0). Here again, as in the `init()` method, an assertion checks that the initial transition goes exactly one level deep in the state hierarchy (line 77).

4.4.5 Static State Transition: The `tranStat()` Method and the `Tran` Class

The static state transition represents an optimization of the dynamic transition in which the complete transition chain is stored in a static instance of class `Tran`. Once initialized, the `Tran` object allows rapid execution of the transition sequence without rediscovering the transition topology.

Listing 4.1, lines 15 through 18 (page 85), shows the declaration of the `Tran` class, which is designed for storage efficiency. This class can store a transition chain of up to eight[19] states. The `myChain[]` attribute stores the states visited at each step, whereas the `myActions` attribute stores the default signals to be dispatched at each step. Because there are only three default signals, it is sufficient to designate only two bits per step to represent the signal. The bit combinations are as follows: (0x1 for `Q_INIT_SIG`, 0x2 for `Q_ENTRY_SIG`, and 0x3 for `Q_EXIT_SIG`).

---

18. Of course, you can change this number to anything you like by redeclaring `entry[]` in line 3 of Listing 4.10.
19. This number is arbitrary, and you can change it for your particular application.

Now you can understand that specifying a transition requires using the preprocessor macro `Q_TRAN()`, rather than directly invoking `tranStat()`, because every transition requires a separate static storage for the associated transition object. As shown in Listing 4.1, line 26, `Q_TRAN()` defines such a static `Tran` object for every transition. To localize the scope of this object to a given transition, the macro wraps it in a dummy (optimized away) `if (1) {...} else` statement, so that you can safely use it as a single instruction terminated with a semicolon (even inside compound `if` statements, without causing the dangling `else` problem).

Listing 4.11   Definition of the static state transition `QHsm::tranStat()`

```
 1 void QHsm::tranStat(Tran *tran, QState target) {
 2     REQUIRE(target != Q_STATE_CAST(top));        // cannot target "top" state
 3     register QState s;
 4     for (s = myState; s != mySource; ) {
 5         ASSERT(s);                               // we are about to dereference s
 6         QState t = TRIGGER(s, Q_EXIT_SIG);
 7         if (t) {                // exit action unhandled, t points to superstate
 8             s = t;
 9         }
10         else {                          // exit action handled, elicit superstate
11             s = TRIGGER(s, Q_ EMPTY _SIG);
12         }
13     }
14     if (tran->myChain[0] == 0) {             // is the tran object initialized?
15         tranSetup(tran, target);                  // setup the transition object
16     }
17     else {        // transition object initialized, execute transition chain
18         register QState *c = &tran->myChain[0];
19         register unsigned short a;
20         for (a = tran->myActions; a; a >>= 2, ++c) {
21             (this->*(*c))(&pkgStdEvt[a & 3]);
22         }
23         myState = *c;
24     }
25 }
```

Listing 4.11 shows `QHsm::tranStat()`, which takes the preallocated static transition object `tran` as an argument. The first step of `tranStat()` (lines 4–13) is identical to the first step in `tran()`. The purpose of this step is to exit the currently active state configuration up to the level of the transition source (which can be different from the active state for inherited state transitions).

In the second step (Listing 4.11 lines 14–24), `tranStat()` executes all the actions associated with the change of state configuration. If the transition object is not initialized (lines 14–16), `tranStat()` initializes it with `tranSetup()` (see next section).

Otherwise (lines 18–24), the transition boils down to traversing the prerecorded state chain myChain and at each step triggering the appropriate signal (encoded in two bits of the myActions bit mask) to the appropriate state handler.

Exercise 4.12 The event processor comprises the methods init(), dispatch(), tran(), and tranStat() and controls all aspects of state machine execution. It is relatively easy to instrument the event processor code by introducing "hooks" (callback methods) that are invoked under specific circumstances. For example, try instrumenting an active-state hook that is invoked whenever the active state changes. Most of the commercial code-synthesizing tools use such hooks, among others, to animate state diagrams during state transitions.

4.4.6 Initializing the **QTran** Object: The **tranSetup()** Method

The static Tran object passed as a parameter to tranStat() (Listing 4.1, line 26) must be initialized the first time a given transition is taken. This initialization is performed in tranSetup().

Method tranSetup() (Listing 4.12) essentially is identical to the second part of the tran() method, except in addition to executing the transition, it also must record the transition in the tran object passed as an argument.

The goal of tranSetup() is to record only the actions actually performed to minimize the length of the transition chain. For example, if a given state handler does not handle entry or exit actions, these actions are not recorded in the tran object (they are optimized away from subsequent executions of this transition).

Listing 4.12 **QHsm::tranSetup() method**

```
1 void QHsm::tranSetup(Tran *tran, QState target) {
2     QState entry[8], p, q, s, *c, *e, *lca;
3     unsigned short a = 0;
4
5     #define RECORD(state_, sig_) \
6         if (TRIGGER(state_, sig_) == 0) {\
7             a |= ((sig_) << 14);   \
8             a >>= 2;               \
9             *c++ = (state_);       \
10        } else ((void)0)
11
12     c = &tran->myChain[0];
```

```
13   *(e = &entry[0]) = 0;
14   *(++e) = target;                                 // assume entry to target
15
16   // (a) check mySource == target (transition to self)
17   if (mySource == target) {
18      RECORD(mySource, Q_EXIT_SIG);                      // exit source
19      goto inLCA;
20   }
21   // (b) check mySource == target->super
22   p = TRIGGER(target, Q_EMPTY_SIG);
23   if (mySource == p) {
24      goto inLCA;
25   }
26   // (c) check mySource->super == target->super (most common)
27   q = TRIGGER(mySource, Q_EMPTY_SIG);
28   if (q == p) {
29      RECORD(mySource, Q_EXIT_SIG);                      // exit source
30      goto inLCA;
31   }
32   // (d) check mySource->super == target
33   if (q == target) {
34      RECORD(mySource, Q_EXIT_SIG);                      // exit source
35      --e;                                      // do not enter the LCA
36      goto inLCA;
37   }
38   // (e) check rest of mySource == target->super->super... hierarchy
39   *(++e) = p;
40   for (s = TRIGGER(p, Q_EMPTY_SIG); s;
41        s = TRIGGER(s, Q_EMPTY_SIG))
42   {
43      if (mySource == s) {
44         goto inLCA;
45      }
46      *(++e) = s;
47   }
48   RECORD(mySource, Q_EXIT_SIG);                      // exit source
49   // (f) check rest of mySource->super == target->super->super...
50   for (lca = e; *lca; --lca) {
51      if (q == *lca) {
52         e = lca - 1;                             // do not enter the LCA
53         goto inLCA;
54      }
55   }
56   // (g) check each mySource->super->super..for each target...
57   for (s = q; s; s = TRIGGER(s, Q_EMPTY_SIG)) {
58      for (lca = e; *lca; --lca) {
59         if (s == *lca) {
```

```
60              e = lca - 1;                        // do not enter the LCA
61              goto inLCA;
62          }
63      }
64      RECORD(s, Q_EXIT_SIG);                            // exit s
65  }
66  ASSERT(0);                                     // malformed HSM
67 inLCA:                    // now we are in the LCA of mySource and target
68  ASSERT(e < &entry[DIM(entry)]);              // new entry e must fit in
69  while (s = *e--) {            // retrace the entry path in reverse order
70      RECORD(s, Q_ENTRY_SIG);                          // enter s
71  }
72  myState = target;                        // update current state
73  while (TRIGGER(target, Q_INIT_SIG) == 0) {
74                      // initial transition must go *one* level deep
75      ASSERT(target == TRIGGER(myState, Q_EMPTY_SIG));
76      a |= (Q_INIT_SIG << 14);
77      a >>= 2;
78      *c++ = target;
79      target = myState;
80      RECORD(target, Q_ENTRY_SIG);                     // enter target
81  }
82  #undef RECORD
83  *c = target;
84  tran->myActions = a >> (14 - (c - &tran->myChain[0])*2);
85  ENSURE(tran->myChain[0] != 0 &&              // transition initialized
86          c < &tran->myChain[DIM(tran->myChain)]);    // check overflow
87 }
```

4.5   C Implementation

The C++ implementation of the behavioral inheritance meta-pattern is funda-mentally object oriented in that it takes advantage of data abstraction (packag-ing data with functions into classes) and inheritance (the capability to define new classes based on existing classes).

You can code such a design in a procedural language such as C, because, as mentioned in the introduction to this chapter, abstraction and inheritance are only relatively low-level meta-patterns, just as behavioral inheritance is. There-fore, they can be used in virtually any programming language, not necessarily an object-oriented one. Appendix A describes techniques for implementing these con-cepts in C as a set of idioms and preprocessor macros that I call "C+."

In fact, "C+" implements the C++ object model so faithfully, that converting the implementation of any C++ design into "C+" involves mostly a mechanical application of simple translation rules. Moreover, the exercises used in Appendix A to illustrate "C+" concepts already prepare most of the elements for the "C+" HSM implementation. Therefore, in this section I just fill in a few missing pieces and high-light only the most interesting parts of the code. The complete "C+" behavioral inheritance implementation is available on the accompanying CD-ROM.

Note: Although I call it by the strange name "C+," rest assured that the implementation is fully portable, ANSI C–compliant code, although it looks very much like C++.

Please note that the C++ version of the QHsm class intentionally avoids poly-morphism because it isn't necessary for the most common uses of HSMs. There-fore, although the "C+" QHsm class supports it,[20] you can ignore polymorphism when you derive your own state machines from it.

Before proceeding any further, you should skim through Appendix A (you can skip the description of polymorphism at first), so that you will understand the "C+" macros, naming conventions, and the idiomatic use of C in this section.

4.5.1   QHsm Class in "C+"

Listing 4.13 shows the "C+" declaration of the QHsm class. Contrast it with the C++ declaration (Listing 4.1). The "C+" QHsm class derives from Object (Listing 4.13, line 5), which means that it inherits the virtual pointer VPTR. The two attributes (state__ and source__) declared in lines 6 and 7 are both private (note the double trailing underscore naming convention). The QHsm class declares the (empty) VTABLE in line 8, which makes it ready for polymorphism. The rest of the elements in the "C+" declaration correspond directly to the C++ implementation.

Listing 4.13   **"C+" declaration of the QHsm class**

```
 1 typedef void (*QPseudoState)(struct QHsm *, QEvent const *);
 2 typedef QPseudoState (*QState)(struct QHsm *, QEvent const *);
 3 typedef QPseudoState QSTATE;          /* return value from a state-handler */
 4
 5 SUBCLASS(QHsm, Object)              /* Hierarchical State Machine base class */
 6    QState state__;                                      /* the active state */
 7    QState source__;                       /* source state during a transition */
 8 VTABLE(QHsm, Object)
 9 METHODS
10 /* public members */
11    void QHsmInit(QHsm *me, QEvent const *e);          /* initial transition */
```

---

20. I will use polymorphism in Chapter 6.

```
12     void QHsmDispatch(QHsm *me, QEvent const *e);        /* take RTC step */
13     int QHsmIsIn(QHsm const *me, QState state);          /* "is-in" query */
14                                             /* static method (no "me" pointer) */
15     char const *QHsmGetVersion(void);
16
17 /* protected members */
18     CLASS(Tran_)                            /* protected inner class Tran_ */
19         QState chain[8];
20         unsigned short actions;             /* action mask (2-bits for action) */
21     METHODS
22     END_CLASS
23
24     QHsm *QHsmCtor_(QHsm *me, QPseudoState initial);           /* Ctor */
25     void QHsmXtor_(QHsm *me);                                  /* Xtor */
26
27     QSTATE QHsm_top(QHsm *me, QEvent const *);           /* "top" state */
28     #define QHsmGetState_(me_) ((me_)->state__)
29     void QHsmTran_(QHsm *me, QState target);         /* dynamic transition */
30     void QHsmTranStat_(QHsm *me, Tran_ *t, QState target);
31     #define Q_INIT(target_) (((QHsm*)me)->state__ = (QState)(target_))
32     #define Q_TRAN(target_) if (1) { \
33         static Tran_ t_;                    \
34         QHsmTranStat_((QHsm *)me, &t_, (QState)(target_));\
35     } else
36     #define Q_TRAN_DYN(target_) \
37         QHsmTran_((QHsm *)me, (QState)(target_))
38 /* private methods */
39     void QHsmTranSetup__(QHsm *me, Tran_ *t, QState target);
40 END_CLASS
```

4.5.2 QHsm Constructor and Destructor

In "C+" constructors and destructors, you need to write code explicitly that a C++ compiler synthesizes behind the scenes. The constructor must explicitly define and initialize the class's VTABLE, construct the part of the object controlled by the superclass, and hook the virtual pointer. The destructor must explicitly destroy the part of the object controlled by the parent. The following code fragment illustrates these elements for the QHsm class.

```
BEGIN_VTABLE(QHsm, Object)              // explicit virtual table for QHsm class
    VMETHOD(Object, xtor) = (void (*)(Object *))QHsmXtor;
END_VTABLE

QHsm *QHsmCtor_(QHsm *me, QPseudoState initial) {              // protected Ctor
    ObjectCtor_(&me->super);                          // construct superclass
    VHOOK(QHsm);                                // hook the VPTR for this class
    me->state__ = QHsm_top;                          // initialize attributes...
```

```
    me->source__ = (QState)initial;
    return me;                                          // return success
}

void QHsmXtor_(QHsm *me) {                               // protected Xtor
    ObjectXtor_(&me->super);                        // destroy superclass
}
```

4.5.3   State Handler Methods and Pointer-to-Member Functions

As described in Appendix A, a class in C corresponds to a C struct combined with C functions that operate on this structure. Per "C+" convention, each class function declares an explicit pointer to the associated structure as the first argument, me. Therefore, in C, a pointer-to-member function is just a regular pointer to a function that takes a pointer to the associated data structure as the first argument.

Lines 1 and 2 of Listing 4.13 can serve as examples. For instance, the QPseudoState pointer to the QHsm member function is declared as follows.

```
typedef void                                      /* return type */
    (*QPseudoState)                  /* name of pointer-to-member */
        (struct QHsm *,       /* class the function is a member of */
         QEvent const *);          /* rest of the argument list */
```

Similarly, the QState pointer-to-member function is declared as follows.

```
typedef QPseudoState                              /* return type */
    (*QState)                        /* name of pointer-to-member */
        (struct QHsm *,       /* class the function is a member of */
         QEvent const *);          /* rest of the argument list */
```

As in the C++ case, the declaration of QState cannot be fully recursive (i.e., the state handler cannot return a state handler [Sutter 01]); instead, the return type is approximated by the QPseudoState pointer-to-member function.

4.5.4   QHsm Methods

Translation from C++ to "C+" for methods of a class is straightforward. You drop the scope resolution operator :: and manually mangle the method name instead (something a C++ compiler also does behind the scenes). You also emulate the __this_call calling convention by providing the me pointer explicitly as the first argument. You use this pointer subsequently to access class attributes. The following example of the QHsmDispatch() method illustrates all these elements.

```
void QHsmDispatch(QHsm *me, QEvent const *e) {
    for (me->source__ = me->state__; me->source__;
        me->source__ = (QState)(*me->source__)(me, e))
    {}
}
```

The most interesting part of this method is the invocation of the state handler (emphasized) based on the pointer-to-member function (*me->source__)(me, ...) followed by the cast of the return type (QPseudoState) to QState.

Exercise 4.13 Using QHsmDispatch() as a template, translate the rest of the QHsm class methods from C++ to "C+."

4.5.5   Statechart Example in C

As an example of a concrete state machine, I'll implement the same statechart I implemented in C++ (Figure 4.3) in "C+." The HSM pattern is applied exactly as in C++ by deriving the state model from the QHsm class. In the concrete subclass, you declare all states as state handler methods. Finally, you define the state machine behavior and topology (state nesting) by implementing the body of the state handler methods.

Listing 4.14   Statechart from Figure 4.3 implemented in "C+"

```
 1 #include "qhsm.h"
 2
 3 SUBCLASS(QHsmTst, QHsm)
 4    int foo__;                              /* private extended state variable */
 5 METHODS
 6    QHsmTst *QHsmTstCtor(QHsmTst *me);
 7
 8    void QHsmTst_initial(QHsmTst *me, QEvent const *e);
 9    QSTATE QHsmTst_s0(QHsmTst*me, QEvent const *e);
10       QSTATE QHsmTst_s1(QHsmTst*me, QEvent const *e);
11          QSTATE QHsmTst_s11(QHsmTst*me, QEvent const *e);
12       QSTATE QHsmTst_s2(QHsmTst*me, QEvent const *e);
13          QSTATE QHsmTst_s21(QHsmTst*me, QEvent const *e);
14             QSTATE QHsmTst_s211(QHsmTst*me, QEvent const *e);
15 END_CLASS
16
17 QHsmTst *QHsmTstCtor(QHsmTst *me) {
```

```
18      QHsmCtor_(&me->super_, (QPseudoState)QHsmTst_initial);
19      return me;
20 }
21
22 void QHsmTst_initial(QHsmTst *me) {
23      printf("top-INIT;");
24      me->foo__ = 0;                /* initialize extended state variable */
25      Q_INIT(QHsmTst_s0);
26 }
27
28 QSTATE QHsmTst_s0(QHsmTst *me, QEvent const *e) {
29      switch (e->sig) {
30      case Q_ENTRY_SIG: printf("s0-ENTRY;"); return 0;
31      case Q_EXIT_SIG: printf("s0-EXIT;");  return 0;
32      case Q_INIT_SIG: printf("s0-INIT;"); Q_INIT(QHsmTst_s1); return 0;
33      case E_SIG:      printf("s0-E;"); Q_TRAN(QHsmTst_s211);  return 0;
34      }
35      return (QSTATE)QHsm_top;
36 }
37 . . .                                    /* other state handlers */
38
39 static QHsmTst test;
40
41 int main() {
42      . . .
43      QHsmTstCtor(&test, (QPseudoState)QHsmTst_initial);
44      QHsmInit((QHsm *)&test, 0);
45      for (;;) {
46          . . .                            /* receive event */
47          QHsmDispatch((QHsm *)&test, &e);  /* dispatch event*/
48      }
49      . . .
50 }
```

Listing 4.14 shows the most interesting implementation details. The state model class (QHsmTst) is declared in lines 3 through 15. Please note that QHsmTst does not declare a virtual table; therefore, it will not support polymorphism. Consequently, there is no definition of VTABLE, and the constructor (lines 17–20) does not hook the virtual pointer (inherited from QHsm). The only initialization that the QHsmTstCtor() constructor performs is the invocation of the QHsmCtor() super-class constructor in line 18. In lines 22 through 26 you see the definition of the initial pseudostate, whereas in lines 28 through 36 you see an example of a state handler, which illustrates, among other things, how a state handler returns its super-state (line 35). Finally, in the test harness, don't forget to invoke the constructor (line 43) explicitly before initialization of the state machine (line 44). You dispatch events to the state machine in the usual way by calling QHsmDispatch(). Please note the explicit type casting (upcasting) used when calling methods inherited from the QHsm class on behalf of the QHsmTst object (lines 44 and 47).

Exercise 4.14 Implement in "C+" the rest of the state machine from Figure 4.3. Execute a test session as logged in Listing 4.7.

Exercise 4.15 Implement in "C+" the Quantum Calculator GUI application from Chapter 1.

4.6   Caveats

The HSM implementation has a few pitfalls, which most often will cause contract violations at run time (see the sidebar "Design by Contract in C/C++" on page 107) but occasionally can lead to subtle bugs. In this section, I point out some malformed HSMs that you could construct by instantiating the behavioral inheritance meta-pattern incorrectly.

Perhaps the most far-reaching assumption of this HSM implementation is that state machine topology is static (i.e., it does not change at run time). This assumption corresponds roughly to statically defined class hierarchy in OOP and, in general programming, to the assumption that code does not modify itself. Whereas normally, state machine topology is indeed fully defined at compile time, some coding styles could lead to unintentional modifications of the transition topology at run time. Consider, for instance, the following state handler.

```
QState MyHsm::stateA(QEvent const *e) {
    switch (e->sig) {
    . . .
    case MYSIG1_SIG:
        Q_TRAN((...) ? (QState)stateB : (QState)stateC);        // WRONG!!!
        return 0;
    . . .
    }
    return (QState)top;
}
```

The MyHsm::stateA() state handler violates the assumption of static state transition because the target of the transition changes at run time. Looking into the Q_TRAN() macro definition, you can see that only one static transition object gets instantiated and that it cannot store two different transition chains. In this case, only one transition chain is recorded in the transition object (targeting whichever state happens to be picked by the condition evaluated the first time through). Subsequently, the condition (choice point) will have no effect. The correct way of coding the choice point is to use two (or more) statically defined transitions as follows.

```
QState MyHsm::stateA(QEvent const *e) {
    switch (e->sig) {
    . . .
    case MYSIG1_SIG:
        if (...)
            Q_TRAN(stateB);
        else
            Q_TRAN(stateC);
        return 0;
    . . .
    }
    return (QState)top;
}
```

The assumption of static transition topology makes implementing the history mechanism (available in UML statecharts) difficult. Consider the following attempt.

```
QState MyHsm::stateA(QEvent const *e) {
    switch (e->sig) {
    . . .
    case Q_EXIT_SIG:
        myHistoryA = getState();            // store the deep history of stateA
        return 0;
    case Q_INIT_SIG:
        Q_INIT(myHistoryA);                                        // WRONG!!!
        return 0;
    . . .
    }
    return (QState)top;
}
```

The idea here is to store the active substate (deep history) of stateA upon exit and restore it in the initial transition. However, this solution makes the initial transition nonstatic (it changes at run time). Please note that you cannot introduce a choice point here as before because choice points (or junctions for that matter) are not allowed on initial transitions. Chapter 5 shows the correct way to implement transitions to history as the History state pattern.

Another potential source of problems is confusing macros Q_INIT() and Q_TRAN(). One could rightfully argue that a single macro (Q_TRAN()) should be sufficient to implement all kinds of transitions, including initial transitions. Indeed, such an implementation is possible, but not optimal. For one thing, using Q_TRAN() in initial transitions would lead to recursive invocation of the underlying QHsm::tran-Stat() method (the transition chain includes drilling into the state hierarchy with initial transitions) and would wastefully allocate static transition objects for initial transitions. For that reason, Q_TRAN() is not designed to be used for initial transitions and vice versa: Q_INIT() is inappropriate for general-purpose transitions. An additional limitation of the Q_INIT() macro is that it can target only direct substates of a given state. This restriction is asserted in the code and will be detected at run time.

Finally, the implementation is vulnerable to mistakes in the state hierarchy specification. For example, it is easy to introduce circular state hierarchies, which would invariably crash the event processor. Consider the following malformed state handler.

```
QSTATE MyHsm::stateA(QEvent const *e) {
    switch (e->sig) {
    . . .
    }
    return (QSTATE)&MyHsm::stateA;                 // Oops! Circular dependency!
}
```

4.7   Summary

So here it is: the optimized behavioral inheritance meta-pattern. Admittedly, it is only a drastically simplified subset of UML state machines, but through its full support for the profound concept of behavioral inheritance (state hierarchy), it forms the foundation for adding other features.

The following bullet items quickly recapitulate how this implementation measures up against the initial goals.

- It is simple to use and maintain. Defining HSMs requires subclassing the QHsm class. Defining states corresponds to adding state handler methods to the derived class, which you can do at any time, even late in the development process. State handler methods are an inexpensive commodity, and there are no limits (except for code space) on how many you can use.

- It allows changing state machine topology easily. In particular, no transition chains must be coded manually. For instance, to change the target of a transition, you modify the argument of the Q_TRAN() macro. Similarly, to change the superstate of a given state, you modify the final return statement in the corresponding state handler. All these changes are confined to one line of code.

- It provides good run-time efficiency and has a small memory footprint. Dispatching events to a state machine involves dereferencing a function pointer and is comparable to the virtual function invocation in C++.[21] The QHsm class adds only two pointers to the subclasses. Complete event processor code requires about 2KB of code space.

- It does not force you to pay for what you don't use. For example, transitions to history and event deferral typically impose memory and run-time overhead, even if not used; therefore, they are not implemented at the fundamental level of the behavioral inheritance meta-pattern. However, you can easily add these features for specific states as state patterns (Chapter 5) and only pay for what you actually use.

Please note that this HSM implementation provides only the event processor component of a state machine, which processes dispatched event instances according to the general semantics of UML state machines. The implementation intentionally omits event queuing and event dispatching mechanisms, which are also necessary components of a hypothetical state machine [OMG 01]. The goal of this implementation is to provide a generic event processor that can be used with any event queuing and dispatching mechanism. This approach allows the behavioral inheritance pattern to fit easily into existing event-driven environments that already support event queuing and dispatching, most notably GUI frameworks (recall the Quantum Calculator GUI application). In Part II of this book, I show you concrete ways in which to implement event queuing and dispatching that is suitable for real-time embedded applications.

---

21. Assuming that the event is handled in the lowest level of nesting, inheriting behavior from superstates requires invocation of *their* sate-handler methods, which incurs some additional overhead.

5

Chapter 5

State Patterns

Science is a collection of successful recipes.
— Paul Valery (1871–1945)

In the previous chapter, you learned how to implement hierarchical state machines (HSMs) in C++ and in C by instantiating the behavioral inheritance meta-pattern. In fact, applying the pattern turned out to be a rather simple one-to-one mapping between a state model and the code. With just a bit of practice, you will forget that you are translating state models into code; rather, you will directly code state machines in C or C++, just as you directly code classes in C++ or Java.

At this point, you will no longer struggle with convoluted if–then–else statements and gazillions of flags. You will start thinking at a higher level of abstraction about the best ways to partition behavior into states, about the events available at any given time, and about the structure of your state machine.

However, coming up with a good structure for nontrivial state machines isn't easy. Experienced reactive-system designers know that a reusable and flexible state machine design is difficult to get right the first time. Yet, experienced designers repeatedly realize good state machines, whereas new designers are overwhelmed by the options available and tend to fall back on convoluted if–then–else statements and the multitude of flags they have used before.

One thing that distinguishes an expert from a novice is the ability to recognize the similarities among problems encountered in the past and to reuse proven solutions that work. To share their expertise, OO designers began to catalog proven solutions to recurring problems as OO *design patterns* [Gamma+ 95]. Similarly, state patterns began to appear [Douglass 99]. In contrast to the OO patterns, which are concerned with optimal ways of structuring classes and objects, the state patterns focus on effective ways of structuring states, events, and transitions.

A state pattern has five essential elements, just as an OO pattern does.

1. The pattern name — a word or two denoting the problem, the solution, and the consequences of a pattern. A good name is vital because it will become part of your vocabulary.

2. The problem — an explanation of the problem the pattern addresses. A problem is often motivated by an example.

3. The solution — a description of the elements (states, transitions, events, actions, and extended state variables) that compose the solution and their relationships, responsibilities, and collaborations.

4. The sample code — a presentation of a concrete implementation of an instance of the pattern. Usually the sample code implements the motivating example.

5. The consequences — the results and trade-offs of applying the pattern.

In this chapter, I provide a minicatalog of five basic state patterns (Table 5.1). The first two are relatively simple state machine solutions to common problems. The other three are just more advanced or expensive features that are found in UML statecharts but are not supported directly in the behavioral inheritance meta-pattern. The leading theme of all these patterns is reusing behavior through behavioral inheritance, in contrast to the state patterns described in the book *Doing Hard Time*, by Bruce Powel Douglass [Douglass 99] that all revolve around orthogonal regions. The other distinguishing aspect of the state patterns presented here is that all are illustrated by concrete, executable code. A state diagram alone is not enough to understand a state pattern because the devil is always in the detail. To be practical, a pattern must be accompanied by a concrete working example that will help you truly comprehend and evaluate the pattern and give you a good starting point for your own instantiation of the pattern.

Many examples in this chapter are implemented as Windows GUI applications because the behavioral inheritance meta-pattern provides only the event processor and lacks the other essential components of a typical event-driven system, such as event queuing. As a reactive system, Windows provides those missing elements. However, the patterns are not at all Windows- or GUI-specific. In particular, they all can be used in conjunction with any other infrastructure to execute a state machine (e.g., the Quantum Framework discussed in Part II of this book).

Table 5.1   **State patterns covered in this chapter**

Pattern Name	Intent
Ultimate Hook (Section 5.1)	Provide a common look and feel, but let clients specialize every aspect of a system's behavior.
Reminder (Section 5.2)	Invent an event and post it to self.
Deferred Event (Section 5.3)	Control the sequence of events.
Orthogonal Component (Section 5.4)	Use state machines as components.
Transition to History (Section 5.5)	Transition to the most recent state configuration of a given composite state.

None of the state patterns described in this chapter captures new or unproven state machine designs. In fact, by definition, a state pattern is a proven solution to a recurring problem that is actually used in successful, real-life reactive systems. However, most of the basic state patterns have never been documented before (at least not with such a level of detail and illustrated with executable code). They are either part of the folklore of various programming communities (e.g., the GUI community or the embedded systems community) or are elements of some successful reactive systems, neither of which is easy for novice designers to learn from. So although these state designs are not new, they are offered here in a new and more accessible way.

5.1   Ultimate Hook

5.1.1   Intent

Provide common facilities and policies for handling events but let clients override and specialize every aspect of a system's behavior.

5.1.2   Problem

Many reactive systems require consistent policies for handling events. In a GUI design, this consistency is part of the characteristic look and feel of the user interface. The challenge is to provide such a common look and feel in system-level software that client applications can use easily as the default. At the same time, the clients must be able to override every aspect of the default behavior easily if they so choose.

5.1.3   Solution

The solution is to apply programming-by-difference or, specifically in this case, the concept of behavioral inheritance. A composite state can define the default behavior (the common look and feel) and supply an "outer shell" for nesting client substates. The semantics of state nesting provides the desired mechanism of handling all events, first in the context of the client code (the nested state) and of automatically forwarding all unhandled events to the superstate (the default behavior). In that way, the client code intercepts every stimulus and can override every aspect of the behavior. To reuse the default behavior, the client simply ignores the event and lets the superstate handle it (the substate inherits behavior from the superstate).

Figure 5.1   **The Ultimate Hook state pattern**

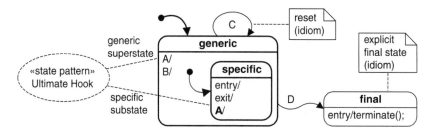

Figure 5.1 shows the Ultimate Hook state pattern using a basic graphical notation adapted from Douglass [Douglass 99]. The dashed oval labeled «state pattern» indicates collaboration among states. Dashed arrows emanating from the oval indicate state roles within the pattern. States playing these roles are shown with heavy borders. For example, the concrete generic state plays the role of the generic superstate of the pattern, whereas the specific state plays the role of the specific substate.

A diagram like this attempts to convey an abstract pattern but can only show a concrete example (instance) of the pattern. In this instance, the concrete generic state in Figure 5.1 handles events A and B as internal transitions, event C as a self-transition, and event D as the termination of the state machine. The concrete specific state overrides event A and provides its own initialization and cleanup (in entry and exit actions, respectively). Of course, another instance of the pattern can implement completely different events and actions.

A few idioms worth noting are illustrated in this statechart. First is the overall canonical structure of the state machine that, at the highest level, consists of only one composite state (playing the role of the generic superstate). Virtually every application can benefit from having such a highest level state because it is an ideal place for defining common policies subsequently inherited by the whole (arbitrary complex) submachine.

Note: As described in Section 2.2.1 in Chapter 2, every UML state machine is a submachine of an implicit top state and so has the canonical structure proposed here. However, because you cannot override the top state, you need another highest level state that you *can* customize.

Within such a canonical structure, a useful idiom for resetting the state machine is an empty (actionless) self-transition in the generic superstate (transition C in Figure 5.1). Such a transition causes a recursive exit from all nested states (including the generic superstate), followed by reinitialization starting from the initial transition of the highest level state. This way of resetting a state machine is perhaps the safest because it guarantees proper clean-up through the execution of exit actions. Similarly, the safest way to terminate a state machine is through an explicit transition out of the generic superstate to a final state (transition D in Figure 5.1) because all pertinent exit actions are executed. The behavioral inheritance meta-pattern does not provide a generic final state. Instead, the statechart in Figure 5.1 proposes an idiom, which consists of an explicit final state with an application-specific termination coded in its entry action.[1]

5.1.4   Sample Code

Listing 5.1 illustrates an implementation of the statechart from Figure 5.1. Lines 1 through 3 declare the signals A through D. The UltimateHook state machine is derived from QHsm in lines 5 through 13. It has three state handlers: generic(), specific(), and final(). The rest of the listing defines the state handler methods. Note, for example, the implementation of the reset self-transition in line 32, the termination transition in line 35, and the signal A override in the Ultimate-Hook::specific() state handler in line 45.

Listing 5.1   Ultimate Hook sample code; the unusual indentation of state handler methods (lines 10–12) indicates state nesting

```
1 enum UltimateHookSignals {                              // declaration of signals
2     A_SIG = Q_USER_SIG, B_SIG, C_SIG, D_SIG, MAX_SIG
3 };
4
5 class UltimateHook : public QHsm {             // "Ultimate Hook" statechart
6 public:
7     UltimateHook() : QHsm((QPseudoState)initial) {}                    // ctor
8 private:
```

---

1.   The Quantum Calculator statechart from Chapter 1 is an example of the canonical state machine structure that uses idioms to reset and terminate.

```
 9      void initial(QEvent const *e);            // initial pseudostate-handler
10      QSTATE generic(QEvent const *e);                      // state-handler
11        QSTATE specific(QEvent const *e);                   // state-handler
12      QSTATE final(QEvent const *e);                        // state-handler
13  };
14
15  void UltimateHook::initial(QEvent const *) {
16      Q_INIT(&UltimateHook::generic);
17  }
18  QSTATE UltimateHook::final(QEvent const *e) {
19      switch (e->sig) {
10      case Q_ENTRY_SIG: exit(0); return 0;        // terminate the application
21      }
22      return (QSTATE)&UltimateHook::top;
23  }
24
25  QSTATE UltimateHook::generic(QEvent const *e) {
26      switch (e->sig) {
27      case Q_INIT_SIG:  Q_INIT(specific); return 0;
28      case A_SIG: printf("generic:A;");   return 0;
29      case B_SIG: printf("generic:B;");   return 0;
30      case C_SIG:
31         printf("generic:C;");
32         Q_TRAN(&UltimateHook::generic);                  // self transition
33         return 0;
34      case D_SIG:
35         Q_TRAN(&UltimateHook::final);     // explicit transition to "final"
36         return 0;
37      }
38      return (QSTATE)&UltimateHook::top;
39  }
40
41  QSTATE UltimateHook::specific(QEvent const *e) {
42      switch (e->sig) {
43      case Q_ENTRY_SIG: printf("specific:entry;"); return 0;
44      case Q_EXIT_SIG: printf("specific:exit;");  return 0;
45      case A_SIG:        printf("specific:A;");     return 0;
46      }
47      return (QSTATE)&UltimateHook::generic;
48  }
```

One option of deploying the Ultimate Hook pattern is to organize the code into a library that intentionally does not contain the implementation of the UlimtateHook::specific() state handler. Clients would then have to provide their own implementation and link to the library to obtain the generic behavior. An example of a design using this technique is Microsoft Windows, which requires the client code to define WinMain() for the Windows application to link.

Another option is to declare the `UlimtateHook::specific()` state handler as an abstract method (a pure virtual function in C++) and force clients to provide implementation for this state handler by subclassing the `UltimateHook` class. This approach combines behavioral inheritance with traditional class inheritance. More precisely, Ultimate Hook represents, in this case, a special instance of the Template Method OO design pattern (refer to Section 6.3.3 in Chapter 6).

Exercise 5.1   Reimplement in C the Ultimate Hook state pattern from Listing 5.1. Hint: Appendix A describes the techniques for realizing classes and inheritance in C, and Section 4.5 of Chapter 4 provides specific guidelines for instantiating the behavioral inheritance meta-pattern in C.

5.1.5   Consequences

The Ultimate Hook state pattern is presented here in its most limited version — exactly as it is used in GUI systems (e.g., Microsoft Windows). In particular, neither the generic superstate nor the specific substate exhibits any interesting state machine topology. The only significant feature is behavioral inheritance (state nesting), which can be applied recursively within the specific substate. For example, at any level, a GUI window can have nested child windows, which handle events before the parent.

Even in this most limited version, however, the Ultimate Hook state pattern is a fundamental technique for reusing behavior. In fact, every state model using the canonical structure implicitly applies this pattern.

The Ultimate Hook state pattern has the following consequences.

- The specific substate needs to know only those events it overrides.
- New events can be added easily to the top-level generic superstate without affecting the specific substate.
- Removing or changing the semantics of events that clients already use is difficult.
- Propagating every event through many levels of nesting (if the specific substate has recursively nested substates) can be expensive.

The Ultimate Hook state pattern is closely related to the Template Method OO design pattern and can be generalized by applying unrestricted inheritance of state machines (see Chapter 6).

5.2 Reminder

5.2.1 Intent

Make the statechart topology more flexible by inventing an event and posting it to self.

5.2.2 Problem

Often in state modeling, loosely related functions of a system are strongly coupled by a common event. Consider, for example, periodic data acquisition, in which a sensor producing the data needs to be polled at a predetermined rate. Assume that a periodic TIMEOUT event is dispatched to the system at the desired rate to provide the stimulus for polling the sensor. Because the system has only one external event (the TIMEOUT event), it seems that this event needs to trigger both the polling of the sensor and the processing of the data. A straightforward but suboptimal solution is to organize the state machine into two distinct orthogonal regions (for polling and processing).[2] However, orthogonal regions increase the cost of dispatching events (see the section "Orthogonal Component" on page 149) and require complex synchronization between the regions (polling and processing are not quite orthogonal).

5.2.3 Solution

A simpler and more efficient solution is to invent a stimulus (DATA_READY) and to propagate it to self as a reminder that the data is ready for processing (Figure 5.2). This new stimulus provides a way to decouple polling from processing without using orthogonal regions. Moreover, you can use state nesting to arrange these two functions in a hierarchical relation to take advantage of behavioral inheritance.[3]

In the most basic arrangement, the processing state can be a substate of polling and can simply inherit the polling behavior so that polling occurs in the background to processing. However, the processing state might also choose to override polling. For instance, to prevent flooding the CPU with sensor data, processing might inhibit polling occasionally. The statechart in Figure 5.2 illustrates this option. The busy substate of processing overrides the TIMEOUT event and thus prevents this event from being handled in the higher level polling superstate.

Further flexibility of this solution entails fine control over the generation of the invented DATA_READY event, which does not have to be posted at every occurrence of the original TIMEOUT event. For example, to improve performance, the

---

2. This example illustrates an alternative design for the Polling state pattern described in Douglass [Douglass 99].
3. Using state hierarchy in this fashion is typically more efficient than using orthogonal regions.

polling state could buffer the raw sensor data and generate the DATA_READY event only when the buffer fills up, Figure 5.2 illustrates this option with the if (...) condition, which precedes the post(DATA_READY) action in the polling state.

Figure 5.2   The Reminder state pattern

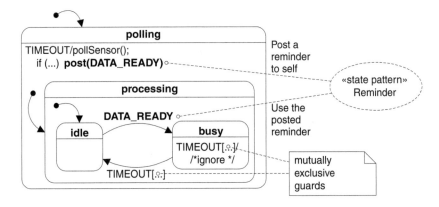

5.2.4 Sample Code

The statechart in Figure 5.2 posts a reminder to self using post(). This operation involves queuing an event and is not supported by the raw event processor of the behavioral inheritance meta-pattern. However, such an operation is available in virtually every event-driven environment.[4] For instance, Windows GUI applications can call the PostMessage() Win32 API to queue a message to self.

Listing 5.2 shows an implementation of the statechart from Figure 5.2 as a Windows GUI application. The initial transition (Listing 5.2, lines 23–29) enters the polling state, which in turn enters the idle substate. Because neither the idle state nor the processing state handle the WM_TIMER signal, the signal is handled initially in the polling superstate (lines 38–55). However, every fourth clock tick, the polling state generates the DATA_READY signal and posts it to self (line 46). This signal causes a transition from idle to busy (line 67). In contrast to the idle state, the busy state overrides the WM_TIMER signal. After two clock ticks (line 78), busy transitions back to idle (line 79), and the cycle repeats.

---

4.   In Part II of this book, I describe a Quantum Framework that supports self-posting of events.

Listing 5.2   Reminder sample code

```
1 enum SensorSignals {
2    DATA_READY = Q_USER_SIG, TERMINATE
3 };
4 class Sensor : public QHsm {
5 public:
6    Sensor() : QHsm((QPseudoState)initial) {}
7 private:
8    void initial(QEvent const *e);
9    QSTATE polling(QEvent const *e);
10       QSTATE processing(QEvent const *e);
11          QSTATE idle(QEvent const *e);
12          QSTATE busy(QEvent const *e);
13    QSTATE final(QEvent const *e);
14 private:
15    int myPollCtr;
16    int myProcCtr;
17    BOOL isHandled;        // flag indicating if the last event was handled
18    HWND myHwnd;                                // the main window handle
19    friend BOOL CALLBACK reminderDlg(HWND hwnd, UINT iEvt,
20                                 WPARAM wParam, LPARAM lParam);
21 };
22
23 void Sensor::initial(QEvent const *) {
24    SendMessage(myHwnd, WM_SETICON, (WPARAM)TRUE,
25                (LPARAM)LoadIcon(inst, MAKEINTRESOURCE(IDI_QP)));
26    myPollCtr = 0;
27    myProcCtr = 0;
28    Q_INIT(&Sensor::polling);
29 }
30 QSTATE Sensor::final(QEvent const *e) {
31    switch (e->sig) {
32    case Q_ENTRY_SIG:
33       EndDialog(myHwnd, 0);
34       return 0;
35    }
36    return (QSTATE)&Sensor::top;
37 }
38 QSTATE Sensor::polling(QEvent const *e) {
39    switch (e->sig) {
40    case Q_ENTRY_SIG: SetTimer(myHwnd, 1, 500, 0);  return 0;
41    case Q_EXIT_SIG:  KillTimer(myHwnd, 1);         return 0;
42    case Q_INIT_SIG:  Q_INIT(&Sensor::processing);  return 0;
43    case WM_TIMER:
44       SetDlgItemInt(myHwnd, IDC_POLL, ++myPollCtr, FALSE);
45       if ((myPollCtr & 0x3) == 0){
46          PostMessage(myHwnd, WM_COMMAND, DATA_READY, 0);
```

```
47        }
48        return 0;
49     case TERMINATE: Q_TRAN(&Sensor::final);  return 0;
50     }
51     if (e->sig >= Q_USER_SIG) {
52         isHandled = FALSE;
53     }
54     return (QSTATE)&Sensor::top;
55 }
56 QSTATE Sensor::processing(QEvent const *e) {
57     switch (e->sig) {
58     case Q_INIT_SIG: Q_INIT(&Sensor::idle);  return 0;
59     }
60     return (QSTATE)&Sensor::polling;
61 }
62 QSTATE Sensor::idle(QEvent const *e) {
63     switch (e->sig) {
64     case Q_ENTRY_SIG:
65         SetDlgItemText(myHwnd, IDC_STATE, "idle");
66         return 0;
67     case DATA_READY: Q_TRAN(&Sensor::busy);  return 0;
68     }
69     return (QSTATE)&Sensor::processing;
70 }
71 QSTATE Sensor::busy(QEvent const *e) {
72     switch (e->sig) {
73     case Q_ENTRY_SIG:
74         SetDlgItemText(myHwnd, IDC_STATE, "busy");
75         return 0;
76     case WM_TIMER:
77         SetDlgItemInt(myHwnd, IDC_PROC, ++myProcCtr, FALSE);
78         if ((myProcCtr & 0x1) == 0) {
79             Q_TRAN(&Sensor::idle);
80         }
81         return 0;
82     }
83     return (QSTATE)&Sensor::processing;
84 }
```

The simple GUI for this application (Figure 5.3) displays the currently active state (busy or idle), as well as the number of times WM_TIMER has been handled in polling and processing, respectively.

Figure 5.3   Reminder sample application GUI

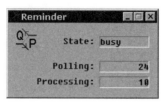

Exercise 5.2   Find the Reminder state pattern implementation on the accompanying CD-ROM and execute it. Next, change the `polling` state to generate `DATA_READY` every eighth, instead of every fourth, clock tick. Recompile and execute again.

Exercise 5.3   Reimplement in C the Reminder state pattern from Listing 5.2. Hint: Appendix A describes the techniques for realizing classes and inheritance in C, and Section 4.5 of Chapter 4 provides specific guidelines for instantiating the behavioral inheritance meta-pattern in C.

5.2.5   Consequences

Although conceptually very simple, the Reminder state pattern has profound consequences. It can address many more problems than illustrated in the example. You could use it as a Swiss Army knife to fix almost any problem in the state machine topology.

For example, consider the artificial limitation of the behavioral inheritance implementation (Section 4.2.1 in Chapter 4), which restricts the initial transition from targeting substates nested deeper than one level[5] (as in Figure 5.4a). The equivalent cascaded initial transitions (as in Figure 5.4b) are sometimes inconvenient because a composite state with the initial transition can never become active without one of its substates being active (see Section 4.4.4 in Chapter 4). Reminder enables you to change the topology of the state machine and replace the initial transition with a regular one triggered by an invented signal, INIT, posted in the higher level initial transition (as in Figure 5.4c).

You also can apply the Reminder idiom to eliminate troublesome *completion transitions*, which in the UML specification are transitions without an explicit trigger (they are triggered implicitly by completion events, aka anonymous events). The behavioral inheritance meta-pattern requires that all transitions have explicit trig-

---

5.   This example is inspired by a suggestion from Paul Montgomery.

gers; therefore, the pattern does not support completion transitions. However, the Reminder pattern offers a workaround. You can invent an explicit trigger for every transition and post it to self. This approach actually gives you much better control over the behavior because you can explicitly specify the completion criteria.

Figure 5.4 **(a) An initial transition penetrating two levels of nesting (not allowed in the behavioral inheritance meta-pattern); (b) the equivalent nested initial transitions; (c) elimination of the innermost initial transition through the Reminder pattern (the ^INIT action indicates the INIT event propagates to self)**

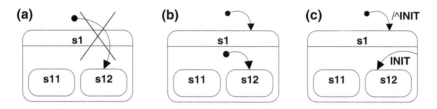

Yet another important application of the Reminder pattern is to break up longer RTC steps into shorter ones. As explained in more detail in Chapter 10, long RTC steps exacerbate the responsiveness of a state machine and put more stress on event queues. The Reminder pattern can help you break up CPU-intensive processing (e.g., iteration) by inventing a stimulus for continuation in the same way that you stick a Post-it®[6] note to your computer monitor to remind you where you left off on some lengthy task when someone interrupts you. You can also invent event parameters to convey the context, which will allow the next step to pick up where the previous step left off. The advantage of fragmenting lengthy processing in such a way is so that other (perhaps more urgent) events can "sneak in" allowing the state machine to handle them in a more timely way.

You have essentially two alternatives when implementing event posting: the first in, first out (FIFO) or the last in, first out (LIFO) policy. The FIFO policy is appropriate for breaking up longer RTC steps. You want to queue the reminder event after other events that have potentially accumulated while the state machine was busy, to give the other events a chance to sneak in ahead of the reminder. However, in other circumstances, you might want to process an uninterruptible sequence of posted events (such a sequence effectively forms an extended RTC step[7]). In this case, you need the LIFO policy, because a reminder posted with that policy is guaranteed to be the next event to process and no other event can overtake it.[8]

---

6. Post-it is a trademark of 3M, Inc.
7. For example, state-based exception handling (see Chapters 3 and 8) typically requires immediate handling of exceptional situation, so you don't want other events to overtake the EXCEPTION event.

5.3   Deferred Event

5.3.1   Intent

Simplify state machines by modifying the sequencing of events.

5.3.2   Problem

One of the biggest challenges in designing reactive systems is that such systems must be prepared to handle every event at any time. However, sometimes an event arrives at a particularly inconvenient moment when the system is in the midst of some complex event sequence. In many cases, the nature of the event is such that it can be postponed (within limits) until the system is finished with the current sequence, at which time the event can be recalled and conveniently processed.

Consider, for example, the case of a server application that processes transactions (e.g., from ATM terminals). Once a transaction starts, it typically goes through a sequence of processing, which commences with receiving the data from a remote terminal followed by the authorization of the transaction. Unfortunately, new transaction requests to the server arrive at random times, so it is possible to get a request while the server is still busy processing the previous transaction. One option is to ignore the request, but this might not be acceptable. Another option is to start processing the new transaction immediately, which can complicate things immensely because multiple outstanding transactions would need to be handled simultaneously.

5.3.3   Solution

The solution is to defer the new request and handle it at a more convenient time, which effectively leads to altering the sequence of events presented to the state machine.

UML statecharts support such a mechanism directly by allowing every state to specify a list of deferred events. As long as an event is on the combined deferred list of the currently active state configuration, it is not presented to the state machine but, rather, queued for later processing. Upon a state transition, events that are no longer deferred are automatically recalled and dispatched to the state machine. Figure 5.5 illustrates a solution based on this mechanism (note the special defer operator in the NEW_REQUEST internal transition in the busy state).

---

8. The Quantum Framework (described in Part II of this book) supports FIFO and LIFO policies through the postFIFO() and postLIFO() methods, respectively.

Note: State nesting immensely complicates event deferral because deferred lists of all nested states of the current state configuration contribute to the mechanism.

Figure 5.5 **Event deferral using the built-in UML mechanism**

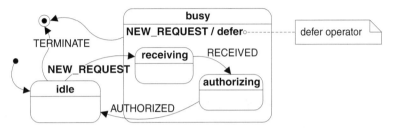

Naturally, the lightweight behavioral inheritance meta-pattern implementation does not support the powerful, but heavyweight, event deferral mechanism of the UML specification. However, you can achieve similar functionality by deferring and recalling events explicitly. Figure 5.6 shows how to integrate these operations into a statechart to achieve the desired effect. The internal transition NEW_REQUEST in the highest level state operational traps any transaction request received in either the receiving or authorizing states. This internal transition triggers the invocation of defer() (a member of the TServer class) to postpone the event. The idle substate of the operational superstate overrides the high-level transition NEW_REQUEST with a regular transition (in state idle, event NEW_REQUEST is no longer deferred). Additionally, the entry action to idle invokes recall(), which posts the first of the deferred events (if present) to the state machine.

Figure 5.6 **Deferred Event state pattern**

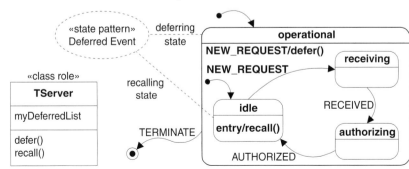

5.3.4   Sample Code

The sample code is a Windows GUI application because recalling deferred events involves posting them to self, which in Windows can be done with a `PostMessage()` Windows API call.

Figure 5.7 shows the simple GUI of this application. As usual, you see the current state in the top row. A check box below indicates whether any request has been deferred. The button at the bottom serves to place a request for a new transaction. You can click this button at any time, including when the system is busy processing your previous transactions.

Figure 5.7   Deferred Event sample application GUI

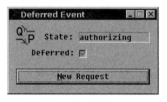

Listing 5.3   Abbreviated Deferred Event sample code

```
 1 class TServer : public QHsm {
 2 public:
 3    TServer() : QHsm((QPseudoState)initial) {}
 4 private:
 5    void initial(QEvent const *e);                    // initial pseudostate
 6    QSTATE operational(QEvent const *e);              // state-handler
 7      QSTATE idle(QEvent const *e);                   // state-handler
 8      QSTATE receiving(QEvent const *e);             // state-handler
 9      QSTATE authorizing(QEvent const *e);           // state-handler
10    QSTATE final(QEvent const *e);                   // state-handler
11
12    BOOL defer(QEvent const *e);                     // defer an event
13    void recall();                        // recall first deferred event
14 private:
15    QEvent myDeferredRequest;              // just one deferred request
16    BOOL isHandled;        // flag indicating if the last event was handled
17    HWND myHwnd;                           // the main window handle
18    friend BOOL CALLBACK DlgProc(HWND hwnd, UINT iEvt,
19                            WPARAM wParam, LPARAM lParam);
20 };
21 BOOL TServer::defer(QEvent const *e) {
22    if (IsDlgButtonChecked(myHwnd, IDC_DEFERRED)) {            // deferred?
23      return FALSE;                        // cannot defer any more events
24    }
```

```
25    myDeferredRequest = *e;                      // save the event (copy by value)
26    CheckDlgButton(myHwnd, IDC_DEFERRED, BST_CHECKED);          // deferred
27    return TRUE;
28 }
29 void TServer::recall() {
30    if (IsDlgButtonChecked(myHwnd, IDC_DEFERRED)) {           // deferred?
31        PostMessage(myHwnd, WM_COMMAND, myDeferredRequest.sig, 0);
32        CheckDlgButton(myHwnd, IDC_DEFERRED, BST_UNCHECKED);
33    }
34 }
35
36 void TServer::initial(QEvent const *) {
37    Q_INIT(&TServer::operational);
38 }
39 QSTATE TServer::operational(QEvent const *e) {
40    switch (e->sig) {
41    . . .
42    case NEW_REQUEST_SIG:
43        if (!defer(e)) {                           // cannot defer the event?
44            Beep(1000, 20);                              // warn the user
45        }
46        return 0;
47    }
48    . . .
49    return (QSTATE)&TServer::top;
50 }
51 QSTATE TServer::idle(QEvent const *e) {
52    switch (e->sig) {
53    case Q_ENTRY_SIG:
54        SetDlgItemText(myHwnd, IDC_STATE, "idle");
55        recall();                         // recall first deferred event (if any)
56        return 0;
57    case NEW_REQUEST_SIG:                      // override the NEW_REQUEST signal
58        Q_TRAN(&TServer::receiving);
59        return 0;
60    }
61    return (QSTATE)&TServer::operational;
62 }
63 QSTATE TServer::receiving(QEvent const *e) { . . . }
64 QSTATE TServer::authorizing(QEvent const *e) { . . . }
```

For simplicity, the implementation shown in Listing 5.3 allows only one deferred event (stored in the myDeferredRequest attribute). In a real application, you might want to replace this attribute with a queue to store more events. However, this is a detail that does not affect the code beyond the concrete implementation of defer() and recall(), shown in lines 21 through 28 and 29 through 34, respectively. Note that defer() must copy the event into local storage, as opposed to storing only the event pointer (line 25). An event instance passed to a state handler is typically destroyed (or goes out of scope) after dispatching. Also, no matter how big you make the deferred event queue, there is always a possibility of overflowing it; therefore, defer() should return the status of the deferral to the caller. This application generates a warning beep when deferring an event fails (line 44).

The application simulates processing delays in states receiving and authorizing with a Windows timer. A timer is created on entry to either state and then destroyed on exit. This example demonstrates how you can use entry and exit actions for guaranteed initialization and cleanup (you don't want to leak a Windows timer!).

Exercise 5.4   Find the Deferred Event state pattern implementation on the accompanying CD-ROM and execute it. Next, set a breakpoint in the exit action from the authorizing state. Start the application, issue the new request, wait until servicing proceeds to the authorizing state, and terminate the application before it transitions back to the idle state. Verify that the exit action from authorizing is executed (and thus the timer is not leaked).

The sample application in Listing 5.3 defers only one type of event: NEW_REQUEST. However, you can easily extend the pattern to defer any number of events. For instance, it might be inappropriate to terminate TServer while it is still processing a transaction; therefore, you can defer the TERMINATE event until the server is idle. To distinguish between deferring and recalling NEW_REQUEST and deferring TERMINATE, you need to create another pair of methods, say deferTerminate() and recallTerminate(), as well as a separate attribute in which to store the instances of the TERMINATE event type (Exercise 5.6).

Exercise 5.5   Reimplement in C the Deferred Event pattern from Listing 5.3. Hint: Appendix A describes the techniques for realizing classes and inheritance in C, and Section 4.5 of Chapter 4 provides specific guidelines for instantiating the behavioral inheritance meta-pattern in C.

Exercise 5.6   Add deferring the TERMINATE signal to the TServer statechart from Listing 5.3 as described in the previous paragraph. Devise and execute a test plan for the new feature.

5.3.5 Consequences

Event deferral is a valuable technique for simplifying state models. Instead of constructing an unduly complex state machine to handle every event at any time, you can defer an event when it comes at an inappropriate or awkward time. The event is recalled when the state machine is better able to handle it. The Deferred Event state pattern is a lightweight alternative to the powerful but heavyweight event deferral of UML statecharts. The Deferred Event state pattern has the following consequences.

- It requires explicit deferring and recalling of the deferred events.

- Concrete state machines (subclasses of QHsm), rather than the event processor, are responsible for storing deferred events and for implementing defer() and recall().

- If a state machine defers more than one event type, it might be appropriate to implement a separate queue for each type, as well as a specific defer???() and recall???() pair for deferring and recalling specific events, respectively.

- Events are usually deferred in a high-level transition (often an internal transition). Conversely, events are typically recalled in an entry action to a low-level state (the state that no longer defers a given event type).

- Recalling an event involves posting it to self; however, unlike deferred events in the Reminder pattern, they are usually external rather than invented.

The real-time object-oriented modeling (ROOM) method [Selic+ 94] supports a variation of the Deferred Event pattern presented here. The ROOM virtual machine (infrastructure for executing ROOM models) provides the generic methods defer() and recall(), which clients need to call explicitly. The virtual machine, however, takes care of event queuing. Methods defer() and recall() in ROOM are not specific to an event type but, rather, to the interface component through which an event was received.

5.4   Orthogonal Component

5.4.1   Intent

Use state machines as components.

5.4.2   Problem

Many objects comprise relatively independent parts that have state behavior. As an example, consider a simple digital alarm clock. The clock performs two largely independent functions: a basic timekeeping function and an alarm function. Each of these functions has its own modes of operation. For example, timekeeping can be in two modes: 12-hour or 24-hour. Similarly, an alarm can be either on or off.

One way of modeling such behavior in UML statecharts is to place each of the loosely related functions in a separate orthogonal region, as shown in Figure 5.8. However, orthogonal regions are a relatively heavyweight mechanism that the current implementation of the behavioral inheritance meta-pattern does not support. More importantly, orthogonal regions aren't often the desired solution because they offer little opportunity for reuse. You cannot reuse the Alarm orthogonal region easily outside the context of the `AlarmClock` statechart.

Figure 5.8   `AlarmClock` **class and its UML statechart with orthogonal regions**

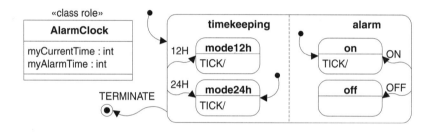

5.4.3   Solution

The solution is to use *object composition* instead of orthogonal regions. In the case of the alarm clock, the alarm function can be included as a separate `Alarm` *component* embedded inside the `timekeeping` *container* object, as shown in Figure 5.9. This solution is based on the universal OO guideline that it is best to construct classes out of high-level components, as opposed to low-level built-in types [Horstmann 95]. If the alarm function of the `AlarmClock` class is so independent that it warrants separation into a distinct orthogonal region, it probably is a component of the `AlarmClock` class. Indeed, as shown at the top of Figure 5.9, the alarm function very naturally maps to the `Alarm` class that has both data (`myAlarmTime`) and behavior (a state machine). Rumbaugh and colleagues [Rumbaugh+ 91] observe that this is a general rule. Concurrency virtually always arises within objects by aggregation; that is, multiple states of the components can contribute to a single state of the composite object.

The use of aggregation in conjunction with state machines raises three questions.

1. How does the container state machine communicate with the component state machines?

2. How do the component state machines communicate with the container state machine?

3. What kind of concurrency model should be used?

Figure 5.9   **Orthogonal Component state pattern; the pattern partitions state behavior as well as extended state variables, as indicated by the class roles at the top of the diagram**

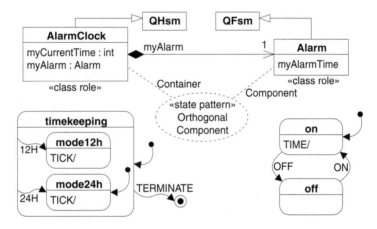

The composite object interacts with its aggregate parts by synchronously dispatching events to them (by invoking dispatch() on behalf of the components). GUI systems frequently use this model because it is how parent windows communicate with their child windows (e.g., dialog controls). Although, in principle, the container could invoke various methods of its components or access their data directly, dispatching events to the components should be the preferred way of communication. The components are state machines, and their behavior depends on their internal state.

To communicate in the opposite direction (from a component to the container), a component needs to post events to the container. Note that a child cannot call dispatch() on behalf of the parent because it would violate RTC semantics. As a rule, the parent is always in the middle of its RTC step when a child executes. Therefore, children need to asynchronously post (queue) events to the parent.

Note: The parent dispatches events *synchronously* (without queuing them) to the children, but the children must post events *asynchronously* (by queuing them) to the parent.

This way of communication dictates a concurrency model in which a parent shares its execution thread with the children.[9] The parent dispatches an event to a child by synchronously calling dispatch() on behalf of the child. Because this method executes in the parent's thread, the parent cannot proceed until dispatch() returns (i.e., until the child finishes its RTC step). In this way, the parent and children can safely share data without any concurrency hazards (data sharing is also another method of communication among them). However, sharing the container's data makes the components dependent on the container and thus makes them less reusable.

5.4.4 Sample Code

The sample code demonstrates the typical code organization for the Orthogonal Component state pattern, in which the component (Alarm) is implemented in a separate module from the container (AlarmClock). The modules are coupled through shared signals, events, and (potentially) variables (Listing 5.4).

Listing 5.4   Common signals and events (clock.h)

```
 1 enum AlarmClockSignals {
 2     TIME_SIG = Q_USER_SIG,
 3     ALARM_SIG, TERMINATE
 4 };
 5 struct AlarmInitEvt : public QEvent {
 6     HWND hWnd;
 7 };
 8 struct TimeEvt : public QEvent {
 9     unsigned currentTime;
10 };
```

Listing 5.5   Alarm finite state machine declaration (alarm.h)

```
 1 class Alarm : public QFsm {
 2 public:
 3     Alarm() : QFsm((QFsmState)initial) {}
 4 private:
 5     void initial(QEvent const *e);
 6     void on(QEvent const *e);
 7     void off(QEvent const *e);
 8 private:
 9     unsigned myAlarmTime;              // time to trigger the alarm
10     HWND myHwnd;                       // window handle
11 };
```

---

9.   Most commonly, all orthogonal regions in a statechart also share a common execution thread [Douglass 99].

Listing 5.5 shows the declaration of the `Alarm` state machine, which derives from the `QFsm` class and therefore uses a slightly different state handler signature. The `Alarm` class encapsulates two attributes — the self-explanatory `myAlarmTime` (line 9) and `myHwnd` (line 10) — to store the window handle that the `Alarm` component needs in the implementation.

Listing 5.6   Abbreviated `Alarm` finite state machine implementation (`alarm.cpp`)

```
 1 #include "clock.h"
 2 #include "alarm.h"
 3
 4 void Alarm::initial(QEvent const *e) {
 5     myHwnd = (static_cast<AlarmInitEvt const *>(e))->hWnd;
 6     . . .
 7     QFSM_TRAN(&Alarm::on);
 8 }
 9 void Alarm::on(QEvent const *e) {
10     switch (e->sig) {
11     case TIME_SIG:
12         if ((static_cast<TimeEvt *>(e))->currentTime == myAlarmTime) {
13             Beep(1000, 20);
14             PostMessage(myHwnd, WM_COMMAND, ALARM_SIG, 0);            // notify
15         }
16         return;
17     case IDC_OFF:
18         . . .
19         QFSM_TRAN(&Alarm::off);
20         return;
21     }
22 }
23 void Alarm::off(QEvent const *e) {
24     char buf[12];
25     unsigned h, m;
26     switch (e->sig) {
27     case IDC_ON:
28         GetDlgItemText(myHwnd, IDC_ALARM, buf, sizeof(buf));
29         if (...) {    // does the user input represent valid alarm time?
30             . . .
31             QFSM_TRAN(&Alarm::on);
32         }
33         return;
34     }
35 }
```

Listing 5.6 shows an abbreviated implementation of the `Alarm` FSM. The first interesting aspect is the `initial` pseudostate (lines 4–8), which uses the event argument to initialize the `myHwnd` attribute (line 5). As described in Chapter 4, the state machine interface intentionally separates the initial transition from the state machine instantiation, which this code exploits. The AlarmClock class, and thus its Alarm component, are instantiated statically before the window handle is allocated. However, the initial transition, which is explicitly triggered much later, offers the container (AlarmClock) an opportunity to initialize the component with the window handle (or any other arbitrary parameters passed in the initializing event).

The other interesting feature is the handling of the TIME signal in (Listing 5.6, lines 11–16). The guard condition for starting the alarm is the match between the current time and the preset alarm time (line 12). Notice the usual downcasting of the generic event pointer to the concrete event class (TimeEvt* in this case). In addition, line 14 illustrates how the Alarm component notifies the container by posting the ALARM_SIG event.

Listing 5.7   Abbreviated AlarmClock hierarchical state machine implementation

```
 1 #include "clock.h"
 2 #include "alarm.h"
 3
 4 class AlarmClock : public QHsm {                    // hierarchical state machine
 5 public:
 6    AlarmClock() : QHsm((QPseudoState)initial) {}
 7 private:
 8    void initial(QEvent const *e);                   // initial pseudostate
 9    QSTATE timekeeping(QEvent const *e);                      // state-handler
10       QSTATE mode12hr(QEvent const *e);                      // state-handler
11       QSTATE mode24hr(QEvent const *e);                      // state-handler
12    QSTATE final(QEvent const *e);                            // state-handler
13 private:
14    unsigned myCurrentTime;                          // current time (in minutes)
15    Alarm myAlarm;                                    // reactive component Alarm
16    BOOL isHandled;
17    HWND myHwnd;                                          // the main window handle
18    friend class Alarm;           // grant friendship to reactive component(s)
19    friend BOOL CALLBACK DlgProc(HWND hwnd, UINT iEvt,
20                           WPARAM wParam, LPARAM lParam);
21 };
22
23 void AlarmClock::initial(QEvent const *) {
24    . . .
25    AlarmInitEvt ie;          // initialization event for the Alarm component
26    ie.wndHwnd = myHwnd;
27    myAlarm.init(&ie);        // initial transition in the alarm component
28    Q_INIT(timekeeping);
29 }
30
```

```
31  QSTATE AlarmClock::timekeeping(QEvent const *e) {
32     switch (e->sig) {
33     . . .
34     case IDC_ON:
35     case IDC_OFF:
36        myAlarm.dispatch(e);           // dispatch event to orthogonal component
37        return 0;
38     }
39     return (QSTATE)top;
40  }
41
42  QSTATE AlarmClock::mode24hr(QEvent const *e) {
43     TimeEvt pe;                               // temporary for propagated event
44     switch (e->sig) {
45     . . .
46     case WM_TIMER:
47        . . .                                  // update myCurrentTime
48        pe.sig = TIME_SIG;
49        pe.currentTime = myCurrentTime;
50        myAlarm.dispatch(&pe);         //dispatch event to orthogonal component
51        return 0;
52     }
53     return (QSTATE)timekeeping;
54  }
```

Listing 5.7 shows the main points of the AlarmClock class implementation. The class aggregates an Alarm object (line 15) and grants friendship to the Alarm class (line 18). The myAlarm component does not make use of the friendship in this particular case, but generally, the friendship is necessary if the container shares data with its components (see Exercise 5.10).[10]

By implementing half of the problem (the Alarm component) as a classical flat state machine and the other half as a hierarchical state machine (the AlarmClock container), an opportunity arises to contrast the nonhierarchical and hierarchical solutions for essentially identical state machine topologies. Figure 5.9 illustrates the different approaches to representing mode switches in the timekeeping HSM and in the Alarm FSM. The hierarchical solution demonstrates the Device Mode idiom [Douglass 99], in which the signals 12H and 24H trigger high-level transitions to states mode12h and mode24h, respectively. The Alarm FSM, on the hand, uses direct transitions ON and OFF between its two modes. Although it is not clearly apparent with only two modes, the number of mode switch transitions in the hierarchical technique scales up proportionally to the number of modes, n. The nonhierarchical

---

10. Components also must "know" their container. If the container is a Singleton, then access is through its static instance() method (see the Singleton pattern in Gamma and colleagues [Gamma+ 95]).

solution, on the other hand, requires many more transitions — $n(n - 1)$, in general — to interconnect all states. There is also a difference in behavior. In the hierarchical solution, if a system is already in mode12h, for example, and the 12H signal arrives, the system leaves this mode and enters it again. (Naturally, you could prevent that by overriding the high-level 12H transition in the mode12h state.) In contrast, if the flat state machine of the Alarm class is in the off state, for example, then nothing happens when the OFF signal appears. This solution might or might not be what you want; however, the hierarchical solution (the Device Mode idiom) offers you both options and scales much better with a growing number of modes.

Exercise 5.7   Change the superclass of the Alarm class from QFsm to QHsm and change the Alarm state machine to use the same structure as the Alarm orthogonal region shown in Figure 5.8. Note that you don't need to change anything in the AlarmClock container class because the QFsm and QHsm classes have equivalent interfaces.

As a container, the AlarmClock class has several responsibilities toward its components. First is the initialization of the Alarm component's state machine, which is best accomplished in the initial transition of the container (Listing 5.7, lines 23–29). Note the use of the initialization event (ie) to pass the window handle to the component. Second is the explicit dispatching of events to the component(s) (lines 36, 50). You can view this responsibility as a liability (errors will result if the container "forgets" to dispatch events in some contexts), but you can also view it as having greater flexibility and as an opportunity to improve performance. Explicit event dispatching offers more flexibility than the event dispatching of orthogonal regions because the container cannot only choose which events it wants to dispatch to its children but even change the event type on the fly. For instance, AlarmClock dispatches events ON and OFF to its myAlarm component as they arrive (lines 34–37). However, the WM_TIMER signal is handled differently (lines 46–51). In this case, AlarmClock synthesizes a TimeEvt event on the fly, furnishes the current time, and dispatches this event to the Alarm component. Note that TimeEvt can be allocated automatically (on the stack) because it is dispatched synchronously to the component.

Complete control over the dispatching of events to components typically allows significant performance gains. For example, in a real digital clock design, the TICK event would probably occur every second so that the clock could display seconds as well. However, the alarm will probably still be specified to within one minute. Therefore, AlarmClock could dispatch only every 60th TICK to the Alarm component (only when the minutes roll over). The UML design with orthogonal regions, on the other hand, would burn many more CPU cycles by automatically dispatching every TICK to every orthogonal region (i.e., to the Alarm region as well).

Figure 5.10 shows the Windows GUI corresponding to the sample code described in this section. The dialog box clearly separates the timekeeping and alarm functions. There is no need to display the states of these components separately because they are readily apparent from the settings of the two groups of radio buttons.

Figure 5.10   Orthogonal Component sample application GUI

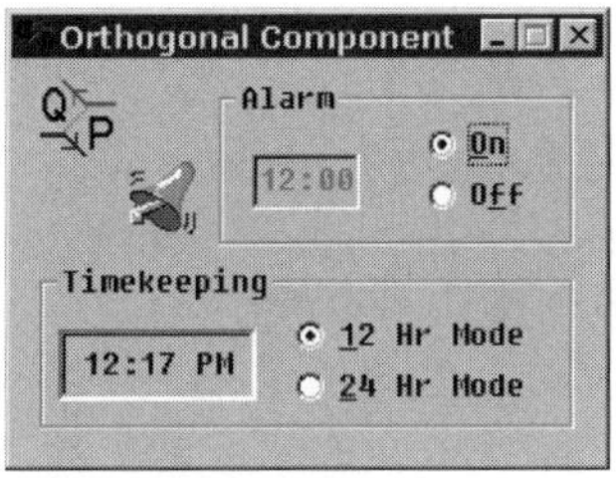

To make this example a little more interesting, I accelerated the clock to tick at a much faster rate than usual (it makes about 20 accelerated minutes per real second). That way you can hear an alarm (a short beep) much more often (about every 72 seconds).

Exercise 5.8   Find the Orthogonal Component state pattern implementation on the accompanying CD-ROM and execute it. Change the timekeeping mode from 24 to 12 hours and the alarm mode from on to off. Notice that only in the alarm-off state can you change the alarm time. Set the new alarm time and turn the alarm back on. Verify that the clock beeps when it reaches the alarm time.

Exercise 5.9   Reimplement the Orthogonal Component state pattern in C. Hint: Appendix A describes the techniques for realizing classes and inheritance in C, and Section 4.5 of Chapter 4 provides specific guidelines for instantiating the behavioral inheritance meta-pattern in C.

Exercise 5.10 Components must often "know" their container. Apply the Singleton design pattern (read about the Singleton pattern in Gamma and colleagues [Gamma+ 95]) to the `AlarmClock` class, and reorganize the `Alarm` class such that it can accesses the `AlarmClock` container through the Singleton's `instance()` method. Remove the `myHwnd` attribute from the `Alarm` class and let it share the window handle of `AlarmClock` instead.

5.4.5 Consequences

The Orthogonal Component state pattern has the following consequences.

- It partitions independent islands of behavior into separate reactive objects. This separation is deeper than with orthogonal regions because the objects have both distinct behavior and distinct data.

- Partitioning introduces a container component (also known as parent–child or master–slave) relationship. The container implements the primary functionality and delegates other (secondary) features to the components. Both the container and the components are state machines.

- The components are often reusable with different containers or even within the same container (the container can instantiate more than one component of a given type).

- The container shares its execution thread with the components.

- The container communicates with the components by directly dispatching events to them. The components notify the container by posting events to it, never through direct event dispatching.

- The components typically use the Reminder state pattern to notify the container (i.e., the notification events are invented specifically for the internal communication and are not relevant externally). If there are more components of a given type, then the notification events must identify the originating component (the component passes its ID in a parameter of the notification event).

- The container and components can share data. Typically, the data is an attribute of the container (to allow multiple instances of different containers). The container typically grants friendship to the selected components.

- The container is entirely responsible for its components. In particular, it must explicitly trigger initial transitions in all components,[11] as well as explicitly dis-

---

11. In C, the container also must call constructors for all its components explicitly.

patch events to the components. Errors may arise if the container "forgets" to dispatch events to some components in some of its states.

- The container has full control over the dispatching of events to the components. It can choose not to dispatch events that are irrelevant to the components. It can also change event types on the fly and provide some additional information to the components.

- The container can dynamically start and stop components (e.g., in certain states of the component state machine).

- The composition of state machines is not limited to just one level. Components can have reactive subcomponents; that is, the components can be containers for lower level subcomponents. Such a recursion of components can proceed arbitrarily deep.

The Orthogonal Component state pattern is popular in GUI systems. For example, dialog boxes are the containers that aggregate components in the form of dialog controls (buttons, check boxes, sliders, etc.). Both dialog boxes and dialog controls are event-driven objects with state behavior (e.g., a button has depressed and released states). GUIs also use the pattern recursively. For instance, a custom dialog box can be a container for the standard File-Select or Color-Select dialog boxes, which in turn contain buttons, check boxes, and so on.

The last example points to the main advantage of the Orthogonal Component state pattern over the and-decomposition of statecharts (orthogonal regions). Unlike an orthogonal region, you can reuse a reactive component many times within one application and across many applications.

Both orthogonal regions and reactive components directly compete in the design space with simple extended state variables. For example, Douglass [Douglass 99] presents a simple Latch state pattern that is applicable to reactive objects that must pass through a specific state in their life cycle in order to proceed with some activity. The proposed solution is to build a latch with an orthogonal region and two states: latched and unlatched. The latch starts in the unlatched state and is forced to the latched state when the object passes through the precondition state. Subsequently, the main state machine of the object uses the IS_IN(latched) operator[12] as a guard on a transition to a state. A simpler solution is to implement the latch as a simple flag, cleared in the initial transition, and set on entry to the precondition state. Subsequently, the object's state

---

12. The IS_IN(foo) operator returns TRUE if any of the orthogonal regions is in the foo state and returns FALSE otherwise. This operator corresponds to the QHsm::isIn() method of the behavioral inheritance meta-pattern implementation.

machine can test the flag in the guard condition. The Latch orthogonal region is overkill here and doesn't add value because it isn't used to capture modal behavior; rather, it only stores information, which is a job for an extended state variable. The litmus test of misusing an orthogonal region as storage occurs when the region is employed only in conjunction with the IS_IN(*state*) operator.

You should apply good judgment and use the Orthogonal Component (or any other) pattern only if it simplifies your designs. Sometimes it is better to use simpler solutions, like extended state variables. Your ultimate goal is to defeat complexity not create clever-looking diagrams.

5.5 Transition to History

5.5.1 Intent

Transition out of a composite state, but remember the most recent active substate so you can return to that substate later.

5.5.2 Problem

State transitions defined in high-level composite states often deal with events that require immediate attention; however, after handling them, the system should return to the most recent substate of the given composite sate.

For example, consider a simple toaster oven. Normally the toaster operates with its door closed. However, at any time, the user can open the door to check the food or to clean the oven. Opening the door is an interruption; for safety reasons, it requires shutting the heater off and lighting an internal lamp. However, after closing the door, the toaster oven should resume whatever it was doing before the door was opened. Here is the problem: What was the toaster doing just before the door was opened? The state machine must remember the most recent state configuration that was active before opening the door in order to restore it after the door is closed again.

UML statecharts address this situation with two kinds of history pseudostates: shallow history and deep history (see Section 2.2.7 in Chapter 2). This example requires the deep history mechanism (denoted as the circled H* icon in Figure 5.11). The behavioral inheritance meta-pattern does not support a history mechanism automatically for all states because it would incur extra memory and performance overheads. However, it is easy to add such support for selected states.

5.5.3   Solution

Figure 5.11 illustrates the solution, which is to store the most recently active substate of the doorClosed state in the dedicated attribute myDoorClosedHistory. The ideal place for setting this attribute is the exit action from the doorClosed state. Subsequently, the transition to history of the doorOpen state (transition to the circled H*) uses the attribute as the target of the transition. Because this target changes at run time, it is crucial to code this transition with the Q_TRAN_DYN() macro, rather than the usual (optimized) Q_TRAN() macro (see Section 4.4.3 in Chapter 4).

Figure 5.11   Transition to History state pattern

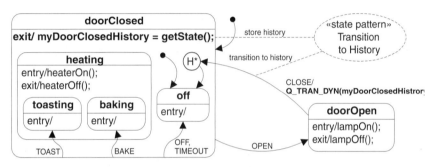

5.5.4   Sample Code

Listing 5.8 shows the complete implementation of the statechart from Figure 5.11 as a console application. The emphasized elements pertain to the history mechanism.

Listing 5.8   Complete implementation of the toaster oven statechart (Figure 5.11)

```
1 class ToasterOven : public QHsm {
2 public:
3    ToasterOven() : QHsm((QPseudoState)initial) {}
4 protected:
5    void initial(QEvent const *e);                  // initial pseudostate
6    QSTATE doorClosed(QEvent const *e);                // state-handler
7       QSTATE off(QEvent const *e);                     // state-handler
8       QSTATE heating(QEvent const *e);                 // state-handler
9          QSTATE toasting(QEvent const *e);             // state-handler
10         QSTATE baking(QEvent const *e);               // state-handler
11   QSTATE doorOpen(QEvent const *e);                   // state-handler
12   QSTATE final(QEvent const *e);                      // state-handler
13 private:
14   QState myDoorClosedHistory; // storage for history of "doorClosed"
15 };
```

```
16
17 enum ToasterOvenSignals {
18    OPEN_SIG = Q_USER_SIG,
19    CLOSE_SIG, TOAST_SIG, BAKE_SIG, OFF_SIG, END_SIG
20 };
21
22 void ToasterOven::initial(QEvent const *) {
23    myDoorClosedHistory = Q_STATIC_CAST(QState, &ToasterOven::off);
24    Q_INIT(&ToasterOven::doorClosed);
25 }
26
27 QSTATE ToasterOven::doorClosed(QEvent const *e) {
28    switch (e->sig) {
29    case Q_ENTRY_SIG: printf("door-Closed;"); return 0;
30    case Q_EXIT_SIG:  myDoorClosedHistory = getState(); return 0;
31    case Q_INIT_SIG:  Q_INIT(&ToasterOven::off); return 0;
32    case OPEN_SIG:    Q_TRAN(&ToasterOven::doorOpen); return 0;
33    case TOAST_SIG:   Q_TRAN(&ToasterOven::toasting); return 0;
34    case BAKE_SIG:    Q_TRAN(&ToasterOven::baking);   return 0;
35    case OFF_SIG:     Q_TRAN(&ToasterOven::off);      return 0;
36    case END_SIG:     Q_TRAN(&ToasterOven::final);    return 0;
37    }
38    return (QSTATE)&ToasterOven::top;
39 }
40
41 QSTATE ToasterOven::off(QEvent const *e) {
42    switch (e->sig) {
43    case Q_ENTRY_SIG: printf("toaster-Off;"); return 0;
44    }
45    return (QSTATE)&ToasterOven::doorClosed;
46 }
47
48 QSTATE ToasterOven::heating(QEvent const *e) {
49    switch (e->sig) {
50    case Q_ENTRY_SIG: printf("heater-On;");   return 0;
51    case Q_EXIT_SIG:  printf("heater-Off;");  return 0;
52    }
53    return (QSTATE)&ToasterOven::doorClosed;
54 }
55
56 QSTATE ToasterOven::toasting(QEvent const *e) {
57    switch (e->sig) {
58    case Q_ENTRY_SIG: printf("toasting;");    return 0;
59    }
60    return (QSTATE)&ToasterOven::heating;
61 }
62
```

```
63 QSTATE ToasterOven::baking(QEvent const *e) {
64     switch (e->sig) {
65     case Q_ENTRY_SIG: printf("baking;");        return 0;
66     }
67     return (QSTATE)&ToasterOven::heating;
68 }
69
70 QSTATE ToasterOven::doorOpen(QEvent const *e) {
71     switch (e->sig) {
72     case Q_ENTRY_SIG: printf("door-Open,lamp-On;"); return 0;
73     case Q_EXIT_SIG:  printf("lamp-Off;"); return 0;
74     case CLOSE_SIG:
75         Q_TRAN_DYN(myDoorClosedHistory);
76         return 0;
77     }
78     return (QSTATE)&ToasterOven::top;
79 }
```

In line 14 of Listing 5.8, you see the declaration of the myDoorClosedHistory attribute that holds the history of the doorClosed composite state. The exit action from doorClosed sets this attribute in line 30 by obtaining the current state from getState() (inherited from QHsm). At this point, the current state is not well defined because the state machine is in the middle of a transition. However, the implementation of the QHsm event processor QHsm::dispatch() is such that the current state pointer (QHsm::myState) is changed only after the whole transition chain completes. So throughout the transition, QHsm::myState still points to the most recently active state, which is the most recently active state and exactly what you want. Finally, the doorOpen state accomplishes a transition to history by means of Q_TRAN_DYN(myDoorClosedHistory) (line 75).

Alongside the history mechanism, Listing 5.8 demonstrates an interesting (proper) use of entry and exit actions that contributes to better robustness and safety of the design. For instance, the heating state disables the heater on exit (line 51), which is safer than doing it in all possible transitions that can lead out of this state. One example of such a transition is triggered by OPEN, but there are more (e.g., OFF).

In addition, the transitions in lines 33, 34, and 35 again demonstrate the Device Mode idiom (Section 5.4.4).

Exercise 5.11 Find the Transition to History state pattern implementation on the accompanying CD-ROM and execute it. You drive the application by injecting events from the keyboard (o = Open, c = Close, t = Toast, b = Bake, f = Off, and e = End). Verify that opening and then closing the door from any of the states baking, toasting, or off leads back to the original state. Modify the implementation to use the Q_TRAN() macro instead of Q_TRAN_DYN(). Recompile and examine how this breaks the desired behavior.

Exercise 5.12 Reimplement in C the Transition to History state pattern from Listing 5.8. Hint: Appendix A describes the techniques for realizing classes and inheritance in C, and Section 4.5 of Chapter 4 provides specific guidelines for instantiating the behavioral inheritance meta-pattern in C.

5.5.5 Consequences

The Transition to History state pattern has the following consequences.

- It requires that a separate QState pointer-to-member function is provided for each composite state to store the history of this state. It is best to use attributes of the concrete subclass of QHsm for this purpose.

- It requires explicitly setting the history variable in the exit action from the corresponding composite state using QHsm::getState().

- It requires the dynamic (not optimized) Q_TRAN_DYN(*<history-variable>*) transition macro to transition to the history of a given state.

- It corresponds to the deep-history, not the shallow-history, pseudostate (see Section 2.2.7 in Chapter 2).

- You can explicitly clear the history of any state by resetting the corresponding history variable.

As a part of the UML specification, the history mechanism qualifies as a widely used pattern. The ROOM method [Selic+ 94] describes a few examples of transitions to history in real-time systems, whereas Horrocks [Horrocks 99] describes how to apply the history mechanism in the design of GUIs.

5.6 Summary

As Gamma and colleagues [Gamma+ 95] observe: "*One thing expert designers know not to do is solve every problem from first principles.*" Collecting and documenting design patterns is one of the best ways of capturing and disseminating expertise in any domain, not just in software design.

State patterns are specific design patterns that are concerned with optimal (according to some criteria) ways of structuring states, events, and transitions to build effective state machines. In this chapter, I described just five such patterns[13] at various levels of abstraction. The first two, Ultimate Hook and Reminder, are at a significantly lower level than the rest, and perhaps I should have called them idioms rather than patterns. However, they are so fundamental and useful that they belong in every state machine designer's bag of tricks.

The other three patterns (Deferred Event, Orthogonal Component, and Transition to History) are alternative (lightweight) realizations of features supported natively in UML statecharts. Each one of these state patterns offers significant performance and memory savings compared to the full UML-compliant realization.

---

13.   You also can find a few useful idioms for structuring state machines.

6

Chapter 6

Inheriting State Models

I have yet to see any problem, however complicated, which,
when you looked at it in the right way, did not become still more
complicated.
— Paul Anderson

Useful reactive classes that you create through instantiation of the fundamental behavioral inheritance meta-pattern frequently have rich state behavior and embed involved statecharts. Coming up with a good statechart that captures a nontrivial behavior is not easy. When you successfully design, implement, and debug a robust reactive class, you want to get the maximum mileage out of it by reusing it in other projects. Seldom, however, can you reuse a class as-is without modifications. You need to be able to inherit from it and refine its behavior in subclasses. Traditional OOP prescribes how to inherit attributes and refine individual class methods,[1] but how do you inherit and refine entire state machines?

The issue is tricky because the behavioral inheritance meta-pattern represents a statechart as a group of interrelated class methods (state handlers) rather than as a

---

1. If you are interested in the C implementation, please refer to Appendix A for an explanation of how to realize inheritance in C.

single method. The challenge is to keep intact the numerous relationships among state handlers in the process of inheriting and refining the derived statechart. The associations among state handlers define the topology of the state machine and come in two flavors: (1) state handlers refer other state handlers as targets of state transitions and (2) state handlers designate other state handlers as superstates. As you will see in a concrete working example, the behavioral inheritance meta-pattern naturally preserves the statechart topology in a derived reactive class and enables easy refinement of the inherited state handlers. However, how it happens is certainly not trivial, and in this chapter, I peek under the hood to find out exactly what's going on.

Another concern associated with inheriting entire state models is compliance with the Liskov Substitution Principle (LSP). According to the traditional LSP, any subclass should be freely substitutable for its subclass. For reactive classes, this means that the behavior refined in any subclass should remain compatible with the behavior of the original base class. At a minimum, this compatibility requires that the subclass must accept all events that can be accepted by the parent, but there is obviously more to it. Although it is generally difficult to define "compatibility of behavior" precisely, this chapter at least enlists design heuristics and practical rules of thumb for inheritance and refinement that comply with the LSP.

In Section 2.2.2 of Chapter 2, I introduced the concept of behavioral inheritance and proposed extending LSP to nested states. Please note that these concepts are distinctively different from the classical class inheritance and the traditional LSP for classes that are the subject of this chapter.

In this chapter, I use the most advanced programming techniques yet in the discussion of statechart implementations. In particular, I rely heavily on polymorphism, which I intentionally have avoided up to this point. Although the techniques presented here can be very useful, they come at the cost of increased complexity and run-time overhead. Please feel free to skip this chapter on the first reading because the material covered here is not necessary to comprehend the other parts of the book.

6.1   Statechart Refinement Example in C++

To illustrate the inheritance and refinement of a nontrivial statechart, consider the Quantum Calculator example introduced in Chapter 1. Figure 1.2 on page 7 is a comparison between the original Visual Basic Calculator and the Quantum Calculator user interfaces. Notice that the Quantum Calculator does not have a % button and consequently does not support calculations of percentages. I have intentionally saved this feature until now so that I can add it through inheritance and demonstrate a nontrivial refinement of the statechart (Figure 6.1). However, I propose to implement percentage calculations differently than in the original Visual Basic Calculator because the Visual Basic implementation is incorrect (Exercise 6.1). The goal is to enable calculations of the type $x + y\%$ gives z (e.g., price + sales tax gives total), wherein the + operator can be replaced by any of $-$, $\times$, or $\div$.

Figure 6.1 **The original Quantum Calculator GUI (a) and the enhanced Quantum Calculator after adding the % button (b)**

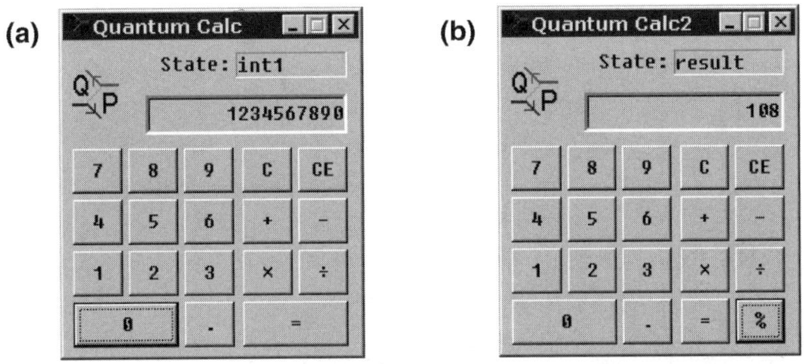

Exercise 6.1 Launch the Visual Basic Calculator application from the accompanying CD-ROM (refer to Appendix C for the structure of the CD-ROM). Try computing 100 + 8% and verify that you don't get the expected result (108). Enter 2, −, −, % and watch the application crash.

From the problem statement, you see that the % button has a function similar to the = button, in that it terminates a two-operand expression. This similarity suggests that the PERCENT event should be handled in the same state context as the EQUALS event — that is, in the operator2 state. This is also the only place it needs to be handled, as shown in Figure 6.2.

This example illustrates a nontrivial refinement to a statechart because it requires modifying the existing operand2 state (by adding a new transition), rather than introducing a new state. The problem is that operand2 is already involved in many relationships (Figure 6.2). For example, it is the superstate of zero2, int2, and frac2, as well as the source of transitions triggered by the signals EQUALS, OPER, and CE. The question is, can you override just the operand2() state handler without breaking all the relationships in which it already takes part? You can if the operand2() state handler is declared virtual in the base class. In other words, the virtual function mechanism of C++ also works for pointer-to-member functions and accomplishes exactly what you want. I'll leave the interesting question of how this is done to Section 6.1.1 and proceed with the example.

Listing 6.1 shows the Calc1 class, which is just a slightly modified version of the original Quantum Calculator Calc class from Chapter 1. The Calc1 class is prepared for inheritance[2] by declaring all state handlers, as well as other helper methods, virtual[3] (e.g., Listing 6.1, line 7). Calc1 also applies the Singleton design pattern [Gamma+ 95] so that any subclass of Calc1 can be plugged in without

Figure 6.2   **Refined statechart of an advanced Quantum Calculator; the refined operand2 state and the new transition triggered by the PERCENT signal are shown in bold**

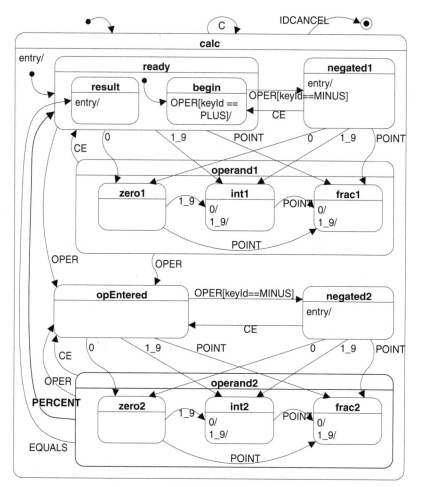

affecting the rest of the GUI code. You just introduce the static member function Calc1::instance() (line 2) and protect the constructor (line 5) to prevent uncontrolled instantiation of Calc1. Other aspects of the implementation of the Calc1 class are identical to the original Calc class, including all the references to the operand2 state (lines 11–22).

2.   The base class Calc originally could have been designed with inheritance and refinement in mind, in which case, creation of the Calc1 class would be unnecessary.

3.   In the fine-tuning phase, you could recover some performance for some methods by selectively removing the virtual keyword.

Listing 6.1 The `Calc1` reactive class prepared for inheritance

```
 1 class Calc1 : public QHsm {
 2    static Calc1 *instance();              // Singleton accessor class method
 3    . . .
 4 protected:
 5    Calc1() : QHsm((QPseudoState)initial) {}         // protected constructor
 6    . . .
 7    virtual QSTATE operand2(QEvent const *e);       // virtual state-handler
 8    . . .
 9 };
10
11 QSTATE Calc1::zero2(QEvent const *e) {
12    . . .
13    return (QSTATE)&Calc1::operand2;                // unchanged from Calc
14 }
15 QSTATE Calc1::int2(QEvent const *e) {
16    . . .
17    return (QSTATE)&Calc1::operand2;                // unchanged from Calc
18 }
19 QSTATE Calc1::frac2(QEvent const *e) {
20    . . .
21    return (QSTATE)&Calc1::operand2;                // unchanged from Calc
22 }
```

The refined Quantum Calculator, represented by the `Calc2` class (Listing 6.2), inherits from `Calc1` and overrides only the `operand2()` virtual state handler (line 3). This state handler method is subsequently defined in lines 6 through 30. This method explicitly handles only one signal, PERCENT (line 18), and delegates all other signals to the original `Calc1::operand2()` state handler (line 29). Handling of the PERCENT signal (lines 9–27) depends on the last operator entered. For the additive operators + and –, the action is to substitute the second operand, `myOperand2`, with the expression `1 ± myOperand2/100.0` and simultaneously to set the operator to multiplication (lines 12–13, 16–17). The following transition (line 26) causes evaluation of the expression in the entry action to `result` (Figure 6.2), which produces the desired result. For the multiplicative operators * and /, the action simply divides `myOperand2` by 100 (line 21) and does not replace the operand. Please note that the potential case of a division by zero (e.g., if the user entered $x \div 0\%$) already is handled in the `eval()` action invoked on entry to `result`.

Listing 6.2   Derived and refined `Calc2` C++ statechart

```
 1 class Calc2 : public Calc1 {
 2 protected:
 3     virtual QSTATE operand2(QEvent const *e);          // overridden handler
 4 };
 5
 6 QSTATE Calc2::operand2(QEvent const *e) {
 7     switch (e->sig) {
 8     case IDC_PERCENT:
 9         sscanf(myDisplay, "%lf", &myOperand2);
10         switch (myOperator) {
11         case IDC_PLUS:
12             myOperand2 = 1.0 + myOperand2/100.0;                 // x*(1 + y%)
13             myOperator = IDC_MULT;
14             break;
15         case IDC_MINUS:
16             myOperand2 = 1.0 - myOperand2/100.0;                 // x*(1 - y%)
17             myOperator = IDC_MULT;
18             break;
19         case IDC_MULT:                          // intentionally fall through...
20         case IDC_DIVIDE:
21             myOperand2 /= 100.0;                              // x*y%, x/y%
22             break;
23         default:
24             ASSERT(0);
25         }
26         Q_TRAN(&Calc2::result);                    // transition to "result"
27         return 0;                                  // event handled
28     }
29     return Calc1::operand2(e);                  // let Calc1 handle other events
30 }
```

The C++ syntax of the pointer-to-member function &*Class*::*method* can be confusing in the context of class inheritance. For example, in lines 13, 17, and 21 of Listing 6.1, state handlers `zero2()`, `int2()`, and `frac2()` return the pointer-to-member function `&Calc1::operand2`, which suggests that they all refer to the `Calc1::operand2()` implementation. In spite of this, when the `Calc2` class inherits these state handlers from `Calc1`, the handlers behave polymorphically by returning the `Calc2::operand2()` implementation. The class name in the fully qualified pointer-to-member function syntax has no effect (i.e., late binding still applies). However, the syntax can be confusing because, in all other circumstances, the fully qualified method name *Class*::*method()* enforces early binding by selecting a specific method implementation (as in Listing 6.2, line 29).

Exercise 6.2   Launch the enhanced Quantum Calculator application qcalc2.exe from the accompanying CD-ROM (refer to Appendix C and the HTML browser on the disc for the description of the CD-ROM). Try computing 100 + 8%, 100 − 8%, 100 × 8%, 100 ÷ 8%, and 100 ÷ 0%. Try event sequences that caused the Visual Basic Calculator to crash in Exercise 6.1.

As you've verified for yourself in Exercise 6.2, the enhanced Quantum Calculator works just fine. The behavioral inheritance meta-pattern not only automatically assimilates the newly defined Calc2::operand2() state handler into the fabric of between-state relationships inherited from the Calc1 base class, but it even allows straightforward reuse of behavior from the original Calc1::operand2() state handler.

Exercise 6.3   The technique presented here allows you to refine all aspects of a state handler. For example, find the VC++ project qcalc2.dsp on the accompanying CD-ROM and add an entry action to the Calc2::opearator2() state handler (e.g., invoke the Win32 Beep()). Rebuild the project and note that only one module, calc2.cpp, needs recompilation. Launch the application and verify that your entry action indeed fires on each entry into the refined operator2 state.

Correct operation under inheritance is an important confirmation that the structure of the behavioral inheritance meta-pattern is indeed flexible and adaptable. This characteristic allows you to take full advantage of inheritance and, once again, the principle of programming-by-difference because refinement of behavior requires that you code only the differences between the reactive base class and its subclass.

6.1.1   How Does It Work?

Something more than traditional bread-and-butter polymorphism is going on with the inheritance of statecharts . Listing 6.3 illustrates the essence of the mechanism.

Listing 6.3   Test case for a pointer-to-virtual-member function

```
1 class Foo {
2 public:
3     typedef void (Foo::*Handler)();
4     virtual ~Foo() {}    // virtual destructor
5     Handler f()
```

```
 6    virtual void g();
 7 };
 8
 9 class Bar : public Foo {
10 public:
11    virtual void g();    // override g()
12 };
13
14 Foo::Handler Foo::f() { return g; }
15 void Foo::g() { printf("Foo::g()\n"); }
16 void Bar::g() { printf("Bar::g()\n"); }
17
18 Foo foo;
19 Bar bar;
20 Foo::Handler h = foo.f();
21
22 void main() {
23    (foo.*h)();
24    (bar.*h)();
25 }
```

Foo::Handler (Listing 6.3, line 3) is a type describing a pointer-to-member function (corresponding to QHsm::QState). Method Foo::f() returns member function g() (line 14), which corresponds to returning a superstate from a state handler. Please note that g() is declared virtual in class Foo (line 6). The value returned from foo.f() is subsequently assigned to the pointer-to-member function h (line 20). If you invoke a method via the h pointer on behalf of the foo object, as in line 23, the instance invoked is Foo::g() (so you would see the text "Foo::g()" on your screen). What happens, however, if you dereference the h pointer on behalf of the bar object, as in line 24? Is Foo::g() still invoked or is it Bar::g()? In other words, does the virtual mechanism work for a pointer-to-member function? It turns out that it is, so you would see the text "Bar::g()" on your screen. The question is *how*?

The pointer-to-member function h must store something other than simply the memory location of Foo::g(), returned from Foo::f() (which would be the case if g() were declared nonvirtual in class Foo). When g() is virtual, the C++ compiler performs a trick that enables polymorphic behavior. Generally, strategies used by different C++ compilers seem to fall into two categories [Lippman 96]. The first strategy is to represent pointer-to-member functions as aggregates that can hold both regular addresses as well as offsets into the virtual table (and provide a mechanism to distinguish between the two). In this case, the pointer-to-member function usually is bigger than a regular function pointer, and every invocation is charged with the cost of checking whether the call is virtual or nonvirtual. The other strategy is to introduce a function-like *vcall thunk* and store its address in a pointer-to-member function.[4] The thunk (which the compiler synthesizes behind the scenes) extracts and invokes the appropriate slot in the associated virtual table. The advantages of this approach are that virtual and nonvirtual invocations are treated transparently and that pointer-to-member functions are the same size as pointers to nonmember functions. Because the behavioral inheritance meta-pattern often manipulates and stores pointer-to-member functions, the thunk technique is much better suited for coding state machines.

Note: Some C++ compilers offer an option to select the internal representation of pointer-to-member functions. For example, GNU gcc provides the command line option -fvtable-thunks to choose the thunk technique, which you should select to improve performance of your state machines [WindRiver 95].

The following machine language output, compiled from Listing 6.3 by the Microsoft C/C++ 32-bit compiler (optimized code), illustrates the vcall thunk technique.[5]

```
; Foo::g()
00401010    push      407040h          ; stack address of "Foo::g()\n"
00401015    call      00401115         ; call printf()
0040101A    pop       ecx
0040101B    ret

; Bar::g()
00401020    push      40704Ch          ; stack address of "Bar::g()\n"
00401025    call      00401115         ; call printf()
0040102A    pop       ecx
0040102B    ret

; main()
004010F0    mov       ecx,4078E8h      ; place foo into ecx (this ptr)
004010F5    call      dword ptr ds:[4078E4h] ; call via pointer h
004010FB    mov       ecx,4078E0h      ; place bar into ecx (this ptr)
00401100    jmp       dword ptr ds:[4078E4h] ; call via pointer h

; thunk
00401110    mov       eax,dword ptr [ecx] ; grab vtable
00401112    jmp       dword ptr [eax+4]    ; jump to offset 1
```

---

4.   Examples of compilers that use this technique include Microsoft C++ and Borland C++ for Intel x86 processors.
5.   The machine code was cut and pasted from a debug session (please note that I intentionally used optimized, non-debug version of code). I've added the comments manually.

```
; Foo::f()
00401E03   mov        eax,[00407E14]
00401E08   test       eax,eax
00401E0A   je         00401E0E
00401E0C   call       eax
00401E0E   push       407024h
00401E13   push       407014h
00401E18   call       00401EEB
00401E1D   push       407010h
00401E22   push       407000h
00401E27   call       00401EEB
00401E2C   add        esp,10h
00401E2F   ret
```

When you step through the Foo::f() method at address 00401E03, you'll find that it returns the address 00401110, which is the address of the compiler-synthesized vcall thunk. This address is subsequently stored in the pointer-to-member function h allocated at 004078E4. A function invocation through pointer-to-member h takes only one machine instruction (e.g., main() performs two such invocations at addresses 004010F5 and 00401100[6]). The vcall thunk itself is very concise. It expects the address of the object (the this pointer) in the ecx register, which the thunk dereferences to find the corresponding virtual table. In the next instruction, the thunk simply jumps to the address pointed to by the appropriate slot in the virtual table (the second slot in this case). Overall, the generated code is beautifully simple and tight.

Exercise 6.4   Execute the test code example from Listing 6.3 and step through the code at assembly level. Subsequently remove the keyword virtual in line 6. Recompile and step through the code again. What difference do you see?

The main points to remember from this discussion are that (1) the C++ virtual mechanism works for pointer-to-*virtual*-member functions, which enables straightforward inheritance and refinement in the behavioral inheritance meta-pattern, and (2) the mechanism incurs some additional overhead for all state handlers declared virtual, regardless of whether they are actually overridden in the subclasses.

---

6. At the address 00401100, you can see the typical function epilog elimination. Because the second method call is the last instruction in main(), the compiler synthesized a jump rather than a call instruction.

6.2   Statechart Refinement Example in C

A C compiler doesn't arrange for polymorphic state handler behavior as a C++ compiler does. In C, you are responsible for constructing the polymorphic state handlers suitable for inheritance and refinement. Section A.2 in Appendix A describes techniques for implementing polymorphism in C as a set of idioms and pre-processor macros that I call "C+." This section uses "C+" techniques[7] to implement polymorphic state machines in C.

6.2.1   Preparing a "C+" State Machine for Polymorphism

As in the case of a C++ implementation, you start by creating a separate reactive base class, `Calc1`, that has behavior identical to the original Quantum Calculator `Calc` class but is polymorphic and applies the Singleton design pattern. As with any poly-morphism-ready "C+" class, `Calc1` needs a virtual table (v-table). This v-table must contain all state handlers, as well as other methods that you might want to invoke polymorphically.

```
SUBCLASS(Calc1, QHsm)
   . . .
   VTABLE(Calc1, QHsm)                          /* v-table for Calc1 extending QHsm */
      . . .
      QState (*operand2)(Calc1 *me, QEvent const *e);
      . . .
METHODS
   Calc1 *Calc1Ctor_(Calc1 *me);                        /* protected constructor */
   Calc1 *Calc1Instance(void);            /* static Singleton accessor method */
      . . .
   QSTATE Calc1_operand2(Calc1 *me, QEvent const *e);
      . . .
END_CLASS
```

Subsequently, you need to initialize the virtual table and then hook the virtual pointer (v-pointer) in the protected constructor `Calc1Ctor_()`.

```
BEGIN_VTABLE(Calc1, QHsm)                  /* initialize v-table of Calc1 class */
   . . .
   VMETHOD(Calc1, operand2) = Calc1_operand2;            /*bind implementation*/
   . . .
END_VTABLE

Calc1 *Calc1Ctor_(Calc1 *me) {
                                        /* construct the superclass (QHsm) */
```

---

7.   Although I use the strange name "C+," the code is plain, highly portable ANSI C, even though it often looks like C++.

```
    if (!QHsmCtor_(&me->super_, (QPseudoState)Calc1_initial)) {
        return 0;
    }
    VHOOK(Calc1);                   /* hook the v-pointer to the Calc1 v-table */
    return me;
}
```

Finally, you need to change all references to state handlers of the `Calc1` class to use dynamic rather than static binding. The following state handler for the `begin` state illustrates how you achieve this.

```
QSTATE Calc1_begin(Calc1 *me, QEvent const *e) {
    switch (e->sig) {
    case IDC_OPER:
        if (((CalcEvt *)e)->keyId == IDC_MINUS) {
            Q_TRAN(VPTR(Calc1, me)->negated1);          /*polymorphic transition*/
            return 0;
        }
        break;
    }
    return (QSTATE)VPTR(Calc1, me)->ready;           /*polymorphic superstate*/
}
```

This state handler demonstrates both ways of referencing state handlers: as targets of state transitions and as superstates. In both cases, you replace the direct reference to a state handler with an indirect reference through the virtual pointer VPTR(*class*, me)->*handler*. The "C+" VPTR() macro (see Appendix A) simply returns the correctly cast v-pointer, through which you can dynamically resolve the desired state handler (i.e., the handler that is characteristic for the given me pointer). This macro exactly emulates the behavior of the C++ vcall thunk but is slightly more efficient (at the expense of code space) because the equivalent of the thunk is synthesized in-line.

6.2.2   Inheriting and Refining the "C+" State Machine

After the groundwork of preparing the base class for polymorphism is in place, implementing inheritance and refinement is straightforward.

Listing 6.4   Derived and refined `Calc2` "C+" statechart

```
1 SUBCLASS(Calc2, Calc1)                      /* derive Calc2 from Calc1 */
2 VTABLE(Calc2, Calc1)                   /* Calc2 needs a separate v-table */
3 METHODS
4     Calc2 *Calc2Ctor_(Calc2 *me);              /* protected constructor */
5     QSTATE Calc2_operand2(Calc2 *me, QEvent const *e);
6 END_CLASS
```

```
 7
 8 BEGIN_VTABLE(Calc2, Calc1)                    /* initialize the Calc2 v-table */
 9     VMETHOD(Calc1, operand2) =                    /* bind the implementation */
10         (QSTATE (*)(Calc1*, QEvent const *))Calc2_operand2;
11 END_VTABLE
12
13 Calc2 *Calc2Ctor_(Calc2 *me) {
14     if (!Calc1Ctor_(&me->super_)) {              /* invoke superclass' ctor */
15         return 0;
16     }
17     VHOOK(Calc2);                 /* hook the v-pointer to the Calc2 v-table */
18     return me;
19 }
20
21 QSTATE Calc2_operand2(Calc2 *me, QEvent const *e) {
22     switch (e->sig) {
23     case IDC_PERCENT:
24         sscanf(me->super_.display_, "%lf", &me->super_.operand2_);
25         switch (me->super_.operator_) {
26         case IDC_PLUS:
27             me->super_.operand2_ = 1.0 + me->super_.operand2_/100.0;
28             me->super_.operator_ = IDC_MULT;
29             break;
30         case IDC_MINUS:
31             me->super_.operand2_ = 1.0 - me->super_.operand2_/100.0;
32             me->super_.operator_ = IDC_MULT;
33             break;
34         case IDC_MULT:                        /* intentionally fall through... */
35         case IDC_DIVIDE:
36             me->super_.operand2_ /= 100.0;                    /* x*y%, x/y% */
37             break;
38         default:
39             ASSERT(0);
40         }
41         Q_TRAN(VPTR(Calc1, me)->result);
42         return 0;                                       /* event handled */
43     }
44                                          /* let Calc1 handle other events */
45     return Calc1_operand2((Calc1 *)me, e);
46 }
```

The points of interest in Listing 6.4 include subclassing Calc1 (lines 1–6), initializing the virtual table (lines 8–11), and delegating unhandled events to the original Calc1 state handler (line 45). The derived Calc2 class defines its own virtual table (line 2) and a new implementation of the operand2 state handler (line 5). Subsequently, this implementation is bound to the method in the virtual table (lines 9–10), and the v-table is hooked in the constructor (line 17). The C implementation of Calc2_operand2() is essentially identical to the Calc2::operand2() C++

counterpart (refer to Listing 6.2). The only differences are in the polymorphic state transition (line 41) and the delegation of unhandled events (line 45). Please note that the delegation cannot be dynamic (an attempt to resolve the call via a v-pointer ends up in endless recursion) and is analogous to the C++ delegation that also uses a static, fully qualified delegation via a call to `Calc1::operand2()`.

Exercise 6.5   Find the C version of the VC++ project `qcalc2.dsp` on the accompanying CD-ROM and add an entry action to the `Calc2_opearator2()` state handler (e.g., the action could invoke the Win32 function `Beep()`). Rebuild the project and note that only the `calc2.c` module needs to be recompiled. Launch the application and verify that your entry action is indeed executed on entry to the `operator2` state.

6.3   Caveats

In most cases, the inheritance of state machines works just fine right out of the box, as demonstrated by the refined Quantum Calculator example. However, problems might arise when you start using inheritance in a more advanced way. This section explains some potential issues and workarounds.

6.3.1   Static versus Dynamic State Transitions

The techniques of inheritance and refinement (in both C++ and "C+") work well for Singletons [Gamma+ 95] — that is, with classes that allow only a single instance in a system, such as in the Quantum Calculator example. In a more general situation, however, you might want to have multiple instances of different subclasses of a given reactive base class. In this case, the optimized transition handling (see Chapter 4) inhibits the fully polymorphic adaptation of the baseline statechart.

For example, suppose you design a generic `Controller` reactive base class that defines a high-level behavior (e.g., a power-on self-test, fail-safe state, etc). Subsequently, you subclass and specialize the generic `Controller` as `ControllerA` and `ControllerB`. Finally, you instantiate a few of both `Controller` subclasses in your system. The problem is that the optimized static transition `QHsm::tranStat()` used inside the `Q_TRAN()` macro (Section 4.4.3 in Chapter 4) prevents the Controller base class statechart from dynamically adapting to potentially conflicting refinements introduced by `ControllerA` and `ControllerB`. The issue is that the optimization relies on calculating the transition chain only once and storing it in a static object (see Section 4.4.5 in Chapter 4). Obviously, this optimization defeats the flexibility needed for refinement via inheritance because you cannot store two (or more) different transition chains in one static variable.

The solution is to forego optimization and recalculate the transition chain dynamically (each time the transition fires) for every polymorphic transition requiring the extra flexibility (e.g., the transitions in the `Controller` base class). The `QHsm` class provides such a dynamic, unoptimized transition method — `QHsm::tran()` (`QHsmTran_()` in C) — which you use through the `Q_TRAN_DYN()` macro.

Exercise 6.6   Replace all occurrences of the `Q_TRAN()` macro with `Q_TRAN_DYN()` in the `Calc1` base class. Recompile and execute the refined `Calc2` application. Verify that it operates as before.

6.3.2   Multiple Inheritance

The C++ implementation of the behavioral inheritance meta-pattern is not compatible with multiple inheritance (MI). The sidebar "C++ Pointer-to-Member Functions and Multiple Inheritance" in Chapter 3 explains the reasons.

Note: Depending on the C++ compiler and the order of the multiple base classes in the declaration, MI might also work with the behavioral inheritance meta-pattern. The point is, the code is not portable.

It is possible to make the behavioral inheritance meta-pattern fully compatible with MI. One such solution[8] is to wrap the naked `QState` pointer-to-member function in a "functor" class, `CQState`. The most important facilities of the `CQState` functor are the redefined state handler signature `QState` and the function call `operator()`.

```
class QHsm {
   class CQState {                                    // CQState functor class
   public:
      typedef CQState (QHsm::*QState)(QEvent const *);
      CQState operator()(QHsm *hsm, QEvent const *e) {
         return hsm->callMemberFn(myPtMF, e, hsm);
      }
```

---

8.   I am grateful to Jeff Claar for contributing this solution. It is somewhat similar to the original GotW problem #57 posted and solved on Usenet [Sutter 01].

```
private:
    QState myPtMF;                  // encapsulated pointer-to-member function
};
    . . .
};
```

The `callMemberFn()` method that the functor invokes is declared as purely virtual in the QHsm base class and subsequently must be overridden in every subclass of QHsm. The following macro automates the definition of this method in each concrete subclass.

```
#define Q_DEFINE_CALL_MEMBER_FN(class_) \
    virtual CQState callMemberFn(CQState::QState fn, \
                                 QEvent const *e, QHsm *hsm)\
    {\
        class_ *c = static_cast<class_*>(hsm); \
        return (c->*fn)(e); \
    }
```

The body of `callMemberFn()` performs all the necessary pointer casting to invoke the `fn` state handler on behalf of a correctly typed QHsm subclass. The functor objects are only temporary objects generated by the `return` statement of `callMemberFn()`. The additional overhead introduced by this technique is thus limited to the polymorphic invocation of `callMemberFn()` and the pointer manipulation inside this method. The function call operator of the functor, on the other hand, should be in-lined and thus optimized to nothing.

Exercise 6.7 Find the MI-compatible version of the extended Quantum Calculator code and add a second base class to the refined `Calc2` class. Note that every state machine class invokes `Q_DEFINE_CALL_MEMBER_FN()` and passes its class name to the macro. Verify that the application compiles and executes correctly.

6.3.3 Heuristics for Inheriting and Refining Statecharts

You can use state machine inheritance for a variety of purposes, including reusing implementations, constructing abstract state machines, organizing code, and fostering consistent behavior (a consistent look and feel). The enhancement of the Quantum Calculator demonstrates a little of all these benefits. It obviously illustrates heavy implementation reuse, but it also takes advantage of abstraction. Inheritance brings better code organization to the calculator "product line" because the different versions of the product (the simple and enhanced calculators) are closely related. The resulting code is much smaller than it would be without inheritance, and its maintenance is easier (e.g., fixing a bug in the simple version of the product fixes it automatically in the more advanced version). Finally, inheritance enforces a consistent look and feel across the product line because any changes propagate automatically from base classes to the offspring (e.g., from `Calc1` to `Calc2`).

However, to reap the benefits of inheritance, class taxonomies need to comply with rules that have been proven by experience, such as the LSP. Generally, compliance with the LSP is much harder to achieve in hierarchies of reactive classes than in classes without state behavior. The following sections give you some ideas of how to refine statecharts, starting with the most strict (and safe) category of refinements through progressively more liberal (and more dangerous) ones. You should strive to stay with the most strict category that accomplishes your goals. Of course, this discussion pertains only to single inheritance (see Section 6.3.2).

Template Method

The simplest — and safest — refinement of a reactive class is not to change statechart topology at all. However, you can still significantly change the behavior of the subclasses by overriding actions and guards that the base class defines as virtual methods. In this case, the reactive base class implements the invariant parts of the behavior (the statechart topology) and leaves it up to subclasses to implement actions and guards that can vary. This is an example of the widely used Template Method design pattern [Gamma+ 95]. In fact, reactive classes make very good natural Template Methods.

The base class has a fine granularity of control over the statechart elements it allows the subclasses to change. The base class can use C++ access control to restrict access to certain methods, or it can refuse to declare certain actions and guards `virtual`, which also effectively prohibits subclasses from overriding them.

The enhanced Quantum Calculator code provides an example of this technique. For example, the actions `clear()`, `insert()`, `negate()`, and `eval()` are all declared `virtual` in the `Calc1` base class and can therefore be overridden by the subclasses.

The technique is even more explicit in the C implementation because the `Calc1` base class uses explicit dynamic binding to invoke the polymorphic actions. The following state handler for the `result` state illustrates the polymorphically invoked protected method `eval_`. In contrast, `Calc1DispState()` is resolved statically because there's no intention to override it.

```
QState Calc1_result(Calc1 *me, QEvent const *e) {
    switch (e->sig) {
    case Q_ENTRY_SIG:
        Calc1DispState(me, "result");
        VCALL(Calc1, eval_, me)END_CALL;
        return 0;
    }
    return (QState)VPTR(Calc1, me)->ready;
}
```

Subtyping

The refinement policy for subtyping restricts statechart modifications to only those that preserve pre- and postconditions of the base class for all events that it accepts, which guarantees the substitutability of subclasses for the superclass.

Because both states and transitions realize the pre- and postconditions for events in a state machine, this policy prohibits removing states and transitions. You can freely add new states and transitions, but you can refine existing states and existing transitions, guards, and actions only as follows [OMG 01].

- You can refine a state by adding new outgoing transitions as well as new sub-states.

- You can refine an outgoing transition to target a direct or transitive substate of the original target state (i.e., the transition can penetrate deeper into the state hierarchy, but it still has to enter the original target state). This refinement guarantees the postcondition established by entry to the original target state.

- You can refine a guard only by strengthening the condition, which weakens any preconditions necessary for the transition.

- You can refine an action sequence by prepending or appending new actions, but you should not alter the original action sequence.

Refinement of the Quantum Calculator falls into the subtyping category. The refined `operand2` state acquired a new outgoing transition triggered by the PER-CENT signal.

Strict Inheritance

Strict inheritance still requires that you only add new features or override existing features; you cannot delete any existing elements. You can alter existing statechart elements as follows.

- You can alter a transition to target a different state that is not necessarily related (via behavioral inheritance) to the original target state. However, you cannot change the source of the transition because this would correspond to removing an outgoing transition from the original source state.
- You cannot change the superstate of any state (reparenting).
- You can change a guard to check a different condition that is not necessarily related to the original.
- You can change an action sequence by dropping some of the original actions, replacing them with others, or prepending or appending new actions. However, you should not alter the sequence of the original actions that remain after the refinement.

Strict inheritance still preserves limited substitutability of subclasses for the superclass. Although the refined behavior is no longer fully compatible, it is often good enough when your objective is reuse of the implementation rather than behavioral compatibility.

General Refinement

In most general cases, you may freely change states, transitions, guards, and actions. You also may remove (or hide) features, which is sometimes called reverse inheritance. However, this freedom will cost you compliance with the LSP.

The behavioral inheritance meta-pattern allows all kinds of statechart modifications, including most general refinements and the removal of features. For example, you can achieve the effect of removing a state by redirecting all incoming transitions away from it and by reparenting all its direct substates. Removing a state transition is even easier. In the refined state handler, you simply return zero for the unwanted transition, which means that the signal is handled but no transition occurs.

6.4 Summary

The behavioral inheritance meta-pattern works correctly under traditional class inheritance, which enables easy reuse and refinement of entire state models. The form of reuse achievable in reactive classes is much higher than is available for nonreactive classes because you inherit behavior in addition to inheriting structure.

The challenge in inheriting state machines is in preserving the numerous associations among states in the inherited and refined state machine topology.

In C++, you enable inheritance of a state machine simply by declaring all its state handlers `virtual`. Your C++ compiler takes care of the correct polymorphic behavior of the whole statechart topology because the underlying pointer-to-*virtual*-member functions act polymorphically. However, in the current C++ implementation, the behavioral inheritance meta-pattern is incompatible with multiple inheritance.

In C, you must explicitly arrange for polymorphism by declaring and initializing the virtual table for the reactive class and by dynamically resolving the reference to each state handler (through the virtual pointer). In this chapter, I demonstrated how to achieve this using "C+" — an OO extension to C (see Appendix A).

In rare occasions, when you anticipate instantiation of different reactive subclasses of a given base class in the same system, you need to be careful to use the unoptimized dynamic transition `Q_TRAN_DYN()` macro in the shared statechart of the base class instead of the optimized `Q_TRAN()` macro. In this case, the optimization built into the `Q_TRAN()` macro inhibits the extra flexibility you need in the shared state machine.

To achieve compliance with the LSP, you should restrict refinements you apply to state machines. In general, you always can add new elements, but you should avoid removing any existing states and transitions.

From a more abstract point of view, the unprecedented degree of reuse achievable by inheriting entire state models results from the unification of Quantum Programming (behavioral inheritance) with traditional object-oriented programming (class inheritance).

PART II

QUANTUM FRAMEWORK

In Part I, I showed you how to implement and use the powerful concept of the hierarchical state machine by instantiating the behavioral inheritance meta-pattern. This meta-pattern intentionally provided only the passive event processor, which must be driven externally to actually process events. In particular, the meta-pattern did not include the standard elements traditionally associated with state machines, such as an event queue, an event dispatcher, an execution context (thread), or timing services. This separation of concerns occurs for at least two reasons. First, unlike the generic event processor, the other elements necessary to execute a state machine depend heavily on the application domain and operating system support. Second, in many cases, these elements are already available. For example, GUI systems such as Microsoft Windows offer a complete event-driven environment for executing passive state machines.

However, the majority of reactive systems, most notably embedded real-time systems, do not provide such an execution infrastructure. In Part II of this book, I describe the Quantum Framework — an event-driven architecture for executing state machines tailored specifically for embedded real-time systems. A real-time framework similar to the Quantum Framework is at the heart of virtually every commercial design-automation tool capable of generating real-time code. In fact, most of these real-time frameworks are based on the model of concurrent state machines that communicate with each other by sending and receiving events. In Part II, I conclude

187

the mission of this book, which is to present a complete solution for programming real-time systems with UML statecharts. The Quantum Framework combined with a preemptive real-time operating system will give you the functional equivalent of a code-synthesizing tool for developing real-time applications.

Chapter 7

Introducing the Quantum Framework

Today I am more convinced than ever.
Conceptual integrity is central to product quality.
— Frederick P. Brooks, Jr.

State machines cannot operate in a vacuum. Apart from the event processor (supplied by the behavioral inheritance meta-pattern), the execution environment for a state machine must provide, at a minimum, the execution context (thread) and the event queuing, event dispatching, and timing services. These elements strongly depend on application domain and operating system support. However, within a given domain, they change little from system to system, and their sufficiently robust representations can be reused in many applications, rather than being developed from scratch each time. For example, you could reuse an event queue or a timeout event generator across many projects. However, you can do even better than merely reuse specific elements as building blocks — you can reuse the whole infrastructure surrounding state machines.

In this chapter, I introduce such a reusable infrastructure for the specific domain of embedded real-time systems. This infrastructure is an example of an *application framework* that I call the *Quantum Framework* (QF). The QF, like any application framework, is a set of cooperating classes that makes up a reusable design for a specific problem domain (embedded real-time systems in this case). The QF captures the overall architecture for executing concurrent state machines in the embedded real-time environment.

Reuse on this level leads to inversion of control between your application and the infrastructure on which it is based. When you use a class library (such as the behavioral inheritance meta-pattern), you write the main body of the application and call the code you want to reuse (e.g., the QHsm::dispatch() method on behalf of a particular state machine object). When you use a framework (such as the QF), you reuse the main body and write the code *it* calls.

You can view a framework as an application skeleton that you need to flesh out to create a complete application. You achieve this by attaching your code to the framework's specifically designed "extension points." You typically customize the framework's behavior by extending classes defined inside the framework. In addition, virtually every framework also incorporates a compatible class library that you can use as a toolkit of components. In this sense, the behavioral inheritance meta-pattern (a toolkit of elements for constructing HSMs) is part of the QF.

The main element of decomposition in the QF is an *active object*. An active object (also known as an *actor*) is a state machine object that executes concurrently with other active objects and communicates with them by sending and receiving events. This concept is not new (see the sidebar "From Actors to Active Objects"). Today, virtually every CASE tool that enables code synthesis for embedded real-time systems incorporates a variant of an actor-based framework. Real-time object-oriented modeling (ROOM) calls such a framework the "ROOM virtual machine" [Selic+ 94]. A visualSTATE tool from IAR Systems calls it a "visualSTATE engine" [IAR 00]. A UML-compliant design automation tool from I-Logix, Rhapsody, calls it an Object Execution Framework (OXF) [Douglass 99].

The QF is a minimal implementation of an active object–based framework with goals similar to the ROOM virtual machine or Rhapsody's OXF. However, unlike the frameworks buried inside CASE tools, the QF is not concerned with facilities for animation or instrumentation of state machines and is not biased toward mechanical code generation. Furthermore, it does not support such advanced, but expensive, features as recursive decomposition of active objects, synchronous communications, multiple active object interfaces, or protocols that restrict certain message types from leaving and entering an active object. The QF implements only the most basic active object–based computing model limited to asynchronous event exchange among active objects in a single level of decomposition.

From Actors to Active Objects

The concept of autonomous software objects communicating by message passing dates back to the late 1970s, when Carl Hewitt and colleagues [Hewitt 73] developed the notion of an *actor*. In the 1980s, actors were all the rage within the distributed artificial intelligence community, much as agents are today. In the 1990s, methodologies like ROOM [Selic+ 94], adapted actors for real-time computing. More recently, the UML specification has introduced the concept of *active object* that is essentially synonymous with the notion of an actor [OMG 01]. Active objects in the UML specification are the roots of threads of control in multitasking systems and engage one another asynchronously via events. The UML specification further proposes the UML variant of statecharts, with which to model the behavior of event-driven active objects.

In Quantum Programming (QP), I will use the UML term "active object," rather than the more compact "actor," to avoid confusion with the other meaning of the term "actor" that the UML specification uses in the context of use cases.

The most important characteristic of an active object is its opaque *encapsulation shell*, which strictly separates the internal structure of an active object from the external environment. The only objects capable of penetrating this shell, both from the outside and from the inside, are event instances. This communication model requires specifically designed intermediate objects (event instances) to carry out all interactions.

7.1   Conventional Approach to Multithreading

Why introduce such severe restrictions on active object communications instead of simply calling methods or communicating through shared variables? The short answer is that the active object–based computing model better addresses the problems associated with concurrency that are found in any multithreading system. To understand why, consider the problems resulting from a conventional approach to multithreading.

7.1.1   Dining Philosophers — Conventional Approach

The classic "dining philosophers" problem posed by Edsger Dijkstra [Dijkstra 65, 71] illustrates the basic challenges of multithreading. As shown in Figure 7.1, five philosophers are gathered around a table with a big plate of spaghetti in the middle. The spaghetti is so slippery that a philosopher needs two forks to eat it. Between each philosopher is a fork. The life of a philosopher consists of alternate periods of thinking and eating. When a philosopher wants to eat, he tries to acquire forks. If successful in acquiring two forks, he eats for a while, then puts down the forks and continues to think. (An alternative oriental version replaces spaghetti with rice and forks with chopsticks.) The key question is: Can you write a program for each philosopher that never gets stuck?

Although mostly academic, the problem is motivated by the practical issue of how to assign resources to processes that need the resources to do their jobs; in other words, how do you manage *resource allocation*. The idea is that a finite set of threads is sharing a finite set of resources, and each resource can be used by only one thread at a time.

Figure 7.1   Dining philosophers

Dining philosophers provide an interesting exercise in controlling what would otherwise be an anarchic group of philosophers all trying to eat at once. The fundamental problem is *synchronizing* access to the forks.

In the simplest (and most naïve) solution, the philosopher threads might synchronize access to the forks using shared memory. To acquire a fork, a philosopher would need to test the corresponding shared flag and proceed only if the flag is cleared. After acquiring the fork, the philosopher would immediately set the corresponding flag to indicate that the fork is in use. However, this solution has a fundamental flaw. If philosopher A preempts philosopher B just after philosopher B acquires a fork but before the flag has been set, then philosopher A could incorrectly acquire the fork that philosopher B already has (the corresponding flag is still cleared). This situation is called a *race condition*. It occurs whenever one thread gets ahead of another in accessing shared data that is changing.

Clearly, the philosopher threads need some method to protect the shared flags, such that access to the flags is mutually exclusive, meaning only one philosopher thread at a time can test and potentially set a shared flag. There are many methods of obtaining exclusive access to shared resources, such as disabling interrupts, performing indivisible test-and-set operations, disabling task switching, and locking resources with semaphores (see Sidebar "Dijkstra's Semaphores"). The solution based on semaphores is, in this case, the most appealing because it simultaneously addresses the problems of mutual exclusion and blocking the philosopher threads if forks are unavailable. Listing 7.1 shows a simple semaphore-based implementation.

Dijkstra's Semaphores

In 1965, Edsger Dijkstra invented semaphores as a protocol mechanism for synchronizing concurrent threads [Dijkstra 65]. Dijkstra defined two primitive operations on semaphores: P() (from Dutch "proberen"—test) and V() (from Dutch "verhogen"—increment). To obtain a semaphore a thread invoks the P() operation on the semaphore, which returns only if the semaphore is available; otherwise the calling thread blocks and waits for the semaphore. The V() operation releases the lock and frees the semaphore to other threads.

Typically, mutlitasking operating systems provide an assortment of semaphores optimized for different functions. The classical counting semaphore maintains the lock counter and is optimized for guarding multiple instances of a resource. A special case of counting semaphore is the binary semaphore, which can be locked by only one thread at a time. A mutex semaphore (or simply mutex) is optimized for problems inherent in mutual exclusion.

Listing 7.1   Simple (and incorrect) solution to the dining philosophers problem implemented with Win32 API. The explicit fork flags are superfluous in this solution because they are replaced by the internal counters of the mutexes

```
1 enum { N = 5};                              // number of dining philosophers
2 static HANDLE fork[N];                      // model forks as mutex semaphores
3
4 void think(long n) {. . . }                 // called when philosopher n thinks
5 void eat(long n) { . . . }                  // called when philosopher n eats
6
7 long WINAPI philosopher(long n) {                    // task for philosopher n
8    for (;;) {                                        // philosopher task runs forever
9       think(n);                             // first the philosopher thinks for a while
10                          // after thinking the philosopher becomes hungry...
11       WaitForSingleObject(fork[(n+1)%N], INFINITE);        // get left fork
12       WaitForSingleObject(fork[n], INFINITE);              // get right fork
13       eat(n);                              // got both forks, can eat for a while
14       ReleaseMutex(fork[(n+1)%N]);                         // release left fork
15       ReleaseMutex(fork[n]);                              // release right fork
16    }
17    return 0;
18 }
```

The solution from Listing 7.1 still has a major flaw. Your program might run for a few milliseconds or for a year (just as the first naïve solution did), but at any moment, it can freeze with all philosophers holding their left fork (Listing 7.1, line 12). If this happens, nobody gets to eat — ever. This condition of indefinite circular blocking on resources is called *deadlock*.

Exercise 7.1   Execute the dining philosophers example from Listing 7.1. Name at least three factors that affect the probability of a deadlock. Modify the code to increase this probability. After the system (dead)locks, use the debugger to inspect the state of the forks and the philosopher threads.

Once you realize the possibility of a deadlock (which generally is not trivial), be careful how you attempt to prevent it. For example, a philosopher can pick up the left fork; then if the right fork isn't available for a given time, put the left fork down, wait, and try again (this is a big problem if all philosophers wait the same amount of time — you get the same failure mode as before, but repeated). Even if each philosopher waits a random time, an unlucky philosopher could starve (never get to eat). *Starvation* is only one extreme example of the more general problem of nondeterminism because it is virtually impossible to know in advance the maximum time a philosopher might spend waiting for forks (or how long a philosopher thread is preempted in a preemptive multitasking system).

Any attempt to prevent race conditions, deadlock, and starvation can cause other, more subtle, problems associated with *fairness* and suboptimal system utilization. For example, to avoid starvation, you might require that all philosophers acquire a semaphore before picking up a fork. This requirement guarantees that no philosopher starves, but limits parallelism dramatically (poor system utilization). It is also difficult to prove that any given solution is fair and does not favor some philosophers at the expense of others.

The main lesson of dining philosophers is that multithreaded programming is much harder than sequential programming, especially if you use a conventional approach to multithreading. The conventional design requires a deep understanding of the time domain and operating system mechanisms for interthread synchronization and communication, such as various kinds of semaphores, monitors, critical sections, condition variables, signals, message queues, mailboxes, and so on. Unfortunately, programmers typically vastly underestimate the skills needed to program with operating system primitives and therefore underestimate the true costs of their use. The truth is that only a relatively limited group of systems programmers is familiar with and comfortable using these mechanisms properly. The majority of us are likely to introduce subtle bugs that are notoriously hard to reproduce, isolate, and fix.

Therac-25 Fatal Incident

On Friday, April 11, 1986, a male patient was scheduled to receive an electron beam treatment from the Therac-25 radiation therapy machine, one of the first fully computer-controlled medical accelerators, at the East Texas Cancer Center. Within a few seconds after the operator turned on the beam, the machine shut down, making a loud noise. The display showed the cryptic message MALFUNCTION 54. The operator rushed into the treatment room, hearing her patient moan for help. The patient began to remove the tape that had held his head in position and said something was wrong. She asked him what he felt, and he replied, "fire" on the side of his face. She immediately went to the hospital physicist and told him that *another* patient appeared to have been burned. Asked by the physicist to describe what had happened, the patient explained that something had hit him on the side of the face, he saw a flash of light, and he heard a sizzling sound reminiscent of frying eggs. He was very agitated and asked, "What happened to me, what happened to me?"

This patient died from the overdose on May 1, 1986, three weeks after the accident. He had disorientation, which progressed to coma, fever to 104°F, and neurological damage. An autopsy showed an acute high-dose radiation injury to the right temporal lobe of the brain and the brain stem [Leveson+ 93].

7.1.2   Therac-25 Story

The problems associated with multithreading are not just academic. Perhaps the most publicized real-life example of the "free threading" approach to concurrent event-driven software is the Therac-25 story. Between June 1985 and January 1987, a computer-controlled radiation therapy machine called the Therac-25 massively overdosed six people. These accidents have been described as the worst in the 35-year history of medical accelerators [Leveson 95]. To attribute software failure as the single cause of the accidents is a serious mistake and an oversimplification. However, the Therac-25 story provides an example of an inherently unsafe and practically unfixable software design that resulted mostly from the (still widely applied) free threading approach to concurrency.

The detailed analysis[1] revealed that the ultimate root causes of all the accidents were various *race conditions* within the Therac-25 software. For example, one such race condition occurred between the processes of setting up the bending magnets in preparation for treatment and accepting treatment data from the console. If a skillful operator could enter all the required data within about eight seconds (the time needed to set up the magnets), then occasionally the machine could end up in an

---

1.   Nancy Leveson performed such an analysis in *Safeware: System Safety and Computers* [Levenson 95].

inconsistent configuration (partially set for X-ray treatment and partially set for electron treatment). These exact conditions occurred on April 11, 1986, when the
machine killed a patient (see the sidebar "Therac-25 Fatal Incident").

Although the Therac-25 software was developed almost three decades ago[2] and
was written in PDP-11 assembly language, it bears many similarities to the Visual
Basic Calculator example discussed in Chapter 1. Both applications are similar, in
that they do not maintain a crisp notion of mode of operation but, rather, represent
modes of operation as a multitude of variables and flags. These variables and flags
are set, cleared, and tested in complex expressions scattered throughout the code so
that it is virtually impossible to determine the mode of the system at any given time.
As demonstrated by the Visual Basic Calculator, this approach leads to subtle bugs in
an application of even a few hundred lines of code. The Therac-25 case, however,
shows that, when additionally *compounded* with concurrency issues, the ad hoc
approach leads to disastrous, virtually uncorrectable designs. For example, in an
attempt to fix the Therac-25 race condition described earlier, the manufacturer
(Atomic Energy of Canada Limited) introduced another shared variable controlled
by the keyboard handler task that indicated whether the cursor was positioned on
the command line. If this variable was set, then the prescription entry was considered
still in progress and the value of the Tphase state variable was left unchanged. The
following items point out some inherently nasty characteristics of such ad hoc solutions.

- Any individual inconsistency in configuration seems to be fixable by introducing
  yet another mode-related (extended state) variable.

- Every new extended state variable introduces more opportunities for inconsistencies in the configuration of the system. Additionally, if the variable is shared
  among different threads (or interrupts), it can introduce new race conditions.

- Every such change perpetuates the bad design further[3] and makes it exponentially
  more difficult (expensive) to extend and fix, although there is never a clear indication when the code becomes unfixable (prohibitively expensive to fix).

- It is practically impossible to know when all inconsistent configurations and race
  conditions are removed. In fact, most of the time during computations, the configuration is inconsistent, but you generally won't know whether it happens during
  the time windows open for race conditions.

- No amount of testing can detect all inconsistencies and timing windows for race
  conditions.

---

2. The Therac-25 software has been reused from earlier versions of the Therac machine.
3. This process is otherwise known as architectural decay.

- Any change in the system can affect the timing and practically invalidate most of the testing.

You might think that the Therac-25 story, albeit interesting, is no longer relevant to contemporary software practices. This has not been my experience. Unfortunately, the architectural decay mechanisms just recounted still apply today, almost exactly as they did three decades ago. The modes of architectural decay haven't changed much because they are characteristics of the still widely practiced bottom-up approach to designing reactive systems mixed with the conventional approach to concurrency.

7.2   Computing Model of the QF

For the reasons just listed and others, operating systems designers have been gravitating toward microkernel architectures. A microkernel operating system (e.g., ChorusOS[4] or QNX Neutrino[5]) is built on top of a small nucleus by adding lightweight concurrent components that communicate among themselves and their application-level clients through message passing.

The message-passing (event exchange) paradigm applied to the realm of objects naturally yields the notion of active objects: concurrently executing, event-driven objects endowed with a light-weight thread of control. In the QF computing model, an application consists of a set of functionally specialized active objects (each embedding a statechart) that collectively deliver the intended functionality. Active objects do not share any data, and the only means of communication among them is the exchange of event instances.

7.2.1   Active Object–Based Multithreading

Active object–based multithreading can achieve the following benefits.

- *Atomic event processing.* Active objects process one event at a time using RTC semantics. As discussed in Chapter 2, discrete and indivisible RTC steps inherently preclude internal concurrency issues. Although it is certainly true that operating system mechanisms, such as critical sections and message queues, serve in the construction of an active object–based framework, application programmers do not need to use these often-troublesome mechanisms directly. Programmers can implement the internal structure of an active object without concern for multithreading. For example, application programmers don't need to know how to use a semaphore or even know what it is. Still, as long as active objects are independent (do not share any data or resources), an active object–based system can

---

4.   To learn more about ChorusOS you can visit the Web site: `http://www.sun.com/software/chorusos`
5.   To learn more about QNX Neutrino microkernel architecture you can visit the Web site:
      `http://www.qnx.com/literature/nto_sysarch/kernel3.html`

reap all the benefits of multithreading. Active objects, executing in separate threads of control, can freely preempt each other, thereby achieving good responsiveness and optimal use of the CPU.

- *Asynchronous event exchange.* An active object can view all event exchanges with its peers as occurring asynchronously. A target active object automatically queues the incoming events when it is busy, without involving the application programmer. Avoiding deadlocks in this way leads to "frictionless" execution with minimal blocking. Blocking can still occur, for example, in active objects that encapsulate I/O devices, but overall, an active object–based system is much more deterministic than an equivalent free-threaded system.

- *Scalability.* New active objects can be added with a minimal effect on other active objects because they are loosely coupled, in contrast to free threading, in which any change can cause dramatic ripple effects.

- *Observability, controllability, and testability.* A running application built of active objects is a highly structured affair. You can gain insight into the system by monitoring event exchanges and active object states and their event queues, which all are under the control of an active object–based framework (such as the QF). From these observations, you easily can produce sequence diagrams and execution traces for individual active objects. Finally, an active object is a natural entity for unit testing, which you can perform easily by injecting events into the active object and observing its state machine.

- *"Thin wire" style of communication.* Because active objects do not share data and communicate only through event instances, they do not need to execute in the same address space. This uniquely qualifies the active object–based computing model for the construction of highly parallel multiprocessor applications, including distributed systems that communicate via networks.

- *Encapsulation of legacy systems.* Active objects lend themselves well to encapsulation of legacy subsystems by providing an opaque shell around them.[6] Because the internal structure of an active object doesn't need to be concerned with concurrency issues, even subsystems designed for single threading can be encapsulated. In many cases, an "actorized" subsystem can be turned from a heavyweight process into a lightweight thread, or from a passive into an active subsystem. For example, an active object encapsulating an I/O device might actively source the incoming data packets in the form of events. Such an active I/O subsystem is much easier to use than a blocking I/O.

---

6. Active objects are ideal Facades (see the Facade design pattern in Gamma and colleagues [Gamma+ 95].)

The benefits of active object–based computing materialize only in correctly designed (loosely coupled) active object systems. Achieving this kind of design is not always easy and occasionally introduces complications (e.g., repetition of information). Moreover, active object–based systems have their own pitfalls — for example, problems caused by overflowing event queues. However, these concerns are relatively easy to resolve and the resulting active object–based systems are much safer, come together more rapidly, and are easier to maintain than alternative designs based on free threading.

7.2.2 Quantum Analogy

The model of interaction based on intermediate communication artifacts (events) is neither new nor specific to software. For example, modern quantum field theory first formulated in the 1930s postulates such a mechanism for all fundamental interactions in nature (see the sidebar "Particle Interaction in Quantum Field Theory"). With the introduction of the active object–based computing model, software engineering seems to follow exactly the developments that occurred in physics three quarters of a century earlier.

In classical physics, which can be compared to traditional OOP, particles interact via continuous fields. For example, according to Newton's law of universal gravitation, every massive object of mass M is surrounded by a continuous force field $f(m, r)$. Any other object of mass m and relative distance r with respect to the object M experiences the force given by $f(m, r) = GMm/r^2$. This interaction model corresponds in programming to direct-method invocation: objects interact by invoking methods such as the $f(m, r)$ "method."

Figure 7.2 **(a) Electron juggling a virtual photon;**
(b) electrons repel by exchanging a virtual photon

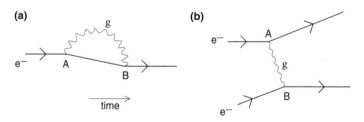

In contrast, all interactions result from particle exchange in quantum field theory. Nature seems to have "invented" specific objects (intermediate vector bosons[7]),

7. Intermediate vector bosons include photons mediating electromagnetic interactions, gluons mediating strong interactions, and bosons W and Z mediating weak interactions.

Particle Interaction in Quantum Field Theory

In Maxwell's theory of electromagnetism, charged particles such as electrons interact through their electromagnetic fields. However, for many years, it was difficult to conceive of how such an action between charges at a distance could come about; that is, how can charged particles interact without some tangible connection? In quantum field theory, such a tangible connection exists: *all the forces of nature are a result of particle exchange*. First, consider the event taking place at point A in Figure 7.2a. An electron emits a photon (the quantum of the electromagnetic field) and, as a result, recoils in order to conserve momentum. It is clearly impossible to conserve energy as well, so the emitted photon is definitely not a real photon. It is a photon with not quite the right energy; physicists call it a "virtual" photon. An electron can nevertheless emit such a photon as long as it is sufficiently quickly reabsorbed. Because of the uncertainty inherent in quantum mechanics, the photon can live for time $\Delta t \leq (\hbar/\Delta E)$, where ΔE is a "borrowed" or missing energy. However, suppose that instead of being reabsorbed by the same electron (as in point B of Figure 7.2a), the photon is absorbed by another electron (as in Figure 7.2b). The latter electron recoils in the act of absorbing the virtual photon at point B. The net result is a repulsive force between the two electrons. In quantum field theory, such exchanges are responsible for Coulomb repulsion of like charges [Halzen+ 84].

The exchanged virtual photons are, in other respects, different from freely propagating real photons encountered in, for example, radio transmission. Virtual photons cannot exist without the charges that emit or absorb them. They can only travel a distance allowed by the uncertainty principle, $c\Delta t$, where c is the velocity of light.

Physicists represent the interactions of quantum particles by Feynman diagrams, like the one shown in Figure 7.2. Feynman diagrams correspond directly to sequence diagrams in software.

whose primary function it is to mediate interactions. The mediating particles are special (quantum theory calls them *virtual*), in that they cannot exist without the interacting objects. In fact, they exist only briefly and disappear as soon as interaction takes place. This more fundamental and accurate model of interaction corresponds to active object–based computing.

The quantum mechanical model immediately explains why interactions can propagate, at most, at the speed of light, whereas the classical interpretation leads to incorrect instantaneous interactions. Incorporating signal propagation delays in the software model becomes increasingly important. With skyrocketing clock speeds in modern electronic devices, it becomes more and more difficult to hide signal latencies from the software. Through the quantum analogy, QP proposes to expose these latencies to programmers, instead of hiding them, as the conventional approach to concurrency does.

7.2.3 Publish–Subscribe Event Delivery

The active object–based computing model encourages breaking up applications into sets of functionally specialized active objects that communicate through asynchronous event exchanges. The central design decision that makes or breaks any active object–based framework is the choice of the mechanism for passing event instances from producers to consumers.

The simplest mechanism lets active objects send events to each other directly. This method requires minimal participation from the framework. However, it requires that active objects intimately "know" each other. The "knowledge" that a sender object needs to communicate is more than merely having a pointer or a reference to a peer object — the sender must also know the kind of events the particular peer might be interested in.[8] This intimate knowledge, distributed among all participating active objects, makes the system difficult to modify and extend. For example, it might be difficult to add new active objects because existing active objects won't know about the newcomers and won't send them events.

To find a better communication mechanism, you could turn to the quantum analogy and investigate how nature has solved this problem. Indeed, quantum field theory reveals a different model of interaction among elementary particles. In the quantum picture, an electron, such as that in Figure 7.2a, constantly juggles virtual photons, regardless of the presence of other particles in the vicinity.[9] However, just being close to the electron does not guarantee that other particles will interact with it. For example, a neutrino can be very close to an electron yet they might not interact because the neutrino is not "tuned" to photons (cannot absorb them). The neutrino is "interested" in other events, such as the emission of virtual bosons W or Z, which the electron also emits, but much less frequently.

The quantum model of interaction that the QF adopts consists of two elements: (1) every elementary particle constantly "publishes" characteristic virtual quanta, and (2) every particle "subscribes" to only a subset of virtual quanta published by other particles. In other words, this is the well-known *publish–subscribe* interaction model. The consequences of this model are as follows.

- Producers and consumers of events don't need to know each other (loose coupling).

- The types of events must be publicly known and must have the same semantics for all parties.

---

8. An alternative is to blindly send every event to all active objects, which is wasteful and as inefficient as unsolicited advertisement (junk mail).

9. This idea is central to all high-energy physics experiments. The experiments probe the "true nature" of elementary particles because they can reveal only those behaviors that happen spontaneously, regardless of whether particles are observed or not. The objective of every experiment is to "catch" a particle doing something interesting, but an experiment cannot induce any particular behavior that does not already exist.

- A mediator is required to accept published events and to deliver them to interested subscribers.

- Many-to-many interactions (object-to-object) are replaced with one-to-many (object-to-mediator) interactions.

The QF plays the central role of the mediator (the quantum vacuum). Upon initialization (e.g., in the initial transition), active objects subscribe to different event types by the QF. Subsequently, they interact only with the QF by publishing event instances, which the QF delivers to all subscribers. Architecturally, the QF combines two design patterns. The QF itself is a Mediator, which mediates events to active objects that act as Observers [Gamma+ 95].

7.2.4   General Structure

The high-level structure of the QF (shown in Figure 7.3) is typical for any active object–based framework. The design is layered with a real-time operating system (RTOS)[10] that provides a foundation for multithreading and basic services like event queues and memory pools. Based on these services, the QF supplies the QActive base class to derive concrete active objects. QActive inherits from QHsm, which means that active objects instantiate the behavioral inheritance meta-pattern. Additionally, QActive gives active objects a thread of execution and an event queue. An application built from the QF extends the framework by subclassing QActive and QEvent. The application uses QF communication and timing services through the QF API; however, the application typically should not need to access the RTOS API directly.

7.2.5   Dining Philosophers Revisited

Section 7.1.1 presented the conventional approach to the dining philosophers problem (DPP). In this section, I show you a design based on active objects and the QF. The purpose of this discussion is to walk you quickly through the main points without slowing you down with the full-blown details. In Chapter 10, I will come back to this example for a closer look at specific QF features and concrete coding techniques.

Active object–based programming requires a paradigm shift from the conventional approach to multithreading. Whereas in the conventional approach you mostly think about shared resources and various synchronization mechanisms, in the active object–based approach, you think about partitioning the problem into active objects and about exchanging events among these objects. Your goal is to break up the problem in a way that requires minimal communication. The generic design

---

10. For simpler designs, the QF can operate without an RTOS (effectively replacing it). See the discussion in Section 7.3.2 and a concrete implementation in Chapter 9.

Figure 7.3   **UML package diagram illustrating relationships among the RTOS, the QF, and the QF application**

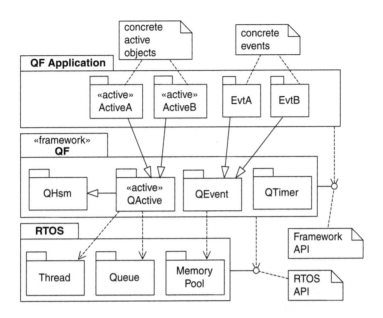

strategy for handling shared resources is to encapsulate them inside a dedicated active object and to let *that object* manage the shared resources for the rest of the system (i.e., instead of sharing the resources directly, the rest of the application shares the dedicated active object).

When you apply this strategy to the DPP (Figure 7.1), you will naturally arrive at a dedicated active object to manage the forks (call it Table for this example). The Table active object is responsible for coordinating Philosopher active objects to resolve contentions over the forks. It's also up to the Table active object to implement it fairly (or unfairly if you choose). A Philosopher active object needs to communicate two things to Table: (1) when it is hungry and (2) when it finishes eating. Table needs to communicate only one thing to a hungry Philosopher: permission to eat. The sequence diagram in Figure 7.4 shows two scenarios of possible event exchange in the DPP. In the case of Philosopher *n*, Table can grant permission to eat immediately. However, Philosopher *m* has to wait in the hungry state until forks become available (e.g., two forks become free when Philosopher *n* is done eating).

Figure 7.4   **Sequence diagram showing event exchange in the active object–based solution of the DPP**

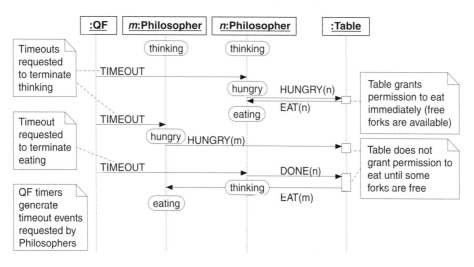

The class diagram in Figure 7.5 shows that the QF application comprises the Table and Philosopher active objects and the specialized TableEvt class. This diagram has a typical structure for an application derived from a framework. Concrete application components (active objects and events in this case) derive from framework base classes (from QActive and QEvent) and use other framework classes as services. For example, every Philosopher has its own QTimer (quantum timer) to keep track of time when it is thinking or eating.

Figure 7.5   **Table and Philosopher active objects and the TableEvt class derived from the QF base classes**

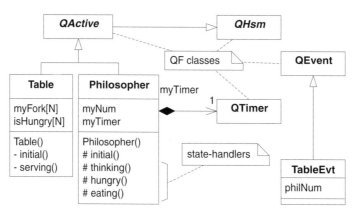

The `Table` and `Philosopher` active objects derive indirectly from `QHsm`, so they are state machines. In fact, your main concern in building the application is elaborating their statecharts. Figure 7.6a shows the statechart associated with `Table`. It is trivial because `Table` keeps track of the forks and hungry philosophers by means of extended state variables (`myFork[]` and `isHungry[]` arrays, Figure 7.5), rather than by its state machine.

The `Philosopher` state machine (Figure 7.6b) clearly shows the life cycle of this active object consisting of states `thinking`, `hungry`, and `eating`. This statechart publishes the `HUNGRY` event on entry to the `hungry` state and the `DONE` event on exit from the `eating` state because this exactly reflects the semantics of these events. An alternative approach — to publish these events from the corresponding `TIMEOUT` transitions — would not guarantee the preservation of the semantics in potential future modifications of the state machine.

Figure 7.6   **(a) Table statechart and (b) Philosopher statechart; the ^DONE(n) notation indicates propagation of the DONE event (publishing the event)**

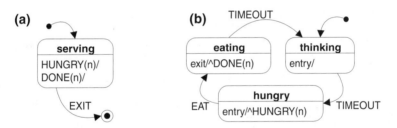

Note that, externally, the active object–based solution makes no reference whatsoever to the forks, only to the philosopher's right to eat (refer to the sequence diagram in Figure 7.4). Interestingly, Dijkstra [Dijkstra 71] proposed a similar solution as the "most natural." His formal analysis of the problem further deduced a need for each philosopher to have an "I am hungry" state, in which the philosopher would wait for permission to eat. Overall, Dijkstra's solution has many remarkable parallels to the active object–based design.

- Each philosopher life cycle goes through `thinking`, `hungry`, and `eating` states (refer to the `Philosopher` statechart in Figure 7.6b).

- Each philosopher has a private semaphore on which to wait when hungry (waiting on this semaphore corresponds to blocking the `Philosopher` thread on the private event queue inherited from the `QActive` base class).

- A philosopher starts eating when in the `hungry` state and neither neighbor is eating (in active object–based design, this is handled by `Table`; refer to the handling of the `HUNGRY` event in Figure 7.4).

- When a philosopher finishes eating, any hungry neighbor starts eating (in active object–based design, this is handled by the `Table` active object; refer to the handling of the DONE event in Figure 7.4)

7.3 Roles of the QF

The most obvious reason to use a software framework such as the QF is the faster development of more robust applications. A framework frees you from making many design decisions so that you, the application implementer, can concentrate on the specifics of your application. However, benefits provided by the QF go further than that. Some of the other characteristics of the QF could turn out to be even more important for you than speedier software development. In the following sections, I suggest other roles that the QF can play in your systems.

7.3.1 Source of Conceptual Integrity

Perhaps the most important contribution of application frameworks in general, and the QF in particular, is the *conceptual integrity* that the derived applications receive from the framework. The role of conceptual integrity is often underestimated. However, conceptual integrity is *the* single factor that distinguishes a clean, coherent, elegant programming product from a poor, inefficient, awkward one. Products with internal conceptual integrity are not only easier to use, but also easier to build, test, maintain, and extend. As Frederic Brooks [Brooks 95] writes:

> ... *conceptual integrity is* the *most important consideration in system design. It is better to have a system omit certain anomalous features and improvements, but reflect one set of design ideas, than to have one that contains many good but independent and uncoordinated ideas.*

One of the most powerful ways to foster conceptual integrity is to use an accurate metaphor. Consider, for example, the desktop metaphor universally used in modern GUIs. Through this metaphor, users find themselves immediately familiar with overlapped windows, cutting and pasting, or dragging and dropping because they already know these concepts from the desktop environment.

The metaphor is not just valuable for users; it is invaluable for software designers[11] because it provides the most difficult part of the design: the conceptual model. With such a model in hand, designers don't need to invent potentially inconsistent policies and behaviors — they can simply consult the real-life model to see how it

---

11. Inventing a metaphor is one of the key practices of eXtreme Programming (XP) [Beck 00].

solves various problems. The metaphor thus serves as an objective arbiter in resolving various design conflicts and ultimately guards the conceptual unity of the design.

In this context, the quantum mechanical analogy (metaphor) is the valuable contribution of the QF, and QP, in general. As explained by means of the hydrogen atom example in Chapter 2 and the virtual photon exchange example in this chapter, the quantum metaphor consists of the following two elements.

- Reactive systems are analogous to quantum systems, in that they are always found in strictly defined discrete states (quantum states) and can change their state only by means of uninterruptible RTC steps (quantum leaps). The states are naturally hierarchical and must comply with the Liskov Substitution Principle (LSP) for states. Behavioral inheritance resulting from state nesting is fundamental because it expresses various symmetries within the system.

- The active object–based computing model is analogous to the quantum field theory, in that the only interaction allowed among reactive objects (hierarchical state machines) is the explicit exchange of event instances (intermediate virtual particles). The quantum model of interaction corresponds to the publish–subscribe model in software.

Admittedly, the quantum metaphor is not as familiar to an average programmer as the desktop metaphor. However, the physics background necessary to benefit from this analogy doesn't go beyond the level of popular science articles. Most importantly, the quantum metaphor is accurate for concurrent reactive systems.

7.3.2 RTOS Abstraction Layer

Whenever your application handles a variety of activities or manages multiple devices, an RTOS can help you simplify the code by separating different tasks. An RTOS is thus an important tool that allows you to divide and conquer [Ganssle 00].

For instance, consider the difficulty of building a global positioning system (GPS) receiver. Without an RTOS, one monolithic hunk of code (often organized into a "superloop") would have to manage signal tracking loop closures, navigation data collection, satellite orbital mechanics calculations, navigation solutions, and communications — all at the same time. An RTOS is a valuable tool because it allows you to partition the code in the time domain (various activities perform concurrently) and in the functional domain (each task handles one thing).

At its simplest level, an RTOS is just a context switcher plus some intertask synchronization mechanisms. The context switcher allocates the CPU to various tasks according to a scheduling algorithm. The tasks can therefore advance at different paces, depending on how many CPU cycles they obtain. An RTOS also provides mechanisms that allow the tasks to synchronize their activities. Examples of such mechanisms include various types of semaphores, mailboxes, and message queues.

Although the basic services provided by RTOSs are very much the same, they are accessible through significantly different APIs. This poses a serious problem for many companies that want to deploy shared application code on different operating systems or don't want to lock their strategic applications into a particular operating system. A common solution to this problem is to create a proprietary RTOS abstraction layer with the sole function of isolating the applications from RTOS differences. Although such indirection layers aren't complicated, they always incur some overhead and add to the problem by introducing yet another proprietary RTOS API.[12]

An active object–based framework such as the QF offers a more elegant solution. As mentioned earlier, applications derived from such a framework don't need to use low-level RTOS primitives directly — the framework effectively isolates applications from the underlying RTOS; that is, changing the RTOS on which the framework is built requires porting the framework code but does not affect applications. At the same time, an active object–based framework is more than just a thin RTOS wrapper because it directly supports active object–based multithreading, as opposed to traditional RTOSs that support only conventional multithreading.

If you use a proprietary homegrown RTOS or just have control over the RTOS source code, you can consider integrating it with the QF into one entity. In fact, RTOSs based on microkernel architecture are already very close to implementing an active object–based framework like the QF. From my experience with several real-time kernels for Motorola 68000, ARM, and ARM/THUMB microcontrollers, integrating an RTOS into the QF is not more difficult than porting the framework to a different operating system (porting the QF is discussed in Chapter 9). Interestingly, because of the spareness of concepts used in the QF, the combined solution is typically smaller than the sum of its parts.

7.3.3 Software Bus

As the number of transistors available on a piece of silicon climbs exponentially according to Moore's Law (see the sidebar "Moore's Law"), more of an electronic system can be incorporated onto a single die. The advantages of higher hardware integration include better system reliability, lower power consumption, smaller size, and lower system cost. The increasingly important problem for the designer community is not to lose these advantages again through the lack of software integration.

Consider, for example, a GPS navigation system. The heart of such a system is a GPS receiver responsible for tracking satellite signals and performing navigation solutions. However, a GPS sensor alone is virtually useless unless it is integrated with other components, such as a GUI, a mapping system, or a vehicle

---

12. For example, the Rhapsody CASE tool from I-Logix uses an RTOS abstraction layer called Abstract Operating System [Douglass 99].

steering system. Although a GPS receiver typically has a powerful 32-bit microcontroller on board that could easily accommodate additional functions,[13] often a closed software architecture forces the designers to implement additional functions in separate hardware. Worse, both the GPS receiver and the extra hardware spend significant resources on communications and are therefore more complex than necessary for the job at hand. In other words, instead of an integrated single-processor design, the system unnecessarily becomes a multiprocessor distributed system and has to cope with all the headaches associated with distributed designs.[14]

Moore's Law

In the 1960s, Gordon Moore [Moore 65] observed that Intel's memory chips were doubling in transistor count with every generation, and a new generation appeared roughly every 18 months. Although Intel has since gotten out of the RAM commodity business, Moore's observation, which the press dubbed Moore's Law, has been remarkably accurate over the last few decades.

The main reason it is not easy for designers to get different functions to share the available hardware is the lack of a "software bus" that would enable tighter software integration, much as hardware buses enable integration of hardware components. Naturally, the concept of a software bus has been around for a long time and has been realized in such software architectures as CORBA, DCOM, and recently .NET. However, these heavy-weight architectures are designed for powerful desktop and server platforms and are unsuitable for most embedded systems. They also address a different need — integrating distributed systems communications over networks.

However, many deeply embedded systems need a simpler, light-weight software bus to integrate various software components efficiently within a single address space. An active object–based framework, like the QF, provides such an *open architecture* as well as the API for integrating software components (active objects). If the framework is based on a preemptive kernel, then adding active objects at a lower priority does not affect the timing of active objects running at a higher priority;[15] thus, it enables hard real-time functions to be integrated alongside soft real-time functions.

In the case of a GPS navigation system, an original equipment manufacturer (OEM) of a GPS receiver can provide the hardware and extensible software, which consists of high-priority active objects implementing the core GPS functions. These core active objects can be provided in compiled form (e.g., as a class library) because

---

13. For example, many GPS receivers already have integrated LCD controllers for graphics applications or pulse-width modulation hardware for vechile steering applications.
14. Refer, for example, to Selic [Selic 00] for discussion of challenges specific to distributed software designs.
15. Active objects do not to share any resources and do not block each other.

the details of GPS signal tracking and interfacing to proprietary GPS correlator hardware are typically among the most guarded trade secrets. The OEM does not have to invent an API to open up the software architecture of the product (the QF already provides such an API), so it can concentrate only on specifying and documenting events (hooks) produced and consumed by the active objects with core functionality. With this specification, third-party designers can use the framework API to integrate additional functionality — such as graphics active objects for a mapping system — without adding any extra hardware or layers of communication.[16] The resulting product is simpler, smaller, more reliable, less expensive and gets to market faster.

7.3.4 Platform for Highly Parallel Computing

The same forces that drive the integration of more and more of a system onto a single die (System-on-Chip) also cause the trend toward putting multiple processors on a chip. For example, network processors integrate one or more RISC (reduced instruction set computing) processors for control with multiple homogeneous or heterogeneous processing elements for data processing. However, developing multithreaded software to drive such processors is the biggest problem — more severe than any of the hardware issues [Merritt 02].

To this end, the active object–based computing model is uniquely suitable for highly parallel hardware. First, the natural breakdown of applications into active objects maps directly to the distributed hardware. Second, the thin wire style of communication among active objects is exactly how the processing elements communicate because they typically share a data bus rather than memory. Finally, the high-bandwidth parallel processing performed in these devices is reactive in nature (e.g., packet switching) and is a natural fit for the state machine formalism.

All this makes active object–based application frameworks, such as the QF, very attractive in this field. Although beyond the scope of this book, extending the QF to span multiple address spaces should be relatively straightforward. More importantly, such a distribution of processing should be almost transparent to the application. Perhaps the most simplifying factor of application design is that communications over data buses (unlike communications over networks) can be considered reliable, which for active objects translates into guaranteed event delivery. As described in Section 8.4.2 in Chapter 8, such a guarantee vastly simplifies any active object–based system because active objects often need to maintain mutual consistency in their state.

---

16. One of the most complex aspects of a commercial GPS receiver is its support for various communications protocols and formats.

Interestingly, the field of network processors has already attracted design automation tool vendors, who offer visual state machine techniques capable of automatic code generation for NPUs [Deshpande 01].

7.3.5   Basis for Automatic Code Generation

When you start using a framework such as the QF, you will notice that much of the code is entirely prescribed by the framework. For example, much of the state machine code resulting from instantiation of the behavioral inheritance meta-pattern (an integral part of the QF) is just housekeeping code (see Chapter 1, Section 1.2.4) and lends itself to automation. Indeed, all code-synthesizing tools are based on this observation, and virtually all use an application framework internally as the underlying structure. Although automatic code synthesis is not the subject of this book (and the QF does not provide it), it is worthwhile to understand and perhaps demystify how most of the commercial CASE tools generate code and, in particular, how they use underlying frameworks to facilitate automatic code synthesis.

As the first example of an automatic code generation tool, consider the application wizard (AppWizard) supplied with Microsoft Visual C++. The wizard relies entirely on the Microsoft Foundation Class (MFC) library, which is the C++ framework for building applications for Microsoft Windows. The MFC App-Wizard is a series of branching path steps in which you choose from the available options. Behind the scenes, the wizard carries out exactly the same operations you would perform to manually derive your application from the MFC framework. These operations include subclassing and specializing the framework classes, creating and naming framework components, setting attributes (properties), and invoking framework services (operations). For example, AppWizard lets you choose between the single-document interface (SDI) or the multiple-document interface (MDI). It then translates your choice by subclassing the main application frame class from either `CFrameWnd` (SDI) or `CMDIFrameWnd` (MDI) MFC classes. You also can choose whether you want to use the Document/View architecture, which the wizard translates into an instantiation of Document/View classes in your application. You can select the frame type for your main application window, which the wizard translates as setting attributes of the main window object. Finally, you can choose to support ActiveX controls, which cause the `AfxEnableControlContainer()` invocation of service from the `InitInstance()` MFC method.

If you have not used the MFC AppWizard before, I encourage you to try it out.[17] When you inspect the generated code, you will notice that the wizard is just a more intelligent cut and paste tool, combined with a global find and replace that uses

---

17. Throughout this book, I assume that you have the Microsoft Visual C++ development suite.

identifiers of your choice rather than generic names. The wizard works by cutting appropriate snippets of code from its internal templates and pasting them into your application according to your preferences. The MFC framework facilitates this approach by prescribing points of customization (framework extension points) and providing much of the default behavior (which does not need generated code). If your application falls into one of the supported categories, automatic code generation can give you a fast head start. However, you will be less lucky if some aspects of your application lie off the beaten path. In all cases, the generated code is only an empty skeleton without any specific behavior.

The automated cutting and pasting techniques found in the MFC AppWizard are the simplest forms of code synthesis. CASE tools that support state machines add significantly more advanced capabilities by generating code pertaining to the specific behavior of the application. This code is almost universally based on the constructive nature of statecharts, which means that statecharts have sufficiently precise semantics to allow translating them to code. A typical CASE tool with these capabilities resembles a specialized graphical editor for drawing state machines. The tool provides a palette of state machine components (states, transitions, pseudostates), which you drop on the drawing pad and manipulate to construct the desired state machine topology. Each of the state machine elements has an associated set of properties that you can modify through specific dialog boxes. For example, properties of the transition component include a trigger, guard, and action. You supply the guard and action by typing source code in a concrete programming language into the dialog box (e.g., C, C++, or Java). Similarly, for the state component, you specify entry actions, exit actions, and internal transitions, again by typing concrete code into the state properties dialog box. The main contribution of the CASE tool is the ability to generate housekeeping code from the graphically defined topology of the state machine by instantiating a state machine pattern similar to the behavioral inheritance meta-pattern of the QF. On the other hand, the tool merely cuts and pastes the snippets of code you attached to state machine components via the dialog boxes.

7.4   Summary

In this chapter, I introduced the concept of the Quantum Framework (QF) — a reusable infrastructure for executing concurrent state machines — which is an application framework optimized for the embedded real-time systems domain.

The QF hinges on the active object–based computing model, in which concurrently executing state machine objects, called active objects, interact with one another by exchanging event instances. This communication model offers many advantages over the free threading approach, which poses many challenges, like race conditions, deadlocks, starvation, and indeterminism, to name just a few. These problems make concurrent programming incomparably more difficult than sequential programming and often lead to arcane, fragile designs that only a handful of expert programmers of a particular system can understand, debug, and maintain.

By design, the active object–based approach avoids most of the problems found in free threading solutions. Perhaps the most important characteristic of active objects is their sequential internal structure (thanks to the RTC semantics), which allows active object–based systems to be designed with purely sequential techniques. At the same time, the system can achieve low latencies and good CPU utilization, which are characteristics of good concurrent designs.

An active object–based framework such as the QF can play several important roles in your projects. It can

- help achieve conceptual integrity through the quantum metaphor,
- serve as an RTOS abstraction layer (indeed, it can event replace an RTOS),
- operate as a light-weight software bus,
- be extended to support highly parallel computing, and
- provide the basis for automated code synthesis.

Chapter 8

Design of the Quantum Framework

The worst buildings are those, whose budget was too great
for the purposes to be served.
— Frederick P. Brooks, Jr.

An active object–based framework, such as the Quantum Framework (QF), sits at the focus of many conflicting forces that the framework must ultimately resolve in the applications' interest. The stakes are high because the applications are so dependent on the framework that any wrong decision in its design or implementation could render the framework inadequate for whole classes of applications. Perhaps nowhere is this more true than in the embedded real-time[1] domain. For example, many embedded systems are extremely cost sensitive, so the framework must be efficient in both memory and CPU utilization. Moreover, real-time systems are particularly intolerant to any form of nondeterminism because it can cause the systems to miss deadlines and fail.

---

1. I intentionally use the terms "embedded" and "real-time" together because, in practice, almost all embedded systems have real-time constraints.

To be effective, the framework must take carefully into account the realities of the application domain it serves. But what exactly are these realities? The embedded software domain is so diverse and fragmented that it is necessary first to define the subset of embedded real-time systems that the QF addresses. Furthermore, it is important to investigate how embedded real-time systems differ from other computer systems because, only then, will you understand the motivation for such important QF policies as error and exception handling, memory management, concurrency handling, event passing, initialization, cleanup, and time management.

Although the focus of this chapter is on the design of the framework, you will also find concrete code for platform-independent components of the QF. In the next chapter, I fill in the platform-dependent elements and explain how to port the QF to different operating systems or to use it stand-alone, without an underlying multitasking kernel.

Code fragments presented in this chapter pertain only to the C++ version of the framework. The C version (available on the accompanying CD-ROM) is essentially identical because it implements the same underlying design. Therefore, even if you are only interested in the C version, you should study the C++ code and explanations because they apply equally to the C implementation. If the idea of object-oriented programming in a procedural language like C is new to you, please refer to Appendix A, which describes a set of techniques and idioms that you can use to implement classes, inheritance, and polymorphism in C.

8.1   Embedded Real-Time Systems

"Embedded" and "real-time" mean different things to different people. First, I need to explanation what *I* mean by these terms so that you understand for which kind of systems the QF might be applicable.

For the purpose of this discussion, an embedded real-time system has the following two main characteristics.

1. It is a combination of computer hardware and software, with perhaps additional mechanical and other parts, designed to perform a specific function [Barr 99].

2. It must respond to external events in a timely fashion, which means that for all practical purposes, a late computation is just as bad as an outright wrong computation.

Vague as it is, this definition can gain the most strength by contrasting embedded real-time systems with general-purpose computer systems (such as desktop PCs), in which the two main characteristics are either nonexistent or far less important. So, you can read embedded to mean "not for general-purpose computing" and real-time to mean "dedicated to an application with timeliness requirements." Either way, the definition emphasizes that embedded systems pose different challenges and require different programming strategies than general-purpose computers.

This distinction is important. Perhaps most (unnecessary) complications commonly introduced into embedded software have their roots in projecting requirements from the desktop onto the embedded real-time domain. I disagree with the opinion that embedded real-time developers face all the challenges of "regular" software development plus the complexities inherent in embedded real-time systems [ObjecTime 97]. Although each domain has its fair share of difficulties, each also offers unique opportunities for simplification, so embedded systems programmers specifically do not have to cope with many problems encountered on the desktop. Attempts to reconcile the conflicting requirements of both the desktop and the embedded real-time domain can turn embedded real-time programming into a daunting process,[2] to be sure, but that just makes your job harder than it needs to be.

Desktop-style Programming for Embedded Systems

Attempts to reconcile general-purpose computing with the embedded domain happen quite often. For example, the recent (fading) hype around embedded Linux has been motivated mostly by the rhetoric: "easy portability of application software and programming skills from desktop Linux." As columnist Niall Murphy [Murphy 00] of the *Embedded System Programming* magazine observes:

> *The last time I heard similar logic was in the early stages of Windows CE marketing. It was as bogus then as it is now. Desktop-style applications can only be used in a tiny minority of embedded designs; admittedly, this refers to large volume applications like set-top boxes. Sharing a skill set is bogus too. The vast majority of embedded software developers have never written a single program to the Unix API (nor the Win32 API, I might add) and asking them to learn one of theses monsters in order to use an RTOS embedded within it is putting a huge onus on the engineer. Will programmers experienced in Linux on desktop machines now be able to turn their hand to embedded systems programming? This would assume that, apart from the knowledge of a particular API, there are no skills necessary in the embedded domain that are not already known to desktop programmers. This is simply not true.*

Usually, an embedded system is a much better defined environment for programming than a general-purpose computer because a typical embedded system has a

---

2. See the back cover of *Doing Hard Time* by Bruce Powel Douglass [Douglas 99].

clear, single purpose in life. In contrast, a desktop system doesn't have such a single purpose — by definition, it must be able to accommodate many different functions at different times or even simultaneously. As far as hardware is concerned, no desktop application can rely on a specific amount of physical memory available to it or on how many and what kind of disk drives and other peripherals are present and available at the moment. The software environment is even less predictable. Users frequently install and remove applications from all possible sources. All the time, users launch, close, or crash their applications — drastically changing the CPU load and availability of memory and other resources. The desktop operating system has the tough job of allocating CPU time, memory, and other resources among constantly changing tasks in such a way that each receives a fair share of the resources and no single task can hog the CPU. This scheme is diametrically opposed to the needs of an embedded system, in which a specific task must gain control *right now* and run until it produces the appropriate output. Fairness isn't part of embedded real-time programming — getting the job done is.

Over the last half century or so, the software community has concentrated mostly on effective strategies to cope with the challenges of general-purpose computing. Perhaps because of this long tradition, the resulting strategies and rules of thumb have become so well established that programmers apply them without giving them a second thought. Yet, the desktop solutions and rules of thumb are often inadequate (if not outright harmful) for the vast majority of embedded real-time applications.

Programmers of embedded systems can be much more specific than programmers of general-purpose computers, and specific solutions are always simpler and more efficient than general ones. The following sections show several areas in which the design of the QF enables you to take advantage of the specifics of embedded systems programming and simplifies the implementation compared to traditional solutions borrowed from the desktop. These areas include (1) handling errors and exceptional conditions, (2) memory management, (3) passing events, (4) initialization and cleanup, and (5) time management, which is pretty much everything there is to it!

8.2   Handling Errors and Exceptional Conditions

Handling errors and exceptional conditions offers perhaps the most opportunities for simplifying embedded real-time code compared to general-purpose computer software. Just think, how many times have you seen embedded designs terribly convoluted by attempts to painstakingly propagate an error through many layers of code, just to end up doing something trivial with it, such as performing a system reset (or worse, somehow sweeping the error under the rug).

By error (known otherwise as a bug), I mean a persistent defect due to a design or implementation mistake. When your software has a bug, you should concentrate on finding and ultimately fixing it, rather than designing a recovery strategy. This situation is in contrast to the exceptional condition, which is a specific situation that can legitimately arise during the system lifetime but is relatively rare and lies off the main execution path of your software. In contrast to an error, you need to design and implement a strategy that handles the exceptional condition.

Embedded systems offer many more opportunities than desktop applications to flag a situation as a bug (that you should prevent from happening), rather than an exceptional condition (that you must handle). Consider, for example, dynamic memory allocation (the next section discusses memory management in detail). In any type of system, memory allocation through `malloc()` (or the C++ operator `new`) can fail. On the desktop, a failed `malloc()` merely indicates that, at this moment, the operating system cannot supply the requested memory. In a highly dynamic general-purpose computing environment, this can happen easily. When it happens, you have options to recover from the situation. One option might be for the application to free up some memory that it allocated and then retry the allocation. Another choice could be to prompt the user that the problem exists and encourage her to exit other applications so that the current application can gather more memory. Yet another option is to save data to the disk and exit. Whatever the choice, handling the situation requires some drastic actions, which are clearly off the mainstream behavior of your application. Nevertheless, you should design and implement such actions because in a desktop application, a failed `malloc()` must be considered an exceptional condition.

In a typical embedded system, on the other hand, the same failed `malloc()` probably should be flagged as a bug.[3] That's because embedded systems offer much fewer excuses to run out of memory, so when it happens, it's typically an indication of a flaw. You cannot really recover from it. Exiting other applications is not an option. Neither is writing to a nonexistent disk. Whichever way you look at it, it's a bug no different from dereferencing a NULL pointer[4] or overrunning an array index.[5] Instead of going out of your way in attempts to handle this condition in software (as you would on the desktop), you should concentrate first on finding the root cause and then fixing it (I would first look for a memory leak, wouldn't you?).

The main point here is that many situations traditionally handled as exceptional conditions on the desktop are in fact bugs in embedded systems. To handle various

---

3.   Embedded systems span such a broad spectrum that there are examples where it makes sense to recover from a failed `malloc()`. In such rare cases, you should treat it as an exceptional condition.

4.   *Thou shalt not follow a NULL pointer, for chaos and madness await thee at its end* — the second commandment for C programmers by prophet Henry Spencer [Spencer 94].

5.   *Thou shalt check the array bounds of all strings (indeed, all arrays), for surely where thou typest 'foo' someone someday shall type 'supercalifragilisticexpialidocious'* — the fifth commandment for C programmers by prophet Henry Spencer [Spencer 94].

situations in your QF applications correctly, you should not blindly transfer rules of thumb from other areas of programming to embedded real-time systems. Instead, I propose that you critically ask the following two probing questions.

1. Can this rare situation legitimately happen in this system?

2. If it happens, is there anything specific that needs to or can be done in the software?

If the answer to either of these questions is "yes," then you should handle the situation as an exceptional condition; otherwise, you should treat the situation as an error.

The other important point is that errors require the *exact opposite* programming strategy than exceptional conditions. The first priority in dealing with errors is to facilitate finding them. Any attempt to handle a bug as an exceptional condition results in unnecessary complications of the implementation and either camouflages the bug or delays its manifestation. (In the worst case, it also introduces new bugs.) Either way, finding and fixing the bug will be harder.

In the following section, I describe how the QF uses assertions to help catch bugs, not so much in the framework, but mostly in applications derived from it. You should extend the same basic strategy to your own code.

8.2.1 Design by Contract

An important aspect of the QF that you, as the framework client, need to understand is the way it uses *assertions*. In this respect, the QF applies elements of the Design by Contract[6] (DBC) methodology pioneered by Bertrand Meyer [Meyer 97]. DBC views a software system as a set of components whose collaboration is based on precisely defined specifications of mutual obligations — the *contracts*. The central idea of this method is to inherently embed the contracts in the code and validate them automatically at run time. Doing so consistently has two major benefits. (1) It automatically helps catch bugs (which manifest themselves as contract violations). (2) It is a great way to document code.

You can implement the most important aspects of DBC easily in C or C++ with assertions [Kapp 00]. The standard library macro `assert()` is rarely applicable to embedded systems, however, because its default behavior, when the boolean expression passed to the macro evaluates `FALSE`, is to print an error message and exit. Neither of these actions makes sense for most embedded systems, which rarely have a screen to print to and cannot really exit either (at least not in the same sense as a desktop application can). In an embedded environment, you usually have to define your own implementation to suit the tools you are using or the error response that fits your system [Murphy 01]. In the QF, I use assertions friendly to embedded systems that are defined in `qassert.h`.

---

6. Design by Contract is a trademark of Interactive Software Engineering.

Listing 8.1   `qassert.h` header file

```
 1 #ifndef qassert_h
 2 #define qassert_h
 3
 4 #ifdef __cplusplus
 5    extern "C" {
 6 #endif
 7
 8 #ifndef NASSERT                       /* assertions enabled (not disabled)? */
 9                                /* callback invoked in case assertion fails */
10 extern void onAssert__(const char *file, unsigned line);
11
12 #define DEFINE_THIS_FILE \
13    static const char THIS_FILE__[] = __FILE__
14
15 #define ASSERT(test_)\
16    if (test_) {         \
17    }                    \
18    else onAssert__(THIS_FILE__, __LINE__)
19
20 #define REQUIRE(test_)    ASSERT(test_)
21 #define ENSURE(test_)     ASSERT(test_)
22 #define INVARIANT(test_)  ASSERT(test_)
23 #define ALLEGE(test_)     ASSERT(test_)
24
25 #else                                          /* assertions disabled */
26
27 #define DEFINE_THIS_FILE extern const char THIS_FILE__[]
28 #define ASSERT(test_)
29 #define REQUIRE(test_)
30 #define ENSURE(test_)
31 #define INVARIANT(test_)
32 #define ALLEGE(test_)\
33    if (test_) {       \
34    }                  \
35    else
36
37 #endif
38
39 #ifdef __cplusplus
40 }
41 #endif
42
43 #endif                                              /* qassert_h */
```

Listing 8.1 shows the complete qassert.h header file, which is designed for C, C++, or mixed C/C++ programming (lines 4–6, 39–41). The main macro ASSERT() (lines 15–18) tests the expression that you pass to it and invokes the callback function onAssert__() when the expression evaluates to FALSE. The empty block in the if statement might seem strange, but you need both the if and the else statements to prevent unexpected dangling-if problems. Other macros — REQUIRE(), ENSURE(), and INVARIANT()[7] — are intended to validate preconditions, postconditions, and invariants, respectively. They all map to ASSERT() (lines 20–22) because their different names serve only to better document the specific intent of the contract.

The callback function onAssert__() (line 10) gives clients the opportunity to customize behavior when an assertion fails. You need to define onAssert__() somewhere in your program. If you define it in a C++ module, be careful to apply the extern "C" linkage specification. Entry to onAssert__() is the ideal place to put a breakpoint if you work with a debugger.

Tip: Install a permanent breakpoint in onAssert__().

ASSERT() invokes onAssert__() (line 18), passing THIS_FILE__ as a parameter, rather than the standard preprocessor macro __FILE__, to avoid proliferation of multiple copies of the filename string, which happens in the standard implementation with the __FILE__ macro. To take advantage of this trick [Maguire 93], however, you have to invoke the DEFINE_THIS_FILE macro (line 12), preferably at the top of every C/C++ file. Every *.C or *.CPP file on the accompanying CD-ROM can serve as an example.

Defining the preprocessor switch NASSERT (line 8) disables assertions. When disabled, the assertion macros expand to nothing (lines 28–31); in particular, they do not test the expressions passed as arguments. The notable exception is the ALLEGE() macro (lines 32–35), which still executes the expression, although when assertions are disabled, it does not invoke the onAssert__() callback. You can use ALLEGE() when the expression has side effects that are important to the normal operation of your program. In general, evaluating contracts should have no such side effects.

The most important point to understand about contracts is that they neither handle nor prevent bugs, in the same way that contracts among people do not prevent fraud. Asserting an outcome of an operation, as for example in ALLEGE((p = malloc(sizeof foo)) != NULL),[8] might give you a warm and fuzzy feeling that you have handled or prevented a bug, when in fact, you haven't. You did establish a

---

7.   The names are a direct loan from Eiffel, the programming language that natively implements Design by Contract.

contract, however, which in this particular situation declares the failed `malloc()` a bug. What does it buy you? It turns every asserted bug, however benign, into a fatal error. If you haven't programmed with assertions before, you might think that this must be backwards: contracts not only do nothing to fix bugs, they also make things worse! This is exactly the cultural difference of DBC. Recall from the previous section that the first priority when dealing with bugs is to help catch them. To this end, a bug that causes a loud crash (and identifies exactly which contract was violated) is much easier to find than a subtle one that manifests itself intermittently millions of machine instructions downstream from the spot where you could have easily caught it.

DBC complements the rest of object technology and is as important (if not more) as classes, objects, inheritance, and polymorphism [ISE 97].[9] DBC is especially valuable for embedded real-time systems because contracts can cover all those situations that, in other domains, would require handling as exceptional conditions. As Bertrand Meyer [Meyer 97b] observes (and I cannot agree more):

> It is not an exaggeration to say that applying Eiffel's assertion-based O-O development will completely change your view of software construction .... It puts the whole issue of errors, the unsung part of the software developer's saga, in a completely different light.

I cannot do justice to the subject of all the creative ways in which contracts can help you detect bugs. The QF will provide you with some concrete examples of strategic, as well as tactical, contracts that are specific to the embedded real-time domain.[10]

8.2.2 State-Based Handling of Exceptional Conditions

Paraphrasing the definition from the beginning of this section, an exceptional condition is a specific situation in the lifetime of a system that calls for a special behavior. In active objects, a change in behavior corresponds to a change in state (state transition). Hence, in active objects, the associated statechart is the most natural way to handle all conditions, including exceptional conditions. Moreover, because of its support for behavioral inheritance, a statechart is ideal for implementing a consistent exception-handling policy. A common superstate can define a general policy that the substates can either accept (inherit) or override (spe-

---

8. Note the use of `ALLEGE()` rather than `ASSERT()`, because the side effect (setting p) is certainly important for proper program operation, even when assertions are disabled. I am still emphasizing asserting `malloc()` because it is such a no-no in desktop programming.

9. It is absolutely amazing that the UML specification does not provide *any* support for such a fundamental methodology as DBC.

10. If you want to know more, the few references I provided here can give you a good start. In addition, the Internet is full of useful links.

cialize). This example is just another instance of the Ultimate Hook state pattern (Chapter 5).

Such state-based exception handling is typically a combination of the Ultimate Hook and the Reminder state patterns (Chapter 5). Whenever an action within an active object encounters an exceptional condition, it generates a reminder event and posts it to self. This event, processed in the following RTC step, triggers the state-based handling of the exceptional condition.

State-based exception handling offers a safe and language-independent alternative to the built-in exception-handling mechanism of the underlying programming language. As described in Section 3.6 in Chapter 3, throwing and catching exceptions in C++ is risky in any state machine implementation because it conflicts with the fundamental RTC semantics of state machines.

Again, language-based exception handling comes from general-purpose computing, where designers of software libraries cannot be specific about handling exceptional situations. Typically, they don't have enough context to determine whether a given circumstance is a bug or an exceptional condition, so they throw an exception just in case a client chooses to handle the situation. In C++, exception handling incurs extra run-time overhead, even if you don't use it. More importantly, exception handling in C++ (even without state machines) is tricky and can lead to subtle bugs. As Tom Cargill [Cargill 94] noticed in his paper "Exception handling: A false sense of security":

> *Counter-intuitively, the hard part of coding exceptions is not the explicit throws and catches. The really hard part of using exceptions is to write all the intervening code in such a way that an arbitrary exception can propagate from its throw site to its handler, arriving safely and without damaging other parts of the program along the way.*

If you can, consider leaving out C++ exception-handling mechanisms from your embedded software (e.g., EC++ intentionally does not support exceptions). If you cannot avoid it, make sure to catch all exceptions before they can cause any damage. Remember, any uncaught exception that unexpectedly interrupts an RTC step can wreak havoc on your state machine.

Exercise 8.1   Add state-based exception handling to the Reminder state pattern implementation described in Section 5.2 in Chapter 5. Introduce a state "fault" and an EXCEPTION event that triggers a transition from the polling to the fault state. Subsequently, invoke the following faulty() function to the entry action of the busy state.

```
void faulty() {
    static int faultCtr = 10;
    if (--faultCtr == 0) {
        faultCtr = 10;
        throw "fault";
    }
}
```

As you can see, faulty() throws an exception every 10th time it's invoked. Surround the invocation of faulty() with a try block and turn the exception into the EXCEPTION event by posting this event to self in the catch (...) block. Confirm that the exception thrown from faulty() causes transition from the polling to the fault state. Verify that the state-based exception-handling mechanism correctly cleans up the Windows timer allocated in the entry action to polling.

8.3 Memory Management

Unquestionably, one of the most important decisions that you will make in designing your embedded application is the memory management policy. The policies used in desktop applications are often not appropriate or applicable to embedded real-time systems, and in this section, I show you why. The QF design carefully enables you to avoid inappropriate memory management mechanisms. At the same time, the QF cannot enforce any particular memory management style, which leaves you much flexibility in this respect.[11] Still, in this section, I recommend a memory management policy that is compatible with the QF and is suitable for embedded real-time systems.

8.3.1 A Heap of Problems

If you have been in the embedded real-time software business for a while, you must have learned to be wary of malloc() and free() (or their C++ counterparts new and delete), because embedded real-time systems are particularly intolerant of heap problems, which include the following pitfalls.

---

11. Including the freedom to shoot yourself in the foot.

- Dynamically allocating and freeing memory can fragment the heap over time to the point that the program crashes because of an inability to allocate more RAM. The total remaining heap storage might be more than adequate, but no single piece satisfies a specific `malloc()` request.

- Heap-based memory management is wasteful. All heap management algorithms must maintain some form of header information for each block allocated. At the very least, this information includes the size of the block. For example, if the header causes a four-byte overhead, then a four-byte allocation requires at least eight bytes, so only 50 percent of the allocated memory is usable to the application. Because of these overheads and the aforementioned fragmentation, determining the minimum size of the heap is difficult. Even if you were to know the worst-case mix of objects simultaneously allocated on the heap (which you typically don't), the required heap storage is much more than a simple sum of the object sizes. As a result, the only practical way to make the heap more reliable is to massively oversize it.

- Both `malloc()` and `free()` can be (and often are) nondeterministic, meaning that they potentially can take a long (hard to quantify) time to execute, which conflicts squarely with real-time constraints. Although many real-time operating systems (RTOSs) have heap management algorithms with bounded, or even deterministic, performance, they don't necessarily handle multiple small allocations efficiently.

Unfortunately, the list of heap problems doesn't stop there. A new class of problems appears when you use heap in a multithreaded environment. The heap becomes a shared resource and consequently causes all the headaches associated with resource sharing, so the list goes on.

- Both `malloc()` and `free()` can be (and often are) non-reentrant; that is, they cannot be safely called simultaneously from multiple threads of execution.[12]

- The reentrancy problem can be remedied by protecting `malloc()`, `free()`, `realloc()`, and so on internally with a mutex semaphore,[13] which lets only one thread at a time access the shared heap (Section 8.4.1). However, this scheme could cause excessive blocking of threads (especially if memory management is nondeterministic) and can significantly reduce parallelism. Mutexes are also subject to priority inversion (see the sidebar "Priority Inversion, Inheritance, and

---

12. You need to consult the run-time library accompanying your compiler to link to the right version of reentrant heap management routines. Be aware, however, that the reentrant versions are significantly more expensive to call.

13. For example, the VxWorks RTOS from WindRiver Systems protects heap management routines with a mutex [WindRiver 97].

Ceiling" on page 231). Naturally, the heap management functions protected by a mutex are not available to interrupt service routines (ISRs) because ISRs cannot block.

Finally, all the problems listed previously come on top of the usual pitfalls associated with dynamic memory allocation. For completeness, I'll mention them here as well.

- If you destroy all pointers to an object and fail to free it or you simply leave objects lying about well past their useful lifetimes, you create a memory leak. If you leak enough memory, your storage allocation eventually fails.

- Conversely, if you free a heap object but the rest of the program still believes that pointers to the object remain valid, you have created dangling pointers. If you dereference such a dangling pointer to access the recycled object (which by that time might be already allocated to somebody else), your application can crash.

- Most of the heap-related problems are notoriously difficult to test. For example, a brief bout of testing often fails to uncover a storage leak that kills a program after a few hours, or weeks, of operation. Similarly, exceeding a real-time deadline because of nondeterminism can show up only when the heap reaches a certain fragmentation pattern. These types of problems are extremely difficult to reproduce.

This is quite a list,[14] and I didn't even touch the more subtle problems yet.[15] So why use the heap at all? Well, because the heap is so convenient, especially in general-purpose computing. Dynamic memory management perfectly addresses the general problem of not knowing how much memory you'll need in advance. (That's why it's called *general*-purpose computing.)

However, if you go down the lists again, you will notice that most of the heap problems are much less severe in the desktop environment than they are in embedded applications. For a desktop application, with only "soft" real-time requirements, all issues (except dangling pointers, perhaps) boil down to inefficiencies in RAM and CPU use. The obvious technique that cures many issues is to massively oversize the heap. To this end, all desktop operating systems these days support virtual memory, which is a mechanism that effects a manifold increase in the size of available RAM by spilling less frequently used sections of RAM onto disk. Another interesting approach, brought recently to the forefront by Java (not that it wasn't known before), is *automatic garbage collection*. You can view garbage collection as

---

14. Why don't you use this list when interviewing for an embedded systems programmer position? Awareness of heap problems is like a litmus test for a good embedded systems programmer.
15. For example, C++ exception-handling mechanism can cause memory leaks when a thrown exception "bypasses" memory deallocation.

a software mechanism to simulate an infinite heap. It addresses the problems of dangling pointers, storage leaks, and heap fragmentation (albeit at a hefty performance price tag). The other issues, especially deterministic execution, remain unsolved and even aggravated in the presence of garbage collection.

For decades, heap problems have been addressed in desktop environments with ever more powerful hardware. Fast CPUs, cheap dynamic RAM, and massive virtual memory disk buffers can mask heap management inefficiencies and tolerate memory-hungry applications (some of them leaking like a sieve) long enough to allow them to finish their job.[16]

Not so in the embedded real-time business! Not only are embedded systems severely limited in the amount of available RAM, but they also must run for weeks, months, or years without rebooting. Under these circumstances, the numerous problems caused by heap-based memory allocation can easily outweigh the benefits. You should very seriously consider not using the heap at all, or at least severely limiting its use in embedded real-time applications.

You should be aware, however, of the far-reaching consequences of such a decision. First, this decision tends to dramatically change your programming style. Second, it severely limits your choice of the third-party libraries and legacy code you want to reuse (especially if you borrow code designed for the desktop). In C, you will have to rethink implementations that use dynamic linked lists, trees, and other dynamic data structures.[17] In C++, the implications are even more serious because the object-oriented nature of C++ applications results in much more intensive dynamic memory use than in applications using procedural techniques. For example, a lack of dynamic storage implies that you will lose many advantages of constructors because the static instantiation of objects happens at a time when you typically don't have enough initialization information. You also will be unable to benefit from the ISO C++ standard libraries (e.g., the Standard Template Library) and from the design techniques they embody.

Nonetheless, deciding not to use the regular heap does not mean that you completely step back into the stone age of programming. In particular, the QF uses dynamic memory — or even a very specific form of garbage collection — to handle events. Before jumping ahead, however, I'll start with the straightforward (stone age) techniques used in the QF.

---

16. That's why it's a good idea to reboot your PC every once in a while.
17. It does not necessarily mean that you cannot use any dynamic data structures. For example, the QF uses internally linked lists, but is no requirement that they be allocated on the heap.

8.3.2 Memory Management in the QF

The basic design philosophy of the QF with respect to memory management is not to commit any memory internally (except for trivial variables). Instead, the QF leaves to the clients the instantiation of any framework-derived objects and the initialization of the framework with the memory that it needs for operation, leaving you the complete flexibility of using the memory mix of your choice. For example, a QF application can use statically allocated memory exclusively, but nothing precludes it from using heap memory or any combination of the two.

I strongly recommend using statically allocated memory wherever you can. The vast majority of embedded applications can be implemented with a fixed number of active objects (threads) and with the entire physical memory available to the embedded application (in contrast to a typical desktop application that must share memory with others). In this case, even if you could allocate storage from the heap, why would you do it? With static memory allocation, your linker (or actually the locator) automatically verifies the worst-case memory use against the available RAM. If you exceed the capacity of RAM, you know it right away because your application won't link. Moreover, the map file shows you exact utilization of each kind of memory in your system. On the other hand, using the heap puts the burden on you to determine correct heap size. The heap leaves you in the dark, and you will not know until run time whether you sized it sufficiently large. Even if you have used the heap judiciously (not causing much fragmentation), in the long run, you end up using significantly more RAM (because of overheads and a safety margin), as well as more code space (ROM) for the routines to manage the heap.

As an example of the QF design philosophy, consider `QActive::start()`, which allows you to initialize and start the thread associated with an active object. The complete signature of this method looks as follows.

```
void QActive::start(unsigned prio, QEvent *qSto[], unsigned qLen,
                    int stkSto[], unsigned stkLen);
```

I'll defer discussion of the first argument (`prio`) to Section 8.6.3 and concentrate here on the other arguments. They have the following semantics: `qSto` is a pointer to the storage for the event queue (Section 8.6.2 discusses event queues), `qLen` is the length of the queue (in units of `QEvent*`), `stkSto` is a pointer to the storage location for the stack,[18] and `stkLen` is the length of the stack (in units of `int`). With this signature, you have the complete freedom to allocate both the event queue and the stack in whichever way you like.

This flexibility could have important performance implications because, often in embedded systems, some RAM is better than other RAM. For example, the AT91

---

18. You typically need to allocate a separate stack for each thread of execution.

family of ARM7TDMI-based microcontrollers from Atmel Corporation provides a small amount (4–8Kb) of high-speed 32-bit on-chip SRAM. This SRAM is too small for most applications, so additional RAM must be added externally. The fast on-chip memory, however, is ideal for placing the stacks, and a failure to do so slows your application significantly. Running with stacks in external RAM is much slower (e.g., four times slower) because the AT91 only has a 16-bit external memory interface (and all ARM cores use a 32-bit stack). Additionally, the external RAM requires more bus cycles, because of wait states, than the fast on-chip SRAM.

Some RTOSs (e.g., VxWorks [WindRiver 97]) don't let you specify the memory for the stack; instead, they allocate the stack themselves (typically on the heap). Ported to such an RTOS, `QActive::start()` needs to be invoked with the `stkSto` argument set to `NULL` (the concrete port should assert that) to avoid doubly allocating memory. This is just one example in which a commercial RTOS could preclude an important performance optimization (e.g., for the AT91 microcontroller family).

8.4 Mutual Exclusion and Blocking

In most real-time systems, different activities have different urgencies. RTOSs typically address this common situation by assigning different priorities to different threads and giving precedence to the threads with the higher priority. The scheduling algorithm embedded inside every RTOS allocates the CPU to threads based on their priorities. One of the most important scheduling algorithms, called the preemptive, priority-based scheduler, always assigns the CPU to the highest priority thread ready to run.

High-priority threads are not always ready to run because they are often blocked. A thread can block for many reasons. One of the most important reasons is the mutually exclusive access to shared resources (recall the dining philosophers problem from Chapter 7).

The following sections discuss various techniques for obtaining mutual exclusion and explain the hazards associated with them. Similar to memory management, the design of the QF carefully avoids inappropriate methods of mutual exclusion internally. At the same time, the QF cannot enforce that your applications stay away from inappropriate mechanisms.

8.4.1 Perils of Mutual Exclusion

In Chapter 7, I listed the methods of obtaining a mutually exclusive access to a shared resource. These techniques include

- disabling interrupts,
- disabling task switching, and
- locking resources with semaphores.

The first two methods are relatively unsophisticated and have serious drawbacks. Disabling interrupts completely cuts the CPU off from the outside world and can increase interrupt latency if the access requires more than a handful of machine instructions. Disabling task switching is less radical, but it prevents indiscriminately the execution of all other threads, including high-priority threads totally unrelated to the resource. A more refined approach is to use a semaphore, because this method affects only the threads actually competing for the resource. Indeed, almost all multitasking operating systems provide an assortment of semaphores specialized for various functions. A semaphore optimized specifically for problems inherent in mutual exclusion is called a *mutual exclusion semaphore*, or simply a *mutex*.

Among all the mutual exclusion mechanisms, the (mutex) semaphore is the most universal. This mechanism is applied quite often inside RTOSs and in various reentrant (thread-safe) libraries, so your application could be using a mutex, even though you do not employ this mechanism directly. For example, the heap management routines discussed earlier, such as `malloc()`, `free()`, `realloc()`, and so on, are commonly protected by a mutex, so that multiple threads can access the (shared) heap resource concurrently. However, in spite of the ubiquity (or perhaps just because of it), mutexes are the most dangerous of all mechanisms (see the sidebar "Priority Inversion, Inheritance, and Ceiling").

Priority inversion can be a show stopper in any real-time system; yet, most less sophisticated RTOSs and real-time kernels don't support any mechanisms to prevent it. Even the high-end systems, which have priority inheritance or priority ceiling built in, don't enable these mechanisms by default because of the high overhead involved.

Priority Inversion, Inheritance, and Ceiling

Priority inversion is the deadly condition in which a low-priority thread blocks a ready and willing high-priority thread indefinitely. Consider the scenario in Figure 8.1a. A, B, and C are threads of low, medium, and high priority, respectively. Threads B and C are blocked, waiting for events. Thread A is running. At time 4, A invokes `malloc()` and acquires exclusive access to the heap through a mutex. In the meantime, an event for the high-priority thread C arrives at time 5. Thread C preempts thread A. After running for a while, C needs memory and invokes `malloc()`. Internally, `malloc()` tries to acquire the mutex and blocks at time 10 because A already holds the mutex. Thread A resumes execution, but because of its low priority, it is vulnerable to preemptions. Indeed, at time 11, B receives an event, unblocks, and immediately preempts A. Thread B does not have any need for memory, so it takes advantage of the contention between C and A and takes a long (indefinite) time to process the event. Even though execution time for `malloc()` might be deterministic, the high-priority thread C cannot run for an indefinite time and misses its deadline at time 20.

Many operating systems recognize the problem and provide workarounds, which rely on augmenting the mutex implementation to prevent intermediate priority threads from running when low- and high-priority threads are competing for access to the shared resource. A mutex can promote a lower priority thread to the higher priority on a temporary basis while it's owned by the lower priority thread using one of two methods: priority inheritance and priority ceiling [Kalinsky 98].

The *priority inheritance mutex* assures that a thread that owns a resource executes at the priority of the highest priority thread blocked on that resource. Figure 8.1b shows an example of the previous scenario, except this time, as soon as the high-priority thread C tries to access the heap (at time 10), the mutex elevates the priority of A, which holds the resource, to the level of C. Thread C blocks as before, but A temporarily inherits its priority and is no longer vulnerable for preemption by B, so A can complete `malloc()` and release the mutex at time 12. As soon as this happens, the mutex lowers the priority of A to its original level. Now C can preempt A, acquire the mutex, and continue. This time, C easily meets its deadline.

The *priority ceiling mutex* also temporarily raises the priority of the thread holding a shared resource, but it uses a fixed priority level (the ceiling priority) that is assigned to the mutex on its creation. The ceiling priority should be at least as high as the highest priority thread working with this mutex. Figure 8.1c shows the scenario. As soon as A calls `malloc()` at time 4, its priority elevates to that of C, so now C cannot preempt A as it receives an event at time 5. Instead, C has to wait until A releases the mutex at time 7 and its priority drops down to the original level. At this point, C runs to completion (and easily meets its deadline), B runs to completion, and finally A runs to completion. Choosing a ceiling priority that is too high will effectively lock the scheduler for other (unrelated) threads. Choosing one that is too low will not protect against some priority inversions. Nevertheless, priority ceiling has some advantages over priority inheritance. It is faster, tends to cause fewer context switches, and is much easier for static timing analysis.

The concepts of priority inheritance and priority ceiling can be combined into a complex, but completely bulletproof (immune even to deadlocks), system-wide solution known as the *priority ceiling protocol* (refer to Sha and colleagues [Sha+ 90] for more information).

A highly publicized example of a system failure caused by priority inversion is the Mars Pathfinder mission from July 1997. The mission (eventually very successful) was saved by remotely enabling priority inheritance in the VxWorks mutex implementation that was originally not activated because of its high overhead (e.g., see `http://www.windriver.com/customer/html/jpl.html`).

Figure 8.1   Timing diagrams for priority inversion (a), priority inheritance (b), and priority ceiling (c)

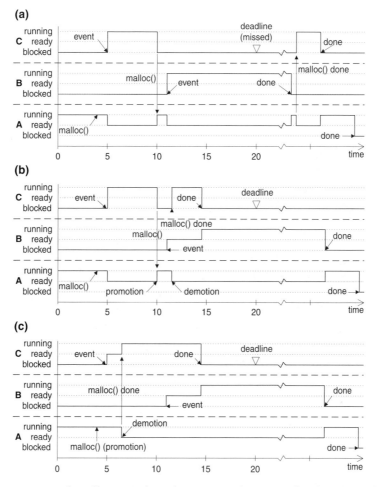

More importantly, all mutual exclusion mechanisms lead to *coupling* among different threads in the time domain. Anytime a high-priority thread, C, shares a resource with a low-priority thread, A, the high-priority thread must take into account delays caused by blocking when A exclusively accesses the shared resource. If A locks the resource for too long, then C might be delayed (and miss its deadline, for example), even if the priority inversion is correctly avoided. Thus the mutual exclusion mechanism couples otherwise independent threads A and C, because any changes to A could have adverse effects on C.

As you will see throughout the rest of this book, the QF consistently helps you to avoid any form of mutual exclusion by handling all the burdens of mutual exclusion internally. In all cases when the QF needs to obtain mutually exclusive access (e.g., to pass events shared among active objects), it uses the simplest safe method (i.e., briefly disabling interrupts), which is not subject to priority inversions.

8.4.2 Blocking in Active Object–Based Systems

In general, active objects block for three reasons: (1) to wait for new events between RTC steps, (2) to wait for other active objects in the middle of an RTC step, and (3) to wait for occurrences not related to other active objects. Type 1 blocking is normal. Type 2 blocking is generally a *bad idea*, and the design of the QF consistently avoids it at the framework level. It is up to you, however, to stay away from this type of blocking at the application level. Type 3 blocking is acceptable and sometimes unavoidable.

As an example of blocking while waiting for active objects in the midst of an RTC step, assume that you allow an active object to block while publishing an event that the subscriber active object cannot accept because its event queue is full. Consider the following scenario: Three active objects, A, B, and C, have priorities low, medium, and high, respectively. High-priority object C is running; objects A and B also have events to process (in fact, the event queue of A is full) but are waiting for their turn to run. At some point, object C publishes an event that happens to be subscribed by object A. At this point, object C blocks (before running to completion), because A's queue is full. But A cannot run and clean its queue because the higher priority object B preempts it and can continue to run indefinitely, effectively preventing high-priority object C from running. You have priority inversion (see the sidebar "Priority Inversion, Inheritance, and Ceiling" earlier in this chapter), however, not in conjunction with a mutex this time but with an event queue. Even if you remedied the problem by applying priority inheritance (or a priority ceiling) to event queues, active objects A and C would still be coupled in the time domain. High-priority active object C would have to take into account delays caused by blocking on A, and any changes in A could have adverse effects on C. But this immediately derails the idea of loose coupling and system extensibility — high-priority object C should not be affected by who will subscribe to its events. That's why (among other reasons) type 2 blocking is a bad idea.

As an example of blocking while waiting for occurrences not related to other active objects, consider an active object whose job it is to handle requests to send data, say, through a serial port. The serial port has a limited throughput, and sending data takes considerable time. Therefore, it is natural for the active object to write a chunk of data to the port (perhaps via a device driver) and block until the transmission completes. Blocking in this case is unrelated to the progress of other active objects and does not introduce couplings among them (typically the blocked active object is released from an interrupt rather than an action in another active object).

The only hazard is that while the active object is blocked, its event queue can over-flow. However, this indicates a sustained mismatch between the volume of application output (production rate) and available bandwidth (consumption rate), which no queue can handle. You should manage this either by reducing the output or by increasing the throughput (perhaps by going to a higher baud rate).

Blocking by mutual exclusion in an active object–based system is the software equivalent of friction in a mechanical system. A well-designed, multitasking system is like a well-lubricated engine that can run smoothly and efficiently without much wear and tear — forever. Excessive blocking in a software system, on the other hand, is like excessive friction in a machine. It can destroy even the best quality parts, and it eventually brings the whole machine to a grinding halt. You don't want this to happen to your software system — lubricate your software machines!

8.5   Passing Events

Event passing is without a doubt the most intricate aspect of the QF, or any other active object–based framework for that matter. The main difficulty is that event instances are the only artifacts explicitly shared among active objects. The quantum metaphor shows you immediately how events differ fundamentally from all other objects. As the mediators of all interactions, events correspond in the quantum picture to so-called virtual particles,[19] which have a very limited lifetime (given by the uncertainty principle $\Delta t \leq (\hbar/\Delta E)$), whereas all other objects correspond to real particles (with unlimited lifetimes).

This qualitative difference demands that you handle events differently from other objects. In general, event instances cannot be static but must be created and destroyed dynamically. Ignore for a moment how to actually implement such dynamic creation and destruction; instead, investigate the mechanism of event exchange. The quantum metaphor offers guidance.

In quantum field theory, when an electron emits a virtual photon, the photon must be absorbed by another electron (electron–electron interaction) or be reabsorbed by the original electron. Either way, the photon *has to* disappear within a very limited time. The destruction of the virtual photon must be guaranteed and automatic (fail-ure to annihilate a virtual particle in time violates the uncertainty principle and ulti-mately energy conservation). An interesting question is: Who "owns" the virtual photon?[20] It is easier to see who doesn't. Definitely, neither the sending electron, nor the receiving electron really own the photon. The recipient cannot, for example,

---

19. See the sidebar "Particle Interaction in Quantum Field Theory" in Chapter 7.

20. This is not really a physical question, but the problem of ownership is interesting from the programming per-spective. In programming, the owner has the responsibility of destroying the object. As in real life, ownership is transferable.

intercept it and explicitly send it to somebody else. Neither of the participants can keep the virtual photon around for any significant time. Rather, the photon is just loaned briefly for the duration of the interaction and then it must disappear into the quantum vacuum.[21]

To translate this scenario into programming lingo, you need to substitute the names of the main actors. You translate "electron" to "active object", and "photon" to "event." Other concepts translate roughly as follows: "virtual" corresponds to "dynamic," "violation of energy conservation" to "memory leak," and "quantum vacuum" to "QF." After translation, the quantum metaphor proposes a mechanism of passing events that requires dynamic creation and automatic destruction of events. Active objects do not own events. They receive events as loans that are valid only for the duration of a single atomic RTC step (a quantum leap). In particular, active objects cannot intercept and retransmit received events. Active objects also have to eventually send out any events that they create, because even these events ultimately don't belong to them. The responsibility for delivering and automatically destroying events rests exclusively with the QF, leading in effect to a specific automatic garbage collection.

Because this model comes from a real-life metaphor, it has a good chance of being coherent. After all, virtual particle exchange has been working flawlessly ever since the Big Bang.[22] To convince you, I will pose a few probing questions. Why must the destruction of events be automatic? Well, if the client code (rather than the framework) were responsible for explicit event destruction, then every event would have to be handled (and eventually explicitly destroyed) by some active object; otherwise, the event would leak. But this contradicts the idea of loose coupling, in which the producer of the event doesn't know who will consume the event (and if at all).

Why can't active objects intercept events and keep them around for future reference? After all, perhaps event parameters contain some information that is useful for longer than one RTC step. If you allowed active objects to intercept events (thus acquiring ownership of events), the framework would have to be notified somehow to spare these events from destruction. In the quantum metaphor, this would correspond to an energy-intensive process of converting virtual particles into real ones, which would lead to a convoluted implementation that nature doesn't favor.

The QF event-passing mechanism that emerges from this analysis involves dynamic event allocation, subscribing to events, publishing events, event multicast-

---

21. If you still need to know who owns that darn photon, then you can think of it as belonging to the quantum vacuum.

22. Okay, the Big Bang itself might be exactly *the* one (pretty big though) violation of the uncertainty principle.

ing (in case of multiple subscriptions), and automatic event recycling. In the following sections, I cover all of these features in turn.

8.5.1   Dynamic Event Allocation

Now that you have an idea of the event-passing mechanism of the QF, you can contemplate implementing dynamic event allocation. If you think that my critique of the heap has caught up with me, you are only partially right. Simpler alternatives exist to the general-purpose, variable-block-size heap. A well-known alternative, commonly supported by RTOSs, is a fixed-block-size heap, also known as a memory partition or memory pool.

Unlike the conventional (variable-block-size) heap, a fixed-block-size heap has guaranteed capacity. It is not subject to fragmentation because all blocks are exactly the same size. Because all blocks have identical size, no header is associated with each block allocated, thus reducing the system overhead per block. Furthermore, allocation through a fixed-block-size heap can be very fast and completely deterministic. This aspect allows you to protect a fixed-block-size heap with a critical section of code (briefly disabling interrupts) rather than a mutex. As explained in Section 8.4.1 briefly disabling interrupts does not cause priority inversion. In the case of a fixed-block-size heap, the access is so fast that interrupts need to be disabled only briefly (no longer than other critical sections in the system), which does not increase interrupt latency and allows access to such a heap, even from ISRs.

Note: A fixed-block-size heap is no different from any other multitasking kernel object. For example accessing a mutex also requires briefly turning off interrupts (after all, a mutex is also a shared resource).

The most obvious drawback of a fixed-block-size heap is that it does not support variable-sized blocks. Consequently, the blocks have to be oversized to handle the biggest possible allocation. Such a policy is often too wasteful if the actual sizes of allocated objects (events in this case) vary a lot. A good compromise is often to use not one, but a few heaps with blocks of different sizes — for example, small, medium, and large.

For the sake of the following discussion, the term "event pool" stands for a fixed-block-size heap customized specifically to hold events. Assume that a quantum event pool class QEPool encapsulates a fixed-block-size heap and provides the myEvtSize attribute for accessing the size of the events managed by the pool. (In Chapter 9, you will find concrete implementations of the QEPool class.) Further assume that the class provides three methods: init(), get(), and put() for pool initialization, event allocation, and event recycling, respectively.

Listing 8.2   Simple QF policy of using multiple event pools

```
1 static QEPool locPool[MAX_POOL];           // allocate MAX_POOL event pools
2                    // The pool pointers keep track of pools actually used.
3                    // The first and last poolPtr are not used (must be 0),
4                    // which is guaranteed by static initialization in C/C++.
5 static QEPool *locPoolPtr[1 + MAX_POOL + 1];
6
7 void QF::poolInit(void *poolSto,
8                   unsigned nEvts, unsigned evtSize)
9 {
10    static unsigned poolId = 0;
11    REQUIRE(poolId < MAX_POOL);                 // cannot exceed the # of pools
12             // please initialize event pools in ascending order of evtSize:
13    REQUIRE(poolId == 0 || locPoolPtr[poolId]->myEvtSize < evtSize);
14    QF_EPOOL_INIT(&locPool[poolId], poolSto, nEvts, evtSize);
15    locPoolPtr[poolId + 1] = &locPool[poolId];       //add *initialized* pool
16    ++poolId;                              // one more pool; (poolId of 0 not used)
17 }
18
19 QEvent *QF::create(unsigned evtSize, QSignal sig) {
20    register unsigned id;
21    register QEPool *p;
22    for (id = 1, p = locPoolPtr[1]; p; p = locPoolPtr[++id]) {
23        if (evtSize <= p->myEvtSize) { //will evtSize fit in this pool?
24            register QEvent *e;
25            e = (QEvent *)p->get();
26            ASSERT(e);                      // the pool must not run out of events
27            e->poolId = id;                         // store pool-ID in the e
28            e->sig = sig;                           // set signal for this e
29            e->useNum = 0;                        // this e is new, not used yet
30            return e;
31        }
32    }
33    ASSERT(0);                  // event too big to fit in any initialized pool
34    return 0;          // should never be reached, just to avoid compiler fuss
35 }
```

Listing 8.2 shows three methods of the QF that implement a straightforward policy for accessing multiple event pools. You use this policy simply to allocate an event from the event pool of the smallest block size that can fit the requested event size. For example, if you initialize two event pools to block sizes of 100 bytes (small-block pool), and 200 bytes (big-block pool), then an event of 68 bytes will be allocated from the small-block pool and an event of 135 bytes from the big-block pool (Figure 8.2).

Figure 8.2   QF with two initialized event pools

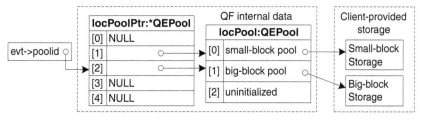

Event pools require initialization through `QF::poolInit()` (Listing 8.2, lines 7–17). According to the general memory management policy of the QF, this method requires storage for the event buffer (in the `poolSto` argument). The other arguments are the number of events in the pool (`nEvts`) and the event size (`evtSize`) in bytes. Internally, the QF maintains two arrays: the array of event pool objects (`locPool[]`) and the array of pointers to event pools (`locPoolPtr[]`). This latter array serves as an indirection layer that (1) indicates which pools are actually initialized and (2) provides mapping between pool IDs and pool objects.

In this design, event instances "remember" which event pool they came from (in the `poolId` attribute) so they can be recycled back to the same pool. A pool ID of 0 has a special meaning (notice that `locPoolPtr[0]` is always NULL in Figure 8.2). It indicates that an event is not coming from any event pool, which is useful for occasional optimizations (e.g., timeout events don't need to be allocated and recycled to event pools).

For possibly quick event allocation (`QF::create()`), the pointers to event pools must be sorted in ascending order of event sizes. Indeed, the indirection layer of `locPoolPtr[]` allows arbitrary mapping between pools and pool IDs (indices into the `locPoolPtr[]` array), and it would be relatively easy to sort the `locPoolPtr[]` array according to the block sizes in the `QF::poolInit()` method. This arrangement would give clients the flexibility of initializing event pools in any order, not necessarily in the ascending order of the block sizes. However, do clients really need such flexibility? Typically, clients initialize event pools on application startup, and it's not an inconvenience to do it in any order, including the desired one. The only problem is that clients should *know* about it. In situations like that, a contract (such as the precondition in line 13 of Listing 8.2) can help. This contract spells out that each invocation of `QF::poolInit()` (except the first one) must initialize the event pool of a bigger block size than the previous one. This *tactical* contract guards against clients forgetting the correct order of initialization (they will find out soon enough, should they forget) and saves `poolInit()` from sorting the `locPoolPtr[]` array, which although straightforward, could easily triple the size of the method. This is just one example of how contracts can lead to simpler code.

The `QF::create()` method (Listing 8.2, lines 19–35) is a straightforward implementation of the event allocation policy discussed earlier. The method scans through `locPoolPtr[]` starting from pool ID = 1, and as soon as it finds a pool that can accommodate the requested size (line 23), it obtains a memory block from this pool (line 25). Subsequently, `QF::create()` asserts that the pool has not run out of blocks (line 26). This is an example of a *strategic* contract. Alternative approaches could be to return an error code, to let clients decide whether this is an error or exceptional condition, or to block on the pool and wait until other active objects release some events (Section 8.4 argues why blocking is a bad idea). The contract in line 26 is an important design decision; it treats running out of pool space as an error not less severe than, for example, running out of stack space.

Typically, you will not use `QF::create()` directly, but through the `Q_NEW()` macro.

```
#define Q_NEW(evtT_, sig_) ((evtT_ *)QF::create(sizeof(evtT_), (sig_)))
```

This macro dynamically creates a new event of type `evT_` (all event types in the QF are subclasses of `QEvent`) with the signal `sig_`. It returns a pointer to the event already downcast to the event type `evT_*`. The contract in line 26 of Listing 8.2 guarantees that the pointer is valid, so you don't need to check the pointer (unlike the value returned from `malloc()`, which you should always check).

8.5.2   Publish–Subscribe Model

As described in Chapter 7, the QF uses the publish–subscribe interaction model — a popular way of decoupling the event producers from the consumers.[23] More specifically, the design of the QF hinges on the combination of Observer and Mediator design patterns [Gamma+ 95], where active objects play the role of Observers, and the QF is the Change Manager (a specific kind of Mediator).

Within the QF, the design patterns work as follows. On startup, each active object subscribes to one or more signals by the framework, thus becoming an observer (the default subject is the QF). From that time on, anything that happens in the application is a direct or indirect result of publishing events. The publication requests to the framework can originate asynchronously from many sources, not necessarily active objects — for example, from interrupts or device drivers. The QF manages all these interactions as the Change Manager. In this role, the QF has three responsibilities:

---

23. For example, the Java 1.1 Event Model is a publish–subscribe architecture for delivering events from event sources (subjects) to action listeners (observers).

- provide an interface for active objects to subscribe and unsubscribe to particular signals (`QF::subscribe()`/`QF::unsubscribe()`),
- provide a generally accessible interface for publishing events (`QF::publish()`), and
- define the event delivery policy (update strategy for subjects).

Figure 8.3   Signal-to-subscriber lookup table and `QSubscrList` data type

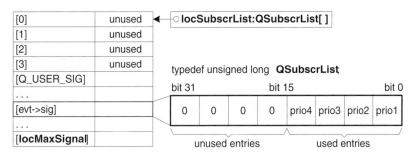

Delivering events is the most frequently performed function of the framework; therefore, it is important to implement efficiently. The QF uses a lookup table to map signals (`e->sig`) to subscriber lists, as shown in Figure 8.3. A subscriber list is a list of active objects that have subscribed to a given signal. The list (`typedef`'d to `QSubscrList`) is just a densely packed bit field storing unique priorities of active objects[24] (more precisely, priorities of the threads associated with active objects; Section 8.6.3). Consequently, the QF requires that clients assign a unique priority to each active object (through `QActive::start()`), even when the QF is based on an operating system that does not support thread priorities in the preemptive, priority-based sense.[25] As will become clear in the next section (covering the policy of delivering events), the priorities stored in subscriber lists serve both to identify active objects and to resolve contentions over events when more than one active object has subscribed to the same event type.

---

24. The current implementation of the QF designates four bits per active object in the 32-bit `QSubscrList`, but you can change both the size of `QSubscrList` and the number of bits per active object.
25. Real-time constraints practically exclude systems that do not support thread priorities. However, the QF can be ported to almost any operating system, not necessarily real-time systems (e.g., Windows), in which case you just make up a unique priority for each active object.

Note:	In severely memory-constraint applications, the size of the subscriber lookup table could become a concern, in which case you might try to reduce the number of different signals and reduce QSubscrList to only 16, or even 8, bits. Typically, however, the table is quite small. For example, the table for a complete real-life GPS receiver application with 50 different signals costs 200 bytes of RAM.

Active objects subscribe to signals through QF::subscribe(), as shown in Listing 8.3. In the precondition (lines 3, 4), the method asserts that the signal is indeed in the range established by QF::init() and that the active object is known to the framework under the priority it claims (the active object becomes known to the framework through QActive::start(), which invokes QF::add(), as discussed in Section 8.6.3). Subsequently, QF::subscribe() enters a critical section of code[26] (line 5) to *atomically* add the new priority to the locSubscrList[sig] subscriber list corresponding to the signal sig. In line 7, the method asserts that the list still has room for new subscribers (the last slot still must be free).

Figure 8.4   **Inserting a new priority into the subscriber list at bit *n* (see QF::subscribe(), Listing 8.3)**

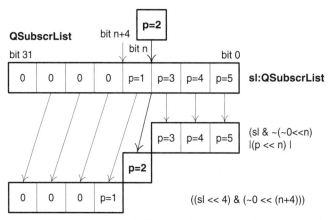

For subsequent efficient event delivery, the method needs to keep the subscriber list sorted in descending order of priorities (i.e., higher priorities at lower bit numbers). This sorting is achieved when the for loop scans for the right slot in which to

---

26. I'm concerned at this point only with the integrity of the subscriber list and not whether the critical section extends the interrupt latency. I assume that subscriptions happen at the startup transient, when interrupt latency does not matter yet.

insert the new priority, as well as in some creative bit shifting and bit masking in lines 10 through 12 (see also Figure 8.4).

Listing 8.3   `QF::subscribe()/QF::unsubscribe()` **pair of methods**

```
 1 void QF::subscribe(QActive *a, QSignal sig) {
 2    register unsigned char p = a->myPrio;        // priority of active object
 3    REQUIRE(Q_USER_SIG <= sig && sig < locMaxSignal &&      // boundary chk
 4          p < QF_MAX_ACTIVE && pkgActive[p] == a);      //consistency chk
 5    QF_PROTECT();                              // enter critical section
 6    register QSubscrList sl = locSubscrList[sig];
 7    ASSERT((sl & 0xF0000000) == 0);           //must have at least one free slot
 8    for (register int n = 0; n < 32; n += 4) {        // find priority slot
 9       if (p > ((sl >> n) & 0xF)) {           // found priority slot?
10          sl = (sl & ~(~0 << n)) |          // part of sl with priorities>p
11             (p << n) |                    // insert p at bit n
12             ((sl << 4) & (~0 << (n + 4)));     // shifted rest of sl
13          locSubscrList[sig] = sl;          // update the subscriber-list
14          break;              // subscriber registered (attached to the list)
15       }
16    }
17    QF_UNPROTECT();                            // leave critical section
18 }
19
20 void QF::unsubscribe(QActive *a, QSignal sig) {
21    register unsigned char p = a->myPrio;        // priority of active object
22    REQUIRE(Q_USER_SIG <= sig && sig < locMaxSignal &&        // boundary chk
23          pkgActive[p] == a);                 // consistency check
24    QF_PROTECT();                              // enter critical section
25    register QSubscrList sl = locSubscrList[sig];
26    for (register int n = 0; n < 32; n += 4) {        // find priority slot
27       if (p == ((sl >> n) & 0xF)) {          // found priority slot?
28          sl =  (sl & ~(~0 << n)) | ((sl >> 4) & (~0 << n));
29          locSubscrList[sig] = sl;          // update the subscriber-list
30          break;              // subscription canceled (removed from the list)
31       }
32    }
33    QF_UNPROTECT();                            // leave critical section
34 }
```

For completeness, the QF provides unsubscribe() (Listing 8.3, lines 20–34), which does the reverse of QF::subscribe(). Please note that both subscribe() and unsubscribe() require an active object as a parameter, which means that only active objects are capable of subscribing to events (only active objects can become Observers).

Publishing events through `QF::publish()` (Listing 8.4), on the other hand, takes an event instance as the sole parameter. This method is designed to be callable from both a task and an interrupt. In the precondition (lines 2, 3), `QF::publish()` checks whether the signal associated with the event is in range and whether the event is not already in use. "In use" here means that the event instance has been published but the framework hasn't recycled it yet. You cannot publish such an event instance because it would conflict with the event-passing mechanism of the QF discussed earlier. This mechanism prohibits, among other things, intercepting events and publishing them again. To remember whether it is in use, every event stores the number of uses in the `useNum` attribute, which must be 0 for an unused event (Sections 8.5.3 and 8.5.4).

Listing 8.4   `QF::publish()` **method**

```
 1 void QF::publish(QEvent *e) {
 2     REQUIRE(e->sig < locMaxSignal &&            // signal exceeding boundary
 3             e->useNum == 0);                    // event cannot be "in use"
 4     register QSubscrList sl = locSubscrList[e->sig];      //table look-up
 5     if (sl) {                                   // any subscribers?
 6         register unsigned char p = (unsigned char)(sl & 0xF);
 7         e->useNum = 1;                          // the first use
 8         ASSERT(pkgActive[p]);                // active object must have subscribed
 9         ALLEGE(pkgActive[p]->enqueue(e));        // queue cannot overflow!
10     }
11     else {                                      // no subscribers
12         QF::annihilate(e);                      // do not leak the event
13     }
14 }
```

Finding a subscriber list corresponding to the signal of the event (`e->sig`) is fast thanks to an efficient table lookup (Listing 8.4, line 4). An empty subscriber list indicates that the signal has no subscribers, and to avoid an event leak, the routine must annihilate the event immediately (line 12). If the signal has subscribers, the routine extracts the first subscriber (the subscriber with the highest priority) from the least significant bits of the subscriber list (line 6). Subsequently in line 8, the method asserts that the subscriber indeed has been registered by the framework (note that the `pkgActive[]` array is in fact another mapping from priorities to active objects). Finally, in line 9, `QF::publish()` places the event on the recipient's event queue.[27]

Inserting an event into the recipient's event queue in line 9 is associated with a strategic contract. This contract declares a failure to enqueue an event (e.g., because of an insufficient event queue size) a bug. In essence, this contract boils down to

---

27. The concrete way of accessing an event queue depends on the platform-dependent implementation.

guaranteed event delivery[28] because an event instance that is successfully placed in a queue is guaranteed to be dispatched and eventually processed. Consequently, with this contract in place, every publisher of an event can safely assume that all subscribers will receive the event. Note that the contract gives no guarantees as to the timeliness of the delivery, only that the event will be delivered and eventually dispatched to the state machines of all subscribers. Still, this guarantee can vastly simplify any active object–based system because active objects often need to maintain mutual consistency in their state.

For example in the dining philosophers problem (Chapter 7), the state of the Table object must match the state of each Philosopher object. If a Philosopher publishes the HUNGRY event (simultaneously entering the hungry state) and the event is not delivered to Table (perhaps because Table's event queue cannot accommodate it at the time), the Philosopher object will surely starve. The Table object will never notice (by changing its state or setting an extended state variable) that the Philosopher object is hungry, so it will never give it permission to eat. Without the guarantee of delivery, a Philosopher object could try to retransmit the HUNGRY event several times, to make sure that the Table object takes notice. (After all, a Philosopher's life is at stake.) This repetition would lead to immense complications in the Philosopher as well as Table state machines because Table would have to distinguish between the original event and the retransmitted copies. The event delivery guarantee avoids all this mess, at the much lower cost of properly sized event queues.[29]

8.5.3   Multicasting Events

In the publish–subscribe mechanism of the QF, it is common for multiple active objects (observers) to subscribe to the same signal. The mechanism is then supposed to multicast identical copies of the event to all registered active objects simultaneously, much as a newspaper publisher is supposed to send out identical copies of a newspaper to all subscribers.

Indeed, the QF keeps track of potential multiple subscriptions to any given signal through the subscriber lists discussed earlier. However, QF::publish(), described in Section 8.5.2, posts the event only to the first subscriber on the list (Listing 8.4, line 9), rather than to all subscribers at once, because the QF is frugal and avoids the costly act of copying events. Instead, the QF circulates a single copy around to all the subscribers. Nonetheless, on a single-processor machine running under a preemptive,

---

28. Strictly speaking, the contract in line 9 of Listing 8.4 only covers delivery to the highest priority subscriber. However, event delivery to other subscribers is also consistently associated with a similar contract (QF::propagate(), Listing 8.5).

29. Chapter 10 discusses the issues associated with sizing event queues.

priority-based schedule (see Section 8.4), this more economical approach is indistinguishable from true multicasting.

A preemptive, priority-based scheduler allocates the CPU to the highest priority thread ready to run. Suppose that the QF truly multicasts several copies of an event to several active objects simultaneously. However, in a single-CPU system, only one thread can execute at a time — the highest priority thread ready to run. After the multicast, it is the highest priority subscriber to the event. It runs to completion and relinquishes the CPU to the next highest priority subscriber, which again runs to completion, and so on. This sequence continues until finally the lowest priority active object on the subscriber list gets a chance to process the event. As you can see, the scheduling algorithm automatically arranges sequential processing, in which only one copy of the event is in use at any given time.

The QF arranges for an identical sequence of processing, as a preemptive, priority-based scheduler would. As you recall from Section 8.5.2, subscriber lists are ordered in the descending order of subscriber priority. The first entry on the list (at the lowest bit number) corresponds to the highest priority subscriber and is the first active object that gets the event in the QF::publish() method. Subsequently, QActive::run() (Listing 8.8 later in this chapter) propagates the event to the next subscriber on the list by invoking QF::propagate().

Listing 8.5   **QF::propagate() method**

```
1 void QF::propagate(QEvent *e) {
2     if (e->useNum > 0) {                        // should QF propagate this event?
3         ASSERT(e->sig < locMaxSignal);              // signal must be in range!
4         register QSubscrList sl = locSubscrList[e->sig];
5         sl >>= (e->useNum*4);          // shift out already serviced subscribers
6         if (sl) {                                  // more subscribers available?
7             register unsigned char p = (unsigned char)(sl & 0xF);
8             ++e->useNum;                                            // next use
9             ASSERT(pkgActive[p]);               // active object must have started
10            ALLEGE(pkgActive[p]->enqueue(e));      // queue cannot overflow!
11            return;                                        // event propagated
12        }
13    }
14    QF::annihilate(e);                 // event not propagated; don't leak it!
15 }
```

Listing 8.5 shows the implementation of QF::propagate(). First, in line 2, the method checks the use number of the event, e->useNum. The number greater than zero indicates that the event is in the middle of the just-described multicasting sequence and needs to be propagated to the next subscriber. An e->useNum of 0, on the other hand, indicates that the event is not intended for multicast (e.g., timeout events fall into this category, see Section 8.8). Such events should be annihilated (line 14).

In line 3, the routine asserts that the signal of the event is in range. In line 4, the routine obtains the subscriber list through the same table lookup as QF::publish(). In line 5, the subscriber list is right-shifted to put the current subscriber into the least significant bit position. In addition, this shift automatically gets rid of the subscribers serviced so far (they "fall off" the least significant bit). If the subscriber list is still not empty (line 6), then QF::propagate() extracts the current subscriber priority in line 7 and increments the event use number, e->useNum, in line 8 to indicate the next use of the event. Lines 9 and 10 are identical to lines 8 and 9 of QF::publish() (line 10 corresponds to the guaranteed event delivery strategic contract).

The sequential multicast mechanism implemented in QF::publish() and QF::propagate() closely approximates a "true" simultaneous multicast only under the following conditions. First, all subscribers must receive the same, unaltered event instance. To this end, the signature of the state handler (Chapter 4) declares the event immutable (QEvent const *e), which should prevent alterations to the event.[30] Second, the sequence of processing exactly follows the priorities of the subscribers only if active objects do not block in the middle of RTC processing. Such blocking (generally a *bad idea*, see Section 8.4) could unpredictably change the processing sequence. Finally, the sequence will be correct only under a preemptive, priority-based scheduler. The QF specifically addresses only this case because no other scheduling algorithm gives a better task-level response; consequently, the preemptive, priority-based scheduler is the most common choice for hard real-time systems. Other scheduling algorithms that could be advantageous in "soft" real-time systems might result in differences between true and sequential event multicasting; then again, these differences should be tolerable for meeting only soft deadlines.

8.5.4 Automatic Event Recycling

The requirement for automatic event recycling is a logical consequence of loose coupling among producers of events (publishers) and consumers (subscribers). The producers should not know or care who will subscribe to their events, including situations when an event won't be subscribed at all;[31] in which case, the published event simply leaks if not automatically recycled.

The event-passing mechanism in the QF has been designed up front with automatic event recycling in mind. All events must funnel through only two framework methods. The first is QF::publish(), which recycles the event in the case of an empty

---

30. Alterations to a received event instance would be like scribbling in a book borrowed from a library.
31. Such a situation can arise easily in the early stages of modeling, when the application is simply incomplete.

subscriber list (Listing 8.4, line 12). The other is `QF::propagate()`, which recycles an event after the last subscriber on the list has processed it (Listing 8.5, line 14).

Listing 8.6   `QF::annihilate()` method

```
1 void QF::annihilate(QEvent *e) {
2    if (e->poolId) {                              // is it a pool event?
3       ASSERT(e->poolId <= MAX_POOL && locPoolPtr[e->poolId]);
4       locPoolPtr[e->poolId]->put(e);        // return event back to the pool
5    }
6    else {                                        // this is not a pool event
7       e->useNum = 0;          // recycle event by clearing the number of uses
8    }
9 }
```

In both cases, the framework invokes `QF::annihilate()` (Listing 8.6). Client code is not allowed to use the `QF::annihilate()` method directly (this method is declared `private` in the `QF` class); rather, the clients must rely on automatic event recycling. `QF::annihilate()` recycles pool events (`e->poolId != 0`, Section 8.5.1) differently than nonpool events. Pool events are always recycled to the pool of their origin (line 4). The nonpool events (`e->poolId == 0`) are recycled by clearing their use number (`e->useNum`).

8.6   Active Objects

From the client's perspective, the most important step in constructing a QF-based application is conceiving the concrete active object classes. As in all other active object–based frameworks, the QF provides a base class for deriving concrete active objects. In the QF, this base class is `QActive`. It combines the following three essential elements: (1) it *is a* state machine (derives from the `QHsm` class),[32] (2) it *has* an event queue, and (3) it *has* an execution thread. The class diagram in Figure 8.5 shows the relationships among these classes.

8.6.1   Internal State Machine

Every concrete active object *is a* state machine because it descends indirectly from the `QHsm` base class, making the whole power and convenience of the behavioral inheritance meta-pattern (the subject of Part I of this book) immediately available for constructing the behavior of active objects. At the application level, you can mostly abstract away all the other aspects of an active object and view it only as a

---

32. For systems with very constrained resources, you might consider deriving `QActive` from the simpler, nonhier-archical state machine `QFsm` (Chapter 3) rather than from `QHsm`.

Figure 8.5   `QActive` **class diagram**

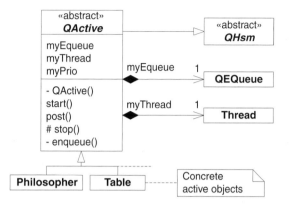

state machine. This abstraction is possible because other elements of an active object, like the event queue or execution thread, work transparently behind the scenes to nurture the embedded statechart with events and CPU cycles.

One of the biggest advantages of the QF is the support for rapid construction of executable models. The framework helps you to put together active objects that make up the application quickly and then to elaborate gradually their internal details (mostly their state machines), keeping the application executable at all times.

8.6.2   Event Queue

Event queues are essential components of any active object–based framework because they allow you to reconcile the asynchronous production of events with the RTC semantics of their consumption. An event queue makes the corresponding active object *appear* always to be receptive to events, even though the internal state machine can accept events only between RTC steps. Additionally, the event queue provides buffer space that protects the internal statechart from bursts in event production that can, at times, exceed the available processing capacity.

You can view the active object's event queue as an outer rind that provides an external interface for injecting events into the active object, protecting the internal statechart during RTC processing at the same time. To perform these functions, the event queue must allow any thread of execution (as well as ISR) to asynchronously insert events, but only one thread — the local thread of the active object — needs to be able to extract events from the queue.[33] In other words, the event queue in the QF needs multiple-write, but only single-read, access (Figure 8.6).

---

33. This mechanism is known in GUI systems as the "message pump."

Figure 8.6   Event queue of an active object holding pointers to event instances

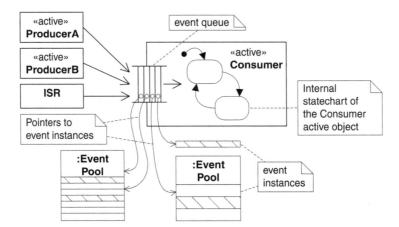

From the description so far, it should be clear that the event queue is quite a sophisticated mechanism. One end of the queue — the end where producers insert events — is obviously shared among many threads and must provide an adequate mutual exclusion mechanism to protect the internal consistency of the queue. The other end — the end from which the local thread extracts events — must provide a mechanism for blocking this thread when the queue is empty. In addition, an event queue must manage a buffer of events, typically organized in a FIFO structure.

As shown in Figure 8.6, the QF event queues do not store actual events, only pointers to event instances. Typically, these pointers point to event instances allocated dynamically from event pools (Section 8.5.1), but they can also point to statically allocated events. You need to specify the maximum number of event pointers that a queue can hold at any one time (the capacity of the queue) in QActive::start() (see the following section). The correct sizing of event queues depends on many factors and generally is not a trivial task. Chapter 10 discusses sizing event queues.

Many commercial RTOSs natively support a queuing mechanism in the form of message queues (sometimes called mailboxes or message mailboxes). A message queue typically maps well to the event queue described here. Standard message queues are far more flexible than required by active objects because they typically support variable-length data (not only pointer-sized data) and allow multiple-write as well as multiple-read access (the QF requires only single-read access). Usually, message queues also allow blocking when the queue is empty and when the queue is full, and both types of blocking can be timed out. (Naturally, all this extra functionality, which you don't really need, comes at an extra cost in CPU and memory usage.) Before you accept the queuing mechanism provided in your RTOS, check how the RTOS implements mutual exclusion in the queue. The right way is to treat the message queue as the first-class kernel object (like a semaphore for example) and to implement mutual exclusion by briefly disabling interrupts. The problematic way is to protect the message queue with a mutex, because this might lead to the priority inversion problem discussed in Section 8.4.1.

In Chapter 9, you will find an example of an event queue built from a message queue of an RTOS, as well as an example of an event queue implemented from scratch.

8.6.3   Thread of Execution

Every active object in the QF executes in its own thread of execution.[34] At some point in the initialization sequence (Section 8.7.1), a QF application needs to call QActive::start() on behalf of every concrete active object in the system to create and start the execution thread associated with that object.

The QActive::start() method, which I mentioned in Section 8.3.2, is one of the central elements of the framework. Unfortunately, it is also one of the most platform-dependent methods, so Listing 8.7 shows only a pseudocode version.[35]

Listing 8.7   QActive::start() method (pseudocode)

```
 1 void QActive::start(unsigned prio, QEvent*qSto[], unsigned qLen,
 2                     int stkSto[], unsigned stkLen)
 3 {
 4    myPrio = prio;                 // store the priority in the attribute
 5    QF::add(this);                 // register "this" active object by QF
 6
 7    // create event queue "myEqueue" of length "qLen"
 8    // create execution thread "myThread" with priority "prio"
 9    //         and stack size "stkLen"
10
11    // postcondition: assert proper creation of event-queue and thread
12 }
```

The first argument of QActive::start() is the priority you must assign to the active object. A high priority means high urgency and has relevance only relative to other priorities. In the QF, every active object must have a unique priority, which you must assign on startup and cannot change later. The QF uses a priority numbering scheme in which priority 1 is the lowest and higher numbers correspond to higher

---

34. In some implementations of the QF, active objects can share a common thread of execution (I'll show an example in Chapter 9). However, the reference design presented here assumes a separate thread for every active object.
35. Chapter 9 shows concrete implementations for specific platforms.

priorities.[36] If the underlying scheduler uses a different priority numbering scheme,[37] then the concrete implementation of start() must remap the QF priority to the priority required by the scheduler before invoking the platform-specific thread creation routine (corresponding to line 8 in Listing 8.7).

Once started, all active objects execute the following thread routine (i.e., all active object threads *share* the following code).

```
/* return type, calling convention */ run(void *a, /*... */) {
    ((QActive *)a)->run();
}
```

The comments in the signature of the thread routine are supposed to denote a platform-specific calling convention (e.g., __cdecl, __near, __far, etc.), return type, and other arguments potentially required by the underlying multitasking kernel. Note that the thread routine is not a method of the QActive class because, typically, only a free function can serve as a thread's entry point.[38] On the other hand, most RTOSs allow you to pass at least one generic pointer to the thread routine, which QActive::start() uses to pass the active object.

Thread processing happens in QActive::run() (Listing 8.8). This method starts by executing the initial transition (line 2) of the state machine associated with the active object (see the QHsm::init() method in Chapter 4, page 107). This transition is an appropriate place to initialize extended state variables, subscribe to events, initialize the hardware managed by the active object, and so on. Subsequently, the thread routine enters a typical endless loop (line 3) of waiting for the event to arrive through the event queue (line 4), before dispatching it for RTC processing through the dispatch() method inherited from QHsm (line 5) and propagating it to other subscribers (line 6). Propagating events is part of multicasting and automatic event recycling, which are discussed separately in Section 8.5.3 and 8.5.4, respectively.

Listing 8.8   Thread routine of an active object

```
1 void QActive::run() {
2     QHsm::init();                        // execute initial transition
3     for (;;) {                                            // for-ever
4         QEvent *e = myEqueue->get();      // get event; block if queue empty
```

---

36. You can think of priority 0 as corresponding to the idle task, which has the absolute lowest priority not accessible to user threads.
37. For example, the VxWorks kernel Wind uses a numbering scheme in which priority 0 corresponds to the highest and 255 to the lowest priority tasks [WindRiver 97].
38. In the C version of the QF, you can use the "C+" class "method" directly because it is already a free function.

```
5        dispatch(e);                     // dispatch event to the statechart
6        QF::propagate(e);                // propagate event to next subscriber
7    }
8 }
```

Please note that all actions associated with the statechart embedded within the active object (including the initial transition) execute in the thread context of the host active object. Consequently, the stack allocated to the thread must be sized sufficiently to accommodate the worst-case nesting of all the actions invoked from the corresponding state handler methods.

Note: To minimize stack use, the behavioral inheritance meta-pattern specifically avoids recursion (which is natural in hierarchical structures like HSM) and judiciously sizes all automatic variables.

8.7   Initialization and Cleanup

Initialization and cleanup of a multithreaded application, such as a set of cooperating active objects, has two main aspects. The first — already discussed — is associated with allocating and recycling memory. The second — described in this section — relates to starting up and shutting down multitasking.

8.7.1   Initializing the Framework

Before you can start active object–based multithreading, you need to perform a basic initialization of the framework itself. You must invoke two methods: QF::init() once and QF::poolInit() for each event pool you want to initialize. The following code fragment illustrates this part of the initialization sequence for just one event pool.

```
enum MySignals {                // enumeration of all signals used in the system
   MY_SIG1 = Q_USER_SIG,
   . . .
   MAX_SIG                                        // biggest signal ever used
};
static QSubscrList subscrSto[MAX_SIG];        // storage for subscriber lists
static MyBiggestEvt evtPoolSto[20];           // array capable of holding 20
                                              // biggest events
int main() {
   QF::init(subscrSto, MAX_SIG);         // init. QF with storage for look-up
   QF::poolInit(evtPoolSto, sizeof(evtPoolSto)/sizeof(*evtPoolSto),
           sizeof(MyBiggestEvt));             // initialize event-pool
   . . .
}
```

Please note the static allocation of storage for the subscriber list (subscrSto) and event pool (evtPoolSto) and the subsequent passing of this memory over to the framework. The QF::init() method is defined as follows.

```
void QF::init(QSubscrList subscr[], unsigned maxSignal) {
    locSubscrList = subscr;              // point to the user-provided storage
    locMaxSignal = maxSignal;            // remember look-up table boundary
    osInit();                            // call OS-dependent QF initialization
}
```

Although correctly sizing the subscriber list lookup table is straightforward (it must accommodate all signals in the system), QF::poolInit() (covered in Section 8.5.1) requires a more tricky decision — proper sizing event pools. In general, the capacity of event pools is related to how many event instances you can "sink" in your system, which is discussed in more detail in Chapter 10.

8.7.2   Starting the QF Application

Starting threads of execution associated with active objects can be problematic because correct initialization can be very sensitive to the sequence and timing of operations.

The QActive::start() method gives you the flexibility to start active objects in any order. The thread created in start() is typically ready to run immediately, so you must be cautious about potential preemption of the current thread by the newly created active object thread. One way to eliminate preemption during the startup phase is to lock the scheduler until all active objects are started (note that disabling interrupts will not do the trick). Some multitasking kernels (e.g., µC/OS) allow you to defer starting multitasking until *after* you start the active objects. Another alternative might be to start active objects from within other active objects, but this choice increases coupling because the active object that serves as the launch pad must "know" all active objects to be launched.

The signature of QActive::start() forces you to make two important decisions for your application to be correct. The first concerns the relative priorities of the active objects of your application. The second decision (which is related to the first) concerns the size of the event queues you preallocated for the active objects. To make these decisions correctly, you need to know the urgency of specific active objects (the real-time constraints), as well as which kind of events they subscribe to (Chapter 10 covers these issues in more detail).

8.7.3   Gracefully Terminating the QF Application

If starting a multithreading application is tricky, then shutting it down gracefully is very tricky. The problem is that the cleanest way to end an active object's thread is to have it stop voluntarily either by returning from its thread routine, or by explicitly calling `QActive::stop()`.[39] Of course to "commit suicide," in that way, the active object must not block (on its own event queue, for example). In addition, before disappearing, the thread should release all the resources acquired during its lifetime. Unfortunately, making a thread stop voluntarily cannot be preprogrammed generically at the framework level and always requires some work on the application programmer's part.

Because the active object's thread routine is organized into an infinite loop (Listing 8.8), the preferred way to end a thread is to call `QActive::stop()` from within the thread. Perhaps the best place to invoke this method is the entry action of the explicit final state (see Section 5.1.3 in Chapter 5).

You can use `QActive::stop()` to terminate one active object at a time. Complete shutdown of the whole application, however, requires waiting until the *last* active object voluntarily stops; only then is the shutdown process complete. This is perhaps the most difficult aspect of the process (how would you know which object is the last?). The shutdown of an application is very important for desktop applications, to be sure, but much less so in embedded systems. The embedded programs almost never have a need to shutdown gracefully because the job of the typical embedded application is never finished. Most embedded applications have to continue as long as the power is on. Therefore, you can simply ignore the graceful shutdown process in most cases.

Note: "Application shutdown" here means complete termination of the embedded application. Entering the "sleep mode" that many embedded devices have is considered just another mode (state) of the application and doesn't count as a complete shutdown.

8.8   Time Management

Time management available in traditional real-time kernels includes timed blocking on various kernel objects (e.g., semaphores, message queues), delaying a calling thread (`sleep()`), and invoking a user-provided callback function after a specified delay using various timers (signals). These mechanisms are not very useful in active object–based systems.[40]

---

39. The concrete implementation of `QActive::stop()` strongly depends on the underlying operating system.
40. Timed blocking on a semaphore might be applicable when blocking an active object thread not related to other active objects (Section 8.4.2).

Instead, to be compatible with active object–based multithreading, time management must be based on a general paradigm in which every interesting occurrence manifests itself as an *event instance*. A clock device capable of generating event instances periodically at every *clock tick* matches this paradigm very well. In fact, every real-time system (regardless of whether it's based on traditional or active object–based multithreading) requires a clock, which typically is an external oscillator that interrupts the CPU at a predetermined (often programmable) rate.[41]

8.8.1   QTimer Class

The QF manages time through *timers* instantiated from the QTimer class. The basic usage model of these timers is as follows. An active object allocates one or more QTimer objects (provides the storage for them). When the active object needs to arrange for a timeout, it arms one of its timers to fire a timeout event. The timer provides two methods for that purpose: QTimer::fireIn() for a one-shot timeout and QTimer::fireEvery() for a periodic timeout event. Each timeout request has a different timer, so a QF application can make multiple parallel requests (from the same or different active objects). When the QF detects that the appropriate moment has arrived, it inserts the requested timeout event directly into the recipient's event queue. The recipient then processes the timeout event just like any other event.

To arm a timer, an active object must provide its this pointer, the timeout signal to deliver, and the number of clock ticks to elapse before delivery. The one-shot request (fireIn()) disarms the timer automatically after firing the event. The periodic timer (armed with fireEvery()), on the other hand, automatically rearms the timer by every timeout for the next shot. You can explicitly disarm any armed timer (periodic or one-shot) at any time by means of the QTimer::disarm() method. After disarming (explicitly or implicitly, as in the case of the one-shot timeout), the timer can be reused for one-shot or periodic timeouts. In addition, as long as the timer remains armed it can be rearmed with a different number of ticks through QTimer::rearm(). For one-shot timers, rearming is useful, for example, to implement *watchdog* timers that need to be periodically "tickled" to prevent them from ever timing out. Rearming might also be useful to adjust the phasing of periodic timers (often you need to extend or shorten one period).

Arming a timer is very much like subscribing to an event. One significant difference is that timeout events are not published globally; rather, they are delivered locally only to the requesting active object. This policy promotes loose coupling among active objects. For example, two different active objects can arm two separate timers to deliver the same signal (say, TIMEOUT_SIG); yet, each object will receive only the requested timeout event, rather than both events.

---

41. Typical clock rates lie between 5 and 100Hz.

8.8.2   Clock Tick, `QF::tick()` Method

To service the armed timers, you need to periodically invoke `QF::tick()`, preferably from the clock tick interrupt. This method (Listing 8.9) manages the open-ended linked list of timers.

Listing 8.9   `QF::tick()` method

```
 1 void QF::tick() {
 2    register QTimer *t, *pt;
 3    QF_ISR_PROTECT();
 4    for (t = pt = locTimerListHead; t; t = t->myNext) {
 5       if (--t->myCtr == 0) {
 6                                                    // queue cannot overflow
 7          ALLEGE(t->myActive->enqueue(&t->myToutEvt));
 8          if (t->myInterval) {                      // periodic timer?
 9             t->myCtr = t-> myInterval;             // rearm the timer
10             pt = t;
11          }
12          else {         // one-shot timer, disarm by removing from the list
13             if (t == locTimerListHead) {
14                locTimerListHead = pt = t->myNext;
15             }
16             else {
17                pt->myNext = t->myNext;
18             }
19             t->myActive = 0;                       // mark the timer free to use
20          }
21       }
22       else {
23          pt = t;
24       }
25    }
26    QF_ISR_UNPROTECT();
27 }
```

At every clock tick, `QF::tick()` scans the linked list of timers (Listing 8.9, line 4) and decrements the `myCtr` down-counter of each timer in the list. When the counter drops to 0, the routine inserts the requested event into the recipient's event queue (line 7). As usual, this operation is associated with the guaranteed event delivery contract. For a periodic timer (with a non-0 `myInterval`), the routine rearms the `myCtr` down-counter to the interval value `myInterval` (line 9). Otherwise, it is a one-shot timer and must be disarmed (lines 12–20). Disarming the timer corresponds to removing it from the linked list. However, because it is only a unidirectional (single-linked) list, the additional `pt` (previous timer) pointer is necessary.

The QF::tick() method is primarily designed for invocation from the interrupt context. For most embedded platforms, the macros QF_ISR_PROTECT() and QF_ISR_UNPROTECT() (Listing 8.9, lines 3 and 26) can translate to nothing because an ISR is always safe from preemptions by a task. For some platforms (e.g., Windows), however, you don't have easy access to the clock tick interrupt and you are forced to invoke QF::tick() from a task context (Chapter 9). A critical section is necessary in this case.

8.9   QF API Quick Reference

As a client of the QF, you need to be concerned only with three framework classes: the QF class, the QActive base class for derivation of concrete active objects, and the QTimer class for instantiating timers.[42] This section briefly summarizes the QF API.

8.9.1   QF Interface

The QF class encapsulates all top-level QF services. The class is unusual (Listing 8.10) because it has only static member functions and no data members. Such a class has only one instance and is equivalent to a module.[43] The use of a C++ class here is only to group related functions to avoid pollution of the global namespace. A specific QF namespace is not used because some older and embedded C++ (EC++) compilers don't support namespaces [EC++ 01]. Table 8.1 summarizes the public interface of the QF class.

Listing 8.10   QF class declaration

```
1 class QF {
2 public:
3     static char const *getVersion();
4     static void init(QSubscrList subscr[], unsigned maxSignal);
5     static void poolInit(void *poolSto,
6                          unsigned nEvts, unsigned evtSize);
7     static void tick();
8     static QEvent *create(unsigned evtSize, QSignal sig);
9     #define Q_NEW(evtT_, sig_) \
10            ((evtT_ *)QF::create(sizeof(evtT_), (sig_)))
11    static void subscribe(QActive *a, QSignal sig);
12    static void unsubscribe(QActive *a, QSignal sig);
13    static void publish(QEvent *e);
```

---

42. The other interesting class QEvent has no methods and so it's not described here.

43. The QF class specifically does not use the Singleton design pattern because it has no need for extensibility by subclassing and the additional cost of accessing the Singleton via the instance() method is not justified.

```
14    static void background();        //for foreground/background systems only
15    static void cleanup();
16 private:                            // internal interface for QActive only
17    static void osInit();                      // OS-dependent initialization
18    static void osCleanup();                        // OS-dependent cleanup
19    static void add(QActive *a);            // register an active object
20    static void remove(QActive *a);         // unregister an active object
21    static void propagate(QEvent *e);       // propagate to next subscriber
22    static void annihilate(QEvent *e);      // annihilate an event instance
23    friend class QActive;
24 };
```

Table 8.1   Brief summary of public QF methods

Method	Description
getVersion()	Return pointer to an immutable version string.
init()	Initialize the framework (requires memory for the subscriber list lookup table). Must be invoked only once.
poolInit()	Initialize the event pool (requires a memory buffer for the pool). Can be invoked several times to initialize event pools of different sizes.
tick()	Process one clock tick (should be called periodically from the clock tick ISR).
create()	Dynamically create an event instance of the specified size. Running out of free events in an event pool causes a contract violation. This method should be used through the Q_NEW() macro, not directly.
subscribe()	Subscribe to a specified signal (should be called by an active object). Multiple active objects can subscribe to the same signal.
unsubscribe()	Unsubscribe a specified signal (should be called by the subscriber active object). Unsubscribing a signal that is not subscribed by the given active object causes a contract violation.
publish()	Publish an event (can be called from a task or interrupt).
background()	Enter an endless background loop (defined only for foreground/background systems, see Chapter 9).
cleanup()	Perform a platform-dependent cleanup (should be called only on application exit).

8.9.2 QActive Interface

The QActive class is the abstract base class for deriving the concrete active objects. As shown in Listing 8.11, QActive derives from QHsm and thus inherits HSM functionality (described in Part I). Table 8.2 summarizes the public and protected methods that QActive adds to the QHsm interface.

Listing 8.11   QActive class

```
 1 class QActive : public QHsm {            // Quantum Active Object base class
 2 public:
 3    int start(unsigned prio, QEvent *qSto[], unsigned qLen,
 4             int stkSto[], unsigned stkLen);
 5    void postFIFO(QEvent *e);         // post event directly (FIFO enqueuing)
 6    void postLIFO(QEvent *e);         // post event directly (LIFO enqueuing)
 7    void run();            // run() is active throughout lifetime of the object
 8 protected:
 9    QActive(QPseudoState initial);                         // protected ctor
10    virtual ~QActive();                                   // virtual xtor
11    void stop();          // stopps the thread; nothing happens thereafter!
12 private:
13    int enqueue(QEvent *e);          // intended to use only by friend class QF
14 private:                                               // data members...
15    QF_EQUEUE(myEqueue)          // OS-dependent event-queue primitive
16    QF_THREAD(myThread)              // OS-dependent thread primitive
17    unsigned char myPrio;            // priority of the active object
18    friend class QF;
19 };
```

Table 8.2   **Brief summary of public and protected `QActive()` methods**

Method	Description
`QActive()`	The QActive constructor, which like the QHsm constructor, takes the initial pseudostate handler as the argument. The constructor is protected to prevent direct instantiation of the QActive class (the class is abstract, i.e., intended only for inheritance).
`start()`	Explicitly start an active object thread of execution. The caller needs to assign a unique priority to every active object in the system (assigning a priority that has already been used causes a contract violation). The priority must conform to the numbering scheme of QF and not to the priority numbering scheme of the underlying operating system. The lowest priority accessible to active objects is 1; higher priorities correspond to higher urgency. The caller also needs to commit memory for the event queue and for the execution stack. Some platforms allocate this memory internally, in which case the concrete implementation of the method could require passing NULL pointers for event queue storage, execution stack storage, or both. The start() method triggers the initial transition in the active object's HSM.
`postFIFO()`	Post an event directly to the active object's event queue using the FIFO policy. The primary intention of this method is to enable the Reminder state pattern (Chapter 5, Section 5.2) and to send notifications from aggregated components to the active object's state machine (Chapter 5, Section 5.4).
`postLIFO()`	Post an event directly to the active object's event queue using the LIFO policy. The primary intention of this method is to enable the Reminder state pattern (Chapter 5, Section 5.2) and to send notifications from aggregated components to the active object's state machine (Chapter 5, Section 5.4).
`stop()`	Stop the execution thread associated with the active object and unsubscribe all signals. The stop() method should be invoked from the context of the terminating active object. Caution: control never returns to the calling thread in this case.

8.9.3 QTimer Interface

The QTimer class (Listing 8.12) is a helper class intended to be used as is, without modifications. Active objects can allocate an open-ended number of timer objects. As with any other object, timers should not be shared. Only the armed timers consume CPU cycles. Table 8.3 summarizes the public methods of the QTimer class.

Listing 8.12   QTimer class

```
 1 class QTimer {
 2 public:
 3    QTimer() : myActive(0) {}                                 // default ctor
 4    void fireIn(QActive *act, QSignal sig, unsigned nTicks);
 5    void fireEvery(QActive *act, QSignal sig, unsigned nTicks);
 6    void disarm();
 7    void rearm(unsigned nTicks);
 8 private:
 9    void arm(QActive *act, QSignal sig, unsigned nTicks);
10 private:
11    QTimer *myNext;                           // to link timers in the list
12    QEvent myToutEvt;                     // timeout event instance to send
13    QActive *myActive;         // active object to send the timeout event to
14    unsigned short myCtr;                  // running clock-tick downcounter
15    unsigned short myInterval;               // interval for periodic-timer
16    friend class QF;
17 };
```

Table 8.3   Brief summary of the public QTimer interface

Method	Description
fireIn()	Arm a timer for a single shot in nTicks number of clock ticks. After timing out, the timer is automatically disarmed and can be reused. Arming a timer that has already been armed causes a contract violation (precondition failure).
fireEvery()	Arm a timer to fire periodically every nTicks number of clock ticks. A periodic timer is automatically rearmed by every timeout. Arming a timer that has already been armed causes a contract violation (precondition failure).

Method	Description
disarm()	Disarm an armed timer (one-shot or periodic) so that it doesn't fire a timeout event. The caller must not assume that no more timeouts arrive after the call because some timeouts could still be in the event queue. Disarming an unarmed timer causes a contract violation (precondition failure).
rearm()	Rearm an armed timer to fire in nTicks number of clock ticks. The method affects only the next shot and does not change the interval of a periodic timer; that is, rearming a periodic timer changes its phasing but not its period. The number of nTicks is arbitrary (but positive) and could exceed the interval (so the method allows both extending and shrinking the next tick). Rearming an unarmed timer causes a contract violation (precondition failure).

8.10 Summary

The design of the Quantum Framework (QF) addresses the particular needs of embedded real-time systems dedicated to a specific function that requires timely responses to external events.

Embedded real-time systems necessitate different programming strategies than general-purpose computers such as desktop PCs. Many established programming techniques and rules of thumb from the desktop are not only inadequate but harmful to the majority of embedded real-time applications. The QF carefully avoids techniques that can be problematic in embedded systems and uses policies that allow you to take advantage of the specific nature of embedded systems programming.

The QF policy for error and exception handling hinges on the observation that, compared to the desktop, the specifics of embedded systems allow you to flag many more situations as errors (which need to be found and fixed, but not handled) than as exceptional conditions (which require handling). To facilitate finding and fixing errors (bugs), the QF consistently applies DBC. To handle exceptions, the QF proposes using state machine–based exception handling instead of the programming language–based technique of throwing and catching exceptions.

The basic design philosophy of the QF with respect to memory management is not to commit any memory internally but leave to the clients the instantiation of any framework-derived objects and the initialization of the framework with memory that it needs for operation. This policy allows you to completely avoid the heap (free store), which often causes problems in embedded real-time systems.

The QF implementation uses only safe (deterministic) mutual exclusion mechanisms (i.e., briefly disabling interrupts) and avoids mutual exclusion semaphores (mutexes) because they can lead to priority inversions. The QF design carefully minimizes the need to block the execution threads associated with active objects. In particular, the QF never blocks active objects when extracting events from event pools or when inserting events to event queues.

The event-passing mechanism of the QF is a publish–subscribe architecture with dynamic event allocation, automatic event recycling, and event multicasting (in case of multiple subscriptions). This design enables the rapid construction and execution of intentionally incomplete applications. For example, publish–subscribe event delivery does not require you to specify the recipients of events, so an application will compile even if some active objects (recipients of events) are missing. Similarly, automatic event recycling allows applications to execute correctly (without memory leaks) even if some published events are never received.

As in all active object–based frameworks, the QF provides an abstract base class, QActive, to derive concrete active objects. QActive inherits the passive event processor from the QHsm class and augments it with an event queue and a thread of execution. Constructing the QF applications consists mainly of deriving concrete active objects and elaborating their internal state machines.

The QF manages time through timer objects (timers) that generate timeout events for active objects. Active objects can arm the timers to obtain either a single timeout (a one-shot timer) or a periodic series of timeout events (a periodic timer). Each timeout request has a different timer, so a QF application can make multiple parallel timeout requests (from the same or different active objects).

Overall, the QF represents a minimal and efficient realization of the active object–based computing model tailored specifically for embedded real-time systems. The design avoids all potentially risky programming techniques internally but does not limit the application designer to only these techniques. The framework has a small memory footprint and executes the applications deterministically. It can be embedded in commercial products.

Chapter 9

Implementations of the Quantum Framework

> *There is no trick in building large systems quickly; the*
> *quicker you build them, the larger they get!*
> — David Parnas

In this chapter, I present concrete implementations of the QF design described in the previous chapter. The primary goal is to fill in the missing platform-dependent pieces of the framework so that you have the complete code ready to use in your applications. This chapter approaches the dilemma — which platform to choose — by describing not one but three implementations of the QF on different platforms. I have chosen diverse platforms to demonstrate how to adapt the QF to a wide range of applications because my secondary goal in this chapter is to show you how to port the QF to the environment of your choice.

I cover the following three concrete implementations of the QF in this chapter.

* DOS — I demonstrate the use of the QF in a foreground/background environment without any underlying multitasking kernel. This implementation could be applicable to simpler embedded systems.

- Windows (32-bit) — I demonstrate the use of the QF in the multithreading environment of a desktop computer, which could be interesting for cross-development, testing, and debugging embedded applications.

- RTKernel-32[1] — This real-time kernel for Intel x86 processors runs in 32-bit protected mode and demonstrates the use of the QF in a true, real-time, multithreading environment with full RTOS support.

As you can see, the implementations span quite a wide range, and most of the systems should fall into one of these broad categories. The platforms have been specifically chosen so that you can use familiar development tools[2] and execute the code on your desktop PC. For the 32-bit Windows and RTKernel-32 ports, I used Microsoft Developer Studio v6.0 for both compiling and debugging (cross-debugging in the case of RTKernel-32). For DOS, I used Visual C++ v1.52. I believe that these choices offer the best prospects for you to experiment with the code.

9.1   The QF as a Parnas Family

It is unnecessary and rarely makes business sense[3] to make every application general and portable. In fact, it often does more harm than good, especially in the embedded real-time domain, where each product has unique hardware and software constraints. At the same time, every application offers specific opportunities for simplification that are lost when you generalize the case. However, this area is exactly where an application differs from a framework. A framework is supposed to capture and explicitly separate commonalities (assumptions that don't change) from variabilities (assumptions that do change). In the domain of embedded real-time systems, platform diversity is exactly the most important variability that a framework, such as the QF, should address up front.

In his seminal paper, David Parnas [Parnas 76] proposed a way to anticipate variability by designing and implementing an entire family of related products (the *Parnas family*). Parnas argues that program development is essentially a path down a decision tree, with each node corresponding to a design decision. Decisions toward the top of the tree are the hardest to change because they require the most backtracking. The trick (and challenge) in designing such a tree is to put near its root those design decisions that are less likely to change (the commonalities).

---

1.   RTKernel-32 is a product of On Time Software. A fully functional evaluation version of this product, as well as documentation, is available on the accompanying CD-ROM.

2.   Throughout this book, I assume that you use Microsoft Visual C++ v6.0. Porting the QF to DOS requires a different (16-bit) compiler. However, because of the tremendous popularity of DOS, I hope that you can find an older C/C++ compiler for DOS relatively easily.

3.   A good rule of thumb is that reusable components will take twice the effort of a one-shot component [Yourdon 92].

In Chapter 8, I constructed the root of the QF design tree by extracting the commonalities in the QF design. In this chapter, I concentrate on the branches and leaves of the tree. These elements are formed by the concrete QF ports, which all make a small Parnas family of the QF.

9.2   Code Organization

Portable code is significantly more difficult to organize than code intended for deployment on a single platform. The difficulties stem from the code structure (both logical and physical partitioning into files) that needs to explicitly separate the commonalities from the variabilities.

The main objective is to deploy the QF as a platform-dependent, fine-granularity class library that clients statically link to their applications. *Platform dependence* means that on each platform you use different files; for example, on the Win32 platform, you use the qf_win32.h header file and the qf_win32.lib library file; on the DOS platform you use the qf_dos.h header file and the qf_dos.lib library file. All the platform-depended header files include a platform-independent (common) header file, qf.h. Similarly, most modules of the library are built from platform-independent (common) source files. However, each port also includes specific platform-dependent elements. *Fine granularity* means that the QF library contains several loosely coupled modules (object files), rather than a single module that contains all functionality. For example, a separate module implements the QF timers; therefore, if your application does not use timer services, the linker does not pull in the timer module. The strategy is to exclude unused parts automatically at link time, rather than to specifically configure and rebuild the framework code for each application.

Each QF port is an adaptable library that does not need to be custom tailored for individual applications on the given platform. You can distribute such a library in a binary format without necessarily disclosing the source code. To this end, the memory management policy of the QF mitigates many traditional reasons for source-level customization. For example, the QF does not need to be preconfigured with a specific number of execution threads, event queues, or timers because the QF does not preallocate memory internally[4] (it leaves the memory configuration to the application — Section 8.3.2 in Chapter 8). This policy avoids wasting memory for the overallocated (preallocated but unused) objects.

This flexibility comes at a price. Specific types of private objects used internally must be revealed to the application level. For instance, the QF internally uses a data type describing the execution thread (inside the QActive class). QF applications do

---

4.   The µC/OS real-time kernel [Labrosse 92a, 92, 99] is an example of a system that internally preallocates memory for kernel objects.

not need to know or care that such a data type even exists; that is, the applications wouldn't care except that they need to instantiate concrete active objects that contain thread instances inherited from QActive. The application code becomes dependent on the details of the framework base classes because, ultimately, the application has to allocate the memory (preferably statically) for all objects. To do so, the C/C++ compiler needs to know the size of each object [Stroustrup 91]. In comparison, systems that preallocate internal objects can better hide platform dependencies and can expose only the platform-independent interface in the header files.

Listing 9.1   Declaration of platform-dependent data members of the QActive class

```
#include "port.h"                    // platform-dependent package-scope interface

class QActive : public QHsm {        // Quantum Active Object base class
public:
   . . .
private:                                        // data members...
   QF_EQUEUE(myEqueue)              // OS-dependent event-queue object
   QF_THREAD(myThread)                // OS-dependent thread object
   unsigned char myPrio;            // priority of the active object
   friend class QF;
};
```

To be more specific, consider again the framework class QActive. As shown in the class diagram in Figure 8.5 (Chapter 8), QActive aggregates by composition a thread of execution (the myThread attribute) and event queue (the myEqueue attribute). These objects are platform dependent; yet, they must be fully specified in the QActive class, not preallocated and hidden inside the framework. Listing 9.1 shows a simple solution that is to declare the platform-dependent data members as preprocessor macros QF_EQUEUE() and QF_THREAD(). These macros are defined in a platform-specific public header file, qf_platform.h.

The QActive class illustrates the way this design handles variability (in this case, platform dependence) in the physical structure of the QF code. The variations are extracted in the form of header files and macros, which are then specialized for each platform.[5]

9.2.1   Directory Structure

Figure 9.1 shows the annotated directory structure of the QF source code. Generally, the code for each QF port consists of three parts.

1. Public header file (e.g., Cpp/Qf/Include/qf_win32.h)

---

5. Conditional compilation (using preprocessor commands #if–#elseif–#else–#endif) is another common way to handle platform dependencies. I try to avoid using this method.

2. Platform-independent header and implementation files
    (`Cpp/Qf/Source/qfpkg.h` and `Cpp/Qf/Source/*.cpp`)

3. Platform-dependent header and implementation files
    (e.g., `Cpp/Qf/Win32/port.h` and `Cpp/Qf/Win32/win32.cpp`)

This structure uses two levels of header files. The public scope header file (e.g., `Cpp/Qf/Include/qf_win32.h`) provides the platform-dependent interface to the QF library. The package scope–level interface (e.g., `Cpp/Qf/Win32/port.h`) includes the public header file and specifies the additional interface (dependencies among QF modules) that is required to build the QF port.[6] Both platform-independent and -dependent implementation files (although located in different directories) belong to the same QF package, and all these modules include the package scope header file `port.h`.

All platform-independent QF source files (in the directory `Cpp/Qf/Source`) include the header file `port.h` without specifying a concrete directory (`#include "port.h"`). The concrete version of `port.h` is chosen automatically by building the QF library in a specific directory (e.g., `Cpp/Qf/Win32` for the Win32 port). The build combines source (`.cpp`) files from two directories: the current platform-dependent directory (`.`) and the platform-independent directory (`../Source`). Typically, you redirect compiler output into a separate build directory (e.g., `./Release`). Furthermore, you must instruct the compiler to include header files from three directories: the current directory (`.`), the public include directory (`../Include`), and the source directory (`../Source`).[7] Note also that both the source code and the build process (the makefiles) use only relative paths with respect to the current directory. This convention allows you to place the QF branch at any level of your particular directory tree without modifying the source code or the makefiles.[8]

9.2.2   Public Scope Header File

Listing 9.2 shows an example of a public scope header file (the platform-dependent QF interface) for the Win32 QF port. The header file starts with the usual protection against multiple inclusion (lines 1–2, 21). In line 4, the file includes the header of the underlying operating system (`<windows.h>` in this case). Lines 7 through 9 define macros, specifying the concrete, platform-dependent data members: the execution thread, the event queue, and the OS event[9] objects (Section 9.5.1). Finally, lines 13

---

6. The division of the interface into package scope (wide) and public scope (narrow) reflects high cohesion within the package and loose coupling to the outside world.

7. Most C/C++ compilers allow you to specify multiple include directories (typically through the `-I` option).

8. Figure 9.1 also demonstrates how you can replicate the same directory structure for multiplatform QF applications (e.g., see the structure of the `QDPP` directory).

9. An OS event object is a platform-dependent attribute of the event queue class (Section 9.3.3) that blocks the active object thread when the queue is empty.

Figure 9.1 **Directory structure and files for multiplatform deployment of QF libraries and QF applications**

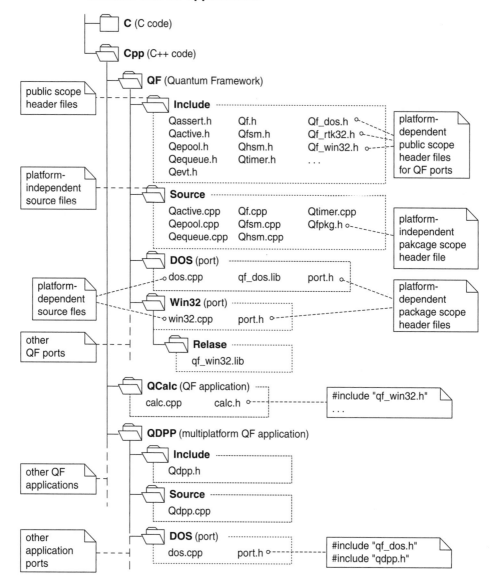

through 19 include various elements of the QF. Note that not all ports require you to include all elements. For example, the RTKernel-32 port (discussed in Section 9.6) does not need either an event queue (qequeue.h) or an event pool (qepool.h) because these elements are based on the native implementation of the underlying RTOS (RTKernel-32).

Listing 9.2   Public scope header file `qf_win32.h` for Win32 port

```
1 #ifndef qf_win32_h
2 #define qf_win32_h
3
4 #include <windows.h>
5
6 // Win32-specific event object, event-queue and thread types...
7 #define QF_OS_EVENT(x_)   HANDLE   x_;
8 #define QF_EQUEUE(x_)     QEQueue x_;
9 #define QF_THREAD(x_)     HANDLE   x_;
10 #define Q_STATIC_CAST(type_, expr_) static_cast<type_>(expr_)
11
12 // include framework elements...
13 #include "qevt.h"
14 #include "qhsm.h"
15 #include "qequeue.h"                      // Win32 needs event-queue
16 #include "qepool.h"                       // Win32 needs event-pool
17 #include "qactive.h"
18 #include "qtimer.h"
19 #include "qf.h"
20
21 #endif                                    // qf_win32_h
```

9.2.3   Package Scope Header File

Listing 9.3 shows an example of a package scope header file (wide interface) for the Win32 QF port. All package scope headers include the public interface (line 4) and the platform-independent package scope header file qfpkg.h (line 5). Subsequently, the header file defines several macros that the shared implementation files (located in the Cpp/Source directory, Figure 9.1) use to code platform-dependent operations. The following sections explain these macros in detail.

Listing 9.3   Package scope header file `Cpp/Win32/port.h` for the Win32 port

```
1 #ifndef port_h
2 #define port_h
3
4 #include "qf_win32.h"
5 #include "qfpkg.h"
6
7 // Win32-specific critical section operations
8 extern  CRITICAL_SECTION     pkgWin32CritSect;
9 #define QF_PROTECT()         EnterCriticalSection(&pkgWin32CritSect)
10 #define QF_UNPROTECT()       LeaveCriticalSection(&pkgWin32CritSect)
11 #define QF_ISR_PROTECT()     QF_PROTECT()
```

```
12 #define QF_ISR_UNPROTECT()     QF_UNPROTECT()
13
14 // Win32-compiler-specific cast
15 #define Q_STATE_CAST(x_)        reinterpret_cast<QState>(x_)
16
17 // Win32-specific event queue operations
18 #define QF_EQUEUE_INIT(q_) \
19     ((q_)->myOsEvent = CreateEvent(NULL, FALSE, FALSE, NULL))
20 #define QF_EQUEUE_CLEANUP(q_) CloseHandle((q_)->myOsEvent)
21 #define QF_EQUEUE_WAIT(q_) \
22     QF_UNPROTECT(); \
23     do { \
24         WaitForSingleObject((q_)->myOsEvent, INFINITE); \
25     } while ((q_)->myFrontEvt == 0); \
26     QF_PROTECT()
27 #define QF_EQUEUE_SIGNAL(q_) \
28     QF_UNPROTECT(); \
29     SetEvent((q_)->myOsEvent)
30 #define QF_EQUEUE_ONEMPTY(q_)
31
32 // Win32-specific event pool operations
33 #define QF_EPOOL                QEPool
34 #define QF_EPOOL_INIT(p_, poolSto_, nEvts_, evtSize_) \
35     (p_)->init(poolSto_, nEvts_, evtSize_);
36 #define QF_EPOOL_GET(p_, e_)  ((e_) = (p_)->get())
37 #define QF_EPOOL_PUT(p_, e_)  ((p_)->put(e_))
38
39               // the following constant may be bumped up to 15 (inclusive)
40          // before redesign of algorithms is necessary
41 enum { QF_MAX_ACTIVE = 15 };
42
43 #endif                                          // port_h
```

9.3   Common Elements

In many ways, adapting the QF to a concrete computing environment is like porting an RTOS to a different microprocessor architecture. Indeed, as described in Chapter 7, the QF is in a sense a replacement for a conventional RTOS. This section covers the common platform-dependent elements of the QF, such as the critical section, the event pool, and the event queue, which typically are provided in an RTOS but might be missing in some implementations.

9.3.1   Critical Section

The QF, like a multitasking kernel, needs to perform certain operations indivisibly. The simplest and most efficient way to protect a section of code from disruptions is to disable interrupts on entry to the section and enable interrupts again on exit. Such a section of code is called the *critical section*.

Note: The time spent in a critical section should be kept to a minimum because this time directly affects the interrupt latency. However, as long as the critical sections introduced in the QF take no more time than when disabling interrupts elsewhere in the system (e.g., inside the underlying kernel or device drivers), the critical sections do not extend the maximum interrupt latency. As you will see, the QF disables interrupts only very briefly, which should not affect the maximum interrupt latency.

For portability of code, the QF defines entry to and exit from a critical section in the QF_PROTECT() and QF_UNPROTECT()[10] macros to protect and unprotect a critical section, respectively (Listing 9.3, lines 9, 10). The definition of these macros depends on the platform and the compiler. For example, on the DOS platform (as on most embedded platforms), the macros can directly switch interrupts off and on. For the x86 microprocessor, use the following macros.

```
#define QF_PROTECT()        __asm{cli}
#define QF_UNPROTECT()      __asm{sti}
```

Here, the macros use in-line assembly to execute x86 instructions. The format is specific to the Microsoft compiler. CLI (clear interrupt flag) and STI (set interrupt flag) disable and enable interrupts, respectively. You could also use _disable() and _enable(), both declared in <dos.h>, to achieve the same effect.

However, on some platforms, you cannot disable and enable interrupts easily, and the operating system provides different ways of protecting indivisible sections of code. For example, the package-level header file for the Win32 port shows the definition of the Microsoft Windows–specific implementation of the critical section (Listing 9.3, lines 9, 10).

9.3.2   Event Pool

In Chapter 8, I introduced the concept of an event pool — a fixed block–size heap specialized to hold event instances. Some RTOSs natively support such fixed block–size heaps (often called memory partitions or memory pools).[11] However, many platforms don't. This section explains how to build your own event pool.

---

10. I used these macros in Chapter 8.
11. For example, RTKernel-32 supports fixed block–size memory pools, which is used later in this chapter to demonstrate an RTOS-based implementation of event pools.

Figure 9.2 **Event pool data structure**

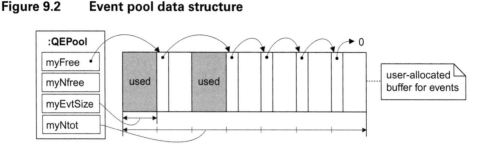

As shown in Figure 9.2, the QEPool class manages a contiguous buffer of memory that the clients use to preallocate storage for events. QEPool tracks memory by chaining all unused memory blocks in a simple linked list (the free list). This technique is standard for organizing stack-like data structures, where the structure is accessed like a stack in the LIFO manner from one end only.[12] QEPool also uses a handy trick to link free blocks together in the free list without consuming extra storage for the pointers [Lafreniere 98, Labrosse 99]. By chaining together free (rather than used) memory blocks, QEPool can reuse the blocks for other things, such as linked list pointers. This use implies that the block size must be big enough to hold a pointer.

Listing 9.4 **QEPool event pool class declaration**

```
 1 class QEPool {                                  // "Quantum" event-pool
 2 private:
 3    void init(QEvent *poolSto, unsigned nEvts, unsigned evtSize);
 4    QEvent *get();                               // get an event from the pool
 5    void put(QEvent *e);                     // put an event back to the pool
 6    void *myFree;                                 // head of the free-list
 7    unsigned short myEvtSize;             // maximum event size (in bytes)
 8    unsigned short myNtot;                     // total number of events
 9    unsigned short myNfree;             // number of free events remaining
10    unsigned short myNmin;              // minimum number of free events
11    friend class QF;
12 };
```

Listing 9.4 shows the declaration of the QEPool class. This class provides three methods — init(), get(), and put() — for pool initialization, event allocation, and event recycling, respectively. Section 8.4.1 in Chapter 8 explains how the QF uses these methods internally — class QEPool grants access to its private interface only to the QF. The data members include the head of the free list (myFree), the event size of this pool (myEvtSize), the total number of events in the pool (myNtot),

---

12. See, for example [Eckel 95, chapter 1].

the current number of free blocks in the pool (myNfree), and the lowest number of free blocks remaining in the pool (myNmin). This last attribute, called the low-water mark, tracks the worst-case pool utilization, which like the worst-case stack utilization provides a valuable data point for the final fine tuning of your application.[13]

Listing 9.5   QEPool class implementation

```
 1 void QEPool::init(QEvent *poolSto, unsigned nEvts, unsigned evtSize){
 2     REQUIRE(nEvts > 0 && evtSize >= sizeof(QEvent));
 3     myFree = poolSto;                  // set head of linked-list of free events
 4     myEvtSize = evtSize;                 // store maximum size of each event
 5     myNtot = nEvts;                       // store total number of events
 6     myNfree = nEvts;                       // store number of free events
 7     myNmin = nEvts;            // initialize the minimum number of free events
 8     register char *block = (char *)poolSto;
 9     while (--nEvts) {                  // chain all blocks in the free-list...
10        *(void **)block = (void *)(block + evtSize);         // set the link
11        block += evtSize;                        // advance to next block
12     }
13     *(void **)block = 0;                        // last link points to 0
14 }
15
16 QEvent *QEPool::get() {
17     register QEvent *e;
18     QF_PROTECT();
19     if (myNfree > 0) {                            // free events available?
20        e = (QEvent *)myFree;                         // get free event
21        myFree = *(void **)e;              // adjust pointer to new free list
22        if (--myNfree < myNmin) {              // one less event in this pool
23            myNmin = myNfree;                 // remember the minimum so far
24        }
25     }
26     else {
27        e = 0;
28     }
29     QF_UNPROTECT();
30     return e;                // return the event or NULL pointer to the caller
31 }
32
33 void QEPool::put(QEvent *e) {
34     QF_PROTECT();
35     REQUIRE(myNfree < myNtot);                   // pool cannot be already full
36     *(void **)e = myFree;              // insert released event into free-list
```

---

13. You can check the myNmin data member in the debugger or through a memory dump.

```
37      myFree = e;                 // set as new head of the free-list
38      ++myNfree;                  // one more free block in this pool
39      QF_UNPROTECT();
40 }
```

Listing 9.5 shows the complete implementation of the QEPool class. The init() method (lines 1–14) takes three parameters: the pointer to the event buffer storage (poolSto), the number of events in the pool (nEvts), and the block size of the pool (evtSize) in units of bytes. To guarantee optimal alignment of the blocks in the pool, you should allocate the event buffer as an array of concrete event objects (pick the biggest event that you want to allocate from this pool), as demonstrated in Section 8.6.1 of Chapter 8.

In the precondition (Listing 9.5, line 2), init() asserts that at least one event is in the pool — the following algorithm breaks if zero events occur — and that the event size can hold at least the base class QEvent, which also means that the event can hold a linked list pointer. The rest of the method initializes the pool attributes, and it chains all memory blocks into a linked list (the free list). Note that internally, the pool treats the free blocks as linked list pointers of type void*, not as events (subclasses of QEvent). Also note that init() does not use critical sections in the initialization of the event pool. Using critical sections is unnecessary because event pools are only initialized with QF::poolInit(), which guarantees that the pool cannot be used before its initialization completes (Listing 8.2 in Chapter 8).

The QEPool::get() method (Listing 9.5, lines 16–31) efficiently retrieves a free block from the pool and returns it to the caller. This method is reentrant (note the use of the critical section), and you can call it from the context of an ISR. If the pool has free blocks (line 19), QEPool::get() quickly unlinks a free block from the free list (lines 20, 21). Subsequently, the routine decrements the free-block counter, checks the counter's value against the current low-water mark, and updates the water mark if necessary (lines 22, 23). Finally, get() leaves the critical section and returns the event to the caller (lines 29–30). Otherwise, if no free events exist, the method sets the event pointer to 0 (line 27) and returns 0 to the caller.

The QEPool::put() method (Listing 9.5, lines 33–40) does the reverse of get(). Just after entering the critical section, the method asserts in the precondition that the pool is not already full (line 35). Subsequently, the method links the returned event to the free list (lines 36, 37) and increments the free-block counter (line 38).

From the data structures and algorithms used in the event pool implementation, it should be clear that writing to an event instance past its declared size has potentially disastrous consequences. Such an overrun can corrupt event parameters or destroy the links of the free list (Figure 9.2). Either way, your application will probably crash.

The way the QF manages event pools mitigates many of the risks associated with using them directly. For example, the QF returns events to the same pool from which they were allocated. Also, allocating events through the Q_NEW() macro (Section 8.4.1 in Chapter 8) is safer than direct invocation of QEPool::get() (actually, QF::create()) because the macro uses event types consistently to allocate an event of sufficient event size from the pool and to type cast (downcast) the returned event pointer. As long as you don't change the type of this pointer (e.g., by explicitly casting it to something else), you should not overrun memory.

9.3.3   Event Queue

Many RTOSs natively support event queues (actually, message queues).[14] However, in case no such support exists or the available implementation is inefficient or inadequate, you might want to supply your own event queue. This section describes an event queue implementation specifically designed and optimized for active objects (Section 8.5.2 in Chapter 8 describes the specifics of event queues in the QF). This implementation omits several commonly supported features of message queues, such as variable-size messages (event queues store only pointers), blocking on a full queue (event queues cannot block on insertion), and timed blocking on empty queues (event queues block indefinitely), to name just a few. In exchange, the implementation is small and probably faster than a full-blown message queue of an RTOS.

Listing 9.6   QEQueue **event queue class declaration**

```
 1 class QEQueue {                                      // event queue-facility ...
 2 private:
 3     int init(QEvent *qSto[], unsigned qLen);
 4     QEvent *get();
 5     int putFIFO(QEvent *e);
 6     int putLIFO(QEvent *e);
 7     // OS-dependent event object to block active object on empty queue
 8     QF_OS_EVENT(myOsEvent)      //platform-dependent primitive for blocking
 9     QEvent *myFrontEvt;         // pointer to event at the front of the queue
10     QEvent **myStart;                     // pointer to start of ring buffer
11     QEvent **myEnd;                         // pointer to end of ring buffer
12     QEvent **myHead;          // pointer to where next event will be inserted
13     QEvent **myTail;          // pointer to where next event will be extracted
14     unsigned short myNtot;              // total # of entries in the buffer
15     unsigned short myNused;             // current # of events in the buffer
```

---

14.   For example, RTKernel-32 supports message queues, which I use later (Section 9.6) to demonstrate an RTOS-based implementation of event queues.

```
16    unsigned short myNmax;            // maximum # of events ever in the buffer
17    friend class QF;
18    friend class QActive;
19 };
```

The declaration of the QEQueue class (Listing 9.6) provides four methods.[15]

1. init() initializes the event queue.

2. get() extracts events from the queue.

3. putFIFO() inserts events into the queue for FIFO processing.

4. putLIFO() inserts urgent events into the queue for LIFO processing.

All these methods are declared private with friendship granted only to the QF and QActive classes (lines 17, 18).

Figure 9.3   Event queue data structure

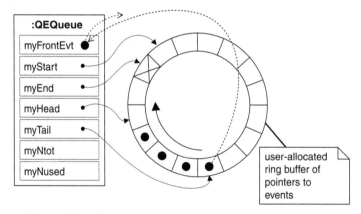

Figure 9.3 shows the roles and relationships among the QEQueue class attributes. All outgoing events must pass through the myFrontEvt data member, which optimizes queue operation by frequently bypassing buffering; in addition, it serves as a queue status indicator (more about that later in this section). The pointers myStart, myEnd, myHead, and myTail manage a ring buffer that the clients must preallocate as a contiguous array of pointers of type QEvent*. Events are always extracted from the buffer at the tail of the queue, the location to which myTail points in the ring buffer. New events are typically inserted at the head of the queue, the location to which myHead points in the ring buffer. Inserting events at the head and extracting from the tail corresponds to FIFO operations (the putFIFO() method). QEQueue also allows you to insert new events at the tail, which corresponds to LIFO operations (the putLIFO() method). Either way, the tail pointer always increments when

---

15. See the discussion following the Reminder state pattern in Section 5.2 in Chapter 5.

the event is extracted, as does the head pointer when an event is inserted. Using the pair of pointers myStart and myEnd confines the range of the head and tail pointers to the ring buffer. When either the myHead or myTail pointer equals myEnd, which points to one location past the preallocated buffer, then the pointers (myHead or myTail) are wrapped around to the myStart location. The effect is a clockwise crawling of the pointers around the buffer, as indicated by the arrow in Figure 9.3.

Other data attributes of the QEQueue class include the total number of events in the ring buffer (myNtot), the current number of events in the buffer (myNused), and the maximum number of events ever placed in the buffer (myNmax). This last attribute (the high-water mark) tracks the worst-case queue utilization, which provides a valuable data point for fine-tuning your application.[16]

Listing 9.7   Initializing the event queue with QEQueue::init()

```
 1 int QEQueue::init(QEvent *qSto[], unsigned qLen) {
 2     if (!QF_EQUEUE_INIT(this)) {        // platform-dependent initialization
 3         return 0;
 4     }
 5     myStart = &qSto[0];
 6     myEnd = &qSto[qLen];                          // qLen is in units sizeof(Evt *)
 7     myHead = &qSto[0];
 8     myTail = &qSto[0];
 9     myNtot = qLen;
10     myNused = 0;
11     myNmax = 0;
12     myFrontEvt = 0;                              // clear front event
13     return !0;
14 }
```

Listing 9.7 shows the event queue initialization through the init() method, which takes the preallocated storage for the ring buffer (an array of event pointers, qSto[]) and the length of the buffer qLen, which is the number of preallocated QEvent* pointers. In line 2, the method invokes a macro to perform platform-dependent initialization of the operating system primitive used to block the calling thread when the queue is empty. (Sections 9.4–9.6 discuss specific definitions of this macro for concrete platforms.) In lines 5 through 12, the method sets the QEQueue attributes to emulate an empty event queue. As in the case of the event pool, QEQueue::init() is not protected with a critical section because the QF initialization timeline precludes accessing an event queue before the initialization is complete.

---

16. You can inspect the myNmax data member in the debugger or through a memory dump.

Listing 9.8 **Extracting events from the event queue with** `QEQueue::get()`

```
1 QEvent *QEQueue::get() {
2    register QEvent *e;                      // event to return to the caller
3    QF_PROTECT();
4    if (myFrontEvt == 0) {                            // is the queue empty?
5       QF_EQUEUE_WAIT(this);              // wait for event to arrive directly
6    }                    // NOTE: QF_EQUEUE_WAIT() leaves the critical section
7    e = myFrontEvt;
8    if (myNused) {                                      // buffer not empty?
9       --myNused;                           // one less event in the ring-buffer
10      myFrontEvt = *myTail;                      // remove event from the tail
11      if (++myTail == myEnd) {
12         myTail = myStart;
13      }
14   }
15   else {
16      myFrontEvt = 0;                                        // queue empty
17      QF_EQUEUE_ONEMPTY(this);         // used only in foreground/background
18   }
19   QF_UNPROTECT();
20   ENSURE(e);
21   return e;
22 }
```

Listing 9.8 shows how the `QEQueue::get()` method extracts events from the queue. This method is called only from the thread routine of the active object that owns this queue. If the owner thread calls `get()` and the queue is empty (the `myFrontEvt` attribute is not set, line 4), the method blocks at line 5 and waits indefinitely for the framework to insert an event into the queue. Blocking is a platform-dependent operation, and the routine handles it through a platform-dependent macro. This macro is designed to be invoked from a critical section and to restore the critical section on its return.[17] At line 7, the queue cannot be empty anymore — it either was not empty to begin with or it just received an event after blocking.[18] The event at the front of the queue is copied for delivery to the caller (line 7). If the ring buffer contains events (line 8), an event is extracted from the tail and moved into the front event (line 10). Otherwise, the front event is cleared, which indicates that the queue is empty (line 16). For nominal (multi-threading) operation, you can ignore the macro in line 17 because it is used only in the case of foreground/background processing, which I cover in Section 9.4. Note

17. For example, Listing 9.3 (lines 21–26) shows a Win-32-specific definition of `QF_EQUEUE_WAIT()`.
18. This is true because only one thread can extract events from the queue.

that QEQueue::get() always returns a valid event pointer to the caller, as asserted in the postcondition in line 20.

Listing 9.9   Inserting events into the event queue with QEQueue::putFIFO()

```
 1 int QEQueue::putFIFO(QEvent *e) {
 2    REQUIRE(e);
 3    QF_PROTECT();
 4    if (myFrontEvt == 0) {                          // is the queue empty?
 5       myFrontEvt = e;                         // deliver event directly
 6       QF_EQUEUE_SIGNAL(this);        // unblock thread waiting on this queue
 7    }        //NOTE: QF_EQUEUE_SIGNAL() must be entered in a critical section
 8    else {              // queue is not empty, leave event in the ring-buffer
 9       if (myNused < myNtot) {          // can the buffer accept the element?
10          if (++myNused > myNmax) {                       // update # of events
11             myNmax = myNused;                  // store maximum used so far
12          }
13          *myHead = e;                  // insert event into the buffer (FIFO)
14          if (++myHead == myEnd) {
15             myHead = myStart;                          // wrap the head
16          }
17          QF_UNPROTECT();
18       }
19       else {                                    // ring-buffer overflow
20          QF_UNPROTECT();
21          return 0;                               // return failure
22       }
23    }
24    return !0;                                  // return success
25 }
```

Two possible variations exist for inserting events into a queue: FIFO (the putFIFO() method) and LIFO (the putLIFO() method). Listing 9.9 shows the implementation of the putFIFO() method. The routine first checks whether the queue is empty (line 4), which is equivalent to inspecting the front event (myFrontEvt). If so, the front event is set directly and the queue is unblocked (line 6). Unblocking a thread is a platform-dependent operation, and putFIFO() handles it through a platform-dependent macro. This macro is designed to be invoked from a critical section and is supposed to leave the critical section on return.[19] If, on the other hand, the queue is not empty, the routine attempts to insert the event into the ring buffer. First, it needs to check whether the buffer can accept one more event (line 9); if so, it inserts the new event at the head (lines 10–16). If the ring buffer is full, the method simply returns failure status (0) to the caller (line 21);

19. For example, Listing 9.3 (lines 27–29) shows a Win32-specific definition of QF_EQUEUE_SIGNAL().

otherwise, the method returns success (line 24). Note that there is no need to leave the critical section before the last return because the QF_EQUEUE_SIGNAL() macro has done it already.

Listing 9.10 **Inserting events into the event queue with QEQueue::putLIFO()**

```
 1 int QEQueue::putLIFO(QEvent *e) {
 2     REQUIRE(e);
 3     QF_PROTECT();
 4     if (myFrontEvt == 0) {                        // is the queue empty?
 5         myFrontEvt = e;                           // deliver it directly
 6         QF_EQUEUE_SIGNAL(this);       // unblock thread waiting on this queue
 7     }                 // NOTE: QF_EQUEUE_SIGNAL() leaves the critical section
 8     else {                      // queue is not empty, leave e in the ring-buffer
 9         if (myNused < myNtot) {        // can the buffer accept the element?
10             if (++myNused > myNmax) {                    // update # of events
11                 myNmax = myNused;                 // store maximum used so far
12             }
13             if (--myTail < myStart) {
14                 myTail = myEnd - 1;                          // wrap the tail
15             }
16             *myTail = myFrontEvt;         // push front e back into the buffer
17             myFrontEvt = e;                              // put event to front
18             QF_UNPROTECT();
19         }
20         else {                                         // ring-buffer overflow
21             QF_UNPROTECT();
22             return 0;                                      // return failure
23         }
24     }
25     return !0;                                         // return success
26 }
```

Listing 9.10 shows the implementation of the putLIFO() method that accesses the queue in the LIFO manner. This method is identical to putFIFO(), except that the event is inserted at the tail rather than the head. Unlike myHead, however, myTail is a full pointer (it points to an occupied location) and must be decremented and wrapped around before inserting the event (lines 13–17).

Having seen implementations of both the get(), putFIFO(), and putLIFO() methods, you can appreciate the role of the myFrontEvt data member. When a queue is empty (which is most of the time), using myFrontEvt bypasses the ring buffer altogether. In other words, passing events usually requires assigning one pointer and unblocking one thread.

9.4   DOS: The QF without a Multitasking Kernel

Multitasking is crucial for fast task-level response and for decoupling different activities in the time domain. Multitasking, however, is essentially an independent concept to the active object–based computing model. In other words, active object–based frameworks can work with a variety of concurrency mechanisms, including mechanisms that share a single thread of execution. In this section, I show how you can adapt and use the QF in a single-threaded environment (such as Microsoft DOS) without an underlying multitasking kernel. More importantly, you learn the kinds of benefits the QF has to offer in this situation.

9.4.1   Foreground/Background Processing

Not all embedded systems need or can afford a multitasking kernel. Simpler, high-volume embedded applications, such as home appliances, electronic toys, vending machines, thermostats, and countless other applications, are typically organized as foreground/background systems (e.g. [Labrosse 92, 99]). As the name suggests, the software consists of two main parts: the *foreground*, which comprises the ISRs that handle asynchronous events in a timely fashion, and the *background*, which is an infinite loop that uses all remaining CPU cycles to perform less time-critical actions. Listing 9.11 shows a typical background loop.

Listing 9.11   Typical background loop

```
main() {
   . . .              // initialization
   for (;;) {         // for-ever
      doA();          // perform action A
      if (...) {
         doB();       // conditionally perform action B
      }
      doC();          // perform action C
   }                  // loop back
}
```

The timing diagram in Figure 9.4 shows a typical execution profile of a foreground/background system. In the absence of interrupts, the background loop (Listing 9.11) executes action A, then B, then C, then loops back to A, and so on. Not all actions in the loop need to execute every time — some might be conditional (such as action B). When an interrupt occurs (Figure 9.4, time 8), the background loop suspends, and the CPU switches context to the foreground (ISR). The foreground typically communicates with the background code through shared memory. The background is responsible for protecting this memory from potential corruption (by disabling interrupts when accessing the shared variables). When the foreground relinquishes control of the CPU, the background always resumes exactly at the point it was interrupted. If the foreground makes some information available to the background, this information (however urgent) must wait for processing until the correct background routine gets its turn to run. In the worst case, this delay can take the full pass through the loop and is called the *task-level response*. Task-level response is nondeterministic because it depends on the conditional execution within the background loop, as well as on the time the foreground preempts the background (as indicated in Figure 9.4 with loop periods T1, T2, T3, etc.). Any change in either the foreground or background code affects the timing.

Figure 9.4   Execution profile of a foreground/background system

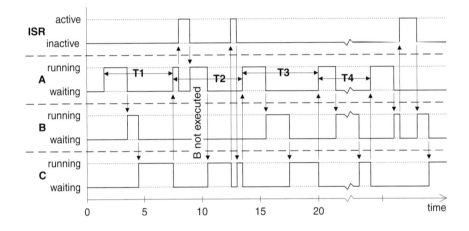

9.4.2   Foreground/Background with the QF

Foreground/background architecture can be adapted to execute independent state machines (active objects) relatively easily. Moreover, the QF naturally replaces traditional circular processing with priority-based event handling. Listing 9.12 shows the structure of the background code modified for the QF.

Listing 9.12   Background processing with the QF

```
main() {
    QF::init(. . .);            // initialize QF
    QF::poolInit(. . .);        // initialize at least one event-pool
    activeA.start(. . .);       // start active object A
    activeB.start(. . .);       // start active object B
    activeC.start(. . .);       // start active object C
    // hook clock tick ISR (platform-dependent)
    for (;;) {                  // for-ever
```

```
    QF::background();    // perform background processing
    // optionally perform other actions (e.g., I/O)
  }
  // optionally perform cleanup (platform-dependent)
}
```

As you can see, background processing starts with a typical initialization of the framework (Section 8.6.1 in Chapter 8) and then enters a for-ever loop that periodically executes only one routine: QF::background().

Listing 9.13   **QF::background() method**

```
 1 unsigned char pkgReadyList;                   // ready-list of active objects
 2
 3 void QF::background() {
 4    static unsigned char const log2Lkup[] = {      // log based 2 look-up
 5       0, 1, 2, 2, 3, 3, 3, 3, 4, 4, 4, 4, 4, 4, 4, 4,
 6       . . .
 7       8, 8, 8, 8, 8, 8, 8, 8, 8, 8, 8, 8, 8, 8, 8, 8
 8    };
 9    if (pkgReadyList) {                          // any events available?
10       register QActive *a = pkgActive[log2Lkup[pkgReadyList]];
11       register QEvent *e = (QEvent *)a->myEqueue.get();
12       a->dispatch(e);                       // dispatch event to the statechart
13       QF::propagate(e);                     // propagate to the next subscriber
14    }
15 }
```

Listing 9.13 shows the implementation of QF::background(). The most important variable of this routine is the package scope ready list, pkgReadyList, which is defined as a byte in line 1. Each bit in this byte represents the state of an event queue associated with each active object (a cleared bit indicates an empty queue). The least significant bit 0 corresponds to the event queue of the active object with priority 1 (the lowest priority), bit 1 corresponds to the event queue of the active object with priority 2, and so on. Finally, the most significant bit 7 corresponds to the active object with priority 8.[20]

With this representation, QF::background() can easily determine in line 9 whether any events are available for processing (at least one bit must be set in the ready list). If so, the ready list is used again to find the highest priority active object with a nonempty event queue (line 10). This action is achieved using a simple lookup table, log2Lkup[], that maps the value stored in a byte (the ready list) to the most

---

20. To use more than eight active objects, you need to increase the size of pkgReadyList (e.g., to 16 bits) and to extend the binary logarithm lookup table accordingly (this action can be expensive, so you might have to use more creative lookup techniques).

Figure 9.5   **Binary logarithm lookup table maps byte value to most significant bit**

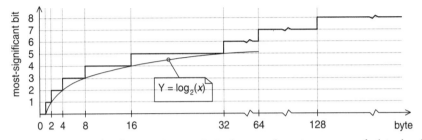

significant bit set in the byte. Figure 9.5 shows the structure of this lookup table, which turns out to be simply the binary logarithm (log base 2). The value returned from the lookup calculation is the priority, which in turn is used to resolve the pointer to the active object. This pointer serves in the next line (11) to extract the event from the queue of the active object. The event is then dispatched to the active object (line 12) and propagated to the other subscribers (line 13). Not surprisingly, these two lines are identical to lines 12 and 13 in the thread routine discussed in Chapter 8 (Listing 8.8), which `QF::background()` replaces in the foreground/background architecture.

The `pkgReadyList` variable is the central element of the design. The event queue implementation in this case must always keep the ready list consistent with the state of the event queues. This requirement implies that `pkgReadyList` is shared between the background and the foreground because ISRs can change the state of event queues by publishing events. (In fact, event passing should be the only way in which the foreground communicates with the background.) As already mentioned in the previous section, the background code is responsible for protecting any shared variables from corruption. Nonetheless, the background loop from Listing 9.13 accesses `pkgReadyList` in lines 9 and 10 without any protection. Generally speaking, you could disable interrupts before accessing `pkgReadyList` (before line 9) and enable them after line 10 (and for completeness, after line 14 as well). In this particular case, however, the critical section can be optimized away, because ISRs can only add events to event queues (by setting bits in the ready list) but can never remove events (by clearing the bits). Therefore, even if an ISR preempts `QF::background()` between lines 9 and 10 (or somewhere in the middle of line 10) and sets some additional bits in `pkgReadyList`, the code handles it just fine. Any bit set in the ready list still corresponds to a nonempty event queue.

The event queue implementation, on the other hand, must protect any access to the shared ready list `pkgReadyList`. Listing 9.14 shows the definition of the platform-dependent macros pertaining to event queues, which appear in the platform-independent event queue code in Section 9.3.3.

Listing 9.14   Definition of platform-dependent macros for DOS

```
 1 #define QF_OS_EVENT(x_)   unsigned char x_;        // see Listing 9.6, line 8
 2 #define QF_EQUEUE_INIT(q_)     (1)                 // see Listing 9.7, line 2
 3 #define QF_EQUEUE_WAIT(q_)     ASSERT(0)           // see Listing 9.8, line 5
 4                                                    // see Listing 9.9, line 6
 5 #define QF_EQUEUE_SIGNAL(q_)  \
 6    pkgReadyList |= (q_)->myOsEvent; \
 7    QF_UNPROTECT()
 8                                                    // see Listing 9.8, line 17
 9 #define QF_EQUEUE_ONEMPTY(q_) (pkgReadyList &= ~(q_)->myOsEvent)
```

The myOsEvent data member of the event queue (Listing 9.14, line 1) is, in this case, just a bit mask with exactly one bit set (the bit corresponding to the priority of the queue). In background processing (Listing 9.13), the event queue can never block because the code extracts events only from nonempty queues. Consequently, the QF_EQUEUE_WAIT() macro should never be invoked, which line 3 of Listing 9.14 asserts. Signaling an event queue corresponds to setting the corresponding bit in the ready list, followed by exiting the critical section (the QF_EQUEUE_SIGNAL() macro in lines 5–7). Finally, extracting the last event from a queue must be associated with clearing the corresponding bit in the ready list (the QF_EQUEUE_ONEMPTY() macro in line 9). Note that every access to the pkgReadyList ready list occurs inside a critical section.

Listing 9.15   Foreground/background-specific implementation of the QActive class

```
 1 int QActive::start(unsigned prio, QEvent *qSto[], unsigned qLen,
 2                    int stkSto[], unsigned stkLen)
 3 {
 4    REQUIRE(0 < prio && prio <= QF_MAX_ACTIVE &&
 5           stkSto == 0);              // f/b does not need per-actor stack
 6    myPrio = prio;
 7    QF::add(this);                    // make QF aware of this active object
 8    if (!myEqueue.init(qSto, qLen)) {
 9       return 0;                                      // return failure
10    }
11    myEqueue.myOsEvent = 1 << (myPrio - 1);    // bit-mask of this actor
12    QHsm::init();                              // execute initial transition
13    return !0;                                 // return success
14 }
15
16 void QActive::stop() { QF::remove(this); }
17
18 int QActive::enqueue(QEvent *e) { return myEqueue.putFIFO(e); }
19
```

```
20 void QActive::postFIFO(QEvent *e) {
21    REQUIRE(e->useNum == 0);                    // event must not be in use
22    ALLEGE(myEqueue.putFIFO(e));                // the queue must not overflow
23 }
24
25 void QActive::postLIFO(QEvent *e) {
26    REQUIRE(e->useNum == 0);                    // event must not be in use
27    ALLEGE(myEqueue.putLIFO(e));                // the queue must not overflow
28 }
```

Listing 9.15 shows the foreground/background-specific implementation of the QActive class. QActive::run() is not implemented in this case. It is not invoked either, so the linker doesn't complain. QActive::start() does not actually start an execution thread. Instead, it just sets the active object's priority (line 6), registers the active object by the framework (line 7), and initializes the event queue (lines 8–11). Specifically, line 11 sets the bit mask that corresponds to the priority of the queue. The last action in QActive::start() executes the initial transition of the active object (line 12). The other platform-dependent QActive methods are straightforward as well. QActive::stop() (line 16) simply removes the active object from the framework (by canceling all subscriptions). QActive::enqueue() (line 18) delegates queuing the event to the event queue object using the FIFO policy, as in the QActive::postFIFO() method (lines 20–23). Finally, the QActive::postLIFO() method (lines 25–28) uses the LIFO policy to queue events.

9.4.3   DOS-Specific Code

The code presented so far is applicable to any foreground/background port of the QF, not just to the DOS platform. Listing 9.16 shows the DOS-specific parts of the implementation.

Listing 9.16   DOS-specific foreground/background code

```
1 #include "qassert.h"
2 #include "port.h"
3
4 // foreground code ...
5 enum { TICK_VECTOR = 0x08 };
6 static void (__cdecl __interrupt __far *dosISR)(void);
7 void __cdecl __interrupt __far ISR(void) {
8    QF::tick();
9    _chain_intr(dosISR);
10 }
11 // background code ...
12 main() {
```

```
13      QF::poolInit(...);
14      activeA.start(...);
15      . . .                                    // start other active objects...
16      dosISR = _dos_getvect(TICK_VECTOR);
17      _disable();
18      _dos_setvect(TICK_VECTOR, ISR);           // hook the clock tick ISR
19      _enable();
20
21      for (;;) {                                             // for-ever
22        QF::background();                      // background processing
23        if (_kbhit()) {                              // any key pressed?
24          break;                        // break out of the loop and shutdown
25        }
26      }
27      QF::cleanup();
28      _disable();
29      _dos_setvect(TICK_VECTOR, dosISR);
30      _enable();
31      return 0;
32  }
```

Listing 9.16 (lines 5–10) pertain to the foreground code, which consists of one ISR — the clock tick. This ISR (lines 7–10) invokes QF::tick() and chains to the standard DOS clock interrupt.

The rest of Listing 9.16 pertains to the background process. After the standard initialization of the framework (lines 13–15), the ISR is hooked up (lines 16–19) and followed by the background loop. The loop invokes QF::background() in line 22 and polls for keyboard input, providing a way to break out of the loop and terminate the application. The DOS-specific cleanup consists mostly of restoring the original interrupt handler (lines 28–30).

Exercise 9.1   Install the evaluation version of On Time RTOS-32 on your PC from the accompanying CD-ROM and port the QF to On Time's RTTarget-32. For the purpose of this discussion, you can view RTTarget-32 as a 32-bit protected-mode DOS. The QF port to RTTarget-32 can use the same source code as DOS, except for system initialization and when connecting the clock tick interrupt. Refer to the On Time documentation [OnTime 01] and to the code of the sample application Serint (both provided in the On Time evaluation kit). Compare your port with the solution on the CD-ROM.

9.4.4 Benefits of the QF in a Foreground/Background System

Employing the QF in a foreground/background system costs you a few hundred bytes of RAM for event queues, event pool(s), and the subscriber lists, as well as a few kilobytes of ROM for the framework code.[21] What do you get in exchange?

First, you gain the power and convenience of hierarchical state machines (described in Part I of this book) and most of the benefits associated with the active object–based computing model (described in Chapter 7).

Second, event queues of active objects act as priority queues and radically change the execution profile of your application. Instead of waiting a full pass through the background loop, a high-priority active object needs to wait only for completion of the currently executing RTC step. This feature dramatically shortens task-level response, which for high-priority active objects is determined only by the longest RTC step in the system rather than the longest pass through the whole loop. In fact, such an execution profile is much more similar to the profile of a cooperative multitasking kernel[22] than to a simple background loop. To reduce task-level response even more, you can use the Reminder state pattern (Chapter 5) to break longer steps up into smaller chunks of processing (at the end of each chunk, you post a reminder to self to trigger the continuation of processing next time around).

Perhaps the most important benefit of the QF, however, is to provide a reliable, hassle-free way to communicate between the interrupt level (foreground) and the task level (background), because ISRs can publish events. This feature significantly reduces the need for ad hoc communication mechanisms via shared memory. You still need to devise mechanisms for the less frequent communication from the task level to the interrupt level (ISRs cannot receive events), but the overall risk of race conditions is significantly reduced.

The small memory footprint required by the QF running in the foreground/background environment makes the QF suitable even for applications severely constrained by resources (including eight-bit micros). Generally, if you can program your system in C (rather than in the native assembly language only), then you probably can use the QF as well.[23]

9.5 Win32: The QF on the Desktop

Although you can use desktop operating systems such as Microsoft Windows for certain classes of embedded applications, you cannot expect fully deterministic

---

21. Code and data in qf_dos.lib for DOS (large memory model, release version) take 5.5Kb.
22. A cooperative multitasking kernel requires RAM for task control blocks and separate per-task stacks, as well as ROM for the kernel code.
23. For smaller systems, you might be more interested in the C version of the QF, which is available on the accompanying CD-ROM.

real-time performance. More importantly, programming general-purpose computers as embedded systems is challenging because it requires reconciling diametrically opposed paradigms. Things that are trivial when you program at the bare-metal level (e.g., disabling interrupts or writing to I/O ports) are often problematic at the level of the desktop operating system. General-purpose computer environments try to insulate applications from the hardware and severely limit the programmer to a specific API (the Win32 API in the case of Microsoft Windows).

Desktop systems, however, are interesting to embedded systems developers not just as potential embedded targets. Desktop systems often make excellent platforms to develop, test, and debug embedded code. This option is especially valuable if you can run the exact code both on the desktop and inside your embedded target. As it turns out, the QF efficiently isolates the application from platform differences. Additionally, loose coupling among application components (active objects) makes it feasible to develop and test active objects in small groups — or, better yet, one at a time on your desktop workstation — and then to recompile the same application code for your embedded target. This approach is often more productive than direct development on the target because the PC lets you work with familiar, powerful, and inexpensive tools and offers excellent visibility into the code, even before the target hardware becomes available. An embedded target, on the other hand, frequently has severe resource constraints and mandates use of expensive, unfamiliar tools operating through a sluggish connection. All of these issues result in slower turnaround of the edit–compile–execute development cycle on the embedded hardware.

The intention of the QF port to the Win32 API is mostly to provide cross-platform embedded development and testing. In particular, this implementation does not attempt to improve the real-time performance of Microsoft Windows[24] — it just sticks to the plain Win32 API.

9.5.1   Critical Section, Event Queue, and Execution Thread

A QF application under Win32 is a single process, with each active object running in a separate Win32 thread. The framework does not use interrupts and handles everything at the task level (including the `QF::tick()` clock tick). Consequently, the Win32 critical-section object (`CRITICAL_SECTION`) is a good mechanism for mutual exclusion.

---

24. Several techniques for improving real-time performance of Microsoft Windows exist (e.g., see [Epplin 98]).

Note: Using the Win32 CRITICAL_SECTION object can lead to priority inversion on Win32 platforms; NT and 9x have different methods of handling it. Interestingly, 9x appears to handle it the proper way by boosting the lower priority thread with the lock to the same priority as the thread that is waiting for the lock. NT randomly boosts priorities of lower priority threads until the lock is released. See Microsoft Knowledge Base article Q96418 for more details [MicrosoftKB 01].

In Section 9.2, you saw the package scope header file for the Win32 port (Listing 9.2). The QF_PROTECT() macro resolves to the EnterCriticalSection() Win32 API call, and QF_UNPROTECT() resolves to the matching call LeaveCritical-Section() (Listing 9.3, lines 9, 10). Because QF::tick() runs in the task context, it also needs to be protected; therefore, the QF_ISR_PROTECT() and QF_ISR_UNPROTECT() macros also resolve to the same Win32 calls. All these macros use only one package scope, critical-section object: pkgWin32CritSect.

The QF port to Win32 demonstrates how to use the event pool and event queue classes (Sections 9.3.1 and 9.3.2) in a multithreaded environment. Porting the event pool class is trivial because the only platform-dependent element is the critical section, which has already been handled. The event queue class, on the other hand, is more problematic because it needs to block the corresponding active object when the queue is empty. To do so, the event queue uses the Win32 event object (not to be confused with the event instances exchanged among active objects). To block the calling thread, the event queue uses the WaitForSingleObject() Win32 call (see the following code snippet of the QF_EQUEUE_WAIT() macro taken from Listing 9.3, lines 21–26). Conversely, to unblock the thread, the QF_EQUEUE_SIGNAL() macro resolves to SetEvent() (Listing 9.3).

```
#define QF_EQUEUE_WAIT(q_) \
    QF_UNPROTECT(); \
    do { \
        WaitForSingleObject((q_)->myOsEvent, INFINITE); \
    } while ((q_)->myFrontEvt == 0); \
    QF_PROTECT()
```

You might wonder why QF_EQUEUE_WAIT() calls WaitForSingleObject() in a loop rather than calling it only once. The reason is that QEQueue::putFIFO() can sometimes signal the event queue more than once between successive invocations of QEQueue::get(). Consider the following scenario. Active object A calls QEQueue::get() to retrieve an event from its queue that holds one event. The queue is now empty, which is indicated by the clearing of its front event, myFrontEvt (Listing 9.8, line 17). After retrieving the event, active object A starts processing. However, active object B preempts A and publishes a new event for active object A. QEQueue::putFIFO() signals active object A's queue (it invokes SetEvent() via the QF_EQUEUE_SIGNAL() macro) because the queue is empty (Listing 9.9 line 6). When active object A comes to retrieve the next event, the queue is not empty (myFrontEvt isn't cleared), so the queue does not attempt to block. This time, nobody inserts events to the empty queue of active object A. When active object A calls QEQueue::get() again, it attempts to block because myFrontEvt is cleared. However, the state of the Win32 event is signaled, and WaitForSingle-Object() returns immediately without blocking. The do-while loop in the QF_EQUEUE_WAIT() macro saves the day by enforcing the second call to WaitFor-SingleObject() — this time truly blocking the active object A until myFrontEvt is set. Note also that the QF_EQUEUE_WAIT() macro tests the myFrontEvent attribute outside of a critical section, which is safe in this case because only one thread (the owner of the queue) can extract events from the queue.

Listing 9.17   Win32 critical section and execution thread integrated into the QF

```
 1 CRITICAL_SECTION pkgWin32CritSect;   // define critical-section object
 2
 3 void QF::osInit() { InitializeCriticalSection(&pkgWin32CritSect); }
 4 void QF::osCleanup() { DeleteCriticalSection(&pkgWin32CritSect); }
 5
 6 static DWORD WINAPI run(LPVOID a) {              // Win32 thread routine
 7    ((QActive *)a)->run();
 8    return 0;
 9 }
10
11 int QActive::start(unsigned prio, QEvent *qSto[], unsigned qLen,
12                    int stkSto[], unsigned stkLen)
13 {
14    REQUIRE(stkSto == 0);        // Windows allocates stack internally
15    if (!myEqueue.init(qSto, qLen)) {
16       return 0;                                      // return failure
17    }
18    myPrio = prio;
19    QF::add(this);              // make QF aware of this active object
20    switch (myPrio) {          // assign Win32 thread priority to "prio"
21    case 1:  prio = THREAD_PRIORITY_LOWEST;        break;
22    case 2:  prio = THREAD_PRIORITY_IDLE;          break;
23    case 3:  prio = THREAD_PRIORITY_BELOW_NORMAL;  break;
24    case 4:  prio = THREAD_PRIORITY_NORMAL;        break;
25    case 5:  prio = THREAD_PRIORITY_ABOVE_NORMAL;  break;
26    case 6:  prio = THREAD_PRIORITY_HIGHEST;       break;
```

```
27    default: prio = THREAD_PRIORITY_TIME_CRITICAL; break;
28    }
29    DWORD threadId;
30    myThread = CreateThread(NULL,                    // Win32 API call
31                            stkLen,         // initial size of the stack
32                            ::run,                        // thread routine
33                            this,              // thread routine argument
34                            0,
35                            &threadId);
36    if (!myThread) {
37       return 0;                                    // return failure
38    }
39    SetThreadPriority(myThread, prio);             // Win32 API call
40    return !0;                                      // return success
41 }
```

Listing 9.17 shows how the QF integrates the Win32 critical section and the Win32 execution thread. Lines 1 through 4 pertain to the critical-section object that needs to be defined, initialized, and cleaned up. In line 6, you see the signature of a thread routine required by the Win32 API. Lines 11 through 41 define QActive:: start(). This method provides an example of remapping the active object priority to the thread priority that the underlying operating system supports. Note that active objects must still have unique priorities, regardless of how many different thread priority levels are actually available in the operating system.

9.5.2   Clock Tick

An ideal place for calling QF::tick() is the clock tick ISR. A clock tick interrupt seems to be universal for both embedded and general-purpose computer systems. Desktop environments, however, are very protective of the interrupts and typically offer only task-level mechanisms for time management. One of the simplest such mechanisms is dedicating an execution thread that invokes the QF clock tick service periodically. The main application thread (the one that runs main()) is convenient for this purpose.

Listing 9.18   Structure of main() in the Win32 QF application

```
#include "qf_win32.h"

main() {
   QF::init(. . .);
   QF::poolInit(. . .);
   activeA.start(. . .);
   . . .
   for (;;) {        // for-ever
```

```
    Sleep(55);      // delay for 55ms
    QF::tick();     // tick
  }
  QF::cleanup();
  return 0;
}
```

Note: The example in Listing 9.18 assumes a Win32 console application. If you want to use the QF in Microsoft Windows GUI applications, you should arrange for a WM_TIMER message to trigger the invocation of QF::tick() from WinMain(). Often, you can use state machines in Microsoft Windows GUIs without the QF (see the Quantum Calculator example in Chapter 1).

Listing 9.18 shows the structure of main() in a QF application under Microsoft Windows. After typically initializing the framework and starting the active objects, main() enters a for-ever loop, which periodically invokes QF::tick(). The tick period is determined by how long the main task delays subsequent QF:tick() invocations (here coded as the Sleep()[25] Win32 call). Note that the clock tick interval in this implementation is subject to additional jitter caused by nondeterministic scheduling of the main thread. This jitter is on top of the usual delay in delivery of the timeout event (see Section 8.7 in Chapter 8).

9.6   RTKernel-32: The QF with a Preemptive Priority-Based Kernel

In this section, I describe the QF port to the environment for which it is primarily designed — a preemptive, priority-based, real-time multitasking kernel.

Such a kernel always executes the highest priority thread that is ready to run. On completion of interrupt handling, the kernel resumes execution of the highest priority thread that is ready to run, which is not necessarily the interrupted thread (an ISR can unblock a higher priority thread by sending it an event). When a thread, rather than an ISR, makes a higher priority thread ready to run (by publishing an event for it), the higher priority thread immediately gets control of the CPU, thus preempting the current thread. The result is a deterministic execution of higher priority threads and an optimal task-level response.

---

25. Sleep() has a resolution of only 18.2Hz (55ms) on Win 9x platforms. The granularity of the system timer in the NT family is much finer (10ms).

To demonstrate this QF port practically, I have chosen RTKernel-32, which is a real-time kernel for x86 processors.[26] I have selected this product because

- it is a true real-time kernel, whose features are characteristic of the commercial RTOS that I want to demonstrate;

- it is designed specifically for x86 processors running in 32-bit protected mode, so you are able to execute the code on virtually any PC or PC-compatible hardware;

- it allows building the code with the same compiler and linker you've been using so far;[27]

- it provides easy-to-use facilities for cross-developing embedded code — in particular, you are able to cross-debug embedded x86 targets directly from a Microsoft Windows host using the Microsoft Developer Studio IDE;

- it offers a fully functional evaluation version, which the company (On Time Software) allowed me to include on the accompanying CD-ROM;

- it comes with comprehensive, detailed documentation, also included on the CD-ROM (this documentation is cited as [OnTime 01]);

- it is, overall, an excellent, royalty-free product with good technical support.[28]

9.6.1 Critical Section and Event Pool

Unlike desktop operating systems (such as Microsoft Windows or desktop Linux), an RTOS leaves you the freedom to disable and enable interrupts directly. RTKernel-32 is a good example on which to demonstrate the three main techniques commonly applied in embedded systems (see also [OnTime 01, Interrupt Handling]). The first, perhaps most straightforward and portable technique is to use functions that you can call from C. For example, RTKernel-32 provides a pair of functions: `RTKDisableInterrupts()` and `RTKEnableInterrupts()` (see Listing 9.19, lines 8, 9). When you step into these functions with a debugger,[29] you find that `RTKDisableInterrupts()` resolves to the `CLI` x86 instruction, and `RTKEnableInterrupts()` resolves to the `STI` instruction (Section 9.3.1). This peek under the hood suggests a second solution, which is to code these machine instructions directly by means of in-line assembly, as in lines 10 and 11 of Listing 9.19, which have been commented out. Finally, some hardware platforms allow interrupts to be masked before they reach the CPU. For example, PC-compatible hardware allows you to

---

26. RTKernel-32 is a product of On Time Software. The accompanying CD-ROM contains a fully functional evaluation version of RTKernel-32 and other On Time products, as well documentation and vendor information (see also http://www.on-time.com).

27. Among other development environments, you can use RTKernel-32 in conjunction with Microsoft Visual C++.

28. I am not associated with On Time Software in any way. I just have used their product and like it.

29. Chapter 10 presents a simple QF application and explains how to cross-debug it with RTKernel-32.

mask interrupts at the level of the programmable interrupt controller, which consists of two cascaded Intel 8089A-compatible chips. You can mask and unmask individual IRQ lines with the RTKernel-32 functions RTKDisableIRQ() and RTKEnableIRQ(), respectively.[30]

Listing 9.19   Package scope `port.h` include file for the RTKernel-32 port

```
 1 #ifndef port_h
 2 #define port_h
 3
 4 #include "qf_rtk32.h"
 5 #include "qfpkg.h"
 6
 7 // RTK32-specific critical section operations
 8 #define QF_PROTECT()           RTKDisableInterrupts()
 9 #define QF_UNPROTECT()         RTKEnableInterrupts()
10 //#define QF_PROTECT()           __asm{cli}
11 //#define QF_UNPROTECT()         __asm{sti}
12 #define QF_ISR_PROTECT()
13 #define QF_ISR_UNPROTECT()
14
15 // RTK32-compiler-specific cast
16 #define Q_STATE_CAST(x_)       reinterpret_cast<QState>(x_)
17
18 // RTK32-specific event pool
19 class QEPool {                                    // "Quantum" Event Pool
20    friend class QF;
21    RTKMemPool myRTKPool;                          // RTK memory pool
22    unsigned short myEvtSize;        // maximum event size (in bytes)
23 };
24
25 // RTK32-specific event pool operations
26 #define QF_EPOOL               QEPool
27 #define QF_EPOOL_INIT(p_, poolSto_, nEvts_, evtSize_) \
28    if (1) { \
29       ASSERT(poolSto_ == 0); \
30       (p_)->myEvtSize = evtSize_; \
31       RTKAllocMemPool(&(p_)->myRTKPool, evtSize_, nEvts_); \
32    } else
33 #define QF_EPOOL_GET(p_, e_) \
34    ((e_) = (QEvent *)RTKGetBuffer(&(p_)->myRTKPool))
35 #define QF_EPOOL_PUT(p_, e_) \
36    RTKFreeBuffer(&(p_)->myRTKPool, e_);
```

---

30. The QF does not use this method to implement a critical section, but the technique is helpful — for example, to mask interrupts while installing an interrupt handler for a particular IRQ.

```
37
38          // the following constant may be bumped up to 15 (inclusive)
39          // before redesign of algorithms is necessary
40 enum { QF_MAX_ACTIVE = 15 };
41
42 #endif                                                      // port_h
```

Commercial RTOSs frequently support real-time memory management in the form of fixed block–size heaps. RTKernel-32 calls them memory pools (see [OnTime 01, Real-Time Memory Management]). The RTKernel-32 memory pools offer almost the entire functionality required by the QF event pools, except for a method to check the block size of the pool. Therefore, the package scope header file (Listing 9.19) wraps the QEPool class around the RTKernel-32 memory pool RTKMemPool (lines 19–23). The QEPool class supplies the missing piece of information in the myEvtSize attribute. Lines 26 through 36 define the platform-dependent event pool operations: initializing a pool, obtaining an event, and releasing an event. All these operations rely on the RTKernel-32 services RTKAllocMem-Pool(), RTKGetBuffer(), and RTKFreeBuffer(), respectively.

Listing 9.20   Public `qf_rtk32.h` include file for the RTKernel-32 port

```
1 #ifndef qf_rtk32_h
2 #define qf_rtk32_h
3
4 #include <rtk32.h>
5
6 // RTK-32-specific event queue and thread types
7 #define QF_EQUEUE(x_) RTKMailbox    x_;
8 #define QF_THREAD(x_) RTKTaskHandle x_;
9 #define Q_STATIC_CAST(type_, expr_) static_cast<type_>(expr_)
10
11 #include "qevent.h"
12 #include "qhsm.h"
13 #include "qactive.h"
14 #include "qtimer.h"
15 #include "qf.h"
16
17 #endif                                                      // qf_rtk32_h
```

9.6.2   Event Queue and Execution Thread

Almost universally, commercial RTOSs support message queues. In RTKernel-32, they are called mailboxes (see [OnTime 01, Mailboxes]). RTKernel-32 mailboxes, as with typical message queues in a commercial RTOS, hold messages of variable size and support indefinite-blocking, timed-blocking, and nonblocking access for both storing and retrieving events. Moreover, unlimited numbers of RTKernel-32 threads can retrieve messages from a single mailbox. As described in Chapter 8, the QF uses only a subset of this functionality.

The public `qf_rtk32.h` include file (Listing 9.20) shows how mailboxes and RTKernel-32 execution threads integrate into the QF. Lines 7 and 8 define the event queue as `RTKMailbox` and the execution thread as `RTKTaskHandle`.

Listing 9.21   RTKernel-32 mailbox and execution thread integrated into the QF; identifiers in boldface indicate RTK-32 function calls

```
 1 static void RTKAPI run(void *a) {
 2     ((QActive *)a)->run();
 3 }
 4
 5 void QActive::run() {
 6     QHsm::init();                         // execute initial transition
 7     for (;;) {
 8         QEvent *e;
 9         RTKGet(myEqu014e, &e);
10         dispatch(e);                      // dispatch the event to the statechart
11         QF::propagate(e);                 // propagate to the next subscriber
12     }
13 }
14
15 int QActive::start(unsigned prio, QEvent *qSto[], unsigned qLen,
16                    int stkSto[], unsigned stkLen)
17 {
18     myPrio = prio;
19     QF::add(this);                        // make QF aware of this active object
20     ASSERT(prio < RTK_MAX_PRIO &&
21            qSto == 0 && stkSto == 0);     // RTK-32 allocates these
22     myEqu014e = RTKCreateMailbox(sizeof(QEvent *), qLen, "");
23     if (!myEqu014e) {
24         return 0;            // failed to create RTK-32 mailbox -- return error
25     }
26     if ((myThread = RTKCreateThread(::run,           // thread routine
27                        prio,                         // thread priority
28                        stkLen*sizeof(int),           // stack size (bytes)
29                        TF_MATH_CONTEXT,              // thread flags
30                        this,                         // thread routine argument
31                        "")) == 0)                    // thread's name
32     {
33         return 0;            // failed to create RTK-32 thread -- return error
34     }
35     return !0;                                       // return success
36 }
```

```
37
38 void QActive::stop() {
39     QF::remove(this);
40     RTKTerminateTask(&myThread);
41 }
42
43 int QActive::enqueue(QEvent *e) {
44     return RTKPutCond(myEqueue, &e);
45 }
46
47 void QActive::postFIFO(QEvent *e) {
48     REQUIRE(e->useNum == 0);                    // event must not be in use
49     ALLEGE(RTKPutCond(myEqueue, &e));
50 }
51
52 void QActive::postLIFO(QEvent *e) {
53     REQUIRE(e->useNum == 0);                    // event must not be in use
54     ALLEGE(RTKPutFrontCond(myEqueue, &e));
55 }
```

Listing 9.21 shows the platform-dependent implementation details. In line 22, QActive::start() creates an RTKernel-32 mailbox capable of holding qLen pointer-sized messages. The active object's thread routine, QActive::run() (lines 5–13), retrieves event pointers from the mailbox by means of the indefinitely blocking call to RTKGet(). QActive::enqueue() (lines 43–45), QActive::postFIFO() (lines 47–50), and QActive::postLIFO() (lines 52–55) are implemented with conditional (nonblocking) calls to either RTKPutCond() or RTKPutFrontCond(). As always in the QF, these calls are associated with the guarantee of event delivery contracts (Section 8.5.2 in Chapter 8).

In lines 26 through 32 of Listing 9.21, QActive::start() creates an RTKernel-32 thread. No remapping of priorities is necessary in this case because RTKernel-32 uses the same priority numbering as the QF. Finally, QActive::stop() (lines 38–41) terminates the thread by means of the RTKTerminateTask() call.

9.6.3   RTKernel-32 Initialization and Clock Tick

Listing 9.22 shows a typical RTOS initialization sequence. The main() routine starts with the RTKernelInit() call (line 12), which is followed by the setup of the custom clock tick handler (lines 15–18). The high-level timer interrupt handler (IRQ 0 on the PC) is customized to invoke QF::tick() (line 7) and then chains to the default RTKernel-32 clock tick interrupt.

After initializing the multitasking kernel, main() initializes the QF as usual and then blocks (in line 28) because a return from main() terminates the whole application in RTKernel-32.

Listing 9.22   RTKernel-32 initialization and setup of the clock tick ISR

```
 1 #include "qf_rtk32.h"
 2
 3 enum { TIMER_IRQ = 0, TICKS_PER_SEC = 100};
 4
 5 static RTKIRQDescriptor rtk32ISR;
 6 static void RTKAPI ISR(void) { //high-level Interrupt Service Routine
 7     QF::tick();
 8     RTKCallIRQHandlerFar(&rtk32ISR);                    // chain to RTK-32 ISR
 9 }
10
11 main() {
12     RTKernelInit(RTK_MIN_PRIO /* this task priority */);
13     KBInit();
14
15     RTKDisableIRQ(TIMER_IRQ);
16     RTKSaveIRQHandlerFar(TIMER_IRQ, &rtk32ISR);
17     RTKSetIRQHandler(TIMER_IRQ, ISR);                   // hook up the custom ISR
18     RTKEnableIRQ(TIMER_IRQ);
19
20                     // set up the ticking rate consistent with TICKS_PER_SEC
21     CLKSetTimerIntVal((unsigned)(1e6/TICKS_PER_SEC + 0.5));
22     RTKDelay(1);                            // wait for the value to take effect
23
24     QF::init(. . .);
25     QF::poolInit(. . .);
26     activeA.start(. . .);
27     . . .
28     getc(stdin);            // block the main thread until the user hits ENTER
29     QF::cleanup();
30     return 0;
31 }
```

Exercise 9.2 Prepare another port of the QF to RTKernel-32 using the QEQueue class instead of the RTKernel-32 mailbox. Apply the RTKernel-32 binary semaphore to block the calling thread when the queue is empty. Compare your port with the solution on the CD-ROM.

9.6.4   Cross-Development with RTKernel-32

With RTKernel-32, you compile and link the code on one machine (called the *host*) but execute the code on a different machine (called the *target*). Embedded applications typically use this method of software development, called *cross-development*.

Figure 9.6   **Cross-development with RTKernel-32**

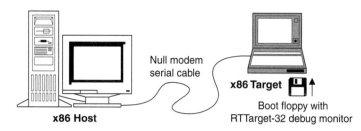

Null modem
serial cable

x86 Target

Boot floppy with
RTTarget-32 debug monitor

x86 Host

Figure 9.6 shows how cross-development with RTKernel-32. In order to execute RTKernel-32 code, you need two PCs — host and target — connected with a null-modem serial cable.[31] The target machine (any PC-compatible hardware in this case) must boot from a specifically prepared boot floppy containing the RTTarget-32 debug monitor and must be connected to the host through COM1. The host machine must be running under Microsoft Windows (95 or NT and above) and must be connected to the target through any configurable COM port.

Exercise 9.3   Prepare both the host and target machines as shown in Figure 9.6 and as described in the On Time documentation for RTOS-32 (included in the RTOS-32 evaluation kit). Follow the On Time documentation [OnTime 01] to prepare the boot floppy and executable for the Hello example application. Next, use Microsoft Developer Studio to download the code to the target and single-step through the code in the debugger.

9.7   Summary

In this chapter, I filled in the necessary implementation details you need to adapt the QF to specific computer platforms. The QF is designed for deployment as a fine-granularity class library that you statically link with your applications. The physical structure of the code anticipates platform dependencies up front and allows an open-ended number of different QF ports.

You have seen QF ports to three very different software architectures, which demonstrates the high portability of the QF and the flexibility of the design. The spectrum of possible QF applications starts with low-end embedded systems without a multitasking kernel, through desktop machines, to real-time systems running under

---

31. In fact, the evaluation version of RTKernel-32 allows you to execute programs only after downloading code from the host to the target (the fully licensed version supports several ways to bootstrap the target).

the control of a commercial RTOS. In all of these areas, the QF has many benefits to offer, and you can use it in commercial products.

Every QF port is provided with full source code and is illustrated with sample applications (described in the next chapter) that you can execute on your PC. Although I discussed only the C++ version of the framework in this chapter, the accompanying CD-ROM provides the equivalent C version as well.

Chapter 10

Sample Quantum Framework Application

The Golden Gate Bridge was built to withstand gales and strong currents,… eleven workers died during the construction completed in May 1937 … over 100,000 cars cross over it every day …
— San Francisco Tourist Guide

In the last two chapters, I dragged you through the internal workings of the Quantum Framework (QF). The way the QF is coded internally resembles the construction of a bridge over turbulent waters, and at times, it is like balancing on the edge of a cliff without a safety net. Virtually every line of code, as with every step on a tightrope, poses risks. Are all possible scenarios of preemptions taken into account? Are all sensitive code fragments protected with critical sections? Are the critical sections short enough? Are priority inversions ruled out? Is the framework code watertight? Well, I sure hope so,[1] but this is neither productive nor the fun way of developing

---

1. I have thoroughly tested the code, but I cannot guarantee that it is correct. If you believe that you've found a bug, please contact me at the address listed in the Preface.

software: it's hard, it's slow, it's risky — it's the conventional approach to multi-threaded programming. However, the struggle is over. The bridge is now open for traffic, so everybody can cross it quickly and comfortably, without taking much risk.

The QF offers you a faster, safer, and more reliable way of developing concurrent software. A QF-based application has no need to fiddle directly with critical sections, semaphores, and other such mechanisms. You can program without the constant fear of race conditions, deadlocks, starvation, priority inversions, and other perils inherent to traditional concurrent programming. Yet, your QF applications can reap all the benefits of multithreading.

My goal in this chapter is to explain how to generate a QF application. First, I explain the implementation of the active object–based solution to the dining philosophers problem (DPP) introduced in Chapter 7, then I show you how to deploy the code on different platforms. As always, every step is illustrated with executable examples.

The second part of this chapter concentrates on the rules, heuristics, caveats, and costs associated with using an active object–based framework in general and the QF in particular. You can think of these issues as a small price to pay for the convenience of application development — like the toll for crossing a bridge.

10.1   Generating a QF Application

Section 7.2.5 in Chapter 7 outlined an active object–based solution to the DPP. This section implements that solution using the QF by (1) declaring signals and events, (2) defining active objects, and (3) initializing the framework and start the active objects.

To keep it simple, the application is text based; that is, it simply outputs text to the screen to report the state of the `Philosopher` active objects. Only the last step (initializing the framework and starting active objects) is dependent on the concrete platform. Consequently, the code is divided into two parts: the platform-independent steps (1 and 2) and the platform-dependent step (3). Figure 9.1 in Chapter 9 shows how the code is physically organized into files and directories.[2]

10.1.1   Signals and Events

The choice of signals is perhaps the most important design decision in any active object–based system. The signals affect the other main application components: events and active objects. Therefore, enumerating signals and devising event classes are good starting points for building a QF application. You can start with drawing sequence diagrams, as in Figure 7.4 in Chapter 7. This activity helps you discover the necessary signals and think about specific event parameters. Naturally, your initial

---

2.   Code organization of a multiplatform QF application mimics the structure of the QF itself.

list of signals and event classes does not need to be complete and almost certainly will grow and change as you progress through the development.

A natural place for declaring signals and event classes is the package scope header file Cpp\Qdpp\Include\port.h (Figure 9.1 in Chapter 9) because all modules need to share these elements.

Listing 10.1   Signals and events used in the DPP application

```
 1 enum DPPSignals {
 2    HUNGRY_SIG = Q_USER_SIG,      //sent by philosopher when becoming hungry
 3    DONE_SIG,                     // sent by philosopher when done eating
 4    EAT_SIG,                      // sent by Table to let a philosopher eat
 5    TIMEOUT_SIG,                  // timeout to end thinking or eating
 6    //... insert new signals here
 7    MAX_SIG                       // keep this signal always *last*
 8 };
 9
10 struct TableEvt : public QEvent {
11    int philNum;                  // philosopher number
12 };
```

For smaller applications, such as the DPP, it is convenient to define all signals in one enumeration (rather than in separate enumerations or, worse, as preprocessor #define macros). An enumeration automatically guarantees the uniqueness of signals[3] (Listing 10.1, lines 1–8). An additional bonus, as the result of an enumeration, is automatic tracking of the total number of signals through the last element in the enumeration (e.g., MAX_SIG in line 7). You need to know the total number of signals to allocate the subscriber list lookup table and initialize the framework (Section 8.5.2 in Chapter 8). Note that the user signals must start with the offset Q_USER_SIG (line 2) to avoid overlapping the reserved signals.

Listing 10.1 defines only one generic EAT_SIG signal (line 4), rather than a specific EAT signal for each philosopher (see Exercise 10.1 for an alternative solution). This design decision represents a trade-off between generality and performance. A generic EAT_SIG signal makes changing the number of participating philosophers easy[4] but requires that each Philosopher state machine filters out only the events pertaining to this particular Philosopher instance. Of course, generating and dispatching events that most subscribers ignore (four out of five) is wasteful and negatively affects performance.

Lines 10 through 12 of Listing 10.1 show an example of an event class with parameters. As described in Section 4.1.1 in Chapter 4, you specify event parameters

---

3.   Overlapping signals lead to especially nasty and hard-to-find bugs.
4.   The other intention is to demonstrate how to multicast events.

by subclassing the QEvent base class. You must derive an event class for every set of specific event parameters in your application. Typically, you will end up with fewer event classes than signals, because not every signal requires a unique set of parameters and some signals don't need parameters at all. For example, the DPP application needs only one specific parameter — the philosopher number declared in the TableEvt class. The TableEvt class is associated with signals HUNGRY_SIG, DONE_SIG, and EAT_SIG, but not with TIMEOUT_SIG, which does not require parameters.

You should keep your event classes simple. In particular, avoid introducing constructors or protecting data members because (as described in Section 4.1.1 in Chapter 4) constructors aren't invoked when you dynamically create events with the Q_NEW() macro. Protecting event data members just hinders access to event parameters from within state handlers. As a reminder of the light-weight character of events, Listing 10.1 uses struct rather than class for TableEvt (line 10).

Exercise 10.1 Change the definition of signals in Listing 10.1 by replacing the generic EAT_SIG signal with a set of signals (EAT0_SIG, EAT1_SIG, ...), representing permission to eat for a specific philosopher. Modify the implementations of the Table and Philosopher active objects accordingly.

10.1.2 Table Active Object

As mentioned in Chapter 7, a general rule for dealing with shared resources (forks in the DPP example) is to encapsulate them inside a dedicated active object. In the DPP case, the Table object encapsulates the forks and manages them for the rest of the system.

Listing 10.2   Declaration of the Table active object

```
 1 class Table : public QActive {                  // Table active object
 2 public:
 3     Table() : QActive((QPseudoState)initial) {}
 4 private:
 5     void initial(QEvent const *e);              // initial pseudostate
 6     QSTATE serving(QEvent const *e);                // state-handler
 7 private:
 8     int myFork[N];              // array of forks (a fork is USED or FREE)
 9     int isHungry[N];         // array of hungry philosophers (TRUE/FALSE)
10 };
```

Listing 10.2 shows the declaration of the Table class. According to Figure 7.6a in Chapter 7, the Table active object embodies a simple statechart with only one serving state. Attributes `myFork[]` and `isHungry[]` represent the quantitative aspects of this state (extended state variables).

Figure 10.1 **Numbering of philosophers and forks (see the `LEFT()` and `RIGHT()` macros in Listing 10.3).**

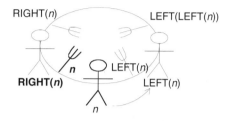

Listing 10.3 **State machine elements of the `Table` active object; boldface indicates the QF services**

```
 1 #define RIGHT(i)  (((i) + (N - 1)) % N)
 2 #define LEFT(i)   (((i) + 1) % N)
 3 enum { FREE = 0, USED = !0 };
 4
 5 void Table::initial(QEvent const *) {
 6     QF::subscribe(this, HUNGRY_SIG);
 7     QF::subscribe(this, DONE_SIG);
 8     for (unsigned n = 0; n < N; ++n) {
 9         myFork[n] = FREE;
10         isHungry[n] = 0;
11     }
12     Q_INIT(serving);
13 }
14
15 QSTATE Table::serving(QEvent const *e) {
16     unsigned n, m;
17     TableEvt *pe;
18     switch (e->sig) {
19     case HUNGRY_SIG:
20         n = ((TableEvt *)e)->philNum;                    // extract sender's ID
21         ASSERT(n < N && !isHungry[n]);          // range and consistency check
22         printf("Philospher %1d is hungry\n", n);
23         m = LEFT(n);                            // left neighbor of philosopher "n"
24         if (myFork[m] == FREE && myFork[n] == FREE) {          // can "n" eat?
25             myFork[m] = myFork[n] = USED;
26             pe = Q_NEW(TableEvt, EAT_SIG);
27             pe->philNum = n;                          // grant "n" permission to eat
28             QF::publish(pe);
29             printf("Philospher %1d is eating\n", n);
```

```
30        }
31        else {                           // philosopher "n" has to wait for free forks
32            isHungry[n] = !0;                        // mark philosopher "n" hungry
33        }
34        return 0;
35    case DONE_SIG:
36        n = ((TableEvt *)e)->philNum;                    // extract sender's ID
37        ASSERT(n < N);                                   // ID must be in range
38        printf("Philospher %1d is thinking\n", n);
39        myFork[LEFT(n)] = myFork[n] = FREE;                 // free-up forks
40        m = RIGHT(n);                               // check the right neighbor
41        if (isHungry[m] && myFork[m] == FREE) {              // should it eat?
42            myFork[n] = myFork[m] = USED;                // pick up its forks
43            isHungry[m] = 0;          // mark philospher "m" not hungry anymore
44            pe = Q_NEW(TableEvt, EAT_SIG);
45            pe->philNum = m;                         // grant "m" permission to eat
46            QF::publish(pe);
47            printf("Philospher %1d is eating\n", m);
48        }
49        m = LEFT(n);                                 // check the left neighbor
50        n = LEFT(m);                                 // left fork of left neighbor
51        if (isHungry[m] && myFork[n] == FREE) {              // should it eat?
52            myFork[m] = myFork[n] = USED;                // pick up its forks
53            isHungry[m] = 0;          // mark philospher "m" not hungry anymore
54            pe = Q_NEW(TableEvt, EAT_SIG);
55            pe->philNum = m;                         // grant "m" permission to eat
56            QF::publish(pe);
57            printf("Philospher %1d is eating\n", m);
58        }
59        return 0;
60    }
61    return (QSTATE)top;
62 }
```

Listing 10.3 shows the implementation of the Table statechart.[5] In the initial transition (lines 5–13), you see how Table subscribes to the HUNGRY_SIG and DONE_SIG signals (lines 6, 7). These signals trigger the internal transitions in the serving state, defined in lines 15 through 62. This ordinary state handler implements a specific policy for resolving contentions over the forks. The numbering convention for philosophers and forks shown in Figure 10.1, as well as the extensive comments in Listing 10.3, should help you understand the algorithm. The novelty here is creating, initializing, and publishing events (in lines 26–28, 44–46, and 54–56, respectively). Note that occasionally the Table object grants two permissions to

---

5.   In Part I of this book, I described techniques for implementing statecharts.

eat in response to one DONE_SIG (see also the sequence diagram in Figure 7.4 in Chapter 7).

10.1.3 Philosopher Active Object

Typically, active objects tend to be Singletons (see the Singleton design pattern in Gamma and colleagues [Gamma+ 95], which means they have only one instance. However, sometimes multiple instances of the same active object class can occur in a system. For example, all philosophers are instances of the same Philosopher class. In order to distinguish between these different instances, the Philosopher class declares the myNum attribute, which is initialized in the constructor (Listing 10.4, line 3). In addition, every philosopher needs to track time while in the thinking or eating state. To do so, each philosopher uses a private QF timer, myTimer (line 11).

Listing 10.4 **Philosopher active object derived from the QActive class**

```
 1 class Philosopher : public QActive {
 2 public:
 3    Philosopher(int n) : QActive((QPseudoState)initial), myNum(n) {}
 4 protected:
 5    void initial(QEvent const *e);                      // initial pseudostate
 6    QSTATE thinking(QEvent const *e);                      // state-handler
 7    QSTATE hungry(QEvent const *e);                        // state-handler
 8    QSTATE eating(QEvent const *e);                        // state-handler
 9 private:
10    int myNum;                              // number of this philosopher
11    QTimer myTimer;                         // to timeout thining or eating
12 };
```

The Philosopher state machine implemented in Listing 10.5 is simple and self-explanatory (especially in conjunction with the state diagram in Figure 7.6 in Chapter 7). Note the use of a QTimer that is armed for a one-shot timeout on entry to the thinking and eating states (lines 12, 42). In both of these states, the timeout signal fires when the timer expires (TIMEOUT_SIG) and triggers the transition to the next state in the life cycle of the state machine. Note that the QF does not publish timeout signals globally; rather, it delivers them directly to each Philosopher instance. Therefore, it is safe to use only one TIMEOUT_SIG signal for all philosophers. In contrast, Table publishes the generic EAT_SIG signal globally and all Philosopher instances subscribe to it in line 5. Therefore, the hungry state needs a guard condition (line 30) to filter out events pertaining to a given instance. Note that the generic EAT_SIG signal is received in all states, not just the hungry state. However, the thinking and eating states ignore this signal (see Exercise 10.2).

Listing 10.5 **Implementation of the `Philosopher` state machine; boldface indicates QF services are accessed**

```
1 enum { THINK_TIME = 7, EAT_TIME = 5 };
2
3 void Philosopher::initial(QEvent const *) {
4    printf("Initializing philospher %1d\n", myNum);
5    QF::subscribe(this, EAT_SIG);
6    Q_INIT(thinking);              // Philosopher starts in the "thinking" state
7 }
8
9 QSTATE Philosopher::thinking(QEvent const *e) {
10    switch (e->sig) {
11    case Q_ENTRY_SIG:
12        myTimer.fireIn(this, TIMEOUT_SIG, THINK_TIME);
13        return 0;
14    case TIMEOUT_SIG:
15        Q_TRAN(hungry);
16        return 0;
17    }
18    return (QSTATE)top;
19 }
20
21 QSTATE Philosopher::hungry(QEvent const *e) {
22    TableEvt *pe;
23    switch (e->sig) {
24    case Q_ENTRY_SIG:
25        pe = Q_NEW(TableEvt, HUNGRY_SIG);
26        pe->philNum = myNum;
27        QF::publish(pe);
28        return 0;
29    case EAT_SIG:
30        if (((TableEvt *)e)->philNum == myNum) {          // guard
31            Q_TRAN(eating);
32        }
33        return 0;
34    }
35    return (QSTATE)top;
36 }
37
38 QSTATE Philosopher::eating(QEvent const *e) {
39    TableEvt *pe;
40    switch (e->sig) {
41    case Q_ENTRY_SIG:
42        myTimer.fireIn(this, TIMEOUT_SIG, EAT_TIME);
43        return 0;
44    case TIMEOUT_SIG:
```

```
45        Q_TRAN(thinking);
46        return 0;
47    case Q_EXIT_SIG:
48        pe = Q_NEW(TableEvt, DONE_SIG);
49        pe->philNum = myNum;
50        QF::publish(pe);
51        return 0;
52    }
53    return (QSTATE)top;
54 }
```

Exercise 10.2 Modify the `Philosopher::eating()` state handler from Listing 10.5 to intercept the generic `EAT_SIG` signal, and assert that the signal is not addressed to this `Philosopher` instance. Hint: assert the converse of the guard in line 30.

10.1.4 Deploying the DPP

In Chapter 9, I discussed the platform-dependent QF code for invoking `QF::tick()`, initializing the framework, and starting active objects in various QF implementations. In every application, however, you need to make several application-specific design decisions. First, you must choose unique active object priorities. For example, you can assign priorities to the `Philosopher` active objects according to their number (1 through N) and assign the highest priority ($N + 1$) to the `Table` active object.

The second group of decisions pertains to sizing various memory buffers (event queues, event pools, and stacks). In general, minimizing memory use requires some nontrivial analysis, which Section 10.4 outlines later in this chapter. However, such analysis is not justified for initial prototyping and for smaller applications (like the DPP). In these cases, you can simply oversize event queues, event pools, and stacks. For example, event queues of length N are definitely oversized in the case of a DPP application. An event pool of size N^2 is oversized as well. The following code fragment shows static memory allocation for the DPP application.

```
enum { N = 5 };
static Table aTable;                              // Table active object
static Philosopher aPhil[] = { 0, 1, 2, 3, 4 };           // 5 Philosophers
static QEvent *tableQueueSto[N];          // oversized event-queue for Table
static QEvent *philQueueSto[N][N];          // event-queues for Philosophers
static TableEvt regPoolSto[N*N];               //event-pool for Table events
static QSubscrList subscrSto[MAX_SIG];              // subscriber-lists
```

Exercise 10.3 Find the DOS version of the QF DPP application on the accompanying CD-ROM and execute it on your PC (qdpp.exe runs in native DOS or in a DOS window on Microsoft Windows).

Exercise 10.4 Find the Win32 version of the QF DPP application on the accompanying CD-ROM and execute it on your PC.

Exercise 10.5 Find the RTKernel-32 version of the QF DPP application on the accompanying CD-ROM. Prepare the host/target environment as described in Section 9.6 in Chapter 9 and download the application for execution on the target machine.

10.1.5 Notes

You might object rightly that the QF-based solution to the DPP is bigger (when measured in lines of code) than a typical traditional solution. However, as I try to demonstrate in the following discussion, none of the traditional approaches to DPP are in the same class as the active object–based solution.

The active object–based solution might be a bit larger than the traditional solution, but the QF-based code is straightforward and free of all concurrency hazards. In contrast, any traditional solution deals directly with low-level mechanisms, such as semaphores or mutexes, and therefore poses a risk of deadlock, starvation, or simply unfairness in allocating CPU cycles to philosopher tasks.

However, what sets the active object–based solution truly apart is its unparalleled flexibility and resilience to change. Consider, for example, how the initial problem could naturally evolve into a more realistic application. For instance, starting a conversation seems a natural thing for philosophers to do. To accomplish such a new feature (interaction among the philosophers), a traditional solution based on blocking philosopher threads would need to be redesigned from the ground up because a hungry (blocked) philosopher cannot participate in the conversation. Blocked threads are unresponsive.

A deeper reason for the inflexibility of the traditional solution is using blocking to represent a mode of operation. In the traditional solution, when a philosopher wants to eat and the forks aren't available, the philosopher blocks and waits for the forks. That is, blocking is equivalent to a very specific mode of operation (the hungry mode), and unblocking represents a transition out of this mode. Only the fulfillment of a particular condition (the availability of both forks) can unblock a hungry philosopher. The whole structure of the intervening code assumes that unblocking can only happen when the forks are available (after unblocking, the philosopher immediately starts to eat). No other condition can unblock the philosopher thread without causing problems. Blocking is an inflexible way to implement modal behavior.

In contrast, the active object–based computing model clearly separates blocking from the mode (hungry) of operation and unblocking from the signaling of certain conditions (the availability of forks). Blocking in active objects corresponds merely to a pause in processing events and does not represent a particular mode of the active object. Keeping track of the mode is the job of the active object's state machine. A blocked philosopher thread in the traditional solution can handle only one occurrence (the availability of the forks). In contrast, the state machine of a Philosopher active object is more flexible because it can handle any occurrences, even in the hungry state. In addition, event passing among active objects is a more powerful communication mechanism than signaling on a semaphore. Apart from conveying some interesting occurrence, an event can provide detailed information about the qualitative aspects of the occurrence (by means of event parameters).

The separation of concerns (blocking, mode of operation, and signaling) in active object–based designs leads to unprecedented flexibility, because now, any one of these three aspects can vary independently of the others. In the DPP example, the active object–based solution easily extends to accommodate new features (e.g., a conversation among philosophers) because a Philosopher active object is as responsive in the hungry state as in any other state. The Philosopher state machine can easily accommodate additional modes of operation. Event-passing mechanisms can also easily accommodate new events, including those with complex parameters used to convey the rich semantic content of the conversation among philosophers.

10.2 Rules for Developing QF Applications

When developing active object–based applications, heed the following few strict rules.

- Active objects cannot share resources. In particular, they cannot share memory.
- Active objects can interact only through an asynchronous event exchange.
- Active objects cannot block in the middle of RTC processing to wait for each other. In particular, they cannot block during event creation (due to an empty event pool) or during event publishing (due to a full event queue).[6]

You should take these rules seriously and follow them religiously. In exchange, the QF can guarantee that your application is free from concurrency hazards,

---

6. The QF does not allow you to block an empty event pool or a full event queue.

including race conditions, deadlocks, priority inversions, starvation, and nondeterminism.[7] In addition, you are able to program in a purely sequential manner, without ever needing to synchronize active objects with troublesome mechanisms, including semaphores,[8] mutexes, condition variables, mailboxes, and message queues.

Still, within these constraints, you can develop responsive applications that make good use of concurrency. In particular, QF applications can be fully deterministic and can handle hard real-time deadlines efficiently.

The rules of using active objects impose a certain programming discipline. In developing your QF applications, you will certainly be tempted to circumvent the rules. Occasionally, sharing a variable among different active objects or a mutually exclusive blocking active object threads might seem like the easiest solution. However, you should resist such quick fixes. First, you should convince yourself that the rules are there for a good reason (e.g., see Chapters 7 and 8). Second, you must trust that it is possible to arrive at a good solution without breaking the rules.

I repeatedly find that obeying the rules ultimately results in a better design and invariably pays dividends in the increased flexibility and robustness of the final software product. In fact, I propose that you treat every temptation to break the rules as an opportunity to discover something important about your application. Perhaps instead of sharing a variable, you will discover a new signal or a crucial event parameter that conveys some important information.

Many examples from other arts and crafts demonstrate that discipline can be good for art. Indeed, an artist's aphorism says, "*Form is liberating.*" As Fred Brooks [Brooks 95] eloquently writes: "*Bach's creative output hardly seems to have been squelched by the necessity of producing a limited-form cantata each week.*"

I am firmly convinced that the external provision of an architecture such as the QF enhances, not cramps, creativity.

Exercise 10.6 Note that only the `Table` active object in the DPP application sends output to the screen by calling `printf()`. Why is calling `printf()` from the `Philosopher` state machine not such a good idea?

---

7.   Of course, these guarantees can be made only when the QF is based on a true, priority-based, real-time kernel with correctly implemented event pools and event queues (see Section 9.3.3 in Chapter 9).

8.   Occasionally, you might use a semaphore to implement blocking on an external device, but never to synchronize with other active objects (see Section 8.5.4 in Chapter 8).

Exercise 10.7 Philosopher active objects in the DPP application think and eat for a fixed number of clock ticks. To make this application more interesting, you might want to introduce random timeouts (by calling rand()). Why is the standard random number generator inappropriate to use in the Philosopher active objects?

10.3 Heuristics for Developing QF Applications

The active object–based computing model has been around long enough for programmers to accumulate a rich body of experience about how to best develop such systems. For example, the real-time object-oriented modeling (ROOM) method of Selic and colleagues [Selic+ 94] provides a comprehensive set of related development strategies, processes, and techniques.

Throughout Part II of this book, you can find several basic guidelines for constructing active object–based systems. Here is the quick summary.

- Active object–based programming requires a paradigm shift from the conventional approach to multithreading. In the traditional approach, you concentrate on shared resources and various synchronization mechanisms, whereas in the active object–based approach, you think about partitioning the problem and about events exchanged among active objects.

- Your main goal is to achieve as loose a coupling as possible among active objects. You seek a partitioning of the problem that avoids resource sharing and requires minimal communication (in terms of number and size of exchanged events).

- The main strategy for avoiding resource sharing is to encapsulate the resources in dedicated active objects that manage the resources for the rest of the system.

- The responsiveness of an active object is determined by the longest RTC step of its state machine. To meet hard real-time deadlines, you need either to break up longer processing into shorter steps or to move such processing to other, lower priority active objects.

- A good starting point in developing an active object–based application is to draw sequence diagrams for the primary use cases. These diagrams help you discover signals and event parameters, which, in turn, determine the structure of active objects.

- As soon as you have the first sequence diagrams, you should build an executable model of it. The QF has been specifically designed to enable the construction and execution of vastly incomplete (virtually empty) prototypes. The high portability of the QF enables you to build the models on a different platform than your ultimate target (e.g., your PC).

- Most of the time, you can concentrate only on the internal state machines of active objects and ignore their other aspects (such as threads of execution and event queues). In fact, generating a QF application consists mostly of elaborating on the state machines of active objects. The powerful behavioral inheritance meta-pattern (Chapter 4) and the basic state patterns (Chapter 5) can help you with that part of the problem.

This list could go on for a long time. In fact, an in-depth coverage of the active object–based paradigm could easily fill entire book. The few basic guidelines listed here are intended just to get you started.

Note: Selic and colleagues [Selic +94] present perhaps the most comprehensive discussion of active object–based computing from a variety of angles, including analysis, design, tools, and process issues. Douglass [Douglas 99] presents unique state patterns, safety-related issues, and a process applicable to real-time development.

Instead of repeating here what you can find elsewhere, I devote the rest of this chapter to the practical issue of sizing event queues and event pools. This subject, although important to any real-life project, is not covered in the literature (at least not in the specific context of active object–based systems).

10.4 Sizing Event Queues and Event Pools

Event queues and event pools are the necessary burden you need to accept when you work with active objects. They are the price to pay for the convenience and speed of development.

The main problem with event queues and event pools is that they consume your precious memory. In order to minimize that memory, you need to size them appropriately. In this respect, event queues and pools are no different from execution stacks — these data structures all trade some memory for the convenience of programming.

Note that the problem with sizing event queues and event pools is common to all active object–based frameworks,[9] not specifically to the QF. For instance, application frameworks that accompany design automation tools have this problem as well. However, the tools handle the problem behind the scenes by using massively over-

---

9. In some active object–based systems, events are allocated from the heap instead of from event pools. Whichever way it is done, the memory must be sized adequately.

sized defaults. In fact, you should do exactly the same thing: create massively over-sized event queues and event pools in the early stages of development.

At some point, however, the problem will catch up with you. Ultimately, you need to deploy the software on production hardware with minimal RAM. Even before that, however, you need to develop a sense of the right size of event queues and event pools in order to know how to oversize them in the first place. For some applications (like the DPP), an event queue of length five is massively oversized, whereas in other cases, such a queue is inadequate.

The correct sizing of event queues and event pools is especially important in QF applications because the QF offers no excuses to overflow an event queue or to run out of events in a pool. These situations are both treated as first-class bugs (Chapters 8 and 9), no different than running out of execution stack space, with potential consequences that are just as disastrous.

10.4.1 Event Queues

One basic fact that you need to understand about event queues is that they work only when the average event production rate $<P(t)>$ does not exceed the average event consumption rate $<C(t)>$. If this condition is not satisfied, the event queue is of no use and always eventually overflows, no matter how big you make it. This fact does not mean that the production rate $P(t)$ cannot occasionally exceed the consumption rate $C(t)$, but that such a burst of event production can persist for only a short time. The bursts should also be sufficiently spread out over time to allow cleanup of the queue.

Some software designers try to work around these fundamental limitations by using message queues in a more flexible way. For example, designers either allow blocking of the producer threads when the queue is full, effectively reducing the production rate $P(t)$, or allow messages to be lost, effectively boosting the consumption rate $C(t)$. The QF views both techniques as an abuse of event queues and simply asserts a contract violation. The basic premise behind this policy is that such a creative use of event queues causes too many potentially dangerous side effects (see Chapter 8).

The empirical method is perhaps the simplest and most popular technique used to determine the required capacity of event queues, or any other buffers for that matter (e.g., execution stacks). This technique involves running the system for a while and then stopping it to examine how much of various buffers has been used. The QF implementation of the event queue (the QEQueue class) maintains the attribute myN-max specifically for this purpose (see Listing 9.6 in Chapter 9). You can inspect this high-water mark easily using a debugger or through a memory dump (see Exercise 10.8). Is this value, however, a good measure of the required capacity? Perhaps not, because seconds or minutes after the end of the experiment, event production can increase dramatically. Even if you apply a fudge factor, such as adding 30 percent extra capacity, you cannot absolutely trust the empirical method [Kalinsky 01].

The alternative technique relies on a static analysis of event production and event consumption. The QF uses event queues in a rather specific way (e.g., there is only one consumer thread); consequently, the production rate $P(t)$ and the consumption rate $C(t)$ are strongly correlated.

For example, consider a QF application running under a preemptive, priority-based scheduler.[10] Assume further that the highest priority active object receives events only from other active objects (but not from ISRs). Whenever any of the lower priority active objects publishes an event for the highest priority object, the scheduler immediately assigns the CPU to the recipient. The scheduler makes the context switch because, at this point, the recipient is the highest priority thread ready to run. The highest priority active object awakens and runs to completion, consuming any event published for it. Therefore, the highest priority active object really doesn't need to queue events (the maximum length of its event queue is 1).

Exercise 10.8 The `Table` active object from the DPP application is the highest priority active object that receives events only from the `Philosopher` active objects, so utilization of the `Table` event queue should not go beyond 1. Verify this fact by using the empirical method. Use the QF RTKernel-32 port from Exercise 9.2 in Chapter 9, because this version is based on the preemptive, priority-based kernel and uses the `QEQueue` class (so you can inspect the high-water mark `myNmax`).

When the highest priority active object receives events from ISRs, then more events can queue up for it. In the most common arrangement, an ISR produces only one event per activation. In addition, the real-time deadlines are typically such that the highest priority active object must consume the event before the next interrupt. In this case, the object's event queue can grow, at most, to two events: one from a task and the other from an ISR.

You can extend this analysis recursively to lower priority active objects. The maximum number of queued events is the sum of all events that higher priority threads and ISRs can produce for the active object within a given deadline. The deadline is the longest RTC step of the active object, including all possible preemptions by

---

10. The following discussion also pertains approximately to foreground/background systems with priority queues (see Section 9.4 in Chapter 9). However, the analysis is generally not applicable to desktop systems (e.g., Microsoft Windows or desktop Linux), where the concept of thread priority is much fuzzier.

higher priority threads and ISRs. For example, in the DPP application, all `Philoso-pher` active objects perform very little processing (they have short RTC steps). If the CPU can complete these RTC steps within one clock tick, the maximum length of the `Philosopher` queue would be three events: one from the clock-tick ISR and two[11] from the `Table` active object.

Exercise 10.9 Apply the empirical method to determine the event queue utilization of `Philosopher` active objects in the DPP application. Verify that the event queues of higher priority philosophers are never longer than those of lower priority philosophers (make sure you run the application long enough). Extend the RTC step of the `Philosopher` state machine (e.g., spend some CPU cycles in a do-nothing loop) and observe when the event queue of the lowest priority philosopher goes beyond 3. Look at the event queue utilization of higher priority active objects.

The rules of thumb for the static analysis of event queue capacity are as follows.

- The size of the event queue depends on the priority of the active object. Generally, the higher the priority, the shorter the necessary event queue. In particular, the highest priority active object in the system immediately consumes all events published by the other active objects and needs to queue only those events published by ISRs.

- The queue size depends on the duration of the longest RTC step, including all potential (worst-case) preemptions by higher priority active objects and ISRs. The faster the processing, the shorter the necessary event queue. To minimize the queue size, you should avoid very long RTC steps. Ideally, all RTC steps of a given active object should require about the same number of CPU cycles to complete.

- Any correlated event production can negatively affect queue size. For example, sometimes ISRs or active objects produce multiple event instances in one RTC step (e.g., the `Table` active object occasionally produces two permissions to eat). If minimal queue size is your priority, you should avoid such bursts by, for example, spreading event production over many RTC steps.

Remember also that the static analysis pertains to a steady-state operation after the initial transient. On startup, the relative priority structure and the event production patterns might be quite different. Generally, it is safest to start active objects in

---

11. Why two? See Section 10.1.2 and the discussion of Exercise 10.9 on the CD-ROM.

the order of their priority, beginning from the lowest priority active objects because they tend to have the biggest event queues.

10.4.2 Event Pools

The size of event pools depends on how many events of different kinds you can sink in your system. The obvious sinks of events are event queues because as long as an event instance waits in a queue, the instance cannot be reused. Another potential sink of events are event producers. A typical event publication scenario is to create an event first (assigning a temporary variable to hold the event pointer), then fill in the event parameters and eventually publish the event. If the execution thread is pre-empted after event creation but before publication, the event is temporarily lost for reuse.

In the simplest case of just one event pool (one size of events) in the system, you can determine the event pool size by adding the sizes of all the event queues plus the number of active objects in the system.

Exercise 10.10 Estimate the event pool size for the DPP application and compare it to the empirical measurement. Hint: inspect the low-water mark (the myNmin attribute) of the QEPool class.

When you use more event pools (the QF allows up to three, see Section 8.4.1 in Chapter 8), the analysis becomes more involved. Generally, you need to proceed as with event queues. For each event size, you determine how many events of this size can accumulate at any given time inside the event queues and can otherwise exist as temporaries in the system.

The minimization of memory consumed by event queues, event pools, and execution stacks is like shrink-wrapping your QF application. You should do it toward the end of application development because it stifles the flexibility you need in the earlier stages. Note that any change in processing time, interrupt load, or event production patterns can invalidate both your static analysis and the empirical measurements. However, it doesn't mean that you shouldn't care at all about event queues and event pools throughout the design and early implementation phase. On the contrary, understanding the general rules for sizing event queues and pools helps you conserve memory by avoiding unnecessary bursts in event production or by breaking up excessively long RTC steps. These techniques are analogous to the ways execution stack space is conserved by avoiding deep call nesting and big automatic variables.

10.5 System Integration

An important aspect of QF-based applications is their integration with the rest of the embedded real-time software, most notably with the device drivers and the I/O system.

Generally, this integration must be based on the event-passing mechanism. The QF allows you to publish events from any piece of software, not necessarily from active objects. Therefore, if you write your own device drivers or have access to the device driver source code, you can use the QF facilities for creating and publishing events directly.

You should view any device as a shared resource and, therefore, restrict its access to only one active object. This method is safest because it evades potential problems with reentrancy. As long as access is strictly limited to one active object, the sequential execution within the active object allows you to use non-reentrant code. Even if the code is protected by some mutual exclusion mechanism, as is often the case for commercial device drivers, limiting the access to one thread avoids priority inversions and nondeterminism caused by the mutual blocking of active objects.

Accessing a device from just one active object does not necessarily mean that you need a separate active object for every device. Often, you can use one active object to encapsulate many devices.

10.6 Summary

The internal implementation of the QF uses the traditional techniques, such as critical sections and message queues. However, after the infrastructure for executing active objects is in place, the development of QF-based applications can proceed much easier and faster. The higher productivity comes from active objects that can be programmed in a purely sequential way while the application as a whole still can take full advantage of multithreading.

Generating a QF application involves defining signals and event classes, elaborating state machines of active objects, and deploying the application on a concrete platform. The high portability of the QF enables you to develop large portions of the code on a different platform than the ultimate target.

Active object–based applications tend to be much more resilient to change than applications based on the traditional approach to multithreading. This high adaptability is rooted in the separation of concerns in active object–based designs. In particular, active objects use state machines instead of blocking to represent modes of operation and use event passing instead of unblocking to signal interesting occurrences.

Programming with active objects requires some discipline on the part of the programmer because sharing memory and resources is prohibited. The experience of many people has shown that it is possible to write efficient applications without breaking this rule. Moreover, the discipline actually helps to create software products that are safer, more robust, and easier to maintain.

You can view event queues and event pools as the costs of using active objects. These data structures, like execution stacks, trade some memory for programming convenience. You should start application development with oversized queues, pools, and stacks and shrink them only toward the end of product development. You can combine basic empirical and analytical techniques for minimizing the size of event queues and event pools.

When integrating the QF with device drivers and other software components, you should avoid sharing any non-reentrant or mutex-protected code among active objects. The best strategy is to localize access to such code in a dedicated active object.

Chapter 11

Conclusion

I would advise students to pay more attention to the fundamental ideas rather than the latest technology. The technology will be out-of-date before they graduate. Fundamental ideas never get out of date.
— David Parnas

For many years, I have been looking for a book or a magazine article that describes a truly practical and reasonably flexible[1] way of coding statecharts in a mainstream programming language such as C or C++. I have never found such a technique.

I believe that this book is the first to provide what has been missing so far — a flexible, efficient, portable, maintainable, and truly practical implementation of statecharts that takes full advantage of behavioral inheritance. This book is perhaps also the first to offer complete C and C++ code for a highly portable statechart-based framework for the rapid development of embedded, real-time applications.

My vision for this book, however, goes further than an explanation of the code. By providing concrete implementations of fundamental concepts, such as behavioral

---

1. I have never been satisfied with the techniques that require explicit coding of transition chains (see Chapter 3) because it leads to inflexible, hard-to-maintain code practically defeats the purpose of using statecharts in the first place.

inheritance and active object–based computing, the book lays the groundwork for a new programming paradigm, which I call Quantum Programming (QP).

This last chapter summarizes the key elements of QP, how it relates to other trends in programming, and what impact I think it might have in the future.

11.1   Key Elements of QP

In the Preface, I defined QP as the programming paradigm based on two fundamental concepts: (1) hierarchical state machines and (2) an active object–based computing model. Although independent in principle, these two ideas work best together. You can realize these concepts in many ways; QP is one of them. Other examples include the ROOM method (considered independent of the ObjecTime toolset) and virtually every design automation tool for developing event-driven software.

What sets QP apart is its minimalist, code-centric, and low-level nature. This characterization is not pejorative; it simply means that QP maps the fundamental concepts directly to the source code, without intermediate layers of graphical representations. QP clearly separates essentials from niceties by implementing the former directly and supporting the latter only as design patterns. Keeping the implementation small and simple has real benefits. Programmers can learn and deploy QP quickly without large investments in tools and training.[2] They also can adapt and customize the Quantum Framework (QF) easily to their particular situation, including to severely resource-constrained environments. They can understand, and indeed regularly use, all the features.

11.1.1   A Type of Design, Not a Tool

The most important point of QP is that the hierarchical state machine (as any other profound concept in software) is a powerful type of design, not a particular tool. The issue here is not a tool — the issue is understanding.

Code-synthesizing tools can have heft and substance, but they cannot replace a conceptual understanding. For over a decade, various authors, in writing about statecharts, have been asserting that the days of manual coding are gone and that statecharts open a new era of automatic programming supported by visual tools. However, with such an era of truly widespread automatic code synthesis still nowhere near in sight, you are left today with no information on how to code statecharts practically. Worse, you cannot access the accumulated knowledge about statecharts because most of the designs exist only on paper, in the form of incomplete state diagrams[3] or, at best, as high-level models accessible only through specific

---

2.   That is, programmers still need to learn the concepts. There is no way around that. However, they can skip learning a tool.

tools. This diffusion of information is unfortunate because instead of propagating a true understanding of the technique, the tool-selling rhetoric creates misconceptions in the software community and makes statecharts, as a type of design, inaccessible to the majority of software practitioners.

The goals of QP are to dispel the various misunderstandings and make statecharts more accessible to programmers. Although tools can help generate code from state diagrams, they are not essential to take full advantage of the most fundamental statechart features. Indeed, it is relatively simple to code statecharts directly in C or C++ and to organize them into fully functional applications founded on a statechart-based application framework (the QF).

11.1.2 A Modeling Aid

Many software methodologists lament that programmers suffer from the rush-to-code syndrome: a pervasive urge to crank out code instead of analyzing, designing, modeling, documenting, and doing the other things that should precede and accompany coding. This syndrome is not necessarily evil. Typically, it reflects the natural and healthy instinct of programmers who want to engage in concrete development instead of producing artifacts whose usefulness they mistrust. Therefore, rather than fighting this instinct, QP helps jump-start the development process by rapidly building high-level, executable models.[4] Such models allow you to perform analysis and design by quickly exploring the problem space; yet, because the models are code, no conflict exists with the rush-to-code syndrome.

QP supports rapid model building in several ways.

1. It lets you work at a high level of abstraction directly with hierarchical state machines, active objects, and events.

2. It has been designed from the ground up so that you can compile and correctly execute intentionally incomplete prototypes successfully. For example, the publish–subscribe event delivery of the QF does not require that you specify the recipients of events, so a prototype still compiles, even if some active objects (recipients of events) are missing. Similarly, automatic event recycling allows the correct execution of applications (without memory leaks), even if some published events are never received.

3. It lets you elaborate statecharts in layers of abstraction; that is, you can intentionally leave the internal structure of composite states unspecified.

---

3. As described in Section 2.2.9 in Chapter 2, state diagrams are incomplete without a large amount of textual information that details the actions and guards.

4. Such models correspond roughly to spike solutions in eXtreme Programming (XP).

4. It lets you modify state machine topology easily at any stage of development. A correctly structured state machine implementation is often easier to modify than the corresponding state diagram.

Through support for executable prototypes, QP offers a light-weight alternative to heavy-weight and high-ceremony CASE tools, for which rapid prototyping has always been one of the biggest selling points. In fact, QP imitates many good features of design automation tools. For example, the QF is conceptually similar to the frameworks found in many such tools. The only significant difference between QP and CASE tools is that the tools typically use a visual modeling language (e.g., UML), whereas QP uses C++ or C directly. In this respect, QP represents the view that the levels of abstraction available in the conventional programming languages haven't yet been exhausted and that you do not have to leave these languages in order to work directly with higher level concepts, such as hierarchical state machines and active objects.

11.1.3 A Learning Aid

Repeatedly, the experience of generations of programmers has shown that to code efficiently and confidently, a programmer must understand how the underlying concepts are ultimately realized.

From my own experience, I recall how my understanding of OOP expanded when I implemented object orientation from scratch in C.[5] I had been using C++ for quite a long time in a very object-oriented (or so I thought) manner. Yet, OOP truly got into my bones only after I saw how it works internally. I started to think about OOP as the way of design, rather than the use of a particular programming language. This way of thinking helped me recognize fundamental OO concepts *as patterns* in many more systems, which, in turn, helped me understand and improve many existing implementations, not just those that are object oriented or coded in C++ or C (but, e.g., in PL/M).[6]

I repeated the experience again, this time with the concepts of hierarchical state machines and the active object–based computing model. I have studied ROOM and have built state models with various tools, but I truly internalized the concepts only after having implemented behavioral inheritance and the active object–based framework.

What worked for me might work for you too. You can use the code I've provided as a learning aid for understanding a concrete implementation of the fundamental concepts. I believe that this book and the accompanying CD-ROM will help you

---

5.   See Appendix A and [Samek 97].
6.   At GE Medical Systems, I had a chance to work with an embedded system with 500,000+ lines of code programmed mostly in PL/M.

through the process[7] in a few short weeks, rather than several years — the time it took me. When you learn one implementation, you practically learn them all because you understand the concepts. Tools and notations come and go, but truly fundamental concepts remain.

11.1.4 A Useful Metaphor

QP owes its name to a powerful analogy between state machines interacting via asynchronous event passing and quantum systems interacting via the exchange of virtual particles. A critique of this analogy might be that programmers are not familiar enough with the physics concepts. However, the physics background necessary to benefit from this analogy is really at the level of popular science articles.

Only recently has the software community started to appreciate the role of analogies and metaphors in programming.[8] A good metaphor is valuable in software for several reasons.

1. It can foster the conceptual integrity of the software.
2. It can improve communications by providing a common vocabulary.
3. It can improve the usability of the end product.
4. It can speed up the learning of new concepts.

Chapter 7 (Section 7.3.1) discusses aspects 1 through 3. Here, I would like to comment only on the last aspect: the role of the quantum metaphor in learning QP.

When people learn new things, they automatically try to map new concepts to familiar ones in the spontaneous process of making analogies. A problem occurs when these spontaneous analogies are incorrect. The new knowledge interferes with the old knowledge (learning interference), and the learning process is more difficult than it would be if the individual did not have the conflicting knowledge in the first place [Manns+ 96]. A correct analogy provided explicitly to the student can speed up the learning process in two ways: by providing correct associations to ease the integration of new concepts with familiar ones and by avoiding learning interference. In this sense, the quantum metaphor can help you learn the fundamental concepts of QP.

11.2 Propositions of QP

As I have indicated throughout this book, none of the elements of QP, taken separately, are new. Indeed, most of the fundamental ideas have been around for at least

---

7. If you are a C programmer interested in QP, you might need to go through the exercises exactly in the order I describe. First, study OOP in C (see Appendix A) and only then study QP in C.
8. Inventing a good metaphor is one of the key practices of eXtreme Programming [Beck 00].

a decade. The contributions of QP are not in inventing new algorithms or new theories of design (although QP propagates a method of design that is not yet mainstream); rather, the most important contributions of QP are fresh views on existing ideas.

Challenging established views is important. An analogy from physics helps illustrate the point. Albert Einstein's [Einstein 1905] famous publication marks the birth of special relativity, not because he invented new concepts but because he challenged the established views on the most fundamental ideas, such as time and space. However, and what is perhaps less well-known, in the very first sentence of his 1905 article, Einstein gives his reason for shaking the foundations — the asymmetry between Newton's mechanics and Maxwell's electromagnetism. Yes, the lack of symmetry was enough for Einstein to question the most established ideas. Ever since, the most spectacular progress in physics has been connected with symmetries.

In this sense, QP pays special attention to symmetries. The hydrogen atom example from Chapter 2 shows how nesting of states arises naturally in quantum systems and how it always reflects some symmetry of a system. This issue alone requires you to consider hierarchical states as fundamental, not merely a nicety, as some methodologists suggest. QP further observes that behavioral inheritance is the consequence of another symmetry — this time between hierarchical state machines and class taxonomies in OOP. Behavioral inheritance and class inheritance are two facets of the same fundamental idea of generalization. Both, if used correctly, are subject to the same universal law of generalization: the Liskov Substitution Principle (LSP) (see Section 2.2.2 in Chapter 2), which requires that a subclass can be freely substituted for its superclass.

The deep similarities among quantum physics, QP, and OOP allow me to make some predictions. The assumption is that QP might follow some of the same developments that shaped quantum mechanics and OOP.

11.2.1 Quantum Programming Language

OOP had a long incubation period. Although the fundamental concepts of abstraction, inheritance, and polymorphism were known already in the late 1960s,[9] OOP came into the mainstream only relatively recently. Without a doubt, the main boost for the adoption of object technology was the proliferation of OO programming languages in the 1980s.[10] These languages included Smalltalk, Object Pascal, C++, CLOS, Ada, and Eiffel [Booch 94].

QP might go a similar route. The fundamental concepts of hierarchical state machines and active objects (actors) were known already in the 1980s. From

---

9.　The first OO language was Simula 67, created in Scandinavia in 1967 to aid in solving modeling problems.

10.　Some of these languages are characterized as being object based rather than fully object oriented [Booch 94].

their inception, these ideas have been supported by visual tools, such as Harel's [Harel+ 98] Statemate. However, as demonstrated in this book, the concepts are viable also with nonvisual programming languages.

At this time, behavioral inheritance and an active object–based computing model are just external add-ons to C++ or C. However, they lend themselves to being natively supported by a quantum programming language, in the same way that abstraction, inheritance, and polymorphism are natively supported by OO programming languages.

The rationale for such a language is the usefulness of QP concepts in programming reactive systems and the relatively low complexity of the implementation. Behavioral inheritance is no more difficult to implement than polymorphism and is probably easier than implementing multiple inheritance with virtual base classes in C++. Yet, language-based support for behavioral inheritance offers arguably many more benefits to programmers, especially to the embedded, real-time software community.

Integration of QP into a programming language could have many benefits. First, a compiler could check the consistency and well formedness of state machines, thereby eliminating many errors at compile time. Second, the compiler could simplify the state machine interface for the clients (e.g., remove some artificial limitations of the current QP implementation). Third, the compiler could better optimize the code.

Many possibilities exist for realizing such a quantum language. One option could be to loosely integrate the QF into a programming language, as with built-in thread support in Java.

11.2.2 RTOS of the Future

Rarely can you find a piece of software truly worth reusing, especially in the fragmented embedded software business. Perhaps the main reason is that reuse is expensive, and there simply are not that many truly general pieces of functionality to justify such expenses. One notable exception has always been a real-time operating system (RTOS). Indeed, as hundreds of commercial and other RTOS offerings can attest, the greatest demand for third-party software in the community is for the operating system.

More opportunities for the reasonable reuse of software exist in conjunction with the functionality traditionally provided by RTOSs. State machines and active object–based computing are truly general and need tight integration with an RTOS. In fact, an active object–based framework, such as the QF, can replace a traditional RTOS.

Benefits of such integration are at least threefold. First, active objects provide a better and safer computing model than conventional threading based on mutual exclusion and blocking. Second, the spareness of concepts necessary to implement the QF eliminates the need for many mechanisms traditionally supported in RTOSs.

Therefore, the integrated system would not be bigger than the RTOS itself, and my experience indicates that it would actually be smaller. Third, such an integrated RTOS would provide a standard software bus[11] for building open architectures.

11.2.3 Hardware/Software Codesign

Advancements in microelectronics have recently enabled the integration of complete, complex systems on a single chip. To cope with the continuously increasing complexity of such systems, designers are considering C and C++ more seriously as languages for describing both hardware and software.[12] The motivation for specifying hardware in C/C++ is at least twofold: (1) to manage the increase in the level of abstraction compared to traditional description languages (e.g., VHDL and Verilog) for hardware design; and (2) to reduce the programming language gap between software and hardware engineers working on the same system.

QP, especially if supported natively by a C-like language, is an ideal platform for uniformly representing both software and hardware, specifically because hardware systems are reactive and concurrent by nature. Although at this time hardware designs have not embraced the concept of hierarchical state machines, they almost inevitably will as hardware rapidly approaches the levels of complexity previously found only in software.

Conversely, increasing clock speeds, power dissipation issues, and the limited memory bandwidth of modern hardware call for a different approach to software. As clock cycles get shorter, some parts of a chip are no longer reachable in a single cycle, and it is increasingly difficult to hide this distributed nature from the software. Moreover, software seems increasingly important for intelligent power management (e.g., clock gating — shutting off the clock in parts of the chip that are not in use).

In many respects, modern hardware starts to resemble relativistic quantum systems, in which the speed of signal propagation from one part of the system to another is no longer instantaneous but limited by the speed of light. A quantum programming language that incorporates the quantum analogy has all the mechanisms to handle such signal latencies built in. A programming paradigm exposes the distributed nature of resources (hardware and software), instead of hiding them, as more traditional software paradigms do. Interestingly, exposing the latencies and resource distribution seems to be exactly what hardware experts are calling for [Merritt 02].

---

11. Section 7.3.3 in Chapter 7 discusses the concept of the QF as a software bus.
12. For example, SystemC is an emerging standard of C/C++ class libraries that also includes a simulation kernel that supports hardware modeling concepts (http://www.systemc.org).

11.3 An Invitation

This book, and even my speculative propositions, has only barely scratched the surface of possibilities that the widespread adoption of fundamental concepts such as behavioral inheritance and active object–based computing can bring. Just think of the explosion of ideas connected with OOP. QP is based on no less fundamental ideas and therefore will eventually make a difference in the software community.

If you are interested in advancing the QP cause, you can become involved in many areas.

- Port the QF to new operating systems and platforms, such as Linux, VxWorks, QNX, eCos, MicroC/OS, and others.

- Provide replacements for conventional RTOSs by tightly integrating the QF with schedulers.

- Use behavioral inheritance meta-pattern to capture and document new state patterns precisely.

- Implement QP in languages other than C and C++ — for example, in Java.

- Explore the possibilities of implementing a quantum programming language, perhaps by modifying an open-source C or C++ compiler.

- Publish reusable, active object components.

- And so much more.

I have opened the official QP Web site at `http://www.quantum-leaps.com`. I intend this site to contain ports, application notes, links, answers to frequently asked questions, upgrades to the QF, and more. I also welcome contact regarding QP through the e-mail address on this site.

Appendix A

"C+" — Object-Oriented Programming in C

C makes it easy to shoot yourself in the foot; C++ makes it harder,
but when you do, it blows away your whole leg.
— Bjarne Stroustrup

Many programmers mistakenly think that object-oriented programming (OOP) is possible only with object-oriented languages like Smalltalk, C++, or Java. However, OOP is not the use of a particular language or tool; it is a way to design programs based on the following fundamental meta-patterns.

- *Abstraction* — the ability to package data with functions into classes.
- *Inheritance* — the ability to define new classes based on existing classes in order to reuse and organize code.
- *Polymorphism* — the ability to substitute objects of matching interfaces for one another at run time.

Although these patterns are traditionally associated with object-oriented languages, you can implement them in almost any programming language, including C[1] and assembly.[2] Indeed, Frederick Brooks [Brooks 95] observes:

> ... *any of these disciplines* [object-oriented meta-patterns] *can be had without taking the whole Smalltalk or C++ package — many of them predated object-oriented technology.*

In fact, hardly any large software system, regardless of implementation language, fails to use abstraction, inheritance, or polymorphism in some form. Easy-to-identify examples include OSF/Motif (the popular object-oriented graphical user interface) and Java Native Interface, both of which are implemented in C. You don't need to look far to find many more such examples.

OOP in an object-oriented language is straightforward because of native support for the three fundamental meta-patterns. However, you can also implement these patterns in other languages, such as C, as sets of conventions and idioms. I call my set of such conventions and idioms "C+"[3] [Samek 97]. The main objective of this particular approach is to achieve performance and maintainability equivalent to that in the C++ object model. In fact, "C+" is, to a large degree, an explicit reimplementation of the C++ object model (e.g., as described in [Lippman 96]).

As you see, the implementation of OO meta-patterns in C is remarkably similar to the behavioral inheritance meta-pattern presented in Chapter 4. In particular, for maximum efficiency, both virtual functions and state handlers rely heavily on pointers to functions. This similarity is not accidental. It is another aspect of the deep analogy between class inheritance and behavioral inheritance.

This appendix offers you an opportunity to peek under the hood and understand the underlying implementation of fundamental object-oriented concepts. Such an understanding will allow you to code more efficiently and with greater confidence.

A.1 Abstraction

As a C programmer, you already must have used *abstract data types* (ADTs). For example, in the standard C run-time library, the family of functions that includes `fopen()`, `fclose()`, `fread()`, and `fwrite()` operates on objects of type `FILE`. The `FILE` ADT is *encapsulated* so that the clients have no need to access the internal attributes of `FILE`. (Have you ever looked at what's inside the `FILE` structure?) The

---

1. The original cfront C++ compiler translated C++ into C, which is perhaps the most convincing argument that all C++ constructs can be implemented in plain C.
2. For example, Borland Turbo Assembler v4.0 [Borland 93] directly supports abstraction, inheritance, and polymorphism; therefore, it can be considered an object-oriented language.
3. I'd like to apologize to Marshall S. Wenrich of Software Remodeling Inc. for stealing the "C+" name from him.

only interface to FILE is through functions (methods), such as fopen(), fclose(), fread(), fwrite(), fseek(), and fpos(). All these methods take a pointer to a FILE object as one of the arguments. You can think of the FILE structure and the associated methods that operate on it as the FILE *class*.

I will quickly summarize how the C run-time library implements the FILE class.

- Attributes of the class are defined with a C struct (the FILE struct).

- Methods of the class are defined as C functions. Each function takes a pointer to the attribute structure (FILE*) as an argument. Class methods typically follow a common naming convention (e.g., all FILE class methods start with f).

- Special methods initialize and clean up the attribute structure (fopen() and fclose(), respectively). These methods play the roles of class constructor and destructor.

The following code fragment declares the QHsm (quantum hierarchical state machine) class. It demonstrates how you can make the association between attributes and methods obvious with the use of a coding convention.

Listing A.1   Declaration of QHsm class

```
1 typedef struct QHsm QHsm;                          /* Quantum HSM */
2 struct QHsm {                              /* attributes of class QHsm */
3    QState state__;                            /* the active state */
4    QState source__;                  /* source state during a transiton */
5 };
6                                              /* methods of class QHsm ...*/
7 QHsm *QHsmCtor_(QHsm *me, QPseudoState initial);   /* protected Ctor */
8 void QHsmXtor(QHsm *me);                              /* Xtor */
9 void QHsmInit(QHsm *me);                    /* execute initial transition */
10 void QHsmDispatch(QHsm *me, QEvent const *e);      /* take RTC step */
11 void QHsmTran_(QHsm *me, QState target);       /* execute transition */
11 QState QHsm_top(QHsm *me, QEvent const *);    /* "top" state-handler */
12                                          /* "inline" function as a macro */
13 #define QHsmGetState(me_) ((me_)->state__)
```

Each class method starts with the common class prefix (QHsm) and takes the pointer to the attribute structure (QHsm*) as the first argument. I consistently call this argument me. In C++, me corresponds to the implicit this pointer. In C, the pointer must be explicit. I could have named it this in an analogy to C++ (which, in fact, was my first impulse), but such a choice precludes using C classes in C++ because this is reserved in C++. (Mixing C with C++ arises easily when you want to share common code between C and C++ projects.) Besides, me is shorter than this, and you will find yourself using many me->... constructs.

Access control is the next aspect that Listing A.1 addresses with a coding convention. In C, you can only indicate your intention for the level of access permitted to a particular attribute or method. Conveying this intention through the name of an attribute or a method is better than just expressing it in the form of a comment at the declaration point. In this way, unintentional access to class members in any portion of the code is easier to detect (e.g., during a code review). Most object-oriented designs distinguish the following levels of protection.

- *Private* — accessible only from within the class
- *Protected* — accessible only by the class and its subclasses
- *Public* — accessible to anyone (the default in C)

My convention is to use the double-underscore suffix (`foo__`) to indicate private attributes and the single-underscore suffix (`foo_`, `FooDoSomething_()`) to indicate protected members. Public members do not require underscores (`foo`, `FooDoSomething()`). Typically, you don't need to specify private methods in the class interface (in the `.h` header file) because you can hide them completely in the class implementation file (declare them `static` in the `.c` implementation file).

Optionally, a class could provide one or more constructors and a destructor for initialization and cleanup, respectively. Although you might have many ways to instantiate a class (different constructors taking different arguments), you should have just one way to destroy an object. Because of the special roles of constructors and destructors, I consistently use the base names `Ctor` (`FooCtor`, `FooCtor1`) and `Xtor` (`FooXtor`), respectively. The constructors take the `me` argument when they initialize preallocated memory, and return pointer to the initialized object when the attribute structure can be initialized properly, or `NULL` when the initialization fails. The destructor takes only the `me` argument and returns `void`.

As in C++, you can allocate objects statically, dynamically (on the heap), or automatically (on the stack). However, because of C syntax limitations, you generally can't initialize objects at the definition point. For static objects, you can't invoke a constructor at all, because function calls aren't permitted in a static initializer. Automatic objects (objects allocated on the stack) must all be defined at the beginning of a block (just after the opening brace '{'). At this point, you generally do not have enough initialization information to call the appropriate constructor; therefore, you often have to divorce object allocation from initialization. Some objects might require destruction, so it's a good programming practice to explicitly call destructors for all objects when they become obsolete or go out of scope. As described in Section A.3, destructors can be polymorphic.

Exercise A.1 Define three preprocessor macros—CLASS(class_), METHODS, and END_CLASS—so that the declaration of class QHsm from Listing A.1 can be rewritten as

```
CLASS(QHsm)
    QState state__;
    QState source__;
METHODS
    QHsm *QHsmCtor_(QHsm *me, QPseudoState initial);    /* Ctor*/
    void QHsmXtor(QHsm *me);                            /* Xtor */
    . . .
END_CLASS
```

Exercise A.2 Using typedef, define QPseudoState as a pointer to the member function of class QHsm, taking no arguments (other than me) and returning void.

Exercise A.3 Using typedef, define another type QState as a pointer to the member function of class QHsm, taking an immutable pointer to QEvent (QEvent const *) and returning QPseudoState.

A.2   Inheritance

Inheritance is a mechanism that defines new and more specialized classes in terms of existing classes. When a child class (*subclass*) inherits from a parent class (*superclass*), the subclass then includes the definitions of all the attributes and methods that the superclass defines. Usually, the subclass extends the superclass by adding attributes and methods. Objects that are instances of the subclass contain all data and can perform all operations defined by both the subclass and its parent classes.

You can implement inheritance in a number of ways in C. The objective is to embed the parent attributes in the child so that you can invoke the parent's methods for the child instances as well (inheritance). One of the techniques is to use the preprocessor to define class attributes as a macro [Van Sickle 97]. Subclasses invoke this macro when defining their own attributes as another preprocessor macro. "C+" implements single inheritance by literally embedding the parent class attribute structure as the first member of the child class structure. As shown in Figure A.1(c), this arrangement lets you treat any pointer to the Child class as a pointer to the Parent class. In particular, you can always pass this pointer to any C function that expects a pointer to the Parent class. (To be strictly correct in C, you should explicitly upcast this pointer.) Therefore, all methods designed for the parent class are automatically available to child classes; that is, they are inherited.

Example of Inheritance in C

Seasoned C programmers often intuitively arrive at designs that use inheritance. For example, in the original μC/OS Real-Time Kernel, Jean Labrosse defines a type OS_EVENT [Labrosse 92]. This abstraction captures a notion of an operating system event, such as a semaphore, a mailbox, or a message queue. The μC/OS clients never deal with OS_EVENT directly, because it is an abstract concept. Such an abstract class captures the commonality among inter-task synchronization mechanisms and enables uniform treatment of all operating system events.

The evolution of this concept in subsequent versions of μC/OS is interesting. In the original version, no OS_EVENT methods exist; the author replicates identical code for semaphores, mailboxes, and message queues. In MicroC/OS-II [Labrosse 99], OS_EVENT has been fully factored and is a separate class with a constructor (OSEventWaitListInit()) and methods (OSEventTaskRdy(), OSEventTask-Wait(), OSEventTaskTO()). The methods are subsequently reused in all specializations of OS_EVENT, such as semaphores, mailboxes, and message queues. This reuse significantly simplifies the code and makes it easier to port to different microprocessor architectures.

Figure A.1   **(a) UML class diagram showing the inheritance relationship between Child and Parent classes; (b) declaration of Child structure with embedded Parent as the first member super; (c) memory alignment of a Child object**

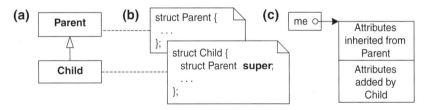

This simple approach works only for single inheritance (one-parent classes) because a class with many parent classes cannot align attributes with all of those parents.

I name the inherited member super to make the inheritance relationship between classes more explicit (a loan from Java). The super member provides a handle for accessing the attributes of the superclass. For example, a grandchild class can access its grandparent's attribute `foo`, as in `me->super.super.foo`, or by directly upcasting it, as in `((Grandparent *)me)->foo`.

Inheritance adds responsibilities to class constructors and the destructor. Because each child object contains an embedded parent object, the child constructor must initialize the portion controlled by the parent through an explicit call to the parent's constructor. To avoid potential dependencies, the superclass constructor should be called before initializing the attributes. Exactly the opposite holds true for the destructor. The inherited portion should be destroyed as the last step.

Exercise A.4   Define preprocessor macro `SUBCLASS(class_, super_)`, so that a class `Calc` (calculator) derived from class `QHsm` can be defined as follows

```
SUBCLASS(Calc, QHsm)
    HWND hWnd_;                      /* the calculator window handle */
    BOOL isHandled_;
    char display_[40];
    char *ins_;
    double operand1_;
    double operand2_;
    int operator_;
METHODS
    Calc *CalcCtor(Calc *me);
    void CalcXtor(Calc *me);
    . . .
END_CLASS
```

Exercise A.5   Provide definition of the `Calc` class constructor `CalcCtor()` and the destructor `CalcXtor()`. Hint: don't forget to explicitly construct/destroy the superclass `QHsm`.

A.3   Polymorphism

Conveniently, subclasses can refine and redefine methods inherited from their parent classes. More specifically, a class can override behavior defined by its parent class by providing a different implementation of one or more inherited methods. For this process to work, the association between an object and its methods cannot be established at compile time.[4] Instead, binding must happen at run time and is therefore

---

4.   Some subclasses might not even exist yet at the time the superclass is compiled.

called *dynamic binding*. Dynamic binding lets you substitute objects with identical interfaces (objects derived from a common superclass) for each other at run time. This substitutability is called *polymorphism*.

Perhaps the best way to appreciate dynamic binding and polymorphism is to look at some real-life examples. You can find polymorphism in many systems (not necessarily object-oriented) often disguised and called hooks or callbacks.

As the first example, I'll examine dynamic binding implemented in hardware. Consider the interrupt vectoring of a typical microprocessor system, an x86-based PC. The specific hardware (the programmable interrupt controller in the case of the PC) provides for the run-time association between the interrupt request (IRQ) and the interrupt service routine (ISR). The IRQ is an asynchronous message sent to the system by asserting one of the pins, and the ISR is the code executed in response to an IRQ. Interrupt handling is polymorphic because all IRQs are handled uniformly in hardware. Concrete PCs (subclasses of the GenericPC class), such as YourPC and MyPC (Figure A.2), can react quite differently to the same IRQ. For example, IRQ4 can cause YourPC to fetch a byte from COM1 and MyPC to output a byte to LPT2.

Figure A.2   YourPC and MyPC as subclasses of the GenericPC class

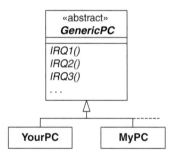

As another example of a system using polymorphism, consider the MS-DOS device driver design shown in Figure A.3. MS-DOS specifies two abstract types of a device: character and block. A *character device* performs input and output a single character at a time. Specific character devices include the keyboard, screen, serial port, and parallel port. A *block device* performs input and output in structured pieces, or blocks. Specific block devices include disk drives and other mass storage devices.

The abstract classes MS-DOS_Device_Driver, CharacterDeviceDriver, and BlockDeviceDriver from Figure A.3 are specified only in the MS-DOS documentation, not a programming language. Still, MS-DOS drivers clearly use the Polymorphism design pattern. As long as device drivers comply with the specification (which is to extend one of the two abstract device driver classes), they can be substituted for one another and are treated uniformly by the operating system.

Figure A.3   MS-DOS device driver taxonomy

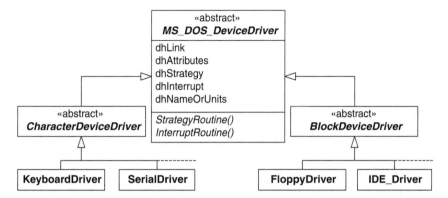

Figure A.4   Dynamic binding in MS-DOS as implemented by the Int 21h functions

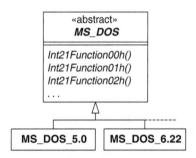

MS-DOS also can be viewed as a abstract superclass for specific implementations, such as MS-DOS v5.0 or MS-DOS v6.22 (Figure A.4). The Int 21h functions provide the portable dynamic binding mechanism used to invoke operating system services from applications. This mechanism allows you to upgrade MS-DOS from v5.0 to v6.22, for example, without affecting the MS-DOS applications.

As you probably noticed in the previous examples, dynamic binding always involves a level of indirection in method invocation. In C, this indirection can be provided by function pointers grouped into virtual tables (VTABLEs; Figure A.5). The function pointer stored in the VTABLE represents a method (a virtual method in C++), which a subclass can override. All instances (objects) of a given class have a pointer to the VTABLE of that class (exactly one VTABLE per class exists). This pointer is called the *virtual pointer* (VPTR). Late binding is a two-step process of (1) dereferencing the VPTR to get to the VTABLE, and (2) dereferencing the desired function pointer to invoke the specific implementation.

Each object involved in dynamic binding must store the VPTR to the VTABLE of its class. One way to enforce this condition is to require that all classes using polymorphism be derived, directly or indirectly, from a common abstract base class,

Figure A.5 **Run-time relationships between objects, VTABLEs, and method implementations**

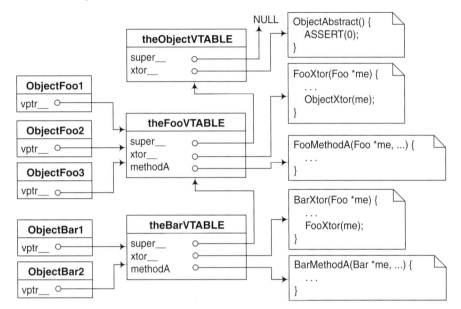

Object (again, a loaner from Java). The VTABLEs themselves require a separate and parallel class hierarchy, because the virtual methods, as well as the attributes, need to be inherited. The root abstract base class for the VTABLE hierarchy is the ObjectVTABLE class. Listing A.2 provides the "C+" declaration of these two base classes.

Listing A.2 **Declaration of the Object and ObjectVTABLE abstract base classes**

```
 1 CLASS(Object)
 2    struct ObjectVTABLE *vptr__;                    /* private vpointer */
 3 METHODS
 4                                 /* protected constructor 'inline'... */
 5 #  define ObjectCtor_(_me_) \
 6          ((_me_)->vptr__ = &theObjectVTABLE, (_me_))
 7                                       /* destructor 'inline'... */
 8 #  define ObjectXtor_(_me_) ((void)0)
 9                   /* dummy implementation for abstract methods */
10    void ObjectAbstract(void);
11                                                   /* RTTI */
12 #  define ObjectIS_KIND_OF(_me_, _class_) \
13          ObjectIsKindOf__((Object*)(_me_), &the##_class_##Class)
14    int ObjectIsKindOf__(Object *me, void *class);
15 END_CLASS
```

```
16
17 CLASS(ObjectVTABLE)
19    ObjectVTABLE *super__;            /* pointer to superclass' VTABLE */
20    void (*xtor)(Object *);            /* public virtual destructor */
21 METHODS
22 END_CLASS
23
24 extern ObjectVTABLE theObjectVTABLE;        /* Object class VTABLE */
```

The Object class is declared in Listing A.2 (lines 1–15). Its only attribute is the private virtual pointer vptr__ (line 2). The Object class is abstract, which means that it is not intended to be instantiated (only inherited from) and therefore protects its constructor ObjectCtor_() and destructor ObjectXtor_(). Other facilities supplied by the Object class include a dummy implementation ObjectAbstract() (line 10), to be used for abstract (pure virtual) methods, and a simple run-time type identification (RTTI), defined as the ObjectIS_KIND_OF() macro (lines 12, 13).

The purpose of the ObjectVTABLE class (Listing A.2, lines 17–22) is to provide an abstract base class for the derivation of VTABLEs. The first private attribute super__ (line 19) is a pointer to the VTABLE of the superclass. You can identify it with the generalization arrow pointing from the subclass to the superclass in the UML class diagram.[5] The second attribute (line 20) is the virtual destructor, which subsequently is inherited by all subclasses of ObjectVTABLE. Consistent with the "C+" convention, it is defined as a pointer to a function that takes only the me pointer and returns void. Although there can be many instances of the attribute class, there should be exactly one instance of the VTABLE for any given class — a VTABLE singleton.[6] This sole instance for any given class Class is called the ClassVTABLE. The VTABLE instance for the Object class (theObjectVTABLE) is declared in line 24.

The hierarchies of the attribute classes (rooted in the Object class) and VTABLEs (rooted in the ObjectVTABLE class) must be exactly parallel. The following macro SUBCLASS() encapsulates the construction of a subclass (see Exercise A.5).

```
#define SUBCLASS(class_, superclass_) \
    CLASS(class_)                     \
        superclass_ super_;
```

---

5. That is why the arrow denoting inheritance points from the subclass to the superclass.
6. Here, I only use the name of the Singleton design pattern [Gamma+ 95] to denote a class with a single instance (lowercase singleton), not necessarily to apply the pattern strictly.

Similarly, building the VTABLE hierarchy and declaring the VTABLE singletons can be encapsulated in the VTABLE() macro.

```
#define VTABLE(class_, superclass_) };              \
    typedef struct class_##VTABLE class_##VTABLE;   \
    extern class_##VTABLE the##class_##VTABLE;       \
    struct class_##VTABLE {                           \
      superclass_##VTABLE super_;
```

VTABLE singletons, as with all other objects, need to be initialized through their own constructors, which the preprocessor macros can automatically generate. The body of the VTABLE constructor can be broken into two parts: (1) copying the inherited VTABLE and (2) initializing or overriding the chosen function pointers. The first step is generated automatically by the macro BEGIN_VTABLE().

Listing A.3   **BEGIN_VTABLE() macro**

```
1 #define BEGIN_VTABLE(class_, superclass_)                    \
2     class_##VTABLE the##class_##VTABLE;                      \
3     static ObjectVTABLE *class_##VTABLECtor(class_ *t)        \
4       register class_##VTABLE *me = &the##class_##VTABLE;   \
5       *(superclass_##VTABLE *)me =                           \
6             *(superclass_##VTABLE *)((Object *)t)->vptr__;
```

This macro first defines the object, which is the ClassVTABLE instance (Listing A.3, line 2), then starts defining the static VTABLE constructor (line 3). First, this constructor makes a copy (by value) of the inherited VTABLE (lines 5, 6), which guarantees that adding new virtual functions to the superclass won't break any subclasses. After adding the attributes or methods to the superclass, no manual changes to the subclasses are required. You only have to recompile the subclass code. Unless a given class explicitly chooses to override the superclass behavior, the inherited or copied virtual functions are adequate. Of course, if a class adds its own virtual functions, the corresponding function pointers are not initialized during this step.

The second step of binding virtual functions to their implementation is facilitated by the VMETHOD() macro.

```
#define VMETHOD(class_, meth_) ((class_##VTABLE *)me)->meth_
```

This macro is an *lvalue*, and its intended use is to assign to it the appropriate function pointer as follows.

```
VMETHOD(Object, xtor) = (void (*)(Object *))QHsmXtor_;
```

Generally, to avoid compiler warnings, you must explicitly upcast the function pointer to take the superclass me pointer (Object* in this case) rather than the subclass pointer (QHsm* in this case). The explicit upcasting is necessary, because the C compiler doesn't know that QHsm is related to Object by inheritance and treats these types as completely different.

If you don't want to provide the implementation for a given method because it is intended to be abstract (a pure virtual in C++), you should still initialize the corresponding function pointer with the ObjectAbstract() dummy implementation. An attempt to execute ObjectAbstract() aborts the execution through a failed assertion, which helps detect unimplemented abstract methods at run time. The definition of every VTABLE constructor opened with BEGIN_VTABLE() must be closed with the following END_VTABLE macro:

```
#define END_VTABLE\
    ((ObjectVTABLE*)me)->super__ = ((Object*)t)->vptr__; \
    return (ObjectVTABLE *)me;                            \
}
```

The attribute and virtual method class hierarchies mostly grow independently. However, they are coupled by the VPTR attribute, which needs to be initialized to point to the appropriate VTABLE singleton, as shown in Figure A.5. The appropriate place to set up this pointer is, of course, the attribute constructor. You must set up this pointer *after* the superclass constructor call because the constructor sets the VPTR to point to the VTABLE of the superclass. If the VTABLE for the object under construction is not yet initialized, the VTABLE constructor should be called. These two steps are accomplished by invoking the VHOOK() macro.

Listing A.4   VHOOK() macro

```
1 #define VHOOK(class_)                                       \
2    if (((ObjectVTABLE *)&the##class_##VTABLE)->super__== 0) \
3        ((Object *)me)->vptr__ = class_##VTABLECtor(me);     \
4    else                                                     \
5        ((Object *)me)->vptr__ =                             \
6                    (ObjectVTABLE *)&the##class_##VTABLE
```

To determine whether the VTABLE has been initialized, the macro VHOOK() checks the super__ attribute (Listing A.4, line 2). If the attribute is NULL (value implicitly set up by the guaranteed in C static pointer initialization), then the VTABLE constructor must be invoked (line 3) before setting up the VPTR; otherwise, just the VPTR must be set up (lines 5-6). Note that because VHOOK() is invoked after the superclass constructor, the VTABLE of the superclass is already initialized by the same mechanism applied recursively, so the whole class hierarchy is initialized properly.

Finally, after all the setup work is done, you are ready to use dynamic binding. For the virtual destructor (defined in the Object class), the polymorphic call takes the form

```
(*obj->vptr__->xtor)(obj);
```

where obj is assumed to be of Object* type. Note that the obj pointer is used in this example twice: once for resolving the method and once as the me argument.

In the general case, you deal with Object subclasses rather than the Object class directly. Therefore you have to upcast the object pointer (on type Object*) and downcast the virtual pointer vptr__ (on the specific VTABLE type) to find the function pointer. These operations, as well as double-object pointer referencing, are encapsulated in the macros VPTR(), VCALL(), and END_CALL.

```
#define VPTR(class_, obj_)          \
    ((class_##VTABLE *)(((Object *)(obj_))->vptr__))
#define VCALL(class_, meth_, obj_) \
    (*VPTR(class_, _obj_)->meth_)((class_*)(obj_)
#define END_CALL )
```

The virtual destructor call on behalf of object foo of any subclass of class Object takes the following form.

```
VCALL(Object, xtor, foo)
END_CALL;
```

If a virtual function takes arguments other than me, they should be sandwiched between the VCALL() and END_CALL macros. The virtual function can also return a result. For example, in

```
result = VCALL(Foo, computeSomething, obj), 2, 3,
        END_CALL;
```

obj points to a Foo class or any subclass of Foo, and the virtual function compute-Something() is defined in FooVTABLE. Note the use of the comma after VCALL().

Exercise A.6   Implement in C+ the classic polymorphic example of geometric shapes. Concrete shapes, such as Rectangle and Circle, derive from the common abstract base class Shape. The shape class provides the abstract method area() that returns the area of a given shape. Concrete shapes implement this method differently (e.g., Rectangle computes its area as a×b, while Circle computes its area as $\pi \times r^2$). Instantiate a few objects of each class and test the polymorphic area() method.

A.4 Costs and Overheads

Any OO programmer can benefit from understanding costs associated with using the OO layer. Abstraction typically incurs no overhead and actually often brings some per-formance boost. If an ADT truly abstracts a useful concept, the OO style of programming typically results in fewer arguments passed to the methods because all attributes are passed as only one me argument.

Inheritance also is mostly free. The invocation of an inherited method on behalf of a distant successor object is exactly as expensive as invocation on behalf of the parent object. The only overhead comes from constructor invocation, which must initialize all parts inherited from superclasses, which, if the hierarchy is deep, could require additional stack space for nested superclass constructor calls.

In contrast, polymorphism always incurs some memory and run-time costs. As far as memory is concerned, each class requires space for its VTABLE. The space required is typically several bytes for function pointers. In addition to this one-time memory cost, each object must contain the VPTR, which is inherited directly or indirectly from the Object class. If many instances of a class exist, the VPTRs in each object can easily add up to something significant.

The run-time cost of virtual call dispatching (dynamic binding) in "C+" is similar to C++. In fact, most compilers generate identical code for "C+" and C++ virtual calls. The following code fragment highlights this overhead for a typical CISC (complex instruction set computing) processor (x86 running in protected 32-bit mode).

```
; static binding: ShapeXtor(c)
    push    ebx                     ; push "me" (in ebx) onto the stack
    call    _ShapeXtor              ; static call
    add     esp, 4                  ; pop the stack

; dynamic binding: VCALL(Object, xtor, c)END_CALL
    mov     eax, DWORD PTR [ebx+0]  ; get VPTR into eax
    push    ebx                     ; push "me" (in ebx) onto the stack
    call    DWORD PTR [eax+4]       ; dynamic call
    add     esp, 4                  ; pop the stack
```

As you can see, dynamic binding requires only one more assembly instruction than static binding. Additionally, you need to dereference VPTR (the me pointer is already in the ebx register) and place the address of the VTABLE into the eax register. The call also requires one more memory access to fetch the address of the appropriate function from the VTABLE.

To complete the picture, now consider the virtual call overhead on a RISC (reduced instruction set computing) architecture using an ARM[7] instruction set.

```
; static binding: ShapeXtor(c)
      mov     a1,v1                 ; move "me" (in v1) into a1 (argument1)
      bl      _ShapeXtor            ; static call (branch with link)


; dynamic binding: VCALL(Object, xtor, c)END_CALL
      mov     a1,v1                 ; move "me" (in v1) into a1 (argument1)
      ldr     a2,[v1,#0]            ; get VPTR into a2
      mov     lr,pc                 ; save return address
      ldr     pc,[a2,#4]            ; dynamically call xtor
```

In this case, the static call is extremely fast, with only two instructions, and does not involve any data accesses, thanks to the ARM branch-and-link instruction bl. Unfortunately, the dynamic call cannot take advantage of the bl instruction because the address cannot be statically embedded in the bl opcode; therefore, an additional instruction that saves the return address into the link register (lr) is necessary. Otherwise, dynamic binding overhead is very similar to that of the CISC processor and involves two additional data accesses (the two highlighted ldr instructions) to dereference the VPTR and to dereference the function pointer.

A.5   Summary

OOP is a design method rather than the use of a particular language or tool. Indeed, as David Parnas [Brooks 95] writes:

> *Instead of teaching people that OO is a type of design, and giving them design*
> *principles, people have taught that OO is the use of a particular tool. We can write*
> *good or bad programs with any tool. Unless we teach people how to design, the*
> *languages matter very little.*

OO languages support OO design directly, but you can also successfully implement OO design in other languages, such as C. Abstraction, inheritance, and polymorphism are nothing but design meta-patterns at the C level. Many C programmers, very likely you as well, have been using these fundamental patterns in some form or another for years, often without clearly realizing it. As with all design patterns, the three patterns combined allow you to work at a higher (OO) level of abstraction by introducing their specific naming conventions and idioms.

In this appendix, you learned "C+," which is one specific set of such C conventions and idioms that achieves performance and maintainability of code comparable

---

7.   ARM is a trademark of Advanced RISC Machines Limited.

to C++. A particularly important feature of "C+" is the high code maintenability. You can add new attributes and methods to superclasses without having to make any manual changes to subclasses. As in C++, after extending the superclass, you only need to recompile the subclass implementation files.

I have been using "C+" successfully in many projects for number of years, and I challenge you to find a more efficient, scalable, portable, and maintainable implementation. However, perhaps the weakest aspect inherent in any attempt to implement OOP in C (not just "C+") is that type safety is compromised. The fundamental problem is that a C compiler does not recognize that some types are generalizations of others and treats related types as completely different. This issue requires a lot of type casting (upcasting), which is awkward and defeats much of the type safety of the language.

Therefore, if you have access to a decent C++ compiler for your platform, I recommend that you consider using it instead of "C+." Contrary to the general view, especially among embedded systems programmers, C++ is not inherently bulky and slow. By sticking only to the essential OO features of C++ and omitting pretty much everything else (Embedded C++ [EC++ 01] provides an excellent example), you can achieve very good performance, elegance, convenience, and full compiler support for OOP.

Appendix B

Guide to Notation

The good thing about bubbles and arrows, as opposed to programs, is that they never crash.
— Bertrand Meyer

In this appendix, I describe the graphical notation that I use throughout the book.[1] The notation should be compatible with version 1.4 of the UML specification[2] [OMG 01]. The timing diagrams are not part of the UML. I adapted them from Douglass [Doublass 99].

B.1   Class Diagrams

A class diagram shows classes, their internal structures, and the *static* (compile-time) relationships among them. Figure B.1 shows the various presentation options for classes.

---

1. In this appendix, I do not include the informal data structure diagrams that show particular C or C++ data structures at run time.
2. I prepared all diagrams with Visio ™ Technical v4.0. The accompanying CD-ROM contains the Visio stencil that I used.

Figure B.1   Various levels of detail, visibility, and properties of classes

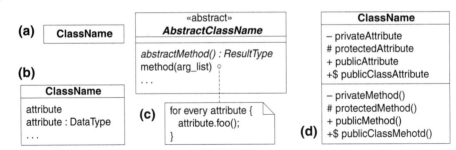

- A class is always denoted by a box with the class name in bold type at the top. Optionally, just below the name, a class box can have an attribute compartment that is separated from the name by a horizontal line. Below the attributes, a class box can have an optional method compartment.

- The UML notation allows you to distinguish abstract classes, which are classes intended only for derivation and cannot have direct instances. Figure B.1c shows the notation for such classes. The abstract class name appears in italic font. Optionally you may use the «abstract» stereotype. If a class has abstract methods (pure virtual member functions in C++), they are shown in an italic font as well.

- Sometimes it is helpful to provide pseudocode of some methods by means of a note (Figure B.1c).

- Finally, a class box can also show the visibility of attributes and methods, as in Figure B.1d.

Figure B.2   Different presentation options for the generalization and specialization of classes

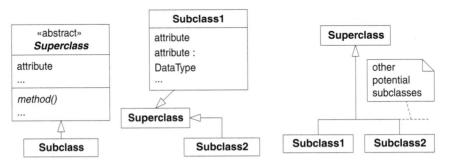

Figure B.2 shows the different presentation options for inheritance (the is-a-kind-of relationship). The generalization arrow always points from the subclass to the superclass. The right-hand side of Figure B.2 shows an inheritance tree that indicates an open-ended number of subclasses.

Figure B.3   Aggregation, navigability, and multiplicity

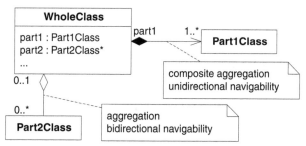

Figure B.3 shows the aggregation of classes (the has-a-component relationship). An aggregation relationship implies that one object physically or conceptually contains another. The notation for aggregation consists of a line with a diamond at its base. The diamond is at the side of the owner class (whole class), and the line extends to the component class (part class). The full diamond represents physical containment; that is, the instance of the part class physically resides in the instance of the whole class (composite aggregation). A weaker form of aggregation, denoted with an empty diamond, indicates that the whole class has only a reference or pointer to the part instance but does not physically contain it. A name for the reference might appear at the base (e.g., part1 in Figure B.3). Aggregation also could indicate multiplicity and navigability between the whole and the parts.

Figure B.4   Design pattern as a collaboration of classes

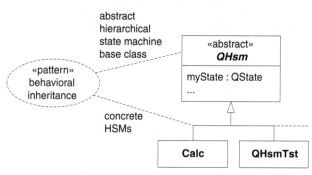

Figure B.4 shows a collaboration of classes as a dashed ellipse containing the name of the collaboration (stereotyped here as a *pattern*). The dashed lines emanating from the collaboration symbol to the various elements denote participants in the collaboration. Each line is labeled by the *role* that the participant plays in the collaboration. The roles correspond to the names of elements within the context for the collaboration; such names in the collaboration are treated as parameters that are bound to specific elements on each occurrence of the pattern within a model [OMG 01).

B.2 Statechart Diagrams

A statechart diagram shows the *static* state space of a given context class, the events that cause a transition from one state to another, and the actions that result.

Figure B.5 **States and a transition**

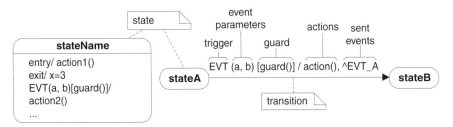

Figure B.5 shows the presentation options for states and the notation for a state transition. A state is always denoted by a rectangle with rounded corners. The name of the state appears in bold type at the top. Optionally, right below the name, a state can have an internal transition compartment separated from the name by a horizontal line. The internal transition compartment can contain entry actions (actions following the reserved symbol `entry`), exit actions (actions following the reserved symbol `exit`), and other internal transitions (e.g., those triggered by EVT in Figure B.5).

A state transition is represented as an arrow originating at the boundary of the source state and pointing to the boundary of the target state. At a minimum, a transition must be labeled with the triggering event. Optionally, the trigger can be followed by event parameters, a guard, a list of actions, and a list of events that have been sent.

Figure B.6 **Composite state, initial transitions, and the final state**

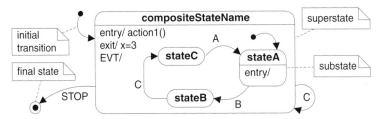

Figure B.6 shows a composite state (superstate) that contains other states (substates). Each composite state can have a separate initial transition to designate the initial substate. Although Figure B.6 shows only one level of nesting, the substates can be composite as well.

Figure B.7   Orthogonal regions and pseudostates

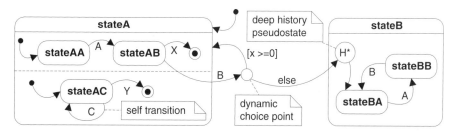

Figure B.7 shows composite stateA with the orthogonal regions (and-states) separated by a dashed line and two pseudostates: the dynamic choice point and deep history.

B.3   Sequence Diagrams

A sequence diagram shows a particular sequence of event instances exchanged among objects at *run time*. A sequence diagram has two dimensions: the vertical dimension represents time and the horizontal dimension represents different objects. Time flows down the page (the dimensions can be reversed, if desired).

Figure B.8 shows an example of a sequence diagram. Object boxes, together with the descending vertical lines, represent objects participating in the scenario. As always in the UML specification, the object name in each box is underlined (some objects are identified only by a colon and a class name). Heavy borders indicate concurrent objects.

Events are represented as horizontal arrows originating from the sending object and terminating at the receiving object. Optionally, thin rectangles around instance lines can indicate focus of control. Sequence diagrams also can contain state marks to indicate explicit state changes resulting from the event exchange.

B.4   Timing Diagrams

A timing diagram shows the explicit changes of state in one or more objects along a single time axis. Timing diagrams are not in the UML standard and are adopted here from Douglass [Douglass 99].

Figure B.9 shows an example of a timing diagram for multiple objects (T1, T2, and T3). The timing diagram has two dimensions: time along the horizontal axis and the object state along the vertical axis. Each object is assigned a horizontal band across the diagram (a "swim lane") separated from other bands by dashed lines. Presentation options include deadlines, propagated events, and jitter.

Figure B.8   Sequence diagram

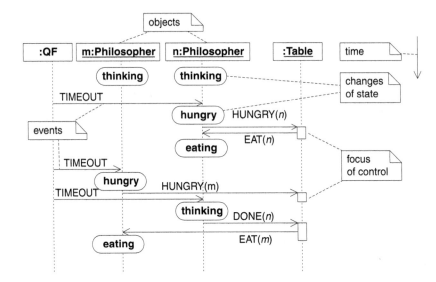

Figure B.9   Timing diagram

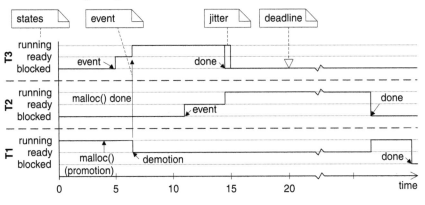

C

Appendix C

CD-ROM

In a double-speed CD-ROM, the pits go flying by the focused spot at a rate of 1,200,000 pits per second. As they do, the servo system adjusts the tracking and the focus of the laser beam so that it remains within about ±0.1μm of the track center and within about ±2μm of the correct focus position even though the CD-ROM disc may be wobbling from side-to-side by ±70μm (44 track diameters) and up-and-down by ±600μm as it rotates. The performance of this opto-electronic system is truly remarkable.
— Murray Sargent III and Richard L. Shoemaker
   The Personal Computer from the Inside Out

The companion CD-ROM contains all the source code and executable images mentioned in the book, including several ports of the Quantum Framework (QF). The disc also includes answers to the exercises scattered throughout the book, the Evaluation Version of On Time RTOS-32 v4.0, Visio™ stencils used to create the diagrams in this book, and several references in Adobe Portable Document Format (PDF).[1]

---

1. A copy of Adobe Acrobat Reader™ is included on the CD-ROM for your convenience.

The CD-ROM is designed for maximum usefulness, even without installing any of it on your hard drive. In particular, you can browse the source code, execute examples, and read PDF documents directly from the CD.

The disc comes with an HTML-based index page, index.htm, in its root directory (Figure C.1). It is automatically activated if the CD autoinsert notification is enabled on your system. You need a Web browser (e.g., Microsoft Internet Explorer or Netscape Navigator) to view the index.

Figure C.1   CD index

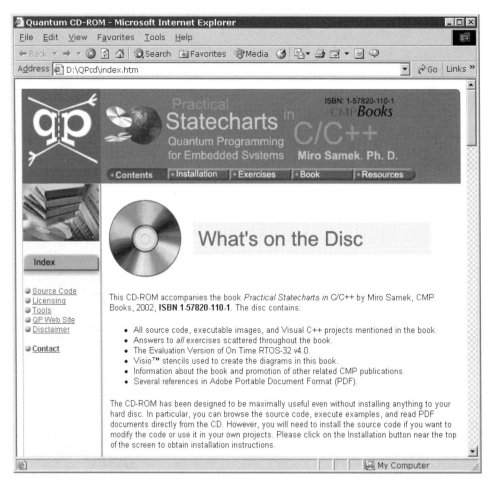

C.1   Source Code Structure

The structure of the source code on the disc does not strictly reflect the chapter structure of the book, so that I would avoid repetition of the central QF implementation. The CD index page lists all the source code directories and describes their contents.

You can browse the code directly on the CD or simply copy selected files to your hard disk for modifications. For your convenience, the disc also contains an installation program, which installs the source code, the projects, and prebuilt libraries.

C.2   Installation

The Installation HTML page on the CD contains links to three self-extracting installation programs, which you can install by simply clicking on the links under Microsoft Windows.

C.2.1   Source Code

The self-extracting installation program `<CD>:\Installations\QPcode.exe` installs the complete Quantum Programming (QP) source code. You will be prompted to select an installation directory and a program group in your Start Menu. The typical setup will install all source code components (the C++, C, and C++ with MI [multiple inheritance]) to your hard disk. The custom setup allows you to selectively install only certain components. The installation creates the same directory structure on the CD-ROM as on your hard drive, so the relative links of the index page will still work correctly. The complete installation requires about 60 Mb of your hard drive because it contains a complete software build (object files, program databases, libraries, etc.).

C.2.2   On Time RTOS-32 Evaluation Kit

On Time's RTOS-32 is a royalty-free, embedded, real-time operating system for x86-compatible CPUs. You need to install the On Time RTOS-32 Evaluation Kit v4.0 if you intend to run the real-time examples from Part II of the book. The file `<CD>:\Installations\RTOS-32.exe` is a self-extracting Windows installation program. The Evaluation Kit can be uninstalled completely and easily.

In order to build QF applications, you also need to define the environment variable RTTARGET and append %RTTARGET%\bin to the execution PATH. On Microsoft Windows 95/98, you need to add the following two lines to the autoexec.bat file.

```
set RTTARGET=<target directory>\RTOS-32
PATH=%RTTARGET%\bin;%PATH%
```

On Microsoft Windows NT/2000, you need to define the environment variable and the path in the corresponding System dialog box.

C.2.3 Adobe Acrobat Reader

The CD-ROM includes several documents in Adobe PDF. To view such documents, you need Adobe Acrobat Reader. If you do not have Acrobat Reader, you can download the latest version free from the Adobe Web site or install version 5.0 from the CD-ROM.

C.3 Answers to the Exercises

The Exercises HTML page on the CD (Figure C.2) contains answers to all of the exercises in the book. The many links to the source code work directly on the CD-ROM or after installation to your hard disk.

C.4 Resources

The CD-ROM contains several of the references (listed in the Bibliography) in PDF. Among others, the documents include the OMG UML Specification v1.4 [OMG 01] and the On Time RTOS-32 Manual [OnTime 01].

For your convenience, the CD also contains the Visio™ stencil and template that I used to draw all the diagrams in this book. One of the main goals of QP is to provide a light-weight alternative to heavy-weight and expensive design automation tools. Such tools typically come with a drawing package to create various diagrams. In fact, most of the tools, if they are used at all, end up as overpriced drawing packages. To this end, a good drawing program does as much for you as a fancy CASE tool.

As described on the Resources page, you incorporate the stencil into Visio by copying `<CD>:\Resources\Visio\Software-UML.vss` to your `Visio\Stencils` directory and `<CD>:\Resources\Visio\Software-UML.vst` to your `Visio\Template` directory.

I have tried both the stencil and the template with the newer version of Visio (Visio 2000), and they seem to work correctly.

Figure C.2   Exercises page

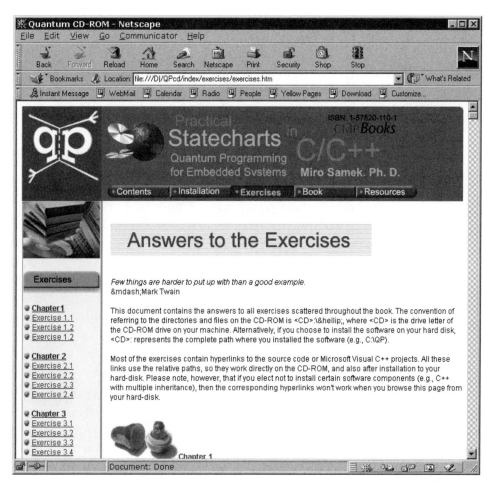

Bibliography

Amber, Scott. 2001. "Debunking Modeling Myths." *Software Development*, August.

Barr, Michael. 1999. *Programming Embedded Systems in C and C++*. O'Reilly & Associates.

Beck, Kent. 2000. *Extreme Programming Explained*. Addison-Wesley.

Booch, Grady. 1994. *Object-Oriented Analysis and Design with Applications*. Addison-Wesley.

Borland. 1993. Borland turbo Assembler v4.0.

Brooks, Frederick P. 1987. "No Silver Bullet: Essence and Accidents of Software Engineering." *Computer*, April, 10-19.

Brooks, Frederick. 1995. *The mythical man-month*. Anniversary ed. Addison Wesley.

Cargill, Tom. 1994. "Exception Handling: A False Sense of Security." *C++ Report*, November-December.

Deshpande, Akash. 2001. Creating advanced network infrastructure based on network processors. *RTC*, October (vol. 10, no. 10), 56–59. (www.rtcmagazine.com)

Dijkstra, Edsger W. 1965. *Cooperating Sequential Processes*, Technology Report EWD-123, Eindhoven, Netherlands.

Dijkstra, Edsger W. 1971. Hierarchical ordering of sequential processes. *Acta Informatica* 1:115–138.

Douglass, Bruce Powell. 1998, State machines and state charts. Pts. 1 and 2. *Proceedings of the Embedded Systems Conference*, Spring. Chicago.

Douglass, Bruce Powell. 1999. *Doing hard time, developing real-time systems with UML, objects, frameworks, and patterns.* Addison Wesley.

Douglass, Bruce Powel. 1999. *Real-Time UML, Second Edition: Developing Efficient Objects for Embedded Systems*, Addison-Wesley.

Douglass, Bruce Powel. 1999. "UML Statecharts." *Embedded Systems Programming*, January, 22-42.

Duby, Carolyn. 2001. Class 203: Implementing UML statechart diagrams. *Proceedings of Embedded Systems Conference,* Fall. San Francisco.

[EC++] Embedded C++ Technical Committee. 2001. www.caravan.net/ec2plus

Eckel, Bruce. 1995. *Thinking in C++.* Prentice Hall.

Einstein, Albert. 1905. Zur Elektrodynamik bewegter Körper. *Annalen der Physik und Chemie.* IV Folge, Band 17, 891–921.

Englebart, D., and W. English. 1968. A research center for augmented human intellect. *AFIPS Conference Proceedings, Fall Joint Computer Conference*, 9–11 December, 395–410. San Francisco.

Epplin, Jerry. 1998. "Adapting Windows NT to Embedded Systems", *Embedded Systems Programming*, June, 44-61.

Fowler, Martin, Kent Beck, John Brant, William Opdyke, Don Roberts. 1999. *Refactoring: Improving the Design of Existing Code*, Addison-Wesley.

Fowler, Martin. 2001. "The Agile Manifesto." *Software Development*.

Gamma, Erich, Richard Helm, Ralph Johnson, and John Vlissides. 1995. *Design patterns, elements of reusable object-oriented software.* Addison Wesley.

Ganssle, Jack G. 2000 *The Art of Designing Embedded Systems*, Newnes.

Halzen, Francis, Alan D. Martin. 1984. *Quarks and Leptons: An Introductory Course in Modern Particle Physics*, John Wiley & Sons.

Harel, David. 1987. Statecharts: A visual formalism for complex systems. *Science of Computer Programming* (no. 8), 231–274.

Harel, David, and Michal Politi. 1998. *Modeling Reactive Systems with Statecharts, The STATEMATE Approach*. McGraw-Hill.

Hejlsberg, Anders. 2001. Simplexity–complexity wrapped in something simple. Acceptance speech for the *Dr. Dobbs Journal*'s Excellence in Programming Award presented at the Software Development Conference West. San Jose, California.

Hewitt, Carl, P. Bishop, and R. Steiger. 1979. "A universal, modular actor formalism for artificial intelligence", *3rd International Joint Conference on Artificial Intelligence*, 235–245.

Horrocks, Ian. 1999. *Constructing the User Interface with Statecharts*. Addison-Wesley.

Horstmann, Cay S. 1995. *Mastering Object-Oriented Design in* C++, John Wiley & Sons.

IAR Systems visualSTATE® http://www.iar.com/Products/VS/

Interactive Software Engineering,
www.eiffel.com/doc/manuals/technology/contract/page.html

Kalinsky, David, 1998. "Mutexes Prevent Priority Inversions", *Embedded Systems Programming*, August, 76-81.

Kalinsky, David. 2001. "Queueing Theory for Dummies", *Embedded Systems Programming*, April, 63-72.

Kapp, Steve. 2000. "Design by Contract for C Programmers", *Embedded Systems Programming*, July, 100-106.

Labrosse, Jean J. 1992a. A portable real-time kernel in C. *Embedded Systems Programming*, May, 40–53.

Labrosse, Jean J. 1992b. Implementing a real-time kernel. *Embedded Systems Programming*, June, 44–49.

Labrosse, Jean J. 1992c. *μC/OS, The Real-Time Kernel*, R&D Publications.

Labrosse, Jean J., *MicroC/OS-II, The Real-Time Kernel*. R&D Publications, 1999, ISBN 0-87930-543-6

Lafreniere, David. 1998. An efficient dynamic storage allocator. *Embedded Systems Programming*, September, 72–80.

Leveson, Nancy, and Clark S. Turner. An investigation of the Therac-25 accidents. *IEEE Computer*, July.

Leveson, Nancy. 1995. *Safeware: system safety and computers*. Addison-Wesley.

Lippman, Stanley. 1996. *Inside the C++ object model*. Addison Wesley.

Maguire, Steve. 1993. *Writing solid code*. Microsoft Press.

Manns, Mary Lynn and H. James Nelson. 1996. "Retraining procedure-oriented developers: An issue of skill transfer." *Journal of Object-Oriented Programming*, November/December, 6–10.

Mellor, Steve. 2000. "UML Point/Counterpoint: Modeling Complex Behavior Simply." *Embedded Systems Programming*, March 2000, 38–42.

Merritt, Rick. 2002. Software model needs overhaul. *EE Times*, 2 January (no. 1199), 5. (www.eet.com)

Meyer, Bertrand. 1997. *Object-oriented software construction*. 2nd ed. Prentice Hall.

Meyer, Bertrand. 1997. "UML: The Positive Spin", *Cutter IT Journal, Volume X, No. 3* (former Ed Yourdon's *American Programmer*).

Meyer, Bertrand. 1997. Letters from readers (response to the article "Put it in the contract: The lessons of Ariane" by Jean-Marc Jézéquel, and Bertrand Meyer), *IEEE Computer*, Vol. 30, No. 2, February, 8–9, 11.

Microsoft. 2001. Microsoft Knowledge Base article Q96418.

Moore, Gordon, E. 1965. Cramming more components onto integrated circuits. *Electronics*, 19 April (vol. 38, no. 8).

Murphy, Niall, 2000. "Open Source Point/Counterpoint: Are Open Source and Innovation Compatible?", *Embedded Systems Programming*, September, 78–86.

Murphy, Niall. 2001a. Assertiveness Training for Programmers. *Embedded Systems Programming*, April, 53–60.

Murphy, Niall. 2001b. Assert yourself. *Embedded Systems Programming*, May, 27–32.

OnTime. 2000. Refer to the On Time documentation on the accompanying CD-ROM.

OnTime. 2001. Refer to the On Time documentation on the accompanying CD-ROM.

Opdyke, William F., "Refactoring Object-Oriented Frameworks", Ph. D. Thesis, University of Illinois at Urbana-Champaign, 1992. NOTE: this document is available in PDF from the accompanying CD-ROM (\Resources\Opdyke92.pdf)

Object Management Group, Inc. 2001. *OMG Unified Modleing Language Specification v1.4*, http://www.omg.org, September.

Parnas, David L. 1976. On the design and development of program families. *IEEE Transactions On Software Engineering* (SE-2, 1), March, 1–9.

Petzold, Charles. 1996. *Programming Windows 95, The Definite Developer's Guide to the Windows 95 API*. Microsoft Press, 1996.

Rumbaugh, James, Michael Blaha, William Premerlani, Frederick Eddy, William Lorenson. 1991. *Object-Oriented Modeling and Design*, Prentice Hall.

Samek, Miro. 1997. Portable Inheritance and Polymorphism in C. *Embedded Systems Programming*. December, 54–66.

Samek, Miro and Paul Y. Montgomery. 2000. State-Oriented Programming. *Embedded Systems Programming*, August, 22–43.

Schlaer, S., Steve Mellor. 1991. *Object Lifecycles: Modeling The World in States*. Yourdon Press.

Sha, L., R. Rajkumar, J.P. Lehocsky. 1990. Priority Inheritance Protocols: An Approach to Real-Time Synchronization. *IEEE Transactions on Computers*, September, 1,175-1,185.

Selic, Bran. 2000. Distributed Software Design: Challenges and Solutions. *Embedded Systems Programming*, November, 127-144.

Selic, Bran, Garth Gullekson, Paul T. Ward. 1994. *Real-Time Object Oriented Modeling*. John Wiley & Sons.

Simons, A J H. 2000. "On the compositional properties of UML statechart diagrams." *Electronic Workshops in Computing: Rigorous Object-Oriented Methods 2000*, series ed. C J van Rijsbergen. British Computer Society.

Spencer, Henry, "The Ten Commandments For C Programmers" (Annotated Edition). (http://www.lysator.liu.se/c/ten-commandments.html#henry).

Stroustrup, Bjarne. 1991. *The C++ Programming Language Second Edition*. AT&T Bell Telephone Laboratories, Inc.

Sutter, Herb, GotW.ca Web site, http://www.gotw.ca/gotw/057.htm

Van Sickle, Ted. 1997. *Reusable software components, object-oriented embedded systems programming in C*. Prentice Hall

WindRiver Systems, Inc. *GNU Toolkit User's Guide*, 2.6, October 1995, Part#: DOC-11091-ZD-01

WindRiver Systems Inc. *VxWorks Programmer's Guide, 5.3.1*, Edition 1, 4 March 1997, Part#: DOC-12067-ZD-00

Yourdon, E. 1994. *Decline and Fall of the American Programmer*. Prentice Hall PTR; November 10.

Index

Symbols

µC/OS 254, 267, 340

A

abstract class 340, 342, 344
    UML notation for 354
abstract method 137, 347–348
    UML notation for 354
Abstract Operating System 208
abstraction 105, 336
    and LSP 34
    as meta-pattern 21, 81, 120, 333, 335–339
    inheritance 32, 105
    levels of 5, 15, 17, 131, 165, 328
    state hierarchy 51, 184
access control 338
    private 338
    protected 338
    public 338
    See also visibility of class members
action 27–30, 41, 43, 49, 53, 55, 59, 67, 224, 253, 327
    coding transitions 98–99
    sequence of 38
    UML notation for 356
    undefined syntax of 41
    See also entry/exit action
    See also internal transition
action listener 240
active object 20, 190–191, 197, 248–253
    as Observer 243
    priority 241
active object computing 191, 315
    and programming discipline 316
    flexibility of 315

heuristics for 317
    rules for programming 315
activity graphs 42
actor 190–191
    See also active object
ad hoc approach 103, 196, 290
additive complexity 35
Adobe Acrobat Reader 362
ADT (abstract data types) 336
AECL (Atomic Energy of Canada Limited) 196
aggregate 63, 86–87
aggregation 151, 355
    UML notation for 355
agile methodologies xii
Agile Modeling xii
ALLEGE() macro 222
Amber, Scott xii
and-decomposition of states 34, 159
    See also orthogonal regions
angular momentum 49, 51–52
    conservation of 50
ANSI C 121
application
    framework 190
    shutdown 255
applicationintentionally incomplete 264
architectural decay 27, 196–197
    and guards 26
ARM (Advanced RISC Machines) 350
    ARM7TDMI 230
    See also Atmel, AT91 microcontroller
arming a timer 256
ASSERT() macro 106–107, 222
assertions 220
asynchronous event
    dispatching 151
    exchange 20, 198
Atmel Corporation
    AT91 microcontroller family 229–230

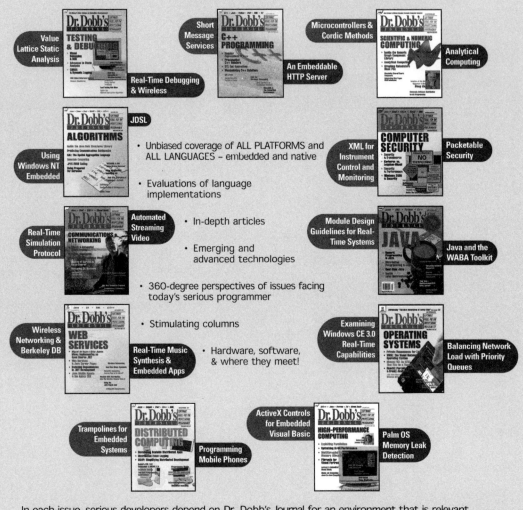

EmbeddedSystems
P R O G R A M M I N G

THE ONLY AUDITED MAGAZINE DEDICATED TO EMBEDDED DESIGN

Embedded Systems Programming has been providing invaluable information to the embedded industry for over 13 years. Our subscribers enjoy high-quality, practical articles on microcontroller, embedded microprocessor, DSP and SoC-based development month after month.

The industry magazine since 1988.

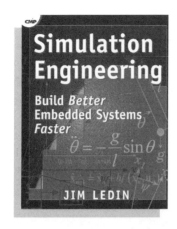

Simulation Engineering

by Jim Ledin

Learn when and how to use simulation methods. The entire range of important techniques are presented, beginning with the fundamentals of mathematical models, how to produce useful results, how to analyze the data and how to validate the models. Each chapter provides step-by-step instructions for developing a working simulation. Includes a review of state-of-the-art tools and administrative guidelines on management and communications. 303pp, ISBN 1-57820-080-6, $44.95

Math Toolkit for Real-Time Programming

by Jack W. Crenshaw

Develop a solid understanding of the math behind common functions — and learn how to make your programs run faster and more efficiently! You get a solid course in applied math from the renowned columnist of Embedded Systems Programming Magazine — and a versatile set of algorithms to use in your own projects. CD-ROM included, 466pp, ISBN 1-929629-09-5, $49.95

What's on the CD?

The companion CD-ROM contains all the source code and executable images mentioned in the book, including several ports of the Quantum Framework (QF). The disc also includes answers to the exercises scattered throughout the book, the Evaluation Version of On Time RTOS-32 v4.0, Visio™ stencils used to create the diagrams in this book, and several references in Adobe Portable Document Format (PDF).[1]

The CD-ROM is designed for maximum usefulness, even without installing any of it on your hard drive. In particular, you can browse the source code, execute examples, and read PDF documents directly from the CD.

The disc comes with an HTML-based index page, index.htm, in its root directory. It is automatically activated if the CD autoinsert notification is enabled on your system. You need a Web browser (e.g., Microsoft Internet Explorer or Netscape Navigator) to view the index.

For more information on the source code structure, installation, answers to exercises, or other CD resources, see Appendix C, beginning on page 359.

---

1. A copy of Adobe Acrobat Reader™ is included on the CD-ROM for your convenience.